A history of Sir John Deane's Grammar School
Northwich

A history of Sir John Deane's
Grammar School
Northwich

1557–1908 by Marjorie Cox, M.A.

with a chapter on later developments
since 1908 by L. A. Hopkins, M.A., Headmaster 1950–73

Manchester University Press

© 1975 The Foundation Governors of Sir John Deane's
Grammar School

Published by
Manchester University Press
Oxford Road, Manchester M13 9PL

ISBN 0 7190 1282 1

Printed in Great Britain
by Western Printing Services Ltd, Bristol

Contents

List of plates

Foreword

It gives me great satisfaction to welcome and commend this book. It is a work of considerable scholarship which places the history of an individual school in a regional and national setting. It will therefore appeal not only to those who know Northwich, Cheshire and the north-west but also to those interested in the elaborating fabric of our education system since the sixteenth century.

Sir John Deane's Grammar School celebrated its quatercentenary in 1957. Since the governors commissioned the book at that time Mrs Marjorie Cox has worked through the archives in the Public Record Office, Somerset House, the Chester Diocesan and County Council archives and the school records. The Chester archives were not, when she started, in their present excellent state of organisation. The school's records too were in disarray; they have recently been deposited with the County Archivist and are now in order. The final chapter dealing with the period since 1908 has been written by Mr L. A. Hopkins, headmaster 1950–73 and also a historian.

This is the story of a Cheshire school which for a period of more than 400 years has affected the lives of thousands of people in mid-Cheshire and through them influenced the character and development of the region. The school never had sufficient funds to go its own way with complete independence and, possibly for this reason, it is evident that teachers and governors remained close to the society they served and sensitive to its opinions while at the same time leading many of its most significant developments. It is a fascinating and finely written study, and a memorable example of how the contemplation of an intimate and small-scale organisation can illuminate the prevailing attitudes and values of the contemporary society.

The governors of the school and the authors are to be warmly congratulated.

J. R. G. Tomlinson
Director of Education
Cheshire County Council

Preface

by Marjorie Cox

This history was undertaken at the request of the foundation governors at the time of the four-hundredth anniversary of the founding of Sir John Deane's Grammar School in 1957. The school possessed records which could form a good basis, but at that date the rich diocesan records, which were essential for a fuller history, were still in a confused and virtually unusable state. Work on the history was delayed until they had been moved to the Cheshire County Record Office (in 1962), where they were gradually sorted and catalogued. The bulk of the research was done in the late 'fifties and early 'sixties, and by 1967 the history was completed to 1908. In 1968, however, a large collection of school records, for which searches had been made unsuccessfully, came to light in Northwich, and this involved some rewriting.

The sources for the school's history, primarily its own records, are not evenly spread throughout its four centuries, and this has determined the shape of the book. The evidence for the earlier centuries, though full, does not lend itself to a narrative of the development of the school, but it is hoped that this will be compensated for by the wealth of evocative detail from the account books. From 1784 to 1884 the minute books provide an almost unbroken thread, but the strange absence of the 1884–1910 minute book leaves a gap which has had to be filled from other sources, mainly the records of the central and local government.

Throughout, the book attempts to place the school in its local setting and to relate its history to the changing local society in which it functioned. The absence of a history of Northwich has been a handicap here, but the printed works and collection of local materials of John Weston, a former governor of the school, have been of great value. This local society was, of course, a part of the whole county of Cheshire, and I am most grateful to Mr John Tomlinson, the County Director of Education, for contributing a foreword. Finally I wish to thank the foundation governors, and especially their chairman, Mr W. D. Yarwood, for their interest and support, and Mr

L. A. Hopkins, until 1973 the headmaster, for his sustained enthu-
siasm and active co-operation.

Acknowledgements

I have received help from many individuals and institutions, to all
of whom, even if not mentioned by name, I should like to express
my gratitude. My greatest debt and warmest thanks are to Mr Brian
Redwood and his staff at the Cheshire County Record Office for
continued, willing and constructive help, without which the book
could not have been written. I should like to express special gratitude, too, to the librarian and staff of the John Rylands University
Library of Manchester, and to the staff of the Public Record Office.

My thanks are due to the librarian of Corpus Christi College,
Cambridge; to the following and their staffs: the Borthwick Institute, York, the British Museum (now the British Library), the Principal Probate Registry (Somerset House), and the Chester City Record
Office, and to the librarians of the following libraries: the Guildhall,
London, Manchester Central Library, Chester Public Library and
the Brunner Library, Northwich. The editors of *The Chester Courant*
and *The Northwich Guardian* kindly allowed me to consult their
files.

For permission to use unpublished theses I wish to thank Mr G. E.
Wilson (and the University of Leeds) for his thesis on Macclesfield
School, Dr P. W. Thomas, who also gave me additional information
on Sir John Berkenhead, Mr E. L. C. Mullins, and the librarian of
the University of Manchester for Mrs Hilda Rooke's thesis.

The late Canon A. W. Maitland Wood, formerly vicar of Northwich, gave me the benefit of his local knowledge and access to the
parish records when they were still in the church: they are now
deposited in the Cheshire Record Office, and for their use I thank
the present vicar, the Rev. G. L. Davies. Lieutenant Colonel J. L. B.
Leicester Warren most kindly allowed me to study documents among
the Tabley MSS. Miss Weston generously allowed me full use of
Mr J. Weston's notebooks and collection of local material. I am indebted for information and help to the late Canon R. V. H. Burne,
the late Mr F. P. White, formerly Keeper of Records, St John's
College, Cambridge, Professor J. S. Roskell, Mr J. H. Hodson, Mr
A. S. Irvine, Mr K. A. Hooper and Mr D. A. Iredale. Dr Alys
Gregory and Professor T. S. Willan were kind enough to read early
drafts of the book and to give much constructive criticism and
practical advice. My husband's support and criticism have been invaluable, and my mother gave constant encouragement to the
writing of the book but, sadly, did not live to see it published.

Note

In quotations the original spelling has been retained, but abbreviations have been expanded and punctuation and capitalisation have been modernised.

To avoid confusion in dates before 1752 the year has been taken as beginning on 1 January and not on 25 March as was then common practice. Thus, for example, dates which appear on the page of the account book reproduced as plate I as in January, February and March (up to the 25th) 1584 are given in the text as 1585.

I wish to thank the President and Fellows of Corpus Christi College, Oxford, for permission to reproduce the extract from the Wase collection as plate II.

Transcripts of Crown-copyright records in the Public Record Office appear by permission of the Controller of H.M. Stationery Office.

The transcript from the Bishop of Chester's register (1525–75), deposited in the Cheshire Record Office, appears by permission of the Cheshire County Council and the Bishop of Chester.

Prefatory note

by L. A. Hopkins

The foundation governors were most fortunate to secure the services of Mrs Cox to write the school history. In accepting their invitation Mrs Cox made one condition: that the period after 1908 should be written by someone nearer to the life of the school and district; and the governors asked me to undertake this task.

Curiously, I found a shortage of basic material. For example, local newspapers could not provide reports of the opening of the new buildings given by Sir John Brunner, and the governors' records are also blank on this event. I have fallen back on the minutes of governors' meetings, and on the quite voluminous correspondence which exists. The official reports written by my two predecessors have also been useful. In addition I have talked to a great number of people who knew the school during this period or for part of it. It is impossible to name them all, but I have been particularly helped by the memories of C. F. A. Keeble and T. Sanderson—both, alas, now dead—as well as other former members of staff. Many former pupils have also talked to me about their schooldays.

The school has been fortunate in many ways: not least in its foundation governors, who were prepared to finance this ambitious project. Even so, because of the steady rise in costs the history would not, in all probability, have been published had not the local authority promised support. This is yet another example of an outstanding characteristic of the school's development during this century—a positive partnership of local independent endeavour and public authority. One can but hope that the spirit of this partnership will survive during the testing years ahead.

Abbreviations

B.N.C. Reg.: Brasenose College Register, 1509–1909 (Oxford Historical Society, LV).

Carlisle: N. Carlisle, *Endowed Grammar Schools in England and Wales*, two vols. (1818)

C.C.R.: Charity Commissioners' Reports (1819–40)

C.P.R.: Calendar of Patent Rolls

C.A.J.: Journal of the Chester and North Wales Archaeological Society

C.D. Recs.: Chester Diocesan Records (deposited in Cheshire County Record Office)

Ches. Co. Rec. Off.: Cheshire County Record Office

C.S.: The Cheshire Sheaf

Chet. Soc.: Chetham Society

D.N.B.: Dictionary of National Biography

Foster: J. Foster, *Alumni Oxonienses* (1887–88 and 1891–92)

Gastrell: Francis Gastrell, *Notitia Cestriensis (Chet. Soc.,* VIII)

Harl. MSS: Harleian manuscripts, British Museum

Hist. Soc. L. and C.: Historic Society of Lancashire and Cheshire

Kay: D. M. Kay, *History of Lymm Grammar School* (1960)

L. and C. Rec. Soc.: Lancashire and Cheshire Record Society

L. and P.: Letters and Papers, Henry VIII

Mun. Glas.: Munimenta alme universitatis Glasguensis: Records of the University of Glasgow from its foundation till 1727, ed. C. Innes and J. Robertson (Maitland Club, 1854)

Ormerod: G. Ormerod, *History of the County Palatine and City of Chester,* second edition, ed. T. Helsby (1882)

Par. Reg.: parish register of St Helen's Church, Northwich, formerly Witton Chapel

P.C.C.: Prerogative Court of Canterbury

P.R.O.: Public Record Office

St John's Coll. Admissions: Admissions to the College of St John the Evangelist, 1629–1802, ed. J. E. B. Mayor and R. F. Scott (1882–1931)

S.I.C.: Schools Inquiry Commission Reports (1868)

Tabley MSS: Manuscripts at Tabley House, Knutsford, catalogued in the National Register of Archives as Letters, strays, box 7, bundle 9

Trinity Coll. Admissions: Admissions to Trinity College, Cambridge, ed. W. W. Rouse Ball and J. A. Venn (1916)

Varley: B. Varley, *The History of Stockport Grammar School* (1957)

Venn: J. and J. A. Venn, *Alumni Cantabrigienses* (1922–54)
Weston *N.P.C.:* J. Weston, *Historical Notes and Records of the Parish Church, Northwich* (1908)
Weston *W.G.S.:* J. Weston, *Witton Grammar School* (two editions, 1885 and 1899)
Weston Notebooks: a series of MS notebooks containing local material
Wilson: G. E. Wilson, 'History of Macclesfield School' (unpublished M.Ed. thesis, University of Leeds, 1952)

I

Northwich in the sixteenth century: an introductory sketch

John Leland's description of Northwich about 1540 is well known—
'a prati market toune but fowle'.* Although neither a chartered
borough nor a parish, it was described early in the seventeenth century as 'a market-town well frequented, gives name to the Hundred,
and seated so near the middest of the county, and so well for
travel every way, that it seems fit, and is oft allotted to the meetings
of the chief governors in the county, for their great affairs'. In 1654
the town was referred to as 'a great thoroughfare', and its geo-
graphical position gave much importance to the various bridges in
and near it: the town bridge over the Weaver, the Dane bridge and
Witton Bridge. Local inhabitants left legacies in their wills for the
upkeep of one or other of the bridges: Thomas Bromfield, in 1558,
left 6s 8d to the reparation of Witton Bridge; Thomas Farmer, the
schoolmaster, left twenty nobles in 1624 for the same purpose, and
Richard Crymes, a London haberdasher of local origin, left a large
sum for the maintenance of the town bridge in 1568.[1] Leland's
comments as he toured England reveal how much a good market
contributed to the importance of a town, and in the late sixteenth
century Northwich was held to be 'a proper town, having every
Friday a market, and yearly two fairs; that is to say, on the day of
Mary Magdalen, and on St. Nicholas' day, being the 6th of
December'. As early as the middle of the fourteenth century specified goods were liable to be taxed at Northwich to help to rebuild the
bridge destroyed in the floods of 1351, and the list shows the variety
of goods on sale in the town: corn, flour, cattle, sheep, goats, pigs,
fleeces, hides, skins, fish, wine, clothing, nails, horseshoes, plough-
clutes,† tin, brass, copper, white glass and coloured glass.[2]

Northwich, however, was not only a market town but one of the
Cheshire production centres of that indispensable commodity, salt.
The salt industry throughout its various vicissitudes and develop-
ments over the centuries was fundamental to the prosperity of

* Miry or muddy.
† Presumably 'clout', an iron plate to protect from wear.

Northwich, and it was also to be of prime importance to that of the town's grammar school. Northwich had produced salt for centuries, but in the sixteenth century it was still far behind Nantwich in the scale of its industry. About 1530 Nantwich had 400 salthouses and under Elizabeth it had 216 of six 'leads' each, making a total of 1,296 leads, while in 1565 Northwich had 113 salthouses, each of four leads, and one odd lead, a lead being a pan in which the brine was boiled. There are no statistics for the population of Northwich in the sixteenth century, but in 1548 Nantwich was described as this 'gret towne' of 1,800 'houseling people', that is, communicants. Some idea of their relative sizes can be gained from Celia Fiennes' descriptions over a century later: Northwich she found 'not very large' and Nantwich a 'pretty large town'.[3]

A late seventeenth-century plan of Northwich shows it as a fraction even of the present central area. The brine pit, foundation of the salt industry, stood on the bank of the river Dane, and parallel to the river ran Seath Street, with the Dane bridge off it to the south. Roughly parallel to Seath Street were four other streets—the High Street, Yate Street, Leach Eye and Leach end or Bakehouse Street. These ran down towards the market place, on the west side of which was the town bridge over the Weaver. Round the market place were some of the more important buildings of the community: the Court House, just before the bridge, the house of correction, the Swan Inn, and the shops. A little distance away was the lead smithy, where the leads were cast to a specified weight, deviation from which was punished by a fine to the manorial lord, and round the corner from it was the lord's bakehouse. Here, by ancient custom, all the inhabitants of the town (unless exempted) were supposed to bake their bread, on pain of a fine. The wich houses lay along Seath Street, High Street, Yate Street, the Leach Eye and what was called the Little Street, otherwise Horsemill Street.* The methods of salt-making fascinated outside observers. Camden earlier in the century described 'the deep and plentiful brine pit' at Northwich 'with stairs about it, by which, when they have drawn the water in their leathern buckets, they ascend half-naked to their troughs and fill them, from whence it is conveyed to the wich houses about which there stand on every side many stakes and piles of wood'. Within the wich houses, according to William Webb, were 'great barrels, set deep into the earth, which are all filled with salt water: and when the bell ringeth they begin to make fire under the leads' or pans. As the salt water seethed, 'the Wallers (which are commonly

* By the end of the century some wich houses were recorded as 'not standing', but the salt-making rights attached to them were exercised in other houses. (A. F. Calvert, *Salt in Cheshire*, pp. 1112–18 and 1050.)

women) do with a wooden rake, gather the salt from the bottoms which they put into a long basket of wicker, which they call a salt barrow—and so the water voideth and the salt remaineth'. It is scarcely surprising that Celia Fiennes should have commented that 'the town is full of smoak from the salterns on all sides'.

This was not, however, the only problem: the piles of fuel by the wich houses, which Leland had noted, were a potential nuisance, and it was laid down that there was to be left a yard and a half between the pile and the crest of the payment, so that 'waynes may have better passage'. A major hazard was fire: Nantwich had been burnt in 1438, and again in 1583 it was 'most part miserably consumed with fire'. Northwich had had a damaging fire in 1306: as a precaution all roads to the water had to be kept open and clear, and no fires were to be lit at night in the wich-house streets. Rural hazards were mingled with industrial hazards in the streets of the town: in 1633 the jury of the manorial lord's court ordered that 'no man inhabiting in this town shall at any time after the first day of March next coming keep any cattell, either kine, oxen, calves or swine to go loose up and down the streets to the hurt or hinderance of the inhabitants of this town, or to the hurt of the brine passage from the brine sheath to the salt houses'. Dunghills and swine cotes 'in the face of the street' were also forbidden, but the very prohibition reveals the lack of separation between urban and rural in sixteenth-century Northwich.

The salt town was highly organised as a community in the sixteenth and early seventeenth centuries under officers elected, with the exception of the lord's steward, by the jury of burgesses at the Court Leet. The most comprehensive record of the customs of the town and of salt-making was that collected by Peter Warburton of Chester, when steward of Northwich, and confirmed by the jury in 1638 and 1641. The processes of salt-making were regulated in minute detail. The brine drawers had to obey their ruler, known as the Lord of the Seath, 'as well when to draw as when to rest'; the wallers were forbidden to put fire under the leads before 'the ringe of the bell or appoyntment of the officer'. The making and boiling of the salt had to begin and cease by order of the Leadlookers, the principal officers of the burgesses' court, and 'not otherwayes'. The Leadlookers seem to have had discretion to allow walling in the early part of the year, but from Palm Sunday until Christmas all was ordered by the sound of the common bell, probably on top of the Court House. Equally, the wallers were to sell the salt 'at the price which the officers sett down to be the common price of the towne'.

Arrangements were made, too, for the communal responsibilities of the town. The 'peeceing' (a 'peeceing' being defined by custom as to wall two days and nights and no more) to be given to the poor was to be agreed on yearly by the greater number of the occupiers assembled in the Court House by toll of the common bell: it was to be set and walled before St Thomas's feast-day (21 December) and the money paid on that day to four honest men for distribution. In 1637 the jury considered the salthouse which had been purchased for the mainten-ance of a Preaching Minister in Witton Chapelry. It had been worth at least £12 originally, but through the decay of trading in salt in the town had become of little value, 'to the greater charge of the whole parish'. The steward and jury agreed then that the walling attached to the house could be set by 'peeceings', and the house itself con-verted to the best advantage.

Northwich in the middle of the sixteenth century was a tight little community, fiercely jealous of the economic rights which its inhabitants asserted strongly against 'foreigners' from Hart-ford and the Cross, otherwise Witton. About 1527, in the course of a dispute between the burgesses and certain 'forayners', several old inhabitants gave evidence that in the past only residents were allowed to make salt, and that, in order to qualify, various indi-viduals living in Hartford and the Cross had come to live or to lodge in Northwich, or alternatively had let their walling to residents: among those who had come to lodge in Northwich 'in the dayes of the old Lord of Darby' were Richard Wynington and Edward Sudlow 'dwelling in the Cros'. A century later similar restrictions on non-residents were recorded in the orders of the town agreed on by the steward and jury in 1638.

In the early sixteenth century some salthouses in Northwich, as well as land in the area, were owned by religious houses. Among these owners were the Augustinian canons of Norton Abbey and three Cistercian houses—Whalley Abbey, Basingwerk Abbey and Vale Royal Abbey. The dissolution of the monasteries by Henry VIII therefore offered opportunities for acquisitions, particularly to local men. By 1565 there were about forty-eight owners of wich houses in Northwich: of these by far the largest was Sutton of Sutton, with forty-six leads; some way behind him was Sir John Warburton with thirty, and then a number of owners of twenty-odd leads—Dutton of Dutton, Mr Leftwich, Laurence Winnington, Starkye of Darlye, Sir Thomas Venables and Mr James Paver. The Earl of Derby had sixteen or eighteen and Mr William Marbury, sixteen and two-thirds, while twenty-five of the owners had four or fewer leads. The Walling book of the same year shows a total of seventy-two makers of salt, of whom only eleven were also owners of wich houses: those who worked on the largest scale were Edward Golborne (twenty-two

leads), Humphrey Yate (twenty-eight, including six of his own),
William Worrall (twenty-four, including two of his own), Hugh
Lowe (twenty), Robert Wynington (twenty-six, including four of his
own), and Roger Torbock (eighteen).[4]

A peculiarity of the urban area was that it was divided between
two manors. The plan mentioned above shows only that part lying
within the manor of Northwich (not more than eight or ten statute
acres), but another part, one street, lay in the manor of Witton,
which was bounded roughly by Witton Brook and Wade Brook on
the north and east, by the Dane on the south, and by the Weaver on
the west, but excluding the manorial township of Northwich. The
manor of Northwich had been given by Richard III in 1484 to
Sir Thomas Stanley, who was created Earl of Derby by Henry VII,
but as early as Domesday Book Witton had belonged to the family
of Venables of Kinderton. This family, which had increased its
holdings of salthouses in Middlewich after the dissolution of the
monasteries, was powerful and active in the area in the mid-
sixteenth century and as late as 1604 had a following of liveried
retainers. In 1530 two Bromfields, Richard and Thomas, both
yeomen and household servants of William Venables, were accused
in Star Chamber of an assault at Northwich Bridge on an enemy of
their master's. Later, in 1564, Sir Thomas Venables, who had been
knighted at Leith in 1544 and was sheriff of the county under Philip
and Mary, was described by an aggrieved tenant as 'a man of worship
and of great power' in Cheshire, while at the same date the Bishop
of Chester reported to the Privy Council that he was 'not favourable
to true religion' as established by the Elizabethan settlement.[5] The
Earl of Derby and the Baron of Kinderton were the most influential
figures in the district, but Northwich was surrounded by lesser
manorial lords. The manor and township of Birches lay east of
Northwich in the Lostock quarter of Witton chapelry and remained
in the Winnington family until the reign of Charles I. Another
branch held the manor of Winnington until a daughter carried it
with her in her marriage to Sir Peter Warburton; Castle Northwich
township and manor were owned by the Wilbrahams, and in Leftwich were the Leftwiches, followed, through a daughter's marriage,
by the Oldfields.[6]

What was commonly known as Northwich church was in fact
physically within the manor and township of Witton, and, strictly,
Witton Chapel. Ecclesiastically it was not a parish church in its
own right but, like Peover, a chapel within the large parish of Great
Budworth. It became a parochial chapel, but up to the middle of
the sixteenth century its curate was probably still appointed by the
vicar of Budworth. The chapelry included a large number of town-

ships, most of them agricultural: Hartford, Winnington, Castle
Northwich, Northwich, Witton and Twambrooke, Lostock Gralam,
Hulse, Lach Dennis, Birches and a small part of Rudheath lordship. It was divided into four quarters—Northwich, Witton, Lostock
and Hartford—each with its own chapel warden. The chapel of
St Helen at Witton, described in the early seventeenth century as
'a very fair church ... mounted aloft upon a bank, that overviews
the town of Northwich', stood among the fields nearly half a mile
from the town centre and was the one building singled out for
mention by travellers. In the later seventeenth century, when there
was a severe infection in the town, the area by the church, where
the school stood, was free from infection for a good while, being
what was considered then 'a prettie distance from the towne'.[7]

For about fifty years from the late fifteenth century extensive
repairs and additions had been made to the chapel, but as yet the
chancel was not battled,* and the surrounding churchyard was considerably smaller than it became in the eighteenth century. Various
families of the local gentry and the town salt-makers gave benefactions to this work. In 1498 Richard Winnington of Winnington had
left 40*s* towards making a stone steeple, and on the roof bosses the
monogram of William Venables and representations of salt barrows
or baskets probably commemorated gifts. The sixteenth-century
windows of the chapel, which have since disappeared, also contained
memorials of local propertied families, often with pleas for prayers
for the souls of those dead and the good health of those living.
In the south windows were the arms of the lord of Witton, Venables
of Kinderton, and a memorial to Sir William Venables, who died in
1541, and to his wife, who died in 1557. In the clerestories on the
north side were a memorial to Richard Leftwich of Leftwich Hall
(living in 1528), and another to Thomas Winnington of Birches, set
up in 1550 by his son, Robert. In another window Richard Winnington of Winnington and his wife were commemorated, together with
their daughter, Elizabeth, and her husband, Sir Peter Warburton.
Apart from these local manorial lords, other influential families, for
the most part also owners of salthouses, were commemorated in the
windows: the Pavers, Bromfields, Maistersons and, from further
afield, Richard Sutton of Sutton Hall, Macclesfield.[8]

Benefactions were not confined to the fabric of the church: in
the early sixteenth century there may have been a chantry of the
Sutton family. Certainly, from time to time, individuals made
provision for commemorative or anniversary services and masses.
In 1518 George Barlowe, a priest in London, left 10*s* for a trental

---

* Embattled or crenellated.

of masses to be said in the parish church of Northwich, where he was born. In 1522 Sir Robert Blagge, a high-ranking royal official resident in the parish of St Bartholomew's, Smithfield in London, not only gave five marks in his will to the chapel works but gave a salary of eight marks for three years to 'an honest preest of good conversacion' to sing masses for the souls of himself, his father, mother and first wife, and of Henry VII in the chapel 'of Witton at the Northwich where I was born'. In 1548 there was in the chapel a very small chantry, modestly endowed with only 16s 8d a year, and without plate, jewels, ornaments or lead. Subsequently it appeared that this was founded by a certain Margaret Knottesford or her trustees to provide in perpetuity anniversary services or obits, and financed by the income from two-thirds of a salthouse in Northwich: she may have been one of the Knottesford family of Twemlow, near by. This endowment compared very poorly with the £7 6s 8d of the chantry at Nantwich church and with the probable average of Lancashire chantries of £5 6s 8d, covering chantries ranging from 30s to £10. The priest who served this obit in 1548 was, according to the Chantry Commissioners, the sixty-year-old Thomas Waller,* although John Deane later mentioned a chantry priest named Thomas Bromfield. Neither of these, however, seems to have had a pension after the dissolution of the chantries. There were other chantry lands belonging to Witton Chapel which were not recorded by the commissioners and so escaped immediate confiscation by the Crown. Later, in 1564 and in 1567, grants were made of these 'concealed lands', which included a tenement in Northwich belonging to 'the late church or chapel of Wilton [*sic*]' and lands in Barnton 'late of the chantry of Wilton alias Vitton called Witton Chapel'.[9]

Like many other Cheshire churches, Witton Chapel, with its mother church of Great Budworth, was appropriated to a monastery. Great Budworth church (the advowson and the tithes) was in the possession of the Augustinian canons of Norton Abbey, and indeed a canon of Norton, William Hardware, held the living by special dispensation from the Pope and later from the Archbishop of Canterbury, until his death about 1550. Witton Chapel was thus closely affected by the dissolution of the monasteries: Norton was dissolved with the smaller monasteries in 1536 and its possessions fell to the Crown. In 1538 the rectory of Budworth, with the chapels of Witton and Peover, was leased to George Cotton. In 1546, however, the King granted it, with the right of presentation to the

---

* In 1541–42 the curate of Witton Chapel was Thomas Wall. (*Clergy List of 1541–2*, ed. W. F. Irvine, *L. and C. Rec. Soc.*, 33, pp. 6–7.) Was there some confusion on the commissioners' part, perhaps?

living, to Christ Church as part of his munificent refoundation of Wolsey's Oxford college, thus establishing an important link between that college and the locality.[10]

These were some of the features of the district from which John Deane sprang. The Chantry Commissioners did not consider it, as they did Nantwich, a society in need of a grammar school, but in the haphazard way in which sixteenth-century charitable endowment operated, Northwich acquired one earlier, thanks to John Deane's generosity and local attachment.

II
The founder

Sir John Deane,* the founder of Witton School, is a shadowy figure
in all that concerns his personality, but he arouses interest and
indeed curiosity by the circumstances of his career. Not always
willingly, and certainly not as an important protagonist, he touched
the dramatic central events of his lifetime. His presence in the heart
of London from the late 1530s to his death under Elizabeth in 1563
guaranteed that he could not escape the impact of the rapid religious
changes of that period. Throughout the latter part of Henry VIII's
reign, the reign of Edward VI, when first moderate and later
extreme Protestant doctrines were established, the reign of Mary
and the Catholic reaction, and the early years of Elizabeth when
the Anglican settlement was initiated, he retained the same living.
This fact throws an interesting light on his personality and beliefs,
particularly as that living was not an obscure or remote country
living but one less than half a mile from St Paul's.

John Deane's living itself, that of St Bartholomew the Great,
Smithfield, had certain special features which enhance our interest
in him.[1] To begin with it was attached to a monastic foundation,
St Bartholomew's Priory of Augustinian canons, which, on the eve
of the dissolution of the monasteries, was one of the wealthiest
monasteries in the City of London. A peculiarity of the priory was
that, having been dissolved under Henry VIII, it was one of a
handful of monasteries which were revived under Mary Tudor,
thus confronting the incumbent of the living with the Marian
reaction in its fullest impact. In another way, too, the holder of the
living of St Bartholomew's, Smithfield, was brought into the closest
contact with the physical realities of the religious changes of the
middle of the sixteenth century, and in a way calculated to instil
acquiescence. Smithfield was the scene of many of the executions

* *Sir* John Deane: the title 'Sir' was frequently placed before the Christian
name of a priest at least until the later sixteenth century. It is ironic that in
the eighteenth century knowledge of the founder was so faint that in official
school documents he was described as 'Sir John Deane, Knight'.

which marked the successive turns of Tudor religious policy. In
1538 Friar Forest was burned in front of St Bartholomew's, Smithfield, in the presence of 10,000 people, for denying the royal
supremacy in the Church after the breach with Rome. In 1546
Anne Askew, with three men, was burned in Smithfield for denying
the doctrine of transubstantiation, and for this event a special
scaffold was erected immediately before what had been the west
front of St Bartholomew's church. Probably a more significant event
for John Deane was the first of the many burnings in Smithfield in
Mary's reign, that of John Rogers, a prebendary of St Paul's, in
1555. From 1550 Rogers had been vicar of St Sepulchre's, a church
which had originally belonged to St Bartholomew's, and whose
parish adjoined Deane's: it was in fact to Rogers' successor, Henry
Atkinson (presented to the living by Philip and Mary in 1556), that
Deane in his will left a lined black gown and 20*s*. In all, during the
reign of Philip and Mary there are records of the burning of forty-
five people in Smithfield.

If the dangers of failure to conform to the current religious policy
were clearly displayed to the incumbent of St Bartholomew's, the
opportunities offered by the large-scale disposal of property following on the dissolution of the monasteries were also peculiarly obvious.
For the first few years after the dissolution sales of monastic lands
were few, but the financial pressure of the war with France resulted
in increasing alienations, and from 1542 vast amounts of Crown
land, particularly monastic land, were sold. The management of the
monastic property and its subsequent sale were in the hands of the
Court of Augmentations, specially created for the purpose in 1536.
Sir Richard Rich, the chancellor of the court from its foundation
to 1544, was the chief parishioner of St Bartholomew's, living in
the prior's house from 1539 or early 1540, and from 1544 the
patron of the living. Furthermore, Rich gathered round him, in
houses in the close of the former priory, various officials of the court.
Not only, therefore, was Deane in close proximity to men deeply
involved in the distribution of monastic property, but he had before
him living examples, pre-eminently Rich himself, of the advantages
to be gained in the process.*

Little is known of John Deane's origin and less of his early life and
career. He was, as he said in the school statutes, one of the sons of
Laurence Deane of Shurlach (described in the early seventeenth
century as a district of 'some freeholders and other good farmers')
in the parish of Davenham, but only about a mile from Northwich,

---

* There is no biography of Rich, but the article on him in the *D.N.B.*
states that 'few were more rapacious or had better opportunities for profiting
by the dissolution of the monasteries'.

where, according to his will, John Deane was born. John Deane's
brother, Richard, was a yeoman by status, and so presumably
was his father, and the family continued in Shurlach and can be
traced until the end of the seventeenth century. (Richard Deane of
Shurlach, gentleman, who died in 1685, seems to be the last traceable
direct male descendant.)* It is possible that the curate of Davenham
about 1542, Roger Deane, was a connection of John Deane,
since the name Roger occurs in the next generation of the Deane
family. There is a sidelight in 1592 on one member of the family,
probably a school feoffee: at the ecclesiastical visitation Richard
Deane (husbandman, of Davenham parish) was 'presented' for
causing his people to work on the 'sabath and holidaies, baking of
bred, braking, stackinge of haie'. The land owned by later generations of the Deane family apparently derived from John Deane, so
that he himself probably sprang from the same sort of stock as
Hugh Latimer, who proclaimed in one of his sermons, 'My father
was a yeoman, and had no lands of his own.'[2] Nothing is known of
Deane's education, except that he had no degree, and that his
learning was very modest. In a report on the archdeaconry of
London in 1561–2 his learning was described in these terms: 'latine
aliquid intelligit', he has some understanding of Latin, and in 1560
a report ran 'non concionatur legit tantum modo', he does not
preach, he reads only so much.[3]

John Deane was ordained priest by the Bishop of Lichfield on 18
June 1519, with the sponsorship of Vale Royal Abbey;† he was then,
probably, twenty-five, the canonical age. He next appears in the
Valor Ecclesiasticus in 1535 as rector of Stanmore Parva, Middlesex,
where his stipend was £6 13s 4d, and where he was, probably,
non-resident. This living was in the gift of the Augustinian Priory
of St Bartholomew's, Smithfield, belonging to the same religious
order as Norton. In 1539 Deane was at St Bartholomew's itself,
and in 1540 he was the parish priest of the church connected with
the former monastery. Among earlier parishioners of St Bartholomew's had been Sir Robert Blagge, who, like Deane, had been
born in Northwich and whose connection with Witton Chapel has
been mentioned. Blagge had been an eminent royal servant, a judge
and administrator: from 1515 he had been joint Surveyor of Crown
lands and in 1519 was Surveyor General in the counties of Chester

* In 1664 his title to gentility, the right to bear heraldic arms, was 'disclaimed' by the heralds at their visitation, but not much can be deduced
from this about his status or aspirations. (J. P. Rylands, 'Disclaimers at the
Heralds' visitations', *Hist Soc. L. and C.* new series, 7.)
† Lichfield *Ordination Register*, B/A/1/14 ii, spelt 'Deyne', but 'Deane'
when made deacon.

and Flint. It has been suggested that Sir Robert was a patron of John Deane, since Deane in his will asked particularly to be buried 'by the righte side of the chappell late Mr. Blages chappell', and some possible backing for this theory is Blagge's bequest, in his will, of 40s to 'Richard Dene my servant'.

While the dissolution of a number of monasteries, including Norton, was accompanied by violence, the surrender of St Bartholomew's was smoothly made in October 1539 by Prior Fuller, who seems to have secured election in 1532 by his usefulness to the King. After the dissolution the thirteen canons were awarded pensions and the prior ended up with a grant for life of almost the whole of the priory's possessions, which he lived to enjoy only until the autumn of 1540. For those like Deane, however, who remained in the former monastic close the physical impact of the dissolution must have been enormous. Though there is no record of it, the church furniture was probably sold at once. Six of the priory's bells were sold to the neighbouring parish of St Sepulchre's; sixteen days after the suppression the monastery's plate and jewels were handed over to Sir John Williams, the King's Master of the Jewels; and, above all, large-scale demolition of the priory church took place. Part of the church—the north transept and Walden's chapel—had been used as the parish chapel, while the main part of the church—the nave and the choir—had been for monastic use. After the suppression it was decided to use the monastic choir as the parish church and to pull down the nave of ten bays and the old parish chapel, a decision thought to have been influenced by Sir Richard Rich. The choir was a convenient size for a parish chapel; the site of the nave made a parochial burying ground, and the old burial ground and north transept increased the space for the profitable Bartholomew's Fair. In addition, the lead and building materials of the nave were more valuable than those of the choir, and by 1544 they had been 'utterly taken away thence', and the lead, stone and timber sold for the Crown's profit. Provision seems to have been made for services for the parishioners between 1539 and 1544, since Deane was described in August 1540 as parish priest of Great St Bartholomew's, and Thomas Hitchyn in 1542 as 'curate of the parish'; nevertheless in 1544 it was stated without qualification that the inhabitants had 'no place where they can and may have divine service and sacraments and sacramentals administered for them as befits Christians'. Such was the church of which Deane was the priest.

There were changes also in the close, the land enclosed by the monastic bounds but outside the range of the monastic buildings. The inhabitants of the close constituted the parishioners of St

Bartholomew's, and numbered in 1544 probably about 250. Before the dissolution they had all been tenants of the priory and convent, but after it the dominant position of Sir Richard Rich gave a new character to the close. Rich had been the Solicitor General associated with Thomas Cromwell in securing the executions of Bishop Fisher and Sir Thomas More, but he managed to survive the fall of Cromwell and became active in persecuting reformers at the end of Henry VIII's reign. In 1536 he was made Chancellor of the Court of Augmentations dealing with the monastic properties, of which he himself acquired a considerable amount, including (in 1544 for the sum of over £1,000) the church and priory of St Bartholomew's, together with the rights of Bartholomew Fair. Round him in houses in the close were many of the Augmentations officials: Burgoyne, an auditor; Sir Edward North, the treasurer and next chancellor (incidentally educated at St Paul's School); the next treasurer, Sir John Williams, and Richard Duke, clerk of the council of the Augmentations, and, from 1545, Walter Mildmay, an auditor. Close to them all was Deane, who, when Rich took over the priory, was the tenant of a house on the eastern side of the close. Another figure linked with the royal court also lived in the close—the eminent doctor, Richard Bartlett, four times president of the College of Physicians, and called in, in 1532, to attend Princess Mary. He and Deane knew each other, certainly in 1539 when both were witnesses to the will of a parishioner. In 1543 both acquired monastic land from the Crown, making payment to their neighbour, Sir Edward North, although Bartlett's purchase was on a much larger scale than Deane's. He acquired a manor and advowson in Gloucestershire for nearly £500.[4] In his will of 1557 Bartlett left to Deane 20s and 'his worstead gowne furred' on condition that he took no money for breaking the ground, and saw his stone laid over him. Deane in his own will left 20s to Katherine 'that dwelt with Mr. Doctor Barthlat'.

At the same time as Sir Richard Rich was granted the priory and church the King appointed John Deane (described as 'curate') to be 'the first Rector and incumbent of the said church for the term of his life', and excused him from payment of first fruits and tenths amounting to £8. After Deane's death the patronage was to lie with Rich and his heirs, and future incumbents were to be inducted in the usual way by the bishop, but there is no record that Deane was so inducted. Whereas his stipend as curate of the parish had been £8, as rector he was to be given lands and property to the value of £11 a year. Five days later, on 24 May 1544, Rich conveyed to Deane and his successors six houses on the west side of the close and a chamber over the south gate of the monastery: these became

the glebe houses, and for them Deane paid 16s yearly tithe to the
King. On 18 June Deane took formal possession in a ceremony
attended by various inhabitants of the close, and by Sir Roland Hill,
alderman of the City. Deane may have lived in one of these houses,
but he leased the rest of them to tenants. John Deane was thus
fully installed in a parish which had a central significance in the
London of the Reformation and Counter-reformation. His chief
parishioner, Sir Richard, later Lord, Rich, was at the heart of
affairs as Lord Chancellor from October 1548 to December 1551,
and Rich's house in the close was an important centre: in 1550
the heretical Joan Bocher was confined there before being burned
in Smithfield, and one of the sessions of the court to try the conservative bishops Bonner and Gardiner was held there. Whatever
his personal religious beliefs, Rich had in him more of the pliable
willow than the oak; he concurred in the council's order command-
ing the destruction of images in churches and in the First Prayer
Book of Edward VI, and although he resigned the Great Seal he was
made Lord Lieutenant of Essex under the Duke of Northumberland,
and signed the proclamation of Lady Jane Grey as Queen.

There is unfortunately no evidence as to how far Deane conformed to the Edwardian religious changes: the relevant records
for St Bartholomew's of the changes in church furnishings to conform with the new doctrinal views are missing, but Bishop Ridley's
visitation of his diocese of London, beginning in May 1550, was
thorough. Every vicar and curate was summoned to his palace at
St Paul's, very close to St Bartholomew's, and, according to Ridley's
latest biographer, when he had finished his visitation not a single
altar, symbolising the old mass, remained in any church of the
diocese.[5] Another fact suggesting that Deane probably conformed
strictly to the religious changes is that he was given ecclesiastical
preferment during the reign of Edward VI. In November 1551
Deane was presented to the prebend of Carlton cum Dalby or
Carlton Kyme in the diocese of Lincoln. Since the see of Lincoln
was vacant at that time he was presented by the Crown and inducted
on an order from Cranmer. He was installed by proxy in January
1552 and there is no evidence that he ever did more than receive
the revenues. A prebendship was 'a place of dignity among the
clergy of the Minster, which had settled on it an endowment for the
maintenance of the prebendary', and it took its name from the
parish in which the estates lay. Deane's prebend was, for the diocese,
of reasonably good middling value. In 1536, however, a predecessor
of Deane had leased the whole of the possessions of the prebend
for forty years to Thomas Dymoke, esq., at a yearly rent of £5 6s 8d,
and since this lease was for a longer period than the lessor's term

of office it was confirmed by the bishop in 1538. It was, therefore, presumably so leased when Deane held it, and he would receive from it annually £5 6s 8d, with no corresponding obligations. All dues payable to Lincoln Minster were to be paid by the lessee, whose responsibility it was to provide two priests to serve at North Carlton and Dalby respectively. This lease, it has been said, illustrates a very bad feature of all impropriated parishes where there was no provision for a permanent vicar: the impropriator (in this case the prebendary), interested in a large rent, laid on the tenant, usually the principal inhabitant, the duty of providing an incumbent and left the parishioners with little opportunity for complaint.[6]

Nine days after the proclamation of Lady Jane Grey as Queen the first proclamation of Mary Tudor was made in London at the Cross in Cheapside on 19 July, and on 3 August Mary entered London. Although her Catholic beliefs were well known, her first pronouncement on religion to her Council on 12 August, was a disclaimer that she wished 'to compel or constrain other men's consciences'; only in the autumn did Parliament enact that after 20 December no service should be used in churches other than that which had been in use in the last year of Henry VIII. Meanwhile Londoners showed their Protestant sympathies. On 13 August Bonner's chaplain, preaching at St Paul's Cross, was attacked by the crowd, and on 11 August, a chronicler recorded, 'This daye an ould preeste sayd masse at St. Batholomewes, but after that masse was done the people would have pulled him in peeces.' In the 1563 edition of Foxe's *Book of Martyrs* the incident is even more vividly described: 'The 11th day of August An.1553 did a priest say masse at St Barthelmews in Smithfield; but before he had half done, he was glad to take him to his legges, for as he was lifting up the bread, there were stones flong at him, and one hit him between the shoulders, as the bread was over his head; so that he would not tary, to make an end of his maske.' It is impossible to say whether this was John Deane himself, but the incident apparently took place in his church and may well have involved him.[7]

During Mary's reign Deane had to meet a more severe test than most parish clergy, even in the diocese of London presided over by Bishop Bonner, who, incidentally, had been rector of Davenham during the 1530s. For the first few years of the reign, until September 1555, he had only to follow the majority of parish clergy in accepting the reversal of the Edwardian legislation, and since he was celibate he was not affected by Mary's campaign against married clergy, which was particularly effective in London. Lord Rich had been an early supporter of Mary, and she had stayed at his house at

Wanstead before her entry into London. He demonstrated his attachment to the old religion in two practical ways besides his zealous persecution of Protestants in Essex. In April 1554 he ordered the first deed of the Felsted foundation, originally a chaplaincy to sing masses and dirges for the dead in Felsted parish church near to his Essex seat and only changed into a school under Elizabeth. Secondly, in December 1555, he granted to the Queen the church and monastic buildings of St Bartholomew's, thereby becoming one of the few who surrendered their monastic spoils. Rich's surrender included also the rectory, the advowson, and the six tenements which he had previously granted to augment Deane's stipend, but it did not include the rights of Bartholomew Fair.

At Easter 1556 the Queen revived the monastery of St Bartholomew's, installing there the Dominicans or Black Friars (English, Spanish and Netherlandish), whose own house at Blackfriars had been demolished. Deane continued in charge of the parish, but his position must have been more testing than that of the average incumbent.* The Dominicans conducted their services in the old monastic choir, which had become the parish church, and seem to have begun some rebuilding. It is thought that Deane may have held his services in a part of the old parish chapel—Walden's Chapel—which had not been demolished, but remained until 1559 or later. The occupation by the friars was, however, short-lived: the prior appointed by Mary died in August 1558, three months before the Queen herself, and though a new prior was elected he never took office. The monastery gradually disintegrated through death and the return of the foreign members to their own countries, until, when the new suppression came under Elizabeth in July 1559, there were only three priests and one young man left.

Deane not only succeeded in coexisting with the Dominicans in St Bartholomew's but even secured another living during the Catholic reaction: this was the living of Coulsdon in Surrey. The advowson of the church there had belonged before the dissolution of the monasteries to Chertsey Abbey, but in 1537 the abbot conveyed it to the King, who granted it to Sir Nicholas Carew, courtier, diplomat and member of the Parliament of 1529. Carew was involved with the Marquess of Exeter in activities which were found treasonable, and was executed in December 1539; his lands were confiscated and the advowson reverted to the Crown. Edward VI granted it to the Archbishop of Canterbury, Cranmer, but Mary,

---

* Rich's surrender of the rectory and glebe houses may account for some confusion as to whether Deane was now curate, as he is described in the Parker certificates of 1560 and 1561, or rector or parson, as he is described by himself in his feoffment of 1557 and in a parishioner's will of 1556.

in recognition of the Carews' loyalty, restored the manor and advowson to Francis Carew, the son of Sir Nicholas. On the death of the existing incumbent, Carew presented John Deane, who was instituted in September 1557: no connection between Deane and Carew has been traced to explain the presentation. (Curiously, a month later the Crown granted letters of presentation to Bonner's chaplain.) Deane held the living until November 1562, when a successor was instituted, presented by the grantees of the late abbey; this suggests that both the Crown and Carew had disregarded some long lease of the advowson. Deane was certainly holding the living at the time of Archbishop Parker's survey in 1561, and he still had some property there in 1563: in the codicil to his will, which itself was dated April 1563, he gave to his cousin Oliver Bradford and his son 'my godson, my mare and cowlte at Culleston'.[8]

Out of the changes and chances of the 'fifties Deane emerged securely. Under Elizabeth's Act of Supremacy of 1559 a visitation took place at which the clergy were required to take the oath recognising the Queen's supremacy in the church. In the diocese of London proceedings began at St Paul's chapter house, and went on to other churches: Deane himself subscribed, signing his name, as curate, at a ceremony in the church of St Lawrence Jewry.[9] By Act of Parliament in the first year of Elizabeth's reign the church of St Bartholomew was restored to its use as the parish church. In February 1560, in consideration of a payment, Rich regained his property and the advowson from the Queen. Deane also seems to have regained his rectorship, for a return made to the Privy Council in 1563 by Grindal, Bishop of London, refers to him as 'Mr. Deane Rector'.[10] While Deane was apparently able to move with each successive religious change, Rich was unable to acquiesce completely in the Elizabethan settlement, and voted against the Act of Uniformity in the House of Lords.

After its vicissitudes under Henry VIII and Mary the fabric of Deane's church was still in danger under Elizabeth. In 1561 the spire of St Paul's Cathedral was struck by lightning and, together with the lead-covered roof, was destroyed by fire. The Bishop of London looked enviously at the lead on St Bartholomew's, and made an appeal to Sir William Cecil, the Queen's secretary: St Bartholomew's church, adjoining Lord Rich's house, he wrote, 'is in decaye and so encreaseth daylye: it hathe an heavie coate off leade, which would do verie goode service for the mother churche off Powles; I have obtyned my L. Riche's good wille, and iff I coulde obteyne my L. chieffe justice off the Kings benche [Catlin, a parishioner] and Sr. Walter Myldemaye's assente, I wolde nott doubte to have the assent also of the whole parisshe ...'. Grindal proposed that the church should be transferred to one of the old monastic buildings, the Fratrie. Cecil, however, seems not to have been favourable, and the matter was dropped. Some repairs must have been going on, or at least projected, to remedy the 'decay' referred to by Grindal, for Deane in a codicil to his will left 26s 8d to the reparations of the parish church.

Deane remained at St Bartholomew's as a priest of only modest qualifications and style, not licensed to preach and not maintaining 'hospitality'. He died in October 1563 and was buried on the south side of the sanctuary in St Bartholomew's.* The wording of his will, dated 6 April 1563, suggests a man of conservative religious views: he followed the traditional Catholic form of bequeathing his soul not only to God and to Christ but also to the Virgin and the company of saints. By the time of his death he was one of a very small number of clergymen in London whose incumbencies had begun under Edward VI or Henry VIII and who still retained their benefices: a year later, in 1564, there were only nine such clergymen. If, as has been said, most of the clergy (for whatever reasons) were 'quite ready to play the part of the Vicar of Bray all through these times', then John Deane was representative of his order.[11]

While he was in London Deane seems to have kept in touch with his native district. He was one of a spreading family: his brother, Richard, had five known children, and his sister, Agnes, had three married daughters. To two of his nephews, both named John, he was godfather: one niece lived in Knutsford, another in Weaverham, and a woman cousin lived in Chester. In addition, various members of the Sudlow family of Northwich were related to him: he left legacies in his will to Edward, William and John, and to Thomas, the son of his cousin, John Sudlow. He had a particular concern for the fatherless children of a deceased Thomas Sudlow, especially for his godson, John Sudlow, to whom he left that part of a house which he himself had occupied. His 'cousin', John Sudlow†, (described in Deane's will as John Sudlow, gent.), actually lived in London, in the other part of the same house, and was made an overseer of his will, while a William Deane lived at Billingsgate, so that there were many family links between Northwich and London. Deane kept up his connection with the town of Northwich

---

* In 1893 the pupils of Witton Grammar School presented to St Bartholomew's a memorial slab to the memory of their founder, now, according to Webb, on the floor near his grave. (E. A. Webb, *The Records of St. Bartholomew's Smithfield*, II, 301.)

† Although the wording of the will is rather obscure he seems to be a different person from the godson of the same name.

as well as with his family. When in 1548, under an Act of Parliament for making inventories of church plate, jewels and bells, a commission, including Sir Thomas Venables, carried out a survey of church goods in Cheshire, it certified to the Court of Augmentations that Northwich church had two chalices, and 'one other in the hands of Sir John Deyne, preste'. Why this should have been is a mystery and there is no suggestion (as at Church Lawton) that the chalice was held as security for a loan, but it does indicate the closeness of Deane's links with the parish.[12] Deane appears to have made periodic visits to Northwich, for in a letter of 1561 he referred to the school statutes having been 'openlye redde in your churche at my last being their'.

At any time when the central government was selling land on a large scale the intimate knowledge of the local man was invaluable in making a purchase. This was shown during the sales of Crown, Church and Royalist lands in the Civil War, and equally in the sixteenth century in the sale of monastic lands. Deane made one purchase of monastic property direct from the Crown. By a grant dated August 1543 he bought property in Northwich formerly belonging to the Cistercian monastery of Basingwerk, and paid £54 for it to the treasurer of the Court of Augmentations, Sir Edward North—a considerable sum for him to have laid out at this stage in his career. The property consisted of 'two salt pits (salinas)* formerly in the tenure of Wm. Sudlowe, and two more in tenure of George Sudlowe', 'with the lead [estimated at 40 'les weightes' in each two] and a messuage [a house with land] in tenure of Thomas Bromfelde'. The Sudlows were old tenants of Basingwerk Abbey: William Sudlow had a forty years lease of the two 'salinas' demised to him by an indenture of 1500, and George Sudlow's salt pans were demised to him for fifty years by an indenture of 1522: each paid twelve cranocks of salt or 12s a year rent.[13] Deane's relationship to the Sudlows may have led him to make this purchase from the King.

Deane was, however, soon involved in litigation to establish his right to part of this property. Some time before 1547 he addressed a complaint to the Chancellor of the Court of Augmentations, which in its judicial capacity dealt with suits involving former monastic possessions. Although the date of the petition is unknown, the Chancellor must have been either Sir Richard Rich or Sir Edward North, both parishioners of Deane's. In his petition Deane com-

---

* *Salinae* were plots of land with buildings on them, one of which must be occupied by any intending maker of salt before he was allowed to take brine from the pits. (J. Varley, *A Middlewich Chartulary*, *Chet. Soc.*, new series, 105, p. 37.)

plained that Alyce Holmes and Thomas Yate had forcibly occupied
one of the salt houses and a 'messuage' granted to him: they had
pulled down the messuage and burned the timber 'so that ther is
no tenemente nor howse leffte opon the grounde'. Deane prayed
for a Privy Seal writ ordering the offenders to appear in the Augmentations Court, but nothing further is recorded of the case.[14]

These four wich houses were those left by Deane in his will to
his nephew, John, the son of his brother Richard, but by the time
the Inquisition on his Cheshire land was taken, six months after his
death, there were only three, and his proper heir was declared to
be his nine-year-old great-niece, Alicia, the daughter of his nephew
Laurence. This procedure followed from the purchase of Crown
property: like most monastic land, it was held by Deane as a tenant-
in-chief of the Crown by the military tenure of knight service—in
Deane's case the twentieth part of a knight's fee—and it came
thereby under the surveillance of the Court of Wards and Liveries
and was subject to various feudal obligations. It was to meet the
considerable charges and fees involved in establishing possession of
land so held that Deane left £20 to his nephew, John, 'towardes
the charges of suinge his lyverie'. Furthermore, because he had
willed away property so held, a pardon of alienation had to be
purchased from the Crown after his death. Finally, the wardship
and marriage of his heir, Alice, a minor, was the Crown's to dispose
of, and in 1567 they were granted, with an annuity of 20s, to
Robert Shawe, a Northwich saltmaker.[15]

The other monastic properties which Deane acquired in Cheshire
he bought at second hand from the original grantee, or at a further
remove. From Basingwerk Abbey again came the land in the Wirral,
a good distance from Northwich but near to holdings of both the
Earl of Derby and Venables of Kinderton. This was a messuage
and tenement at Larton, in the parish of West Kirby, held under a
deed of 1503 by the Warrington family, who paid the monastery a
rent of 20s a year. In March 1553 it was included in a great rag-bag
of grants of land scattered throughout various counties made by
Edward VI to Leonard Browne, gentleman, of Skymande, Lincolnshire, and Anthony Trappes, gentleman, of London, for a total
sum of over £1,000. (Browne, incidentally, had links with the Dean
and Chapter of Lincoln, who in 1558 appointed him Receiver
General.) At some date between then and 1557, when he made
the feoffment for the school, Deane bought this isolated parcel of
land.[16] From the possessions of Norton Abbey Deane acquired lands
in Barnton and 'a crofte of lande now or late in the tenure of
Randoll Torbocke called Shaies Crofte or Cannons Crofte' in
Witton, which he left by will to his nephew. This croft, known also

as 'Shawe's crofte' and 'Jermins croft', was sold by the Crown as late as June 1554, together with a large number of other properties, to William Morgane of Pentrebagh, Monmouthshire, and Jerome Halley, gent., of London. Between then and 1563 it passed to Deane, and, unlike his earlier monastic purchase, this land was not held of the Crown by the onerous knight service but 'as of the manor of East Greenwich', a fictional tenure not involving the same feudal burdens whereby the land was made more attractive to a would-be purchaser.[17]

A good deal of Deane's Cheshire property and the bulk of his endowment of the school was, however, not monastic but chantry land. The dissolution of the chantries, which had been founded and endowed in great numbers in the later Middle Ages for religious, educational and charitable purposes, had been planned by an Act of Parliament under Henry VIII but interrupted by his death. The seizure of their property was put into effect by an Act of the first year of Edward VI, and to that end a survey was made in the next year by royal commissioners of all chantries and obits or anniversary services for the dead. The chantry at Witton has been described, and there seems no way of resolving the problem of the name of the chantry priest, which was given by the Cheshire commissioners as Thomas Waller, while Deane in 1557 referred to Thomas Bromfield, 'late chantry priest' (canteriste); possibly the commissioners did not enquire strictly into such a small endowment. The two-thirds of a salthouse from which the chantry's income derived was included in June 1549 in a grant of a large number of properties by the King to Nicholas Bacon of London, mercer, and John Crymes of London, clothworker. The King's two parts of a salthouse divided into three parts, 'in tenure of Thomas Bromefield in Northwych Cheshire . . . All which premises came to the king by the Act of I Edward VI' were granted to Bacon and Crymes 'as fully as they were held by . . . any chaplain of the Chapel of Wytton within the parish of Budworth'. They were to be held not by the burdensome knight service but by free socage as of the manor of Acton.* At a date between June 1549 and December 1551, probably in 1549, Deane bought this property from Bacon and Crymes. John Crymes's name suggests that he had links with Northwich: in 1568 Richard Crymes of London, haberdasher, a considerable speculator in monastic lands, left a bequest to Witton and referred to those bearing his name living near Northwich. Furthermore, John Crymes himself

---

* Before it became customary later in Edward VI's reign to use the fictional tenure of the royal manor of East Greenwich to enable purchasers to hold of the Crown by non-military tenure, the nearest royal manor to the land involved was used. (J. Hurstfield, *The Queen's Wards*, p. 21.)

had a married daughter named Alice Sudlowe, who was possibly
the wife of Edward Sudlow, one of the original feoffees of Deane's
school.[18]

Deane, however, had trouble also with this property, which was
to form a major part of the school's endowment. Between his
purchase and December 1551 he addressed to the Lord Chancellor,
then Lord Rich, a petition against Thomas Bromfield and Thomas
Newall, who were withholding the rents and profits of the salthouse
from him. The suit had to be brought in the equitable Court of
Chancery and not at common law, because Bromfield and Newall
possessed the legal documents by which Margaret Knottesford or
her feoffees had given the property for an obit, and 'by color of
havyng the same have entred into the premisses and do deteyne
the rents and proffitts of the same from your saide Oratour'. Deane
petitioned for a writ of sub-poena on Bromfield and Newall com-
manding them to surrender the deeds and to pay the 33*s* 4*d* rent
due at the previous Michaelmas, that is, two years' rent. Since no
more was heard of the case, and since Deane was able to include
the property in his feoffment of 1557, Bromfield and Newall presumably surrendered, and in 1557 Thomas Bromfield, 'late chantry
priest', was still the tenant. It has not been possible to identify this
man, though he may have been the son of Thomas Bromfield of
Little Witton, who included Thomas Newall among the executors
of his will, dated August 1558, and left to his master, Sir Thomas
Venables, 'three silver cupps guilt'.[19]

The great college of St John the Baptist in Chester had been
much favoured by chantry founders, and became a rich quarry of
lands after its dissolution in the first year of Edward VI's reign.
From its possessions in Chester the King, in 1552, gave a considerable grant to the grammar school at Macclesfield, founded fifty
years before, and thereby doubled the value of its endowments.
Within the precincts of the collegiate church there was a chapel of
St Anne, belonging to the fraternity of St Mary and St Anne.
These fraternities were characteristic of late medieval towns: this
one was already in existence in 1361, and was refounded in 1393,
when it included many wealthy citizens. Later it received generous
endowments with which it maintained a chantry served by two
chaplains, and by 1547 owned a large amount of house property
in Chester. In May 1553, together with other property to a total
purchase price of over £1,700, the King granted various possessions
of the fraternity and the college to Thomas Sydney of Walsingham,
Norfolk, described as 'the King's servant', and Nicholas Halswell
of Gotehurste, Somerset. Among them were several of the premises
with which Deane later endowed his school: these were 'the messuage

and garden called "the signe of the Swanne" in the street called
Foregatestrete in Chester in tenure of Peter Nicholas and Alice his
wife and the close of land in tenure of Peter Nicholas, which
belonged to the late fraternity of St. Anne in Chester'; 'other three
messuages in tenure of John Hankeye, assignee of Hugh Hankey
and Margaret his wife, in Chester, which belonged to the said
fraternity of St. Anne there' (this was what Deane described as the
Saracen's Head); and 'the croft of land in tenure of Thomas Ball
upon le "Deye Bankes" in the fields of the city of Chester . . .
which belonged to the late College of St. John Baptist in Chester'.
We do not know when, between 1553 and 1557, Deane bought
these properties or how he came to choose them.* He may have
bought the land in Barnton occupied by Thomas Lytloner and
formerly belonging to Norton Abbey from these same grantees,
Sydney and Halswell, but another item in Sydney and Halswell's
grant has a special interest. After reciting the grant to Deane, in
1543, of four salt pits in Northwich to be held 'for ever, of the
King in chief by the service of the twentieth part of one knight's
fee and a rent of 4s yearly at the Augmentations', the new grant
transferred this rent, payable by Deane, to Sydney and Halswell.
Very little is known about the way in which these enormous grants
of scattered properties were made up and how they were subsequently redistributed, so that this point of contact within the same
grant between the grantees and one of the ultimate purchasers is
of interest.[20]

Deane does not seem to have confined himself to buying monastic
and chantry lands. Among the petitions to Nicholas Heath, Archbishop of York, when he was Lord Chancellor (between 1556 and
1558), is one from 'John Deane, clerk' who, in the Cheshire context,
is very probably John Deane of St Bartholomew's. The petitioner
related how one Gilbert Grene, a clergyman and an ex-monk of the
suppressed monastery of Combermere, had sold him his pension of
£5 a year granted out of the abbey lands (according to witnesses,
in December 1551) but had failed to fulfil his verbal promise to
complete the transfer in writing, intending to defraud the petitioner
not only of the pension but also of the purchase money which he
had already paid. In the absence of any writing Deane had no
remedy at common law and had to appeal to Chancery. Gilbert
Grene replied by asserting that Deane had got possession of the
letters patent granting the pension on the death of one Edward

* Deane had a cousin, Alice Barlow, in West Chester (i.e. Chester) who
may have had some link with the Swan: in 1586 the school feoffees paid
£6 13s 4d to an 'Alles Barlow' in consideration of her surrender of the lease
of the Swan.

Bury, to whom he had given them to be kept safely for his own use, and that Deane had for about four years received the pension in Grene's name: he absolutely denied any sale of the pension to Deane. There is a 'replication' from 'Sir John Dean Clerk' re-affirming his charges, and a rejoinder from Grene, persisting in his denials, together with depositions in 1556 by several of Deane's witnesses.* A pension list of Combermere Abbey in 1556 has John Deane as assignee for Grene's pension, and it seems strange, if Deane's case was untrue, that Grene had not himself taken legal action earlier.[21]

Deane's activities in the land market and the property, both landed and personal, which he left at his death suggest that he was a man of some substance. His income derived from various sources, some ecclesiastical and some private. From his living at St Bartholo-mew's he had a stipend of £11 a year; his prebend in Lincolnshire was leased at £5 6s 8d a year, and in addition, for a few years, he had the living of Coulsdon, valued in 1535 at almost £22. This was at a time when £20 has been described as 'the pay of a well-paid canon'. But Deane also had property in his own right. At his death his property in Northwich and district (apart from that with which he had endowed his school) was leased out to tenants at an estimated annual return of nearly £3. His London house property had previously belonged to the monasteries of St Bartholomew and of Hounslow, and was estimated to be worth close on £5 a year, and he drew Grene's pension of £5 a year for some time. As parish priest, too, Deane had been the recipient of a number of bequests from his parishioners. Dr Richard Bartlett left him 20s and his 'worstead gowne furred'; Edward Corbett, gentleman, left him 13s 4d in 1549, together with the £10 which he owed him. Dame Dorothy Paver, a widow living in the close from 1543 at least, left him a 'gilte pece', the lease of her house, and 20s for his work as exe-cutor of her will of 1548. She was undoubtedly connected with the Northwich family of Paver, one of whom was appointed by Deane as his attorney in the school feoffment.† Probable links with Deane's family are to be found in her bequests to John Deane (not *Sir* John Deane), Margaret Bradford, Anne Deane, and to her 'servant' Agnes Deane, a co-executor with Deane, and very probably his sister, later Agnes Bradford.[22]

---

* One of the witnesses was Robert Moyses, of the parish of Great St Bartholomew's, a servant of Sir Walter Mildmay.

† The two-thirds part of a salthouse with which Deane endowed his school was on the same site as the third owned by the heirs of James Paver of Watford, a place with which her will shows that Dame Dorothy Paver was connected. (Calvert, *op. cit.*, p. 1111.)

In his own lengthy and complicated will, made in April 1563, Deane was lavish in his monetary bequests, which totalled over £100 (a large amount for a priest), the largest single bequest being the £20 to his nephew towards suing his livery. Five families were each left £5 and one over £6 to buy mourning clothes. There were numerous charitable legacies on a conventional pattern: 20s was left to the poor householders in the parish of his burial; five marks to the poor householders in Northwich; 20s to the 'pore folkes in St. Bartillmew's Spitle suche as have most neede in the same howse'. Further, there were bequests similar to those found in several of his parishioners' wills to the prisoners of Newgate, Ludgate, the King's Bench and Marshalsea prisons. One beneficiary under his will was charged to distribute each Christmas Eve for ever, out of the profits of his legacy, 10s in coal, wood or money to the poor house-holders of St Bartholomew's, with the advice of the churchwardens; failure to distribute the charity meant immediate loss of the pro-perty bequeathed by Deane, but there is no record of anything ever having been paid out. A similar charity was made the condition of a bequest in Northwich to John Deane and his heirs male: out of the profits of the property they were 'yearlie for ever [to] geve, distri-bute and bestowe amongest the pore schollers and pore folkes of my free scole and parishe of Wytton Xs. in the vigill or even of the birthe of oure Lorde God'. It is not known if this charity was ever distri-buted, but Deane had taken the precaution of making the bequest public knowledge by advertising it at the end of his statutes for the school, and as these were to be read out regularly it is probable that the money was distributed.

In addition to gifts of money Deane gave a quarter's rent to every one of his London tenants, with the exception of Augustine Turner, who owed two quarters' rent and was forgiven one. He left to rela-tives and friends certain specified articles which are of some interest: to John Deane he left a ring of gold 'havinge the twoo letters of my name graven therin'; to his executor, Richard Durante, a neighbour and parishioner, he left 'my velvet jacket and a ringe of gould wayinge three poundes* havinge a deathes heade to turn aboute in yt'; to his cousin, Alice Barlow of West Chester, 'a girdle with a pen-dante of silver parcell gilte'; to 'Sir Henry of St. Pulchers [St Sepulchre's] a lyned blacke gowne', and to Bryan Storke, 'myne hoste', and his wife 'all the moveables that shall remayne in the perloure where I lye at the time of my deathe' and 'my second coverlett'. His livestock, his cow and his mare and colt at Coulsdon, were also carefully allotted. The impression given by the will, which

* See Ormerod, I, 525, fn. referring to a chain of gold weighing about xxx li (meaning sovereigns), mentioned in a will of 1579.

is occasionally carelessly drafted, is of a kindly man anxious not to
forget any of his numerous relations, godsons and friends, including
in some instances their servants too: 10s to each servant of his tenant
of the Half Moon Inn, Bryan Storke, 'that shall serve in his house
at the time of my death', and 40s to his own boy, Thomas Temple.
He did, however, ignore completely the relation who proved to be
the legal heir of his Cheshire property, his great-niece, and he
willed away all his landed property when by law a tenant-in-chief
of the Crown could dispose freely of only two-thirds.

   John Deane displayed a strong local patriotism very characteristic
of his period, and also in his various pronouncements a touch of the
authority of the conscious local benefactor, benefiting his native
district out of the proceeds of his own efforts. In his own community
he had indeed raised himself into the ranks of the fairly substantial
wich house owners in Northwich. In the 1565 list he appeared with
twelve leads, well below the really large owners like Sutton and
Sir John Warburton, well below Sir Thomas Venables, James Paver,
'Mr. Leftwich', and Laurence Winnington, but on a level with
Leigh of Adlington, and above Robert Bromfield (son of Thomas)
and Winnington of Birches. He was considerably above the
general run of owners such as Peter Paver, Raffe Done, esquire,
Richard Litler and Humphrey Walley. As late as 1619 the memory
of his purchases was enshrined in the official list of salthouses: 'Roger
Deane of Shurlach 2 [wich-houses] ... now they are John Deanes
landes purchased by parson Deane': 'Thomas Sudlowe of Witton
late Simcock's land purchased by parson Deane'. (Alicia Deane
married Arthur Symcock, and they established their claim in 1574
to the third of Deane's Northwich property which, under the Statute
of Wills of 1540, had to descend to the legal heir of a Crown tenant-
in-chief. Their son, George, established his claim by a similar writ
of livery in 1596.[23]) Quite apart from his foundation of the school,
therefore, John Deane, parson of Great St Bartholomew's, Smithfield, left his mark on his native community, and a not inconsiderable
one for a member of the lower clergy at that date.

III
The foundation

With the founding of Witton grammar school in 1557 by Sir John Deane, priest, Northwich had its share in a country-wide movement which gave an impetus to education in the sixteenth and early seventeenth centuries. In his study of charitable foundations in Lancashire in the later sixteenth century Professor Jordan drew attention to 'the pervading influence' of London, and the large role played by Londoners who had been born in Lancashire. In Cheshire, too, two grammar schools, at Stockport and Macclesfield, had already been founded by rich London merchants of local origin. Sir Edmund Shaa, founder of Stockport grammar school by his will of 1488, and Sir John Percival, founder of Macclesfield grammar school in 1502, were merchants of such eminence that each had held the office of Lord Mayor of London. Rich merchants remembering their native towns or villages were frequent founders of schools in the sixteenth century, and so were high-ranking clergymen, from Dean Colet of St Paul's and Bishop Hugh Oldham of Manchester grammar school early in the century to such later founders or re-founders of Lancashire schools, as Archbishop Parker at Rochdale, Dean Alexander Nowell at Middleton and Bishop James Pilkington at Rivington. To find a member of the lower clergy as a benefactor of his native town is, however, rarer, and in this Witton is unusual, although it has been suggested that when the London lower clergy did make benefactions they were especially concerned with education.[1] Within Cheshire itself John Deane had two recent royal examples to follow: the foundation in 1541 by Henry VIII of the free school of Chester, connected with the cathedral of the newly created diocese, and the re-endowment in 1552 by Edward VI of Macclesfield grammar school. The latter actually set a precedent for Deane to follow by granting to the school property in Chester which had belonged to the College of St John the Baptist.

In London, too, Deane was very near to the fountain-head of the stream of educational foundations. St Paul's school, re-founded in 1509–12 by Dean Colet, lay close to Deane's church, so much so that in his statutes Colet forbade his pupils to engage in 'disputing at Sent Bartilmews', a custom described by John Stow in his *Survey of London*, published in 1598. 'The arguing of the schoolboys about the principles of grammar hath been continued even till our time,' wrote Stow, 'for I myself in my youth, have yearly seen, on the eve of St. Bartholomew the Apostle, the scholars of divers grammar schools repair unto the churchyard of St. Bartholomew's, the priory in Smithfield.' These disputations 'surceased' after the surrender of the priory to Henry VIII, but Deane may well have seen them himself.[2] Individuals, too, in the official circles with which Deane was in contact were involved in founding or re-founding grammar schools: in 1551, Chelmsford grammar school was re-founded at the request of several Essex chantry commissioners, including Thomas and Walter Mildmay, while in his will of 1559 Sir John Williams, a treasurer of the Court of Augmentations, was to found such a school at Thame. Sir Rowland Hill, who had been one of the witnesses of Rich's conveyance of the glebe property to Deane, founded in 1556 a free school in his native town of Drayton in Shropshire, with the churchwardens of the parish as his trustees.* In such a milieu Deane would have had no difficulty in finding the 'godlye and discrete advise of the learned' which he used in drawing up his statutes, and it is not surprising that he wished his scholars to keep the customs of what he called 'great scoles'.

The feoffment

A month after John Deane was instituted to the living of Coulsdon—that is, on 26 October 1557—he drew up, 'for the good and Christian education [institucione] of boys within the township of Witton near Northwich in virtue and good letters', an indenture in Latin enfeoffing twelve men from the locality with properties in Chester, Northwich, Agden, Peover and Larton in the Wirral,† and appointing two attorneys to deliver possession to the feoffees on his behalf. The deed was witnessed by the Recorder of London and three others, and attached to it was a schedule reciting in English the purposes for which the feoffment was made.‡ This lengthy and verbose legal document recites how

---

* Hill had, incidentally, two interesting Cheshire connections. He leased lands from the Abbot of Combermere from 1537, and after the dissolution he acquired, in 1541, the manor of Darnhall, near Northwich, formerly belonging to Vale Royal monastery. See G. Chesters in *The Cheshire Round*, vol. I, 4, p. 108, and Ormerod, II, 180.

† For these see Appendix II and pp. 57–61.

‡ See Appendix II.

I the sayd Sir John Deane, perceyvinge and well consyderinge howe very godly, vertuous and necessary itt is to provyde that youthe shall and maye be brought uppe in vertue, learninge and good order and obedyence, wherbye they maye the better knowe and serve God and proffitt ther countrey, have fullye determyned with mye self by goddes furtherance, to ordeyne, take order and establyshe that a free grammar scoole shalbe by me founded and erected within the towneshipe off Wytton nere to the sayd vylledge off Northwyche.

The duties of the feoffees were laid down, together with arrangements for the choice and maintenance of 'one good able and sufficient scoolemaster teachinge grammer scoole' and, if the finances allowed, of an usher or assistant master. This method of founding a school by making a charitable trust was a common one: letters patent from the Crown, making possible incorporation, were probably expensive and perhaps needed an influential friend at court.[3]

Deane's deed appointed Peter Paver of Northwich and Richard Wilbram of Crosse, yeoman, attorneys to hand over the property to the feoffees, and on 6 November, twelve days after the signing of the deed by Deane, they delivered possession to two of the feoffees, Robert Wynington of Northwich and George Sudlowe, acting on behalf of their co-feoffees, after the deed and schedule had been read in English. The undertaking of the trust took place in the presence of thirteen named local men (including four 'gentlemen') and of others unnamed, and was thus accepted before the community.* The list of feoffees named by Deane began with his brother, Richard, yeoman of Shurlach, and his three sons. It included two Sudlows—Edward, a yeoman of Lostock, who was doubtless the man to whom Deane left 40s in his will and who, in 1565, held four 'leads' of Deane's property, and George, a yeoman of Crosse, probably the man mentioned in Deane's will as holding part of the four wich houses owned by Deane in Northwich.† Of the two other yeomen among the feoffees, William Walley of Hartford was probably the tenant of land in Shurlach left by Deane to his nephew. John Deane, but nothing is known of Hugh 'Cowe' of Cross.‡ The original feoffees included also Philip Downes, mercer, of Northwich, Robert Wynington of Northwich, gentleman, a salt owner and

* See Appendix II.
† He may have been the George Sudlowe described as 'of Northwich, gent', whose son entered the Middle Temple in 1565.
‡ Both the nearly contemporary copy of the feoffment in the Bishop's Register at Chester and Randle Holmes's copy in the British Museum give this name as 'Hugh Cowe', but a nineteenth-century copyist altered it to 'Hugh Lowe', who appears in the Walling Book of 1565 as a substantial saltmaker. The name 'Lowe' certainly appears later among the feoffees, but a 'John Coe' appears in the feoffment of 1578.

maker, Thomas Masterson of Winington, gentleman, and John Wynington, kinsman and heir of Robert Wynington of Birches. The last four were men of proved substance or status: Robert Wynnyngton of Northwich, Philip Downes and John Wynnyngton of Birches were rated in the subsidy roll of 1559, and in 1580, at the herald's visitation of Cheshire, a Masterson of Winington (and Nantwich) and a Winington of Birches appeared to affirm their status of gentility and to enter their pedigrees.[4] It is noteworthy that the feoffees did not include the lord of the manor of either Northwich or Witton.

John Deane's relations were particularly prominent among the feoffees, and later, in the statutes, Deane explicitly stated that 'as often as iiij of the feoffees bee deade, the reste of the feoffees survivinge, within one quarter of a year, shall assemble them selves at the schoolehouse aforesaid and shall not onlye then and their elect and choose iiij others of the founder's next kynsfolke . . .': only for lack of such were they to choose 'foure of the mooste honeste, sage and discretest persons beynge inhabytants of the parisshe of Wytton'. (Even for the post of schoolmaster Deane, in his statutes, favoured his kinsfolk, if equally qualified, over other applicants.) This preference for the founder's kin was not uncommon in Tudor grammar schools and made for an inbred group, but Deane provided, even in his original deed, some external control over his feoffees. They were to pay over each year on the feasts of St Michael and of the Annunciation* (beginning with the following Michaelmas, i.e. 1558), or within twelve days of each, to the churchwardens of the church of Northwich £12 in two equal parts, 'which somme I wyll shalbe holly bestowed by the sayd churchwardens for the tyme beynge' for the master's wages. Moreover, if the income of the property could be increased above £12, the excess was to be used, at the *churchwardens'* discretion, either towards finding an usher 'or ells to some other suche good purpose as they, the same churchwardeins for the tyme beynge, shall thinke good and necessary for the preservacion, maynetenance and contynuance off the sayd free scoole forevermore'. There was thus a built-in system of checks and balances between the feoffees and the wardens in the administration of the school's income, for the former were authorised by Deane to use part of the rents for upkeep and repairs. In the appointment of the schoolmaster Deane decreed in the schedule that during his own lifetime the master was to be 'named, examined, appointed, placed, removed and removeable from tyme to tyme' by himself or an assignee: after his death the duty was to devolve on the Bishop and

* 29 September and 25 March.

schoolmaster of Chester. For the future, therefore, there was to be a closer external supervision than the ordinary episcopal licensing.

The statutes

Although the school does not possess the original deed by which John Deane founded it, it is fortunate in still possessing one of the original copies of his statutes.* In his letter of August 1561 on the choice of a master, Deane stated that 'the same statutes, hanginge in the scole, were openlye redde in your churche at my last beinge their', and continued, 'I praie you send me upp the statuts hither to London to th'intent I maye set my hande to them in confyrmacion, and in the meanetyme those that you have to hange theym upp in the scole'. The framed copy which now hangs in the school is apparently the one which was sent up to Deane and signed by him.† It is written on parchment in a good hand, with characteristic mid-sixteenth-century floral decoration, and it opens with a 'portrait' of the founder, which is, however, probably only a conventional representation.‡ Deane is shown wearing a fur-trimmed gown, a cap and a stole or scarf: in one hand he holds a book and from the other comes a scroll bearing the words 'Miserere meum Deus et averte faciem tuam peccatis meis', taken from Psalm 51, one of the seven penitential psalms which Deane required his scholars to recite every Friday.

The statutes had an eventful history. They were of supreme importance to both feoffees and masters of the school, since they were the standard of conduct by which both would be judged in any legal dispute. They were also in constant use: they had to be read at the installation of a master and at the admission of a pupil, and they were taken over to the church of St Helen to be read 'at every feaste before the breaking upp of the schoole to all the schollers to th'intent the schollers maie the better theirby remember their duetie in the tyme of their absence'. It is therefore not surprising to find the accounts of the feoffees punctuated with items for renewing and safeguarding the copies of the statutes. John Deane had ordered that one set should hang in the school, and in 1579, at the beginning of the surviving accounts, the feoffees paid 4s 10d for 'wrytinge of the statute the frame and lynen cloth to hange them in the schole'. In 1598 5s 6d was paid to a scrivener for engrossing the statutes and in 1602 3s 4d for binding them. In 1617 the statutes were ingrossed

---

* See Appendix II.
† The signature strongly resembles the signature on Deane's application to purchase his salthouses, P.R.O. E 318/359.
‡ See frontispiece.

at a cost of £1; in 1621 they were set in a frame and 1s was spent at setting up the statutes. No more is heard of them until the mysterious entry in 1662: 'paid to Parson Dayne that he spent regaineing the statutes of the school that had been taken away by Jeffrey Harrison 1s 2d.'* The statutes needed engrossing again in 1667, and the feoffees paid the large sum of £2 6s 8d for this. It seems to have been a major event in the management of the school at this time. In February 1667 the feoffees spent 2s 8d on 'Mr. Richard Baker and his friends that came with him to shew us the schoole statutes after he had fairly ingrossed them'. In July the bailiff feoffees went to Chester to see about the setting of the statutes in a new frame of wood, with two lids or covers, costing 8s, and coloured and laid with oil for 2s. An ex-schoolmaster, then resident in Chester, saw to the carriage of the statutes in their frame from the painter's house to a salter who brought them safely to Northwich at a cost of 2s 6d plus entertainment. In 1682 a lock and rod of iron were bought for the statutes, and in 1687 a key.

It is possible that some verbal tradition of this recovery and recopying survived into the nineteenth century. When, in 1818, Nicholas Carlisle published his survey of grammar schools based on information received from the schools, his information from Witton was that the founder's 'excellent *Statutes*, which seem to have been recovered by accident in a mutilated condition, were recopied and handed down to posterity by the two Bailiff Feoffees in 1666'. Carlisle also stated that 'there is likewise added to them a list of the *Feoffees* acting in 1744, probably with the intent to show the number at that period in existence, since the Founder's Statutes have left that point undefined'. A torn paper copy of the statutes with a reference to 1666 and a list of the feoffees of 1741 is among the school papers, but the framed copy has no such list and is of earlier date: it was presumably kept in custody by the feoffees, while the second copy was in general use and needed frequent renewal.

The vicissitudes of the statutes were not ended by 1818. J. Weston, who in the last century collected together some materials for the history of the school, noted on 25 September 1872, 'I have before me the recovered statutes of Sir John Deane engrossed on two skins of parchment, they were purchased by Rev. Henry Linthwaite headmaster from 1857 to 1872 from a London bookseller to whom they were sold from some solicitor's office together with a lot of ancient pleadings in Chancery—1834 etc., ... Mr. Linthwaite, who now, September 1872, has removed to Durham having lately accepted a benefice there declines to sell this locally historical treasure which I

---

* See below, Chapter VI, p. 115.

hope will not leave the neighbourhood for very long time.' Weston's hope was fulfilled, for Mrs Greenall, widow of Archdeacon Greenall, bought the documents, and the governors had the statutes framed in October 1874. How Linthwaite learned of the whereabouts of the original copy of the statutes is not known: it seems that through some extraordinary carelessness it was not returned to the feoffees after use as evidence in the Hand Chancery case, but must have remained in a London solicitor's office unclaimed after the end of the case. Some repairs and re-touching seem to have taken place in 1901.[5]

The statutes which Deane drew up have generally been assumed to date from 1558, but in fact they are not dated: the only date mentioned in them is that of the 'erection' of the school at Michaelmas 1558, so they were clearly drawn up later. Statutes were by no means always drawn up at the time of the foundation of a school: even where authority to make them had been granted, years might elapse before they were made—three years at Hawkshead, for instance, eight at Grantham and over a hundred at Birmingham. Deane's statutes should most probably be read in conjunction with his letter, dated 30 August 1561, to an unknown recipient or recipients, which was found at the bottom of the school chest in 1708 by one of the bailiff feoffees.* Faced with disagreements over the choice of a schoolmaster, Deane, 'as one to whome me thinke, the thinge beinge by me founded, apperteyneth', required that attention should be paid to 'my meanynge in the foundacion'. He urged the electors, leaving their affections aside, to bind their election simply upon the statutes which were hanging in the school and had been read openly in Witton Chapel during his last visit. When the requirements had been carefully considered, Deane asked for the statutes to be sent up to London to receive his signature in confirmation, while a second copy was hung in the school. In addition to underlining the procedure for choosing the master, Deane in his letter also clarified the arrangements for the management of the school property by the two bailiff feoffees in association with the churchwardens. Finally, he ordered—it is hardly too strong a word—that the letter should be read in the church so that the whole parish should understand his intentions. Deane's desire to add his signature to the statutes and to clarify their meaning by having his letter read out in church strongly suggest that they had not long been drawn up. The curious, and strictly irrelevant, 'special remembrance' at the end of the statutes suggests a date towards the end of Deane's life. In it, after publicising the bequests under his will to the poor of the parish and the poor scholars of the school, he ends with a solemn

* See Appendix II.

valedictory message, 'And thus I bid you all farewell and desire you all to pray for me.'

It is noteworthy that in the statutes Deane made slight alterations in the arrangements for managing the school as laid down in the schedule to the feoffment, changes which showed a more detailed and businesslike approach. Instead of waiting until eight feoffees had died before making up the number to twelve, a new feoffment was to be made when only four had died. The management of the finances was given to two bailiff feoffees elected by their fellows and the churchwardens: they were to hold office for two years only and were to render account yearly to the other feoffees and the wardens 'uppon Jhesus even', presumably the day before 'Jhesus daie'. Further, the master was to be paid his salary quarterly instead of twice yearly.

The statutes laid down by the founder had binding force at law, and this was, of course, a reason for drawing them up. 'For that nothinge can endure and contyneue longe in good ordre without lawes and statutes' (a quotation from Colet's statutes for St Paul's), Deane drew up 'certeyne orders, rules, statutes and lawes to be observed and kepte for ever', to provide against any 'rulers or teachers as eyther thrughe a singularytie or els necligence wolde not observe such good customes, ordres, statutes and lawes as their predecessors have used, and as are used in the great scoles, to the great hinderance of the scollers'. Among Cheshire grammar schools Witton was unusual in having written statutes: neither Stockport nor Macclesfield had statutes, and although Edward VI's charter to Macclesfield authorised the governors, with the bishop's advice, to make statutes from time to time, no composite list was ever made.[6] In the early years, particularly, detailed statutes were undoubtedly of value, and the repeated reading of them to the masters and scholars instilled the traditions of the school. But as centuries passed written statutes, especially if too specific on detail, could become a check on development and provide material for legal controversy: unlike Colet, Deane did not give his trustees discretionary power to alter the statutes. Equally, any ambiguities in the wording of statutes could be exploited in the event of a dispute: the various references to the role of the churchwardens in Deane's feoffment, statutes and letter were such as to confuse the issue if differences existed between the feoffees and the wardens. Moreover, explicit as they were on certain points, Deane's statutes were inadequate on two important matters. He did not define the 'freedom' of the school exactly, that is, how many free scholars there were to be, if they were to be limited, and what the exact qualification was to be, apart from kinship to the founder regardless of place of habitation; and although he mentioned an usher in the schedule to the foundation deed he made no reference to him in the statutes, and did not state clearly by whom he was to be chosen.*

Six of the sixteen statutes concerned the schoolmaster. The first statute of all very properly dealt with the 'qualities of the Scolemaister', since in many towns the school *was* the master. Deane required for his school a master 'lerned, sobre, discrete and unmaryed' with an Oxford or Cambridge degree or degrees, 'ondefamed and of th'age of thirtie yeres at least'. In another statute he willed that if any of his kindred were 'hable and meete to teach or comparable to those which may be gottin when the place is voide, that theye shalbe preferred'; failing them, a qualified man born in the parish or brought up in the school was to have preference. Not many school statutes were specific about whether the master should be married or single. Several, including St Paul's, left the matter open, but Manchester Grammar School had the same requirement of celibacy as Witton.[7] (It will be remembered that Deane himself had remained a celibate priest.) Arrangements were laid down for admitting the master to the school (a ceremony in which the schoolmaster of Chester was to take part); for removing the master, with due notice on either side; for his stipend, and for his annual leave of thirty days (with the feoffees' licence) 'to recreate hymselfe', 'soo it be for reasonable occasions and urgent busynes', and provided that 'his schollers loose no tyme in his absence, but that they be occupyed and exercysed at their bookes till his returne, at his chardges'. (The relation of these thirty days to terms and vacations is rather obscure, but the reference to paying a substitute seems to imply term time.†) Deane was explicit on the faults disqualifying a master, apart from negligence or inefficiency: he was not to be 'dissolute in maners, a drunkerde, a horemaister, or intangeled with other occupacions repugnaunt to his vocation'. Finally, Deane made sensible provision to protect the master against interference by parents of children whom he had disciplined.

In the election and admission of the master Deane associated with the feoffees 'certeyn honeste men of the parisshe of Wytton'. This is a vague term, but it was clearly intended as a means to interest and involve the local community in the working of the school. Similarly, at the installation of the master the churchwardens were to distribute among the feoffees, 'th'other honest men of the parisshe of Wytton' and the Chester schoolmaster 40*s* 'for their paynes' in

* See below, Chapter VII.
† *Cf.* Darnhall School, whose foundation was influenced by Witton, where the thirty days' absence allowed to the master was specifically of 'school time'. (*C.S.*, third series, IV, 105–7.)

acquainting him with the school, its rules and property. If, on leaving, the master failed to give the required six months' notice
'openlye in the church' on Sunday or a festival day, the feoffees
were to retain 40*s* of his wages for distribution among forty poor
people of the parish. The founder intended his school to be an
integral part of the local community.

Deane founded his free grammar school, as he stated in his feoffment, for the education of boys 'infra villam de Wytton iuxta
Northwyche', Witton being, like Northwich, a township within the
chapelry of Witton. In the schedule to the feoffment he referred to
the churchwardens of the church of *Northwich*, but in the statutes
describe them as the churchwardens of *Witton*, wrote of the parish
of *Witton*, but referred to his school as the free grammar school at
Northwich. This confusion of terminology drew comment during
the two Chancery cases in which the school was involved in the
nineteenth century. The names 'Witton School' and 'Northwich
School' were both in use: a master's will referred to the school in
Witton and an old pupil's to the free school in Northwich. In the
entrance records of Cambridge colleges Northwich School was the
usual title, but Witton occasionally appears, while in the school's
own records although Witton School was in regular use the alternative occurs.* However, despite these confusions, what is clear is
that the school, like so many contemporary foundations, was
intended to serve a restricted area: Deane's kinsfolk, 'whearsoever
they dwell', were to be freely taught; otherwise the freedom, though
not explicitly defined, had patently a local basis. Within this locality
the school was for all ranks of society: in the statute on discipline
Deane insisted that 'all the scollers *of what estate, condicion or
degree so ever they be*' should submit to the master's correction,
while in his will he provided for the distribution of 5*s* a year to the
poor scholars of his school (my italics).

There was indeed no provision made for paying pupils, but for
all pupils there was an entrance, or more exactly an enrolment, fee
of 4*d*. This was the amount charged at St Paul's School: elsewhere
entrance fees varied from 1*d* to 12*d*. The child, of at least six years
of age, had to be presented to the master by his friends, who were
to promise that he would abide by the rules which the master read
out; thereupon the master would admit him and write his name in a
roll of parchment. If the parents or friends would not pay the
entrance money willingly, the child was to be refused. The only
other payment which Deane exacted from the scholars to the master
was 'on the firste Thursdaie after the begynnyng of schoole after

* The first surviving accounts refer to the stock of the 'schole of Northwiche'.

Christmas, of every scholler a penny commonlye caulled a cock-pennye'. A cock-penny was a gratuity given to the master, usually at Shrovetide and especially in schools in the north of England, to purchase his consent to the sport of cock-fighting, and to defray the expenses of it. At Warrington free school, according to the statutes of 1526, the master was allowed to take a cock-penny in the quarter after Christmas, but at Manchester Grammar School the master and usher were required (in 1524) to teach freely without any cock-penny or suchlike reward. Colet had forbidden cock-fighting altogether at St Paul's, but in this respect Deane did not follow him.[8] Deane's school, therefore, was a 'free' school in the sense defined by A. F. Leach: 'entrance fees, and all sorts of extras and luxuries, such as fires, light, candles, stationery, cleaning, whipping, might have to be paid for; but a free School meant undoubtedly a School in which, because of the endowment, all, or some of the scholars, the poor or the inhabitants of the place, or a certain number, were freed from fees for teaching'.[9]

The boys were to come to John Deane's school at 7 a.m. winter and summer alike: this was the most common time for starting school, and, whatever we may think of it, it was a rather more humane hour than that of some schools which began at 6 a.m. in the summer. The break for dinner was from 11 a.m. to 1 p.m., after which there were four more hours of school until 5 p.m. These hours were kept six days a week, but Deane decreed that on Thursday and Saturday afternoons the scholars should 'refresshe themselves', as also on 'hollydaies'—that is, saints' days and holy days—specifying the free time to avoid disagreement between master and pupils. This was a generous provision for recreation compared with many schools, which, although they observed holy days, had only one half day a week, usually Thursday. The number and season of vacations varied between schools, and Deane was not explicit, but the arrangements for 'barring out' before Christmas and Easter suggest that the school may originally have had only two vacations, probably amounting in all to about five weeks, apart from scattered holy days. By the late seventeenth century, however, and possibly earlier, there was a Whitsuntide vacation too.*

Deane tried to regulate the behaviour of his scholars during the holidays as well as in term, decreeing that the statutes should be read to them in the church 'at every feaste before the breaking upp of the schoole',

---

* The breaking up of the school at Whitsuntide is mentioned in the accounts in 1687. See also Chapter VII, pp. 141 and 143, and *cf.* Darnhall School (*C.S.*, third series, IV, 106) and Audlem (B. Redwood, *C.A.J.*, new series, 51, p. 48).

to thintent the schollers maie the better theirby remembre their duetie, in
the tyme of their absence. And that the Schoolemaister do gyve them an
exortacion in the schoole before they break upp schoole, howe they shall
ordre them selves till their returne. At which tyme I will that foure of the
feoffees and the churchewardeyns be present to thintent they maie gyve
warninge to suche schollers as they shall see to offend against the said
exortacion or against enny of theis estatutes.

The requirement evokes the close-knit, all-seeing local community,
reflected also in the presentments for moral disciplining before the
ecclesiastical courts. In a way very characteristic of Tudor government enactments Deane specified the games to be played by the
boys while on holiday or at play: archery, but not such unlawful
games as bowls, quoits, cards and dicing. Archery was favoured
as developing a sturdy population capable of self-defence, and therefore encouraged and indeed enforced by law. The other games were
presumably condemned as an occasion for gambling: John Earle
in his *Microcosmographie* of 1628 described a bowling alley as a
place 'where there are three things thrown away besides bowls, to
wit, time, money and curses'.

The custom of 'barring out' the master has been described as
'probably the most popular event of the year where it was tolerated'.
At Witton it was actually sanctioned by the statutes: 'I will that . . . a
weeke before Christynmas and Easter accordinge to the olde
custome, they barre, and keepe forth of the schoole the schoolemaister in suche sorte as others scollers doo in great schooles.' By
this custom the boys, under the head boy, barricaded the master
out of the school, only admitting him on condition that all past
offences were forgiven. The schoolmaster and educationist Charles
Hoole, writing about 1640, thought it a custom worth retaining, with
certain conditions: the master was to be warned in advance; the
boys were to 'behave themselves merrily and civilly'; their petition
[for pardon] was to be presented 'writ fairly in Latin', and the
master was to agree to it in front of witnesses before being allowed
in, when he would receive 'a short congratulatory oration, and
dismiss them to play'. This was probably a counsel of perfection: Dr
Johnson, who had himself experienced this licensed safety valve for
schoolboy energy, described it as 'a disorderly privilege which at
that time prevailed in the principal seminaries of education'. It was
still observed at Burnley Grammar School in the early nineteenth
century, and as late as 1876 was recorded at the National School of a
village near Accrington.[10]

It has been frequently pointed out that Deane's rules for the
curriculum of his school bear a strong resemblance to those of Colet,
drawn up in 1518 for St Paul's School. Colet's statutes formed the

pattern for many foundations, but this resemblance is of special
interest in view of Deane's own very modest learning. Colet's articles
on the curriculum are reproduced here for comparison with Deane's
seventh statute.*

As touching in this school what shall be taught of the Masters and learned
of the scholars, it passeth my wit to devise and determine in particular, but
in general to speak and somewhat to say my mind, I would they were
taught alway in good literature, both Latin and Greek, and good authors
such as have the very Roman eloquence joined with wisdom, specially
Christian authors that wrote their wisdom with clean and chaste Latin
other in verse or in prose, for my intent is by this school, specially to
increase knowledge and worshipping of God and our lord Christ Jesu and
good Christian life and manners in the children.

And for that intent I will the children learn first above all the catechism
in English, and after, the Accidence that I made, or some other, if any be
better to the purpose, to induce children more speedily to Latin speech.
And then *Institutum Christiani Hominis* which that learned Erasmus made
at my request, and the book called *Copia* of the same Erasmus. And then
other authors Christian as Lactantius, Prudentius, and Proba and Sedulius
and Juvencus and Baptista Mantuanus, and such others as shall be thought
convenient and most to the purpose unto the true Latin speech. All barbary,
all corruption, all Latin adulterate which ignorant blind fools brought into
this world and with the same hath distained and poisoned the old Latin
speech and the very Roman tongue, which in the time of Tully and Sallust
and Virgil and Terence was used, which also St. Jerome and St. Ambrose
and St. Austin [Augustine] and many holy doctors learned in their times,
I say that filthiness and all such abusion which the later blind world
brought in, which more rather may be called bloterature than literature,
I utterly banish and exclude out of this school, and charge the Masters
that they teach alway that is best and instruct the children in Greek and
reading Latin, in reading unto them such authors that hath with wisdom
joined the pure chaste eloquence.[11]

The preamble in Deane's statute on 'authors to be read in school'
follows Colet's almost word for word and must certainly have been
copied. The conclusion similarly followed Colet's, although it
omitted his more forthright denunciation of the 'Latin adulterate
which ignorant blind fools brought into this world' and his witticism
'bloterature'. Greek, though coupled with Latin literature in the
preamble, is not specifically mentioned again by Deane.

When it came to prescribed authors Deane's statute was rooted in
Colet's, although he made certain adaptations and omissions. It
forms a classic example of the sixteenth-century grammar school and
its aims, derived from the Pauline model. The catechism which

---

* Since this quotation is for comparison only, I have modernised the
spelling.

Deane prescribed has been thought to be the *Latin* catechism, such
as was prescribed at certain other schools, but it is unlikely that
Deane intended to   depart from Colet's rule which specified the
catechism in English.[12] After this religious basis the other fundamental work in the curriculum was the Latin grammar. This was
the foundation of the learning which it was the function of the
grammar schools to impart, and the first two or three years of a
pupil's school life would be spent in getting the grammar by heart.
The Latin grammar must be thought of in the humanist terms of the
century as the most up-to-date weapon for the conquest of the world
of knowledge and of action. In Leach's words, 'The diplomatist, the
lawyer, the civil servant, the physician, the naturalist, the philo-
sopher, wrote, read, and to a large extent spoke and perhaps thought
in Latin. Nor was Latin only the language of the higher professions.
A merchant, or the bailiff of a manor, wanted it for his accounts;
every town clerk* or guild clerk wanted it for his minute book.
Columbus had to study for his voyages in Latin; the general had to
study tactics in it. The architect, the musician, everyone who was
neither a mere soldier nor a mere handicraftsman wanted, not a
smattering of grammar, but a living acquaintance with the tongue,
as a spoken as well as a written language.' The Latin grammar
authorised by Henry VIII for use in schools to the exclusion of all
others, and confirmed by Elizabeth I in her Injunctions of 1559,
was William Lily's *Grammar*. This embodied Colet's *Accidence* and
had been approved by Erasmus; in the form of the Eton Grammar
it was used in schools beyond the middle of the nineteenth century,
having gone through three hundred editions. It has been described
as about the size of a modern prayer book ($5\frac{1}{2}$ in. $\times$ $3\frac{1}{2}$ in.), paper
covered, and with two hundred pages of small, crabbed type.[13]

Erasmus dominated the Witton curriculum, and in this Deane was
following the educational fashion of his day. Through Colet the
Erasmian conception of education—'pietas litterata', virtue combined with learning, Roman eloquence together with Christian
wisdom and conduct—became the ideal of the English grammar
schools. Not only did Erasmus lay down the principles, he provided
the textbooks for putting them into practice. The *Institutum
Christiani Hominis* was a little religious pamphlet prepared by
Erasmus for the boys of St Paul's in 1514. His *Colloquies* were
designed to teach Latin by means of dialogues on a variety of
subjects, often relating to school life: 'The Schoolmaster's admoni-
tions, sports, the whipping master, saying a lesson and making a

---

* Peter Tarbocke of Witton, who was appointed Town Clerk of Liverpool
in 1611 (J. Touzeau, *The Rise and Progress of Liverpool*, 1, 146), may well
have been a pupil at Witton School, but no proof exists.

quill pen' were among the topics. They contained incidentally outspoken comments on ecclesiastical matters which led equally to their condemnation by the University of Paris in 1528 and the Council of Trent in 1564, and to their adoption as a school book in countries influenced by the Reformation. Erasmus's *Copia verborum et rerum*, dedicated to Colet, who had persuaded him to write it for St Paul's, was the leading school book of the time on the principles of Latin composition, dealing with both style and matter.

Colet had implied approval of certain classical writers for study— Tully (Cicero), Sallust, Virgil and Terence, but the authors whom he actually prescribed were early and later Christian writers and poets—Lactantius, Prudentius, Proba, Juvencus, Sedulius and Mantuan. Only one of these Christian writers remained in Deane's statutes—Mantuan, otherwise Baptist Spagnuoli, a Carmelite friar in sixteenth-century Mantua, who wrote a number of eclogues. He, it has been said, 'had the honour of fixing his first line on Shakespeare's mind', and figured as Holofernes' 'good old Mantuan' in *Love's Labours Lost*. Otherwise, Deane prescribed the original classical writers mentioned (but not prescribed) by Colet, with the addition of Ovid and Horace. In this he followed the custom which had become widespread by the middle of the century, and derived from Wolsey's statutes for his school at Ipswich.[14]

It is not known how many of these books the boys would actually have possessed, but one book Deane required his scholars to 'have and use in the churche'. This was the primer 'wherin is conteyned the vii psalmes,* the psalmes of the passion and such like'. Throughout the Middle Ages the primer was the service book used by the laity in their devotions, but it was also much used in the education of children, the whole or part of it being learned by heart. Chaucer's Prioress, in *The Canterbury Tales*, described the 'litel child his litel book lerninge / As he sat in the scole at his *prymer*'. After the Reformation it retained its function, particularly as it was available in English, and was a standard book in elementary education, being often combined with the ABC. Simplified and shortened versions were published for use in schools, but Deane seems to be referring to the more traditional form for use as a service book.[15] School life was permeated by religious observances laid down in the statutes. The boys should

thrise a daie serve god within the schoole, rendring hym thanks for his goodnes doon to theym, craving his specyall grace that they maie profyte

---

* The seven psalms referred to the seven deadly sins: they, together with everything relating to prayers for the dead, e.g. the Dirge and Commendation, were omitted from primers based on Edward VI's (1553), so that Deane clearly intended the more traditional form based on Henry VIII's (1545).

in vertuose lernynge to his honor and glorye. Prayinge for the soull of their founder by name, and for the soules of his father and mother, and all Christian soules, and onste every week, that is to saie on the Frydaye, to saie the seven penytencyall psalmes, with the latenye, [litany] suffrags and collects, and every seconde Frydaie the psalmes of the passion, with the psalmes of mercy and de profundis, with a collet at thende theirof.

These prayers, comparable with those at the earlier pre-Reformation foundations of Manchester and Stockport grammar schools, show Deane as a man of conservative religious habits as well as of up-to-date educational principles.

Deane linked his school very closely with a central institution of the local community, the parochial chapel of St Helen at Witton. In a general way very characteristic of his age he declared in his statutes that 'myne entente is by foundinge of this schoole, specyallye to encrease knowleage and worshipp of God and our Lorde Jhesus Christe'. The school was erected in the name of Jesus (possibly following the dedication of St Paul's to the child Jesus), and once a year 'uppon Jhesus daie in thafternone'* the scholars were 'in the parisshe church aforesaid to saie the dirige and commendacions'. These were both part of the Latin burial and commemorative services, and recitation of them had been among the duties of chantry chaplains. The church was also to be the scene of the reading of the statutes before breaking up and of the schoolmaster's announcement of his intention to leave.

The endowment

In his statute on the admission of the master Deane laid it down that not only should he have the rules and statutes read to him but he should be shown 'the lands and houses apperteynynge to the scoole, wheare they lye and in whoose handes and occupacion they are, and what interest and yeres the tenantes and occupyers have in them'. Witton School was described by William Webb in the early seventeenth century as 'endowed with good lands', among which he singled out for mention the Saracen's Head, in Chester, presumably an inn of some note. The capital value of the property in 1596 has been calculated as £429.[16]

John Deane had indeed left his school fairly well provided for as school foundations of the time went. At Macclesfield the grammar school had by its original endowment in 1502 lands to the annual value of £10 17s 8d, and in 1552 it received a royal grant of property worth £10 7s 4d, a total of £21 5s 0d of which £1 5s 0d had to be paid to the Crown. More exalted ecclesiastics than Deane, such as

* Probably the feast of the name of Jesus, 7 August, but see below, pp. 142–3.

Bishop Pilkington and Dean Alexander Nowell, were founding or re-founding schools in Lancashire with incomes of that order or rather higher.[17] The first evidence of the value of the Witton endowment dates from some twenty years after the foundation, when the rental of the school lands was given in the accounts as follows:

Mr. John Hankey	[The Saracen's Head]	53s	4d
Peter Nycolas	[The Swan]	27s	0d
Thomas Waryngton	[Larton]	20s	0d
Mr. Balle	[Ball's Croft]	3s	4d
Anne Wood	[Peover]	6s	0d
Mr. Venables of Agden	[Agden]	3s	4d
Ellen Tarbocke	[wich-house stead]	2s	0d
The Chamber rent		10s	0d
Total		£6	5s 0d

In the same year the profits from the two parts of a salthouse amounted to £9 5s 0d, giving a total of £15 10s 0d. The school's income was, however, rather more than this, since there was interest from the lending out of the school stock: in the early 'eighties the income from all sources averaged about £21. Deane had stipulated that the master of his school should have a salary of £12, 'a reasonable and a competente stypende', as he put it. It was perhaps rather below the average in the reign of Elizabeth, but it was comparable with Macclesfield's £13 6s 8d and Stockport's £10.

The handing over of the first revenues to the churchwardens for the payment of the schoolmaster at Michaelmas 1558 coincided, according to the statutes, with the erection of the school building. The delay of nearly a year from the granting of the lands presumably left time for the feoffees to organise their affairs and to put up the building near Witton Chapel.* This original building was in use until the middle of the eighteenth century, when, having become 'quite ruinous and decayed', it was taken down. Unfortunately, with the passage of time accurate memories of it lapsed and much about this building and its exact site is obscure.† In the statutes Deane made provision for keeping up the number of feoffees lest 'the schoole-house wante suche furnyture as appertayneth', and also arranged for the newly appointed master to be shown 'the commodyties of the scoole and his lodginges their', but there is no mention of this building in any school feoffment or survey of

---

* The statement made by A. M. Stowe, *English Grammar Schools in the Reign of Queen Elizabeth*, p. 137 n., that Witton School was held in the parish church is based on a careless interpretation of the statute dealing with the reading of the statutes before breaking up.

† See Appendix IV for a discussion of the problem.

property. At one Lancashire school, Rivington, the lease of the school was granted by its owner to the schoolmaster, and by him to the governors, for a thousand years for a nominal payment:[18] possibly some such transaction at Witton was recorded in the earliest accounts, now no longer in existence. Certainly, though the feoffees regularly paid rent for the master's chamber, later his house, they never paid any rent for the school itself.

A previous school?

Not only was there some doubt by the nineteenth century about the site of the first school, but in the course of a lawsuit the feoffees cast doubts on Deane's erection of the school and put forward a theory that he had merely adopted an existing school. This theory was given credence in the report in 1850 of the Master in Chancery dealing with the case: Sir George Rose stated that he found from the evidence laid before him that, 'in and about the year 1558, the said testator, Sir John Dean either adopted the school then in existence in the said Ville of Witton, or caused a new School to be erected therein; and that the said School so adopted or founded, was afterwards used as the School of the said Testator'.[19]

One piece of contemporary evidence may lend support to this theory: in his will, dated April 1563, Deane referred to 'a crofte of lande now or late in the tenure of Randoll Torbocke called Shaies Crofte or Cannons Crofte lyinge and beinge nighe a lane called the schole masters lane in Northwiche aforsaide'.* It has unfortunately not proved possible to identify the site of this croft, but it is arguable that this customary name could not have established itself in the five years in which Deane's own foundation had existed. If, however, we ask what kind of a school might have existed, we meet with difficulties. In 1548 Edward VI's chantry commissioners had recorded at Macclesfield a church, a grammar school, and three priests serving chantries to the value of over £7; at Knutsford they noted a chapel and a grammar school, while at Nantwich they drew attention to the need for a grammar school. At Northwich they recorded only the existence of a very small, poorly endowed chantry served by one priest. Before 1548 injunctions to teach children to read and write had been addressed to chantry priests: these may have been obeyed at Witton, but there is no evidence of it, and in any case it would not constitute a

---

* A copy of the will among the school records has 'land', but that in Somerset House has 'lane'. For its location the will gives Northwich, while the *inquisition post mortem* gives Witton: Deane seems to have used the names interchangeably.

grammar school such as Deane set up. After 1548 similar injunctions were directed to vicars and curates, and it is after a change of incumbent at the chapel and after the dissolution of the chantry that there are some indications of a school at Witton before John Deane's.

There is a strong, though not long-standing,* local tradition that the first master of John Deane's school was John Bretchgirdle (Bratchgirdill, Brechgirdle or Bracegirdle), curate at Witton from about 1548, whose chief claim to fame is that, as vicar of Stratford on Avon, he baptised Shakespeare. Bretchgirdle's life was investigated by the Rev. E. Fripp as part of an intensive study of Shakespeare's local background.[20] Bretchgirdle, according to Fripp, was a native of Baguley, who went up to Christ Church College, Oxford, 'a nest of Protestant heresy', in or about 1540. He took his B.A. in 1545 and his M.A. in 1546, but remained at Christ Church until 1547. In March 1547 he had a dispensation from the Archbishop of Canterbury allowing him to take orders without letters dismissory from his diocesan, and in or about 1548 he returned to Cheshire as perpetual curate at Witton Chapel. A contemporary of his at Christ Church, Thomas Boswell, was presented by his college in 1551 to the living of Great Budworth. John Bretchgirdle may well have been connected with the locality through a relative of the same names who was a stipendiary priest at Budworth in 1541–2, when he himself was not yet ordained and was, presumably, at Oxford. In the lists of clergy of Great Budworth parish (a very large one, with several subsidiary chapels) in May 1548 and in 1554 *two* John Bretchgirdles (Brachgirdill) appear, and in the 1554 list both are attached to Witton.† (After each name there is a word, but these two words have proved difficult to decipher with certainty: a possible reading is 'senior' and 'junior'.)

John Bretchgirdle, M.A., settled himself in Witton, leasing for life from the lord of the manor, Sir Thomas Venables of Kinderton, about 1549 (he was vague about the date, having lost the lease) a 'messuage' or dwelling house, a croft, and a piece of land of about half an acre adjoining Witton churchyard. He spent £20 on repairs of the existing buildings and on the erection of a new chamber. As an unmarried clergyman he was undisturbed during Mary's reign, and shortly before her death he was presented by his college to the vicarage of Great Budworth, where he was instituted in December 1558: his signature on a bond at his institution still

* Weston, writing in the late nineteenth century, makes no mention of Bretchgirdle.

† Fripp was apparently unaware of the existence of two men of the same name.

remains in the diocesan records. He retained this living until May
1560, when his successor, Richard Eaton, was appointed. It is not
clear why his successor was appointed before he himself had been
appointed elsewhere, but it is conjectured that he retained the
curacy of Witton after ceasing to be vicar of Great Budworth.
What is certain is that in January 1561 he was appointed vicar
of Stratford on Avon, where he had a cousin, and in February
he was admitted to his charge. His Protestant leanings can be
deduced from the fact that his Romanist predecessor at Stratford,
Roger Dyos, had been practically dismissed by the corporation.

   Whether or not Bretchgirdle retained the curacy at Witton up
to the end of 1560, he certainly retained his rented property there
as late as 1564. In October 1564 he petitioned the Lord Keeper
in the Court of Chancery for redress against his landlord, Sir
Thomas Venables, who at the previous Whitsuntide had taken a
gelding worth 40s from his land and had held it until it died of
hunger: since then, so Bretchgirdle alleged, he had harried him
and his servants in the occupation of the property and had sought
to deprive him of it. The suit was not brought at common law
since Bretchgirdle had by misfortune lost his original lease, which
had come into the hands of Venables, and further, as he said in
his petition, Venables was 'a man of worship and of greate power
in the said shyre', and thus capable of influencing a lesser court.
No details of the outcome of the case survive; indeed, it probably
collapsed with the death of Bretchgirdle in June 1565.[21]

   The inventory of Bretchgirdle's goods taken after his death included books to the value of £10, which has been taken to mean
that he probably had three or four hundred volumes. By his will
Bretchgirdle left a number of specified books to boys of Stratford
and of Northwich and district. The books are proof of his humanist
learning, and they correspond significantly with those mentioned
in Deane's statutes for Witton School. The chief beneficiaries in
Stratford were the sons of Alderman Smith, ranging from six
months to twelve years of age: among other books they were left
Erasmus's *Copia Verborum* (for Richard, aged ten), Tully's *Offices*
in English (for Robert, aged six), and Sallust and Justin (for John,
aged eight). Several bequests go back to Bretchgirdle's time at
Witton: Edward Winnington, a godson, received a Greek lexicon,
and his brother, Hugh, a copy of Josephus 'de antiquitatibus
Judeorum bello';* Robert Venables, another godson, was left 'my

---

   * Edward Winnington may have been the man of that name who went to
Brasenose College, Oxford, in 1565, taking his B.A. in 1567; Hugh Winnington was almost certainly the son of Robert Winnington, one of the original
school feoffees, and himself elected a feoffee in 1578.

Encheridion in Englyshe and Laten', Erasmus's famous and influential work. One other boy possibly came from Bretchgirdle's years in Cheshire: George Marson, a godson, was left a Virgil with commentary and a Horace.[22]

In addition to these individual bequests Bretchgirdle left his Cooper's Latin dictionary* to Stratford grammar school, where a few months before, his friend John Brownswerd, to whom he also left two books, had become master. Brownswerd was then in the early stages of his career as an eminent schoolmaster whose reputation as a teacher of grammar lasted into the next century. After a time as master at Wilmslow he had been appointed master at Macclesfield in January 1561, but moved to Warwick in 1564 and from there to Stratford. After the two years there for which he had been engaged he returned to Macclesfield and died, much honoured, some twenty years later, in 1589. He was succeeded at Macclesfield by a pupil, Thomas Newton, who in 1590 published a volume of Brownswerd's Latin poems which gained him a contemporary reputation. It is from some of these poems that the evidence is drawn that Bretchgirdle kept a school at Witton.[23]

Latin versification, modelled on the classics, was a regular part of the curriculum of the grammar schools, and three of Brownswerd's poems, dedicated to Bretchgirdle, 'quo non alter amicior/Mortale spirit', clearly grew out of the school exercises to which he refers:

> Brunsuerdus, Olim qui tibi cognitus,
>   Lusi proterva multa procax fide,
>   Lesbiacae modulis puellae,
>   Doctae cum strepui molestus auri.

I, Brownswerd, who once known to you did disport myself greatly, impudent in my wanton confidence while I chattered on in the measure of the Lesbian maiden, [i.e. Sappho], a burden to your cultured ear.†

The first poem (of twenty-one stanzas, in the metre of Horace, *Odes*, I, 2—the Sapphic ode form referred to) is described by Fripp as a school exercise in the form of a hymn, with a prayer for the master and scholars, and he attributes it to the time when Brownswerd was still a pupil at Witton. After a prayer to God to protect Bretchgirdle, Brownswerd describes him thus:

> Qui feros cura meditatur omni
> Atque acri mores cruciare lima:
> Ora Norvicum placido, erudito
>   Ore reformans

---

* See below, p. 68.
† I am grateful to Mr A. N. Marlow for his translations of Brownswerd's verse.

Who takes great pains to chasten [literally 'crucify'] brutish manners with a keen file, refashioning Northwich with his gentle and learned speech.

After a eulogy of the master, Brownswerd turns to exhort the pupils:

> Tuque Norvicensis ager iuventus
> Quam nutrit, doctum ex animo magistrum
> Optime de te meritum, verere am—
>   plectere, adora

And you, O youth, nurtured by the fields of Northwich, revere, embrace, adore from your heart the learned master to whom you owe so much.

A second poem (of twenty-six stanzas in the metre of Horace, *Odes*, 1, 6) is thought by Fripp to have been written at Poynton, soon after Brownswerd left Witton. It is a good example of pedantic Renaissance verse-making of the kind spoken by the Player King in *Hamlet*:

> Bis sex flammifera concitus orbita
> Phoebus proripuit signa per aurea
> Cursus, ac toties emicuit vaga
> Accensa facie soror:
> Nostram dum pietas perpetuo tua
> Aurem personuit, castaque pectoris
> Docti simplicitas, et studium tetri
> Erroris tenebras fugans.

Twice six times did Phoebus rising in his fiery orbit hurry his course through the glittering constellations, and as often did his wandering sister shine forth, her face enkindled, [by his light] while your goodness sounded perpetually in my ear, and the chaste simplicity of your learned heart, and your zeal dispelling the darkness of shameful error.

Fripp took this to mean that for twelve years and twelve lunar months Brownswerd had been a pupil of Bretchgirdle, but this may be forcing the meaning of the poetic phraseology. At any rate, for twelve (or perhaps thirteen) years Brownswerd was under Bretchgirdle, and this strongly indicates a period from 1547 or 1548 to 1559 or 1560, remembering that in January 1561 he was appointed at Macclesfield. Brownswerd pays tribute to the discipline of those years, painful though it may sometimes have been:

> Felix ille tuae qui ferulae manus
> Submittit teneras et tolerat piae
> Vitam militiae qui virides tuo
> Annos transigit in sinu

Happy he who holds out tender hands to the rod and endures a life of devoted discipline, who passes the fresh years [of boyhood] in your care.

The last and longest poem (of thirty-one stanzas) is dated by Fripp not long before Christmas 1560 and is in part a plea by Brownswerd for support in advancing his career. It provides the information that Bretchgirdle was still at Witton:

Te solitis fidibus saluto,
Norvici patriae decusque nostrae

I salute you with my wonted lyre, glory of Northwich and of our land.

In the poem Brownswerd speculated on the present activities of his old master: was he happy in the company of the Muses, poring (with grave face) over Zeno, Aristotle or Socrates, walking the spacious halls of Solomon, or at the shrine of Plato? There was no doubt, however, that he was tirelessly pursuing the tasks of a schoolmaster from morning to night. Beneath the stilted, allusive Latin there emerges a nostalgic picture of an inspiring and conscientious master, proficient in Hebrew and Greek as well as Latin, to whom Brownswerd sent his volume of poems for correction, and whom he followed to the midlands, only to lose almost at once.

There can be no doubt that Bretchgirdle taught at Northwich and that he taught grammar and not merely elementary instruction. The dates for his teaching there are rather tentative, but most probably he had his school there from about 1548 to 1560: it is perhaps significant that Deane referred not to *school* lane but to *schoolmaster's* lane, suggesting an individual teacher rather than an established school. What is not so self-evident as Fripp makes out is Bretchgirdle's connection with Deane's foundation, and there is a good deal of supposition in his account. Deane's school was 'erected' at Michaelmas 1558, just before Bretchgirdle was appointed to Great Budworth but over two years before he went to Stratford. In his Chancery petition Bretchgirdle referred to his own peaceable and quiet occupation and enjoyment of the property he had rented from Sir Thomas Venables 'by the space of vii yeres'. Fripp assumed that this period, from 1549–50 to 1556–7, was ended by Bretchgirdle's move into lodgings provided by Deane for the master of his school and referred to in the statutes, but there is no evidence at all for this, and the change may just as easily have been connected with Bretchgirdle's appointment to Great Budworth. Fripp argues that 'to fail to recognise continuity between Bretchgirdle's work and interest and the school of John Deane is sheer scepticism. Obviously his school became the Free Grammar School of Witton and he was elected its first headmaster.'

It is of course unlikely in the extreme that there would have been two different people teaching grammar at the same time in

a place the size of Northwich and Witton: unfortunately the visitation records which survive for the 'fifties make no mention of
schoolmasters at Witton. If Brownswerd's poem will bear the interpretation given about the length of time he spent under Bretchgirdle
(and this seems acceptable), then most probably Bretchgirdle taught
in Deane's school. Circumstantial evidence supports this conjecture:
there is the appearance of the same classical texts among Bretchgirdle's books and in Deane's statutes (though these were only
the common humanist texts), and in addition Deane's letter of
August 1561 implies that this was the first election of a master
by the feoffees. Deane had earlier reserved the choice during his
lifetime to himself or an assignee, and it would have been very
natural for him to have chosen the experienced man who was
already teaching in Northwich. There may be some support for
this assumption in the fact that Bretchgirdle was instituted at
Stratford in February 1561 and in August Deane was chiding the
electors for quarrelling. This is as far as the evidence allows us to
go in seeking for the original master at Witton, and it is noteworthy
that in the late seventeenth century memory in the school did not
reach back beyond the appointment of Thomas Farmer in 1586.*

The first known master

Bretchgirdle's link with the school presents great problems but
the tracing of the next master is also difficult. It has in the past
been stated definitely that when Bretchgirdle left Witton he was
replaced in the curacy by Henry Birchinhead, but that the feoffees
chose as his successor in the school one Stephen Lambert.[24] The
burial of 'Sir Henrie Byrchenhead' is recorded in the parish register
in January 1563, and there is evidence that in 1563 the curate was
Hamlet Tailiour or Taylor. In the visitation record of 1563, however, the schoolmaster at Witton was given as Richard Mather.†
It is unlikely that Mather became master before 1563, since he
did not gain his B.A. at Cambridge until early in 1563, having
matriculated at St John's College at Easter 1560.[25] We are left
with a gap between Bretchgirdle's departure and Mather's appointment, and with Deane's letter of August 1561 urging the electors
to hasten their choice. However, it can be positively stated that
Stephen Lambert was not the master at Witton at this or any later

---

* See Chapter VI, p. 71.
† The name is lightly scored out, though no other name is inserted. The
list contains similar alterations elsewhere, and W. F. Irvine, who transcribed
it, attributed the alterations to 1569.

time. No man of this name graduated at Oxford or Cambridge at this time, and it was inherently improbable that in the lifetime of the founder his academic requirements for a master should have been disregarded. In fact Stephen Lambert, the name given by Fripp and Weston and probably derived from Ormerod, is more correctly Stephen Limbert. Furthermore his connection with Witton turns out to have been based on a misunderstandng.

In 1586 Geoffrey Whitney of Nantwich published a book of poems, *A Choice of Emblems and Devices*, which included one addressed to the youth of Audlem School, where he had been a pupil. Another poem was dedicated to 'Doctissimo viro D. STEPHANO LIMBERTO Nordouicensis Scholae Magistro'. This led to a supposition, which appeared in Ormerod's *History*, that Whitney had been a pupil not only at Audlem but also at Northwich or Witton. As early as 1859, however, it was pointed out that 'this conjecture turns on the meaning of the word *Nordouicensis* which may denote either Northwich, in Cheshire, or the city of Norwich, in Norfolk'. Inquiry showed that *Dominus* Stephen Limbert was master of King Edward's School, Norwich, from 1570 to his death in 1589, that is, at the time of Whitney's dedication. He had graduated B.A. at Cambridge from Magdalene College in 1565, and M.A. in 1568. Whitney himself had links with Norfolk, holding the post of under bailiff of Great Yarmouth until 1586.[26] The mysterious 'Stephen Lambert' must therefore be removed from the list of masters of Witton School. There may have been an appointment between Bretchgirdle's departure and Mather's appointment after his graduation at the beginning of 1563, or perhaps the curate, Sir Henry Birkenhead, although he was without the required degree, may have officiated temporarily, following his predecessor's custom of combining the two offices. For the shadowy period before the school records begin in 1578 only the names of Bretchgirdle, rather tentatively but very probably, and of Richard Mather, perhaps more certainly, emerge.

A note on Great Budworth school

Some confusion seems to have been caused by the entry in Bishop Gastrell's *Notitia Cestriensis* under Great Budworth, in which he stated, writing about 1719,

Here is a school, built about 100 years agoe upon part of the churchyard, to which Mr. Pickering of Thelwall gave 100 *l* [the] interest for the Master, who is nominated by the Vicar. This school was founded by John Dean, Rector of Great St. Bartholomews, near Westminster.

Unfortunately the surviving returns on which Gastrell based his statement do not include those for Great Budworth. No evidence has been discovered of any link between Deane and the school at Great Budworth, and the date given by Gastrell would not fit with a foundation by Deane.

There may well have been a school at Great Budworth as early as 1563, for in the list of clergy and schoolmasters for that year, two masters (apart from the one at Witton) were recorded for Budworth parish. They were James Roe and Richard Wode, and it is known that John Bruen of Stapleford, who lived with his uncle, Master Dutton of Dutton, attended Roe's school, which was aparently a grammar school. Budworth was, of course, an enormous parish containing several chapels, but it seems likely that one of these masters was at the headquarters of the parish. Certainly by 1578 there was a school at Budworth, at which Thomas Farmer taught before moving to Witton: Farmer's presence there suggests that it was a grammar school. Evidence about its foundation was given in 1633 at the visitation of the Archbishop of York. The parishioners excepted against the then schoolmaster, James Knott, on the grounds of his misbehaviours and of his attempt to combine the mastership with the curacy, and in the course of the proceedings it was stated that the school was 'erected here for the use of the inhabitants of that parish at their owne charge'.[27]

The school appears as a grammar school in later visitation records but when, in 1778, the vicar replied to visitation queries he made no mention of any foundation by Deane, referring only to benefactions from Mrs Pickering and Mrs Dorothy Glover, and he further stated that there was no free school in the parish.[28] It must be assumed either that Gastrell was misinformed or that, in assembling the material, some confusion arose between Great Budworth as a place and as a parish including the chapelry of Witton.*

* In the Charity Commissioners' report of 1837 Witton's school and charities appeared under 'Great Budworth'.

IV

Early prosperity, 1578-1643

The school and the community

John Deane's school was thus settled close to the chapel of St Helen, and it remained for it to establish its place in the society of Northwich and Witton, and its links with the local community. Professor Jordan has shown how the grammar school founded at Ashton in Makerfield in 1588 benefited from the activity of the ordinary inhabitants of the rural community, whereby its original small endowment was augmented within a generation by numerous relatively modest sums; similarly at Ormskirk the school enjoyed from its foundation in 1611 'the warm and generous support of the whole community'.[1] By the time that William Webb was making his perambulation of Cheshire, about 1621, Witton School had become a noteworthy part of the community: he recorded, after a description of the town and its government, that 'there is also a free Grammar School, endowed with good lands, founded by Sir John Dayne, Priest, born in Shurlach . . .'. The formalities of the annual account rendering symbolised the connection with the parochial community. They probably always took place in Witton Chapel, though this was only occasionally stated: in the late seventeenth century a payment is recorded to a man for carrying the account book from the school to the church. During this period the ready money and securities were handed over to the new bailiff feoffees and the accounts yielded up regularly, almost always in the presence of, and on a few occasions *to*, the churchwardens, whose signatures or marks appear in the account book. Gradually the account making was followed by some celebration. In the early years the amount spent at the making of the accounts was small: it started in 1579 at 4*d* for drink, but in 1603 43*s* 4*d* was spent at the feoffees' dinner and in subsequent years costs ran from 25*s* to over £2. In 1625 they even included a payment for 'musicke', but this was perhaps a special occasion, since it was the first for the new master, Richard Pigott, and the dinner included his 'companie'. The entry of a gift of 2*s* to the poor at the dinner of 1633 may represent either greater generosity on the feoffees' part or stricter accounting.

The salt-making community of Northwich was still highly organised in the early seventeenth century, although there were already signs of a declining yield from some existing wich houses. In the careful lists of salthouses and their owners drawn up between 1565 and 1638 the school figured regularly as the owner of what were variously described as two parts of four leads, two leads and two-third parts of a lead and two-third parts of four leads. In 1605 the list specified the services and chief rents due from certain salthouses to the lord of the manor of Northwich: the school land fell into this category of 'unfree occupation and payeth yearly to the Lord of the manner for Lead fine' 5s 4d and for chief rent 3d.[2] There does not seem to be any record of either payment being made by the feoffees in normal times; possibly they were exempted as a charitable foundation.

The recognition of the school by the community was signified by the insertion into the salt-making rules of certain exceptions in its favour. To the rule, confirmed by the jury in 1638, that it should be in the discretion of the Leadlookers for the time being to bind by the ring of the bell one quarter of the town 'and more or less as they shall think fit' was added the qualification '(except it be any Town peeceing,* Schoole peeceing or other contrary peeceing of any man that is behind with his walling'). Furthermore the bailiff feoffees of the school lands could set their 'peeceings, being twelve in number yearly; that is three in every quarter, of the Schoole lands themselves to the most benefitt of the school Master'. The feoffees were thus apparently not bound by the communal price-fixing arrangements. While the school was favoured, the schoolmaster was restricted. An interesting rule, aimed presumably at securing a division of functions, laid down that 'no spirituall person, apprentice or schoole-master, single-woman nor any waller (except widowes) nor any bryne drawer shall wall or occupy walling or making of salt (except it be such as shall be left or come unto them by gyfte or death of their parents or friends)'.[3]

There is in the school accounts only one reference to officials of the salt borough: the record in 1579 of a gift to the feoffees of 26s 8d 'of good will' from 'the lead-lookers of the North-wich'. This was an early tangible appreciation of the school's place in the community, but apart from this, and from the privileges quoted, the community made no formal provision for the school. Such benefactions as it received (and they were few) came not from the community as a whole but from individuals, and the links with the local society were embodied in the feoffees.

* See p. 4.

The feoffees

The feoffees who administered the school's affairs were drawn from among the leading inhabitants of Northwich and the chapelry of Witton and some from further afield in the parish of Great Budworth; periodically, as in 1586, small payments were made to messengers who went to summon the country feoffees. The feoffees' standing is shown in the parish records and in the lists of jurors in the lord's court at Northwich. Robert Fox, a feoffee from 1597 and bailiff in 1601–2, who died of the plague which hit Northwich in 1604–5,* was described in the parish register as 'one of the burgesses of Northwich, at the time of his death the supervisor of the ' "leads", a most honourable man'. William Robinson, bailiff three times between 1597 and 1612, was described at his death in 1623 as 'a very honourable man', 'mourned by all'. The entry of the burial of Lawrence Roe in January 1605 seems to be the first to specify that a man had been a feoffee of the school. Feoffees who were among the jurors in the 1630s were Paul Winnington, William Leftwich Sr, and Jr, and Peter Venables, and those among the signatories of the guarantee of the preaching minister's income were John Johnson, Peter Venables, Robert Pownall, William Leftwich and William Hewitt. Of the twelve feoffees chosen in 1626, four appeared in the subsidy book.[4]

From time to time the number of feoffees for the trust had to be made up in accordance with Deane's rules. This happened infrequently before 1665, when the rule in the feoffment schedule was followed and elections took place only when eight feoffees had died, and much more frequently afterwards, when, in accordance with the statutes, they occurred when four had died. (Curiously, until the feoffment of 1641 the four surviving feoffees elected twelve *new* ones instead of eight to make up the number.) Sometimes, as in 1626, the choice of feoffees and the feoffment involved several meetings. Members of John Deane's family were, of course, to be found regularly among the feoffees, especially during the first century of the school's history. Richard Deane was bailiff twice in the later sixteenth century, while John, younger son of Roger Deane, who was chosen a feoffee in 1597, improved on this record by holding the office five times between 1601 and 1622. Both Richard, who died in 1617, and John, who died in 1625, were without sons, and the male line of 'Sir' John Deane's family continued in Richard (the only son of their brother Roger), who was eleven in 1626,

---

* No echo of this catastrophe, which was said (in an entry in the Parish Register of 13 July 1604) to have killed 'almost all the men and women of good estate and condition', appears in the school accounts.

when he was chosen a feoffee, but did not become a bailiff until 1666.* Other relations of the Deane family were among the feoffees: Thomas Symkocke or Simcock was doubtless a connection of Alicia Simcock, heir of John Deane, clerk, and in the early years Thomas Sudlow followed George Sudlow.[5]

Regularly, from generation to generation, the family names of two of the original feoffees recur—Winnington of Northwich and of Birches: Hugh Winnington and Julius Winnington of Birches were the only two bailiff feoffees to be distinguished in the account books before the Civil War as 'gentlemen'. Hugh Winnington, the son of Robert, of Northwich (one of the original feoffees), was elected about 1578 and acted as bailiff feoffee three times. He entered the Inner Temple in 1573, and became a barrister and a much-consulted legal adviser 'of singular humanity and gentlenesse'. Although he moved away from Northwich after inheriting the Hermitage estate in Cranage township in 1591, he retained property there including salthouses and a house in Castle Northwich held by the minister of Witton Chapel, Richard Walker; he remained a feoffee until 1597, and his son, Benjamin, was a pupil under Richard Pigott.[6] George Winnington was twice a bailiff, although his account-keeping was not infallible, as a note in the 1593-4 accounts suggests:

forasmuch as the ij last accompts in this booke were mystaken by George Wynington (who dealt therin on the behalfe of Hugh Wynington one of the bayliffes by reason of his absence furth of the countrey) & others that cast the same, namely both in the somes conteyned in the billes, accompting xlviii li. vis. xd. for xlix li. xiiid. as may appeare by the foote of the last accompt & the billes hereunder writen, and also miscast otherwise. Therfore the foresayd last accompts for the yeres 1593 & 94 are defaced & made void & theis two next followyng set downe in steyd therof . . .

He was also the earliest known benefactor of the school, leaving it a legacy of £3 which was fetched from Chester in 1599. The family of Winnington of Birches continued to be represented. Julius Winnington, a feoffee from 1597 until his death, acted as bailiff four times, and at the feoffment of 1626 his brother, Paul, succeeded him as a feoffee.

The tendency in the early seventeenth century for the office of bailiff feoffee to revolve among a few individuals—John Deane and Ralph Nickson (probably a half-brother of Thomas Sudlow) had five two-year tenures, Julius Winnington and Henry Pickmere four, and Thomas Simcock three—was mainly caused by the deaths

* Stowe, *op. cit.*, p. 25, cites an example at Tiverton, where two infants (sons of two relations of the benefactor) were named among the original feoffees of a school in case they were not subsequently elected.

of four of the feoffees soon after their election. Henry Pickmere's will (proved in 1633) nevertheless illustrates the closeness of the local circle: in it he referred to his good friends and neighbours Paul Winnington of Birches, Randle Birchenhead Sr (the usher at the school) and Thomas Litler: Richard Pigott, the master, was a witness.[7]

The finances

Financially the school's fortunes were linked with those of the town of Northwich by its share in the salt production. The school's wich house was situated on the north side of what was then known as the Leach Eye: this later became the Swine Market, and in the late nineteenth century the site became the south-west corner of the Market Hall. At the end of the sixteenth century the school land lay between a tenement belonging to Peter Warburton of Arley and one belonging to Thomas Starkey of Stretton: beyond Starkey's land lay that of Hugh Winnington, esq., and just beyond that, the Earl of Derby's bakehouse.[8] The price at which the feoffees were able to set their piecings (most frequently twelve) varied from time to time. At the beginning of the accounts it was 15s 6d; in 1585 it was 14s, with the exception of one piecing, which had been set to William Birchenhead at 14s, but he became bankrupt about St Andrew's tide (30 November) and it was set 'upon St. Thomas Even before Christmas' (21 December) to Randle Yate, as the piecings were then set in the town, that is, for only 10s. After slight fluctuations the rate remained constant from 1601 to 1632 at £1, giving a firm financial basis for the school. In the decade before the Civil War, however, it fluctuated, falling to 10s in 1635, significantly at the time that measures had to be taken to assure the income of the preaching minister out of the parish leys if his salt rights failed to yield the promised amount.

The income from salt thus varied with the rate, beginning at about £9, dropping occasionally as in 1594 to £6 12s 8d and in 1635 to £6, but between 1601 and 1632 running at £12. It did not give rise to much difficulty in this period, but in 1601 there were charges in the accounts in a suit against Julius Winnington, a bailiff feoffee of the previous year, about a school piecing for his brother. A small addition to the school's income from its salthouse was provided by the rent of the 'wich-house stead', for it appeared by the list of 1593 that the salthouse was 'not standing'.* The 'stead'

---

* At Middlewich if the structure of a salthouse was not standing it was sometimes termed a 'wich house place'. As time went on many salthouses ceased to have a territorial significance and came to mean merely brine shares. (J. Varley, *A Middlewich Chartulary*, p. 37).

brought in 2*s* a year, although in 1596 the bailiff feoffees recorded that they could not let it. After that it was let only intermittently, and not at all after 1620, but in 1632 it seems to reappear as a barn, and subsequently as two-thirds parts of a barn, regularly let for 3*s* to John Broome, a saltmaker, who later leased the whole of the school's walling.

The most distant of the school lands had in fact the most stable history: this was the farm at Larton. The school had inherited the tenants with the land from Basingwerk Abbey, for the Warrington family had been there certainly since 1503, when a lease was made to Robert Warrington and his son, John, for their lives at a rent of 20*s* a year: Robert was still the tenant in 1536 and his son was there in 1551. The farm remained in the male line until the middle of the seventeenth century.[9] Thomas Warrington paid the school 20*s* in 1579, as did Robert Warrington in 1597 and William in 1630. The Warringtons seem to have been very good tenants, coming over regularly to Northwich with their rent, and on occasion being given a dinner or a gift of money by the feoffees. The rent, it will be noted, remained constant from 1503 onwards in a time of steeply rising prices, when many landlords were raising their rents. But the feoffees made their profit on the fine, an occasional payment made on the renewal of a lease, and, to a much lesser extent, on the heriot payable on the death of a tenant. In 1609, when Robert Warrington died, a heriot of 33*s* 4*d* was paid, and when a new lease to his son, William, was sealed at the same rent a fine of £30 was paid in three instalments between 1610 and 1612. This must have been a short-term lease, for in 1624 a new lease was sealed, and William Warrington paid a fine of £8 5*s* 0*d*.

The Chester property had a more complicated history than the Larton farm. The largest of the properties was the Saracen's Head, an inn situated on the north side of Foregate Street* and deriving its name from the crest of the Warburton family, who owned property in Chester at an early date: the site covered an area of ten roods by four (a rood here meaning six to eight yards) and the size of the building can be judged from the fact that it had fifty-three bays. What sort of a state it was in when Deane bought it is not known, but in 1593 the feoffees went to view the 'wants of reparation' of the Saracen's Head, and a survey made for them in 1606 referred to it as an 'antient Inn house', and listed a formidable number of 'decays and ruins'. Among them were:

* Nos. 39–45 and a corner of the Commercial Hall. (*Cheshire Sheaf*, third series, xxxiv, 104.)

Item one Stable joining to the Garden the walls floor and roof decayed.
Item a Malt house and Kilne joining to the said Stable, the walls, floor
and roof decayed.

... Item the hoslery. Item the Chamber over the Hoslery, the Walls and
Roof decayed. Item a Room of 3 Bays between the Brewhouse and the
Hoslery, the Walls decayed and the Roof fallen down. Item the Brewhouse
of 2 Bays in some decay. Item the Kitchen. Item the Chamber over the
kitchen and the Chamber next unto it much decayed. Item the Chamber
between the old hall and the kitchen in decay. Item the old Hall the rain
comes in on both sides.

... Item the Coventree Chamber, the Wall ready to fall down. Item the
princes Chamber the Wall plate broken and rotten. Item the flower de luce
Chamber the floor and Roofe decayed.[10]

In 1579 John Hankey, the tenant mentioned in Deane's feoffment,
and an alderman of the city of Chester, was paying £2 13s 4d in
rent, and continued to do so until 1590, when John Brerewood
paid the same sum; successive tenants paid the same rent until 1634.
In that year the feoffees spent the enormous sum of £66 18s 5d
on repairs, and were subsequently able to let out the building in
parts: the main tenant and holder of the inn itself, John Cottingham,
paid an annual rent of nearly £14; the tenant of two chambers
paid £1, of a chamber and a kiln £4 6s 8d, and of 'the lower kiln'
£2 13s 4d, so that at this stage the feoffees looked in a fair way to
recouping their outlay. An entry in 1638 records that the bailiff
feoffees went to Chester to survey the Saracen's Head, and to see
'whether the wainscote, bedsteads, tables, formes, court-cupboards,
shelves, grates, racks and mangers belonginge to the house were
to be had'.

Although the feoffees had already spent a large sum on repairs
at the Saracen's Head, it seems probable that two interesting
entries in the accounts of 1637 refer to one of the two inns owned
by the school in Chester. They are as follows:

spent by mr Winington and myself when we sett the playhouse
to be repaired   5s 0d

for makinge one brick Chimney with 3 pipes and stone for
silling one side of the play house with barridges   £4 11s 0d

Altogether a total of over £30 was spent on this work in material
and labour: the place is not specified, but various facts establish
that it was in Chester, and the chances certainly are that it was in
one of the two inns owned by the school, since dramatic performances frequently took place in inn yards and buildings connected
with inns. Some of the timber seems to have been supplied by two

Chester tenants of the school (Richard Ley and 'Mr. Sallisbury'),
and the work was carried out under a head workman, Arratt Watt,
who figures in the accounts of Chester cathedral, doing work in
'the new school' when the King's School moved into the refectory
and in the cathedral itself.[11] But although Watt was paid £2 10s 6d
for fifty days' work and a half, the greater part of the work was
apparently done by John Fairchild and his two men, who were
paid £6 7s 6d for fifty-one days' work. Watt, however, was allowed
8s, that is 2d a day, 'in admitting Fairechilde to worke'. Fairchild,
as appears elsewhere in the accounts, was a Northwich man who
did carpentry work at the school itself, and in 1637 his travelling
expenses had to be covered, as well as horse hire 'to carry the
carpenters tooles'. Unfortunately no other reference to the 'playhouse' occurs, so that we are left with this tantalising hint of the
school's connection with the theatre in Chester. Very little seems
to be known about dramatic performances in Chester in this period
(other than the Chester mystery plays), but in 1615 the corporation
heard complaints about disturbances caused by performances at
night, since servants and apprentices resorted to inn-houses to see
them; it therefore restricted them to the daytime.[12]

The earliest rental, of 1579, shows that originally the other
Chester properties were of considerably less value than the Saracen's
Head. The Swan, on the south side of Foregate Street, had a rent
of 27s a year, while Ball's Croft brought in only 3s 4d.* Unlike the
Saracen's Head, however, the rents of these properties increased
during the sixteenth century. By 1585 the several tenants of the
Swan property were paying over £5 between them, and in 1590
the rent of Ball's Croft had doubled. In the first half of the
seventeenth century the Swan frequently brought in over £6, for
though smaller than the other inn it was in much better order,
and the survey of 1606 listed no 'decays'. (Curiously, from 1609
it was described as 'the old Swan'.) The only occasional payments
received for the Swan seem to have been heriots on the death of
tenants, and the only expenditure (unless the 'playhouse' was there)
28s 6d for building a brick chimney in the feoffees' chamber in 1611.
Ball's Croft, a holding of about an acre on the banks of the Dee,
produced 10s a year from 1616, and had as its tenant between
1634 and 1641 the Earl of Derby. Each year one or more of the
bailiff feoffees went over to Chester to collect the rents at each
quarter, but occasionally they were brought by a Northwich
tradesman coming home from Chester.

The feoffees had a certain amount of trouble with their Chester

* The Swan property occupied Swan Court and Nos. 48–52 Foregate
Street. Ball's Croft is now part of Grosvenor Park.

property. They were involved in various suits with their tenants, and in 1613 there was a tithe case about Ball's Croft in the Consistory Court. On several occasions the feoffees were put to some trouble and expense to establish their ownership of their property. Under Elizabethan statutes to safeguard charitable bequests the Lord Chancellor had authority to appoint commissioners to investigate abuses in the management of trust property and to rectify them by decree. Witton School property was the subject of four such investigations in the seventeenth century, three of which concerned the Saracen's Head and seem to have arisen from attempts to deny the school's ownership. The investigations were often long drawn out: for the commission which ended in the decree of 1615 the feoffees paid 3s for six men's dinners in 1612 at the first Commission for Pious Uses at Chester, and 5s 9d at the second commission for 'horse meate and man's meate'. The commission ended with a judgement that the three Chester properties had been given by John Deane to trustees for the school. Another dispute arose in the late 1620s and the first sign seems to be in the accounts of 1627 when the bailiff feoffees went to 'speake with the Auditor about the conceled house in Chester'. The bailiff feoffees had to attend sessions of the Commission for Pious Uses at Grappenhall in 1628 and at Warrington in 1629, and finally in 1630 spent 1s 4d on 'a pottell* of wyne to the Jurors when the [sic] put there hands to the Inquisition'. The inquisition, taken on 26 August 1630, found that the house in Foregate Street in tenure of Peter Marshall was part of the lands purchased by Deane for the school 'and hath bene comonly reputed and taken to be part and parcell of the Saracen's Head therewith by the said feoffees set let occupied and enioyed and was parte of the dissolved monastery of St. Anne's in Chester'. The commission ordered that the rents and profits of the house should henceforth be paid to the feoffees for the use of the school 'and no otherwise'.[13]

The remaining properties of the school, at Agden and Peover, remained in the hands of the same two families, Venables and Wood, who paid their small rents pretty regularly up to the Civil War, despite legal disputes in 1574 and 1630 respectively. In 1579, however, there was a change when Venables of Agden covenanted to pay his chief rent out of his tenement in Hartford in the tenure of 'Rauffe Bostocke'.[14] The only payments to the State recorded before the Civil War were two feudal levies, revived by James I, for the knighting of his son, Prince Henry, and the marriage of his daughter to the Elector Palatine. In 1609 the feoffees paid 6s 8d

---

* A pottle was two quarts. (R. V. H. Burne, *Chester Cathedral*, p. 70.)

for the lands in Chester and Wirral and 2*s* 6*d* for the lands in
Northwich 'for the princes ayde', and in 1612 2*s* 6*d* 'for the La:
Elizabethes Aide' for the Northwich lands, paying presumably in
their capacity as Crown tenants-in-chief. (In 1665 the feoffees went
to Nantwich to certify to the King's auditors that there was no
chief rent due to the Crown for Witton School lands, but this was
after the abolition of feudal incidents after the Restoration.)

The school's total income, however, exceeded the salt profits and
the rents, since there was in addition the interest from capital lent
out. This amounted to a considerable sum in the early seventeenth
century, and must have formed an important source of small loans
in Northwich and district: in 1597 there were nine borrowers, but
in 1609 there were forty-eight. Charity stock has been recognised
as a source of capital at a time when this was not easy to come by.[15]
Witton School stock was lent out for the most part in small sums of a
few pounds or less: sums of over £10 were lent occasionally even
as early as 1594, but £15 was about the limit and these larger loans
were unusual. From 1598 to 1602 the schoolmaster, Thomas Farmer,
had a loan of £4 and in 1607 among the debtors, for 40*s*, was
'Rodger Tovye Clarke', curate of Witton, still on the list in 1621.
The loans, starting in 1570 with thirteen and rising by 1628 to
over sixty, were mostly to local salt-house owners, gentry, yeomen,
tradesmen and craftsmen: when two men of the same name were
borrowers their trades were specified, and the list of 1602 names
three shoemakers, and a carpenter. This was for over two centuries
the feoffees' method of investing their capital, for not until 1797
did they invest £170 in government funds, and they bought no
land with the accumulation.

The total amount of money in the bailiff feoffees' hands increased
steadily. The stock handed over at the first account was £31; in
1592 besides their rents and interest the feoffees had over £42
in two bills; in 1603 the money lent out at interest amounted to
over £78, and in 1625 there was over £220 lent out under sealed
contract. The margin between income and expenditure was quite
small, but the capital grew. In 1634, however, there came a check
to this increase: the expensive repairs to the Saracen's Head ate
up over £66, and in 1636 the accounts contained a mysterious payment to a Mr Tilston, 'with interest and charges', of £111 7*s*,
following on a law suit and an attachment against the feoffees.
John Tilston, ar., brought his suit in the Chester Exchequer Court
in December 1635 against William Leftwich and William Rowe,
the two feoffees who had acted when the debt was incurred,
apparently in 1633. They confessed to a debt of £100 remaining
from a greater sum, and, after delays, repaid it. John Tilston was

described as one of the serjeants attending the court, but there is no indication of the origin of the debt, and the borrowing does not figure in the accounts. The large expenditure on the Saracen's Head and on this repayment was met by holding back the master's salary in 1636 and 1637 and not employing an usher, by borrowing £25 from Robert Pownall from 1636 to 1638, but above all by reducing the school's capital.[16]

Just before the Civil War, therefore, the bailiff feoffees handed on to their successors in March 1642 the sum of £61 6s 11d. Of this only £2 4s 9d was in ready money; the rest consisted of stock lent out, unpaid interest and rents, and showed a sad depletion of capital. The cash was kept by the feoffees in a 'Congleton purse' bought for the purpose for 10d in 1633: Congleton was noted in the seventeenth century for its leather goods. The securities (bonds or contracts under seal known as specialties) were kept in a chest, the opening of which was clearly a formal occasion: in 1624 2s 10d was spent 'when the feoffees met to goe into the chest to looke on writings' connected with a commission, and a further 3s was spent 'in goinge into the cheste' when several bonds were renewed.

The letting out of money on interest was later to prove a precarious business, and even in this period of the school's history it was troublesome. A curious instance of this is to be found in the accounts for 1589: Richard Kay

payd in corne growing his dett of xxiiij s. which afterwarde being shorne did not extend therunto by viii s. for yt was shold in the eyiar [ear] for xvj s. which yf wee had taken and payd for carriage, threeshing and windowing and such lyke charges would have growen to as greate a losse and so wee crave out of our charge allowance of viii s.*

A more common source of trouble, especially as borrowers multiplied, was non-payment of interest or stock: in 1627 unpaid interest amounted to over £22, one debtor owing for eleven years, and another for three, and seven of his grandfather's. In the first half of the seventeenth century the feoffees were constantly involved in expenditure on writs, attachments and court charges against their debtors. Costs could be high, although recoverable if the suit was successful; in 1639 costs of a suit against Richard Deane for 'Mr Litler's' debt of £2 13s 4d were over £4. The number of courts in which the feoffees prosecuted their suits is remarkable: they included the Exchequer at Chester, the 'County Court', the Pentice Court at Chester, and the various manorial courts of the neighbourhood—Crosse, Kinderton, Northwich, Middlewich and Halton.

* I am grateful to Mr J. H. Hodson for help in deciphering this passage and certain others.

Although the sums lent out were not large and the interest (originally at the legal rate of 10 per cent) for each individual debtor small, the arrears of unpaid interest mounted up as high as £30 10s 6d in 1634. During the 'thirties the feoffees were active in prosecuting their debtors, whatever their rank, even to the point of sequestration, and by 1642 the unpaid interest stood at just under £15, but two debtors owed interest for twenty-five years. The accounts of 1599 are enlivened by a Latin tag placed at the head of the list of debtors: 'Veritas non querit angulos'. What it meant to the writer is obscure: it appears to be a Latin translation of a late sixteenth-century English proverb, 'Truth seeks no corners', and a century later it is given as a proverb by Adam Martindale (a Cheshire Puritan and father of a Witton master) in his autobiography, and runs 'Truth seekes not corners, but some causes need shifts'.[17]

The school buildings

The feoffees were constantly making outlays for the upkeep of the school buildings, and, as in so many school accounts, glazing and mending of locks and hinges figured frequently. In 1591 the school-house was inspected by John Bowdon, doubtless the master builder in charge of the building of the stone steeple at Nether Peover in 1582. The first substantial repairs recorded were in 1584–5, when some slating was done at the schoolhouse, and timber was brought from Darnhall for the school floor: in the course of the work the church spade was broken and the feoffees had to pay 6d for it. Again in 1589 two of the feoffees went over to Darnhall to choose timber in Dutton Park the carriage of which cost 26s, while in 1625 a man was paid 3s for 'leading' boards from Tabley Wood. In spite of Weston's statement that the school was a thatched building, there seems no doubt from a study of the accounts that it had in fact a slate roof: in 1629 there is a specific entry 'To the slater for mend-inge the roofe of the schoole'. There were various visits from the slaters, who were not natives of the town, and in 1640 the feoffees paid 1s for the slaters' beds and 2s 8d for eight days' and nights' grass for the slaters' horse. In 1640, incidentally, the three loads of slate cost 18s but the cost of their carriage was £1 7s.

The walls of the school were of wattle and daub, and frequent repairs were made by 'windings': in this process flexible twigs of hazel were woven round upright staves called 'clamstaves', a term also found in the accounts of Chester cathedral.[18] The walls were then plastered and lime-washed: in 1639 the feoffees spent several pounds on repairs—'windings', plastering, whiting and rough-casting. (The plaster seems to have been kept in the church, for there is a payment for leading the 'plaister' into the steeple door and another for cleaning the church.) In 1608 the 'payntores of Budworth' were paid 24*s* 4*d* for 'whitinge and layeing the postes about the scoole in collores'. There is evidence in the accounts that there was some sanitation at the school by the mid-seventeenth century: in 1629 the master, Richard Pigott, gave £1 'towards the makinge the howses of office'. (Early in 1653 they were blown down and new ones had to be put up.)

There is little in the accounts of this period to enable us to picture the interior of the school, but occasional references, together with what is known of other schools, make a sketch possible. The school room was normally a long room on the ground floor, where both the master and the usher taught. Although in the late eighteenth century, in the second school building, the master taught in the ground-floor room and the usher in the upper room, in the original school both apparently taught in the same room, the master having his seat at the upper end of the school. The furniture was simple: in 1602 the feoffees paid 14*s* 'for a table to the schoole', and in 1626 for mending two tables. The pupils would sit on forms round the sides of the room: when the school floor was re-laid in 1585 the forms had to be set up, and there are occasional entries for mending or making a form. In 1608 the feoffees paid Daniell, the painter, for 'writing sentences in the school', most probably maxims painted round the top of the walls.* Above the school room at Witton there was more than one room.[19] Payments for cleaning the school were few and far between, and usually followed repairs or decorating: in the ordinary way at Witton, as at some other schools, the poorer pupils probably swept out the school. A curious entry in 1628 seems to show a concern for the pupils' comfort: 4*d* was paid for 'kids' (i.e. faggots) and 'kindinge' the way for the scholars.

It has been assumed in the past that the master at Witton lodged in the school, above the school room, as many masters did. The statute on the admission of the master may perhaps support this belief, as the feoffees were to 'show him the commodities of the school and his lodging there . . .', but the evidence from the accounts, beginning in 1578, contradicts that impression, although there may have been a change in the arrangements. The accounts show that, whereas the roof of the school was of slate, the master's chamber was periodically thatched. Moreover, while no rent was ever paid for the school, the feoffees regularly paid rent for the master's chamber to the Venables, barons of Kinderton: in the early years 6*s* 8*d*, but in 1601, and for fifty years after, 8*s*. Originally, however, the feoffees

---

* See the illustration of Hawkshead village school in W. G. Hoskins, *Local History in England* (1959), p. 68.

sub-let the chamber, and in the first complete accounts the rental of school lands included 10s for the chamber. In 1580 and 1581 the tenant was 'Raffe Sempoole', undoubtedly Ralph Saintpoole, the curate of Witton Chapel.[20] In the following two years the master paid the feoffees 6s 8d rent for the chamber, and in 1584 his widow paid half a year's rent. In 1586 the rent of the chamber for three quarters of a year was paid by John Rostorne,* but when, in 1586, Thomas Farmer was appointed master, the feoffees improved and furnished the chamber for him. They paid 14s 6d at Chester for a bed, and other charges for carriage, setting it up, and for cords for it. Further, they paid for making a pair (i.e. flight) of stairs for the chamber, for a lock and key, and 'for the amending of the cloase aboute the chamber'—proof that it was a ground floor building. They continued, at first, to charge Farmer rent, but after 1589 he made no further payment and the chamber became a perquisite of his office. This did not necessarily mean that he always occupied it: in 1615 there is a payment for repairs at the school to 'Richard of the Chamber'.

Some more light is shed on the master's chamber by later accounts: the composite accounts for 1642–9 record a payment for 'takeinge up the stones where the ould chamber stood' and later for 'laying the stone for the chamber'. In the same account £1 12s was spent on dinners for the workmen at the 'rearing' of the chamber.† This was perhaps some temporary rebuilding or alternatively the nucleus of the new house which was built in 1653 for the master, at considerable expense. The rent paid to the Baron of Kinderton, however, continued to be the same 8s until 1658, when, though still described as the chamber rent, it was raised to 10s; in 1659 it became the chamber and 'yoord', and in 1660 was described as the schoolmaster's house and yard. All this suggests strongly that the house was built on the same site as the chamber.

The curriculum and the library

Although we know from the statutes the texts which were to be used in the school, we have no evidence from Witton itself at this date of how the curriculum was organised. However, we know that Witton was at its foundation a one-master school (though an usher was envisaged if the funds allowed) modelled on St Paul's and that in

* In 1594 J. Rostorne was paid for 'setting down and writing up the accounts' and in 1592 the payment was made to 'the Clerke', possibly the parish clerk.

† The previous item is for making a pair of stairs 'at the end of the schoole', but there is no reason to think that this is connected with the chamber.

the sixteenth century there was considerable uniformity among grammar schools. Two one-master schools founded almost at the same time as Witton and modelled on St Paul's were Tideswell and Guisborough, both founded by Robert Pursglove, an ex-prior and a former pupil at St Paul's. Their statutes (of which Guisborough's are more detailed) show the stages of learning through which the pupils passed, and may be taken as a guide to Witton. The school was organised in four forms. The first form consisted of beginners, commonly called 'Petitts', who remained in that form until they could read perfectly and pronounce their words plainly and distinctly. The master was not bound to teach them, but could delegate the work to a senior pupil. This presupposes that the boys on entering the school were unable to read English; requirements in schools varied: some required reading and writing in English, some readiness to begin Latin, and others even some knowledge of Latin. It is impossible to tell what the position was at Witton originally, as there were no requirements in Deane's statutes.

The ground is, however, firmer when dealing with the classical instruction: the second form at Guisborough was to be taught by the master the parts of speech, conjugation of verbs and declension of nouns 'every way backward and forward', and when they had learned every part 'not by rote but by reason' they were to proceed further in grammar, and on to certain 'little books' containing not only eloquence of the tongue but also 'good plaine lessons of honesty and godliness whereby they may be induced also to perfect pronunciacion'. (The combination of aims echoes Deane's statutes.) When they had mastered this stage the boys passed into the third form, where they were taught the authorised Latin grammar, Terence, Aesop's fables, Virgil and Tully's epistles. Finally, in the fourth form the scholars were to have daily practice in translation to and from Latin besides studying Sallust, Ovid, Horace, Tully's *Offices* and Erasmus's *Copia*. The master was to teach Latin versification to apt pupils and the art of numbering by arithmetic, and in the third and fourth forms pupils were to speak nothing but Latin in school. This gives an idea of the ladder of learning at small grammar schools comparable with Witton and using the same books. Within the diocese of Chester the episcopal requirements as shown in Bishop Chadderton's visitation articles of 1581 were confined to instruction in godliness and virtue 'and especially in Master Nowels Catechisme lately set forth': in addition the schoolmasters were expected to 'cause their children to resort unto the Church to heare divine service and sermons'.[21]

There is little evidence in the account books of any school books provided by the school. In 1585 two books, both dictionaries, were

bought at a cost of 8s 10d: they were Baret's dictionary, which was
an 'Alvearie or Triple Dictionarie in Englishe, Latin and French . . .'
first published in 1573 (with a second edition in 1580) by John Baret,
a fellow of Trinity College, Cambridge, and 'Cowper's' [Cooper's]
dictionary, an improved and enlarged edition of the Latin dictionary
compiled by Sir Thomas Elyot in 1538, and the book which
Bretchgirdle had left to Stratford Grammar School. (It is interesting
to see, in the accounts of the Dean and Chapter of Chester, that in
1589 the master of Chester School was given 20s to buy a dictionary
for the school, and that the carriage of 'Cowper's dictionary' from
Cambridge cost 9d.) At the same time the Witton feoffees paid 7d
for two chains to hang the dictionary in, and the next year, when
two calves' skins were bought for them, John Sworton was paid 6d
to hang them up in chains. This seems to have been a common
practice: at Boston, for example, in 1578, it was resolved 'that a dictionary shall be bought for the scholars of the Free School, and the
same book to be tied in a chain and set upon a desk in the school,
whereunto any scholar may have access as occasion shall serve'.[22]
Not until 1707 is there any record of any other book being bought by
the feoffees, and again it was a dictionary, costing 6s 8d.

The school, however, was fortunate in that as early as 1631 it
had a library: in that year £3 18s 2d (a large sum) was paid to
Thomas Deane for 'makinge the librarie', presumably presses to
hold the books. Macclesfield School's library, of which a catalogue
exists, was founded in 1681, and drew on various benefactors in the
county, including Peter Venables of Kinderton. All but one of
Witton's benefactors are unknown, if indeed there was more than
one, but from the accounts it looks as if the books which were fetched
from Bunbury in 1630 were the nucleus of the library. The only
known donor was a distinguished old scholar of the school, Thomas
Pierson, a Puritan minister and writer, in sympathy with the
religious views of the then master, Richard Pigott. A *Life* of Pierson
states that 'At Northwich in Cheshire, there being a free schoole,
where first he was brought up [in] learning, he in his life time had
taken care, that there should be a place fitted for a library, which he
furnished with some bookes, such as he then thought convenient for
the use of the schoolmasters and scholars'. The books from Bunbury
may well be connected with Pierson, since in 1609 he had married
the widow of the Rev. Christopher Harvey of Bunbury.* He himself,
after some time in Witton and Weaverham, held the living of
Brampton Bryan in Herefordshire. In 1632 Pierson sent two books to

---

* In his will Harvey left books to the value of £42 13s 10d, all his goods
being divided equally between his wife and his son. (*Cheshire Sheaf*, new
series, I, 6.)

the school, and in 1634 the sum of 6s was paid for the carriage of Mr Pierson's books, which came via Congleton. These were the books which Pierson had left to the school in his will. By the will, dated 15 October 1633 (he died later that month), he left books from his library to the value of £4 for the use of the school of Kington, Herefordshire, where his stepson had been master briefly, and to the value of £20, a considerable sum, 'to the use of the free schoole in Northwitch in the countie of Chester', where he was educated. The distribution of the books was to be done by Sir Robert Harley, his ecclesiastical patron, Humphrey Walcot, Richard Moore and Christopher Harvey, his stepson and the author of a poem, *The Synagogue*, often bound up with George Herbert's *The Temple*. Pierson's library was described as 'far better than is usual amongst private country ministers', and the books which he left to Witton were 'partly in Divinity, partly in Humanity,* for the benefit of the preachers and schoolmasters there': the joint use for school and chapel is noteworthy. Such a munificent gift must have made the school a centre of learning in the district, and it is a pity that no catalogue survives.[23]

The masters

After Richard Mather, probably master in 1563, the first known master was Henry Webster, whose name appears in the accounts of 1580. He was, without doubt, the Cheshire man of that name who entered as a sizar and graduated as B.A. from Mather's college, St John's, Cambridge, in 1573. He was admitted as master at Witton at the visitation of the Archbishop of York in 1578. He did not fulfil Deane's requirements about celibacy: a daughter of his, 'Margeirie', was baptised in March 1580 and a son in 1582. Shortly afterwards Webster died, being buried in Witton Chapel in February 1584, and in 1585 the feoffees paid the arrears of his wages to his widow, Margery.[24]

Webster's death was followed by a period of confusion and complication before the feoffees finally acquired a satisfactory master. Detailed items in the accounts throw an interesting light on the process of appointment. In 1584 a 'Mr. Albright' from Chester was installed as master with some ceremony—dinners for the feoffees, churchwardens and some parishioners—and taken to Manchester to be presented to the bishop. The presentation to the bishop (and the fact that previously five of the feoffees had been to see the bishop at Ashton under Lyne) is evidence that Northwich was an exception

* The study of the Latin language and literature, a term still used in Scottish universities.

to the general state of Lancashire and Cheshire which was reported
to the Privy Council about 1591, when it was stated that 'the
youth are for the most part trained up by such as profess papistry; no
examination is had of schools and schoolmasters'.[25]

John Albright must have seemed a good choice: he had been a
scholar at Christ's College, Cambridge, and after taking his B.A.
in 1579 had been a minor canon of Chester Cathedral from 1582 to
1584. In that year, however, his name disappeared from the
treasurer's record at the cathedral, and 'Mr. Albright' appears at
Witton. He seems to have lodged in the town, but after the payment
of his midsummer wages he left the district and the feoffees nego-
tiated with him for his return. A 'Mr. Dicson' then appeared on
the scene with a letter of recommendation from the Earl of Hunt-
ingdon, then President of the Council in the North, and a great
Puritan patron, who had shown his interest in education by drawing
up statutes for schools at Leicester and Ashby de la Zouch and at
his death was to leave benefactions to Emmanuel College, Cambridge. The feoffees found it necessary to take counsel from 'Mr.
Warburton' on the matter, and there followed an agreement
between Albright and Dicson: the feoffees paid Dicson 30*s* to pay
Albright on his departure. Albright's further career was a roving
one and of some interest. He took an M.A. at Magdalene College,
Cambridge, in 1588, and then returned to be a minor canon at
Chester again. In 1592 he became headmaster of the King's School
there, but in 1594 was summoned to appear before the Archbishop's
Chancery Court at York to answer a charge of libelling Robert
Rogers, Archdeacon of Chester. Albright abandoned his post at
Chester, but for a year, on the presentation of the Bishop of Chester,
was Vicar of Bolton. He resigned in 1595, and went to Ireland,
where he began as a Vicar Choral of Christ Church Cathedral,
Dublin, and secured further preferment from both Elizabeth and
James I. It is obvious that Witton was but a stepping stone in a
chequered career.[26]

Dicson was forthwith installed and several payments to him were
recorded, including 20*s* when he 'went into Yorkshire',* a benevo-
lence as well as his wages at Michaelmas 1584 and £14 in 1585,
but by 1586 the feoffees were negotiating with a 'Mr. Tilman' to be
master. Tilman came from Ashton in Makerfield, and may
possibly have had the backing of Lord Strange, the Earl of Derby's
heir; at any rate the negotiations included a meeting between him
and four feoffees in the presence of Lord Strange. Although Tilman

---

* This suggests a possible identification with Robert Dickson of Yorks.,
pleb. Queen's Coll., Oxford, B.A. February 1579, M.A. from Queen's or
Brasenose 1581. Perhaps vicar of Burnsall, Yorks., 1587. (Foster.)

was hired and the feoffees paid the charges of two men and four horses to fetch him and 'his stuffe', there are no payments of wages to him recorded. The fault may well have lain with Tilman, for in the same year the feoffees received from Lord Strange 10s as a gift towards their charges in relation to Tilman. They themselves were involved in soliciting a 'Mr. Greenehill' to be master, bestowing a quart of wine on Mr Starkey of Lancashire 'when his sonne should have beine our scoolemaster', and negotiating with a 'Mr. Cawfeld' who was backed by the Earl of Derby. The parson of 'Mobley' (Mobberley) was consulted about 'Cawfeld', who was eventually paid 20s 'for a pleasure to dessist his sute'. During the absence of a school master the feoffees paid 23s 4d to 'Sir homfrey Venables' 'for thenstructing of the youth'.[27]

After this unsatisfactory and disturbed period, reminiscent of the divisions of 1561, the feoffees' choice fell on Thomas Farmer, with whom they had apparently been in touch in 1584, probably for advice. Farmer had been the schoolmaster at Great Budworth since 1578, and when he came to Witton the feoffees went over to Great Budworth for the hiring of a new master there; at his admission to Witton School he was accompanied by a number of Budworth parishioners. Farmer came originally from Tettenhall in Staffordshire, to the poor of which he left £10 in his will, and thus, unlike many of the masters, he was not a local man. Almost certainly he had been at St John's College, Cambridge, like his two known predecessors, and he graduated there in 1576. (Although recorded only as a B.A. at Cambridge, Farmer was described on his tombstone as M.A.) He was born about 1545, and thus admirably fulfilled Deane's stipulation as to the master's age, being over forty at the time of his appointment. He did, however, marry in 1593 Margaret Burton, who died ten years later leaving him without any children: in his will he left to Margaret Birchinhead, the inn-keeper and wife of his usher, 'to dinner and supper unpaid for ten pound'.[28] Farmer gave great satisfaction to the feoffees, and from 1592 to 1610, in almost every year, they gave him 40s extra above his salary of £16, 'of good will'. In 1611 he was paid a salary of £18, and from 1612 to 1615, £20; after several years of lower and irregular payments the £20 was resumed in 1619.

Thomas Farmer was the first master to leave any traceable impress on the school and on the community of Northwich, and when, in the late seventeenth century, the Witton schoolmaster was answering a questionnaire on the school, he asserted that Farmer was the first master and that he 'continued 40 years'.* Farmer was a man

* See Chapter VI, p. 120.

of both substance and public spirit. When in 1622 the clergy and schoolmasters of the diocese of Chester paid contributions towards the recovery of the Palatinate, where James I's daughter, Elizabeth, had lost her throne early in the Thirty Years War, the list in Frodsham deanery included the curate of Witton, Mr Walker, who gave 5s, the schoolmaster at Budworth, Mr Key, who gave 3s, the schoolmaster at Halton, Mr Piggott, who gave 6s 8d, and Farmer, who gave 10s. At his death in January 1625 he left monetary bequests of over £200, and his goods were valued at over £354, some £330 of which was in bills, bonds and ready money. The rest of his goods included three 'kyne' valued at £7, his bed, furniture and clothes at £10, his books at £3, and his brass and pewter at £1 13s 4d. His will reveals him as a man of public and private generosity: besides gifts to his own nephews and nieces he had a particular care for the daughters of Richard Skelhorn, between whom he left £60, and he remembered also his four godsons, Thomas Sudlow, Thomas Birchinhead (without doubt the son of Randle, baptised in 1607), Thomas Hyd and Matthew Symcock. His public bequests were twenty marks for the 'battelling of the Chancell' of Witton Chapel, 'if it be done with in the space of foure yeares after my death'; twenty nobles towards the maintenance of Witton Bridge, 26s 8d 'to the poore of the Wich' (Northwich), and 20s 'to the poore of the Crosse' (Witton). There is a curious entry in the ecclesiastical Correction Book for 1619–28 of a charge of usary against Farmer and George Tarbocke, a feoffee. It was, however, answered by the appearance of Tarbocke, who alleged that he was an executor and employed the money for 'poore infants', after which the case was dismissed. It seems to be evidence rather of Farmer's position of trust in local society than of any misdemeanour.[29]

Unfortunately, nothing is known of the conduct of the school under Farmer, who taught for fifteen years without an usher,* but the feoffees regularly gave him bonuses. The names of two of his pupils survive: one, Thomas Pierson, who went up to Cambridge in 1590, was a distinguished clergyman; the other, Peter Jackson,† who went there in 1620, was obscure—possibly a local curate. Nevertheless Farmer's benefaction to the school is sufficient evidence of his devotion and care for learning, and there can be little doubt that if the names of schools sending pupils to Cambridge colleges survived for this early date Witton would have been among them. Farmer's attachment to the school is symbolised by his desire to be

* The record in the accounts of 1591 of an agreement between the master and the curate, Sir Henry Wyddenstall, formerly curate at Great Budworth, remains mysterious and may not refer to teaching.

† I owe the name of Peter Jackson to Mr C. D. Rogers.

buried on 'the bank before the scoole doore', and he willed to each
of the scholars at the time of his death an unspecified number of
pence—careless drafting, perhaps due to his age. His special claim to
Witton's gratitude lay, however, in the following bequest:

> I give to the scoole of Wytton fiftie pounds to be disposed by the feoffees
> and the church wardens for the tyme beinge in this manner (to weett) that
> if aney poore scholler be brought up in the scoole of Witton till he be suffi-
> cient & a scoller fitt for the University, that the he [*sic*] to have the use of
> it till he be Maister if he tarrie so long in the University; yf not then an
> other; and if there be noe scoller my will is that it be bestowed upon the
> marriage of poore wenches that marrie in the feere of god, within the
> Chappendry of Wytton. Also my desire is that the Curat for the tyme
> beinge see thexecution here of till there be a scoller.

The first scholar, Richard Wrench, was subsidised in 1634 and he
was the only one of the nine holders of Farmer's exhibition (at
Oxford, Cambridge and Trinity College, Dublin) to go up before
the Civil War; Wrench was a native of Davenham parish, and this
may be connected with the dispute which arose as to which 'poore
and towardly schollar' was to be preferred. The matter was
referred to a Commission of Pious Uses to determine the 'mind of
Thomas Farmer'; for 'the defect of the testator's expression in his
written will, what schollar and of what place should bee preferred'
in the case of competition had led to contention and expense. The
commission found in March 1640 that Farmer 'did in words by way
of codicill' specify that 'if any poore schollar borne within Witton,
that is within the towneship of Witton, Northwich, Hartford or
Lostock' were educated at the school until fit for the university, he
should have preference over one born elsewhere, and that he 'added
withall that hee hoped Mr. Pigot and the feoffees would have a care
thereof'.[30]

Farmer's bequest is one of the few known benefactions to the
school in its first three centuries, and only his and Peter Cotton's
(in 1716) were on this generous scale. It is fitting that the school
should still possess the metal plate which was on his tombstone: it
was taken off when thieves tried to steal it in the mid-nineteenth
century and nailed behind the great door of the school, where it
remained until the demolition of that building in 1869. Owing to
damage the Greek inscription is incomplete, but the headmaster
who, at prize-giving in 1887, referred to the old Greek motto over
the door—'An honourable man in his life pursues learning honour-
ably'—gave a reasonable translation of what remains and was
probably referring to it. (The translation given by Weston which
adds 'More worthy is the man, who, dying, is of service to the
living:—such this man', may represent a tradition of the total.)[31]

The death of Thomas Farmer after almost forty years as master
must have been a great loss to the school, but the feoffees were
fortunate in their choice of his successor. Richard Pigott (the name
is variously spelt Pigot, Piggot and Piggott), the son of Richard, of
Northwich, was chosen in Farmer's lifetime and was almost certainly
educated at Witton. He had matriculated in 1614 as a sizar at
Christ's College, Cambridge (of which he was later a modest benefactor), and graduated B.A. in 1618 and M.A. in 1621. Before he
came to Witton he taught at Halton School, and one of his pupils
there, Benjamin, son of Hugh Winnington of Cranage (doubtless
the school feoffee) followed him to Witton. According to custom,
Pigott was shown the statutes and taken with them to Wigan to be
presented to the bishop. To judge by the number of pupils he
entered at Cambridge colleges he seems to have been an extremely
successful teacher. Northwich was fortunate that it did not lose him
to Macclesfield soon after his arrival: in 1630 his name was among
those considered by the governors of Macclesfield School for the post
of master, which went in the end to Thomas Bold of Middlewich.
Pigott's distinction is attested further by his appointment by the
corporation during the Civil War as master of Shrewsbury School,
and even more strikingly by his confirmation there after the Restoration by the legal patrons, St John's College, Cambridge. The
historian of Shrewsbury School finds it curious that St John's confirmed the man intruded by the Puritan corporation in 1646, but
Pigott's record at Witton suggests that this was merely a recognition
of his ability.[32]

Richard Pigott as schoolmaster had an important share in the
Puritan influence which was so strong at Northwich in the two
decades before the Civil War. This influence had a tradition in the
town of which it is possible that an early instance was the indictment
of Witton at the visitation of the Archbishop of York in 1578, that
'The masters and parents send not their children to be taught in the
catechisme'. Certainly from 1599 to 1601 Witton Chapel had had as
'lecturer' (an unbeneficed clergyman appointed solely to preach) the
Witton School pupil, Thomas Pierson, who edited works of William
Perkins, the influential Cambridge Puritan divine. Furthermore the
town supported a 'preaching minister' by a communal gift of salt
rights. Pigott was described by the Puritan annalist Calamy as 'an
able, prudent and religious man', and was a friend of Richard
Baxter, to whose influence, it is surmised, he owed his appointment
at Shrewsbury. After his removal to Shropshire he played a leading
part in both the ecclesiastical and the civil organisation of the
county. In 1647 he was declared fit to be a lay member of one of
the Shropshire *classes*, the Presbyterian committee system which

replaced the Anglican hierarchy. Later, in 1654, he became a commissioner for Shropshire.[33]

This influence at the school combined easily with that of the contemporary clergy at Witton and Budworth. At Great Budworth the Puritan Richard Eaton was followed in 1615 by a distinguished Puritan, John Ley, an active preacher and pamphleteer. The Puritan ministers in Cheshire were well organised and their monthly preaching Exercises were held at Northwich as well as at a number of other towns. (Such Exercises had existed with episcopal approval in the diocese in the late sixteenth century, when they were attended by schoolmasters as well as clergy.) At Witton Pigott's term of office coincided with that of Richard Mather, who was curate from 1628 to 1640: both men had been presented at the archiepiscopal visitation of 1630 for not exhibiting their licences annually, but the case had been dismissed when they appeared at the visitation. In 1633 Mather was presented for not wearing a surplice, not reading prayers on Wednesdays and Fridays, and not reading the Book of Common Prayer; the entry of his burial in the parish register bears witness to his Puritan emphasis on preaching the word of God: translated, it runs, 'Richard Mather, Master in Arts, a dear servant of God, who for twelve years most faithfully exercised the sacred function of preaching to this people of Witton', buried 'with the deepest mourning of all good men'. It was for the duration of Mather's ministry that the leading burgesses agreed to make the falling yield of the minister's salt rights up to £10 a year out of the 'leies' of the parish. The Pigotts and Mather were close friends: Pigott's sister, Margery, left by her will (proved in 1639) 20s to Mather, 'preacher of god's word at Witton', while Mather appointed Pigott as an overseer of his will.

Mather left to each of the overseers of his will and to certain other friends a number of selected books. The bequests point to a circle of Puritan ministers and laymen in the district. It included 'Mr. Burrows', vicar of Runcorn and later Presbyterian minister of Christleton; Pigott himself, who was to have Roger's *Catechism* and *Treatise of the Sacraments*; Thomas Robinson (presumably the future County Commissioner under the Commonwealth), who was left 'Elton upon the 8th of Romans'; Peter Venables of Lostock Gralam* (possibly a later feoffee), who was to have 'such a booke as Mr Pigot shall thinke fitt', and 'Mr Robert Venables the younger', undoubtedly the son of Robert Venables of Antrobus and the future Parliamentarian general, who was left a book by 'Renalls'. Other books for relatives and friends were to be chosen by Pigott. When

---

* He was presented at the visitation of the Archbishop of York in 1630 for not kneeling at communion. (*York Diocesan Records*, R VI A 22.)

Mather died in 1640 he was succeeded by Richard Holford, a noted
Puritan, and in July 1642, when the Parliamentarian party organised
opinion in the county in the form of remonstrances in favour of the
unity of King and Parliament, the first six signatories of the Northwich declaration were the two Robert Venables, father and son,
William Bentley, physician and leading school feoffee for many
years, John Partington, Richard Holford and Richard Pigott.[34]

Pigott was a successful master sending a succession of pupils to
Cambridge and several to Oxford. He sent only two from Witton to
his own college, Christ's, one in 1627 and one in 1646, and since he
had already sent a boy from Halton to Christ's in 1625 the stream of
boys he sent from Witton to St John's College suggests the existence
of an established link between the school and Farmer's college. He
remained at the school until Michaelmas 1643, although he did not
get the £24 15s 6d due to him for arrears until 1649 or 1650. He
was, in addition, a leading and influential member of the local
community. Before he left, the Civil War had begun, and he seems
to have played some part in the military organisation of the town
by the Parliamentarians. In November 1643 'Mr. Richard Pigot'
and two others (including the minister) were repaid for what 'they
had expended in Northwiche upon the publiq occasions there, they
beinge entrusted for the securinge of that garrison, duringe the
absence of Capt. Leigh and Capt. Gerrard then forth with our
army against Chester'. About the same time 'Mr. Richard Pigate'
received from the constables of Hartford £2 levied on the inhabitants for the payment of a dragooner for six weeks.[35]

After a successful period at Shrewsbury School, Pigott survived
the Restoration and was confirmed as master there, but in July 1662,
with other prominent Puritans, he was imprisoned in Shrewsbury
Castle, and though released after a few days was deprived of his
post in September under the Act of Uniformity and died in the
following year. Like Thomas Farmer, Pigott was a man of some
wealth: among the composition papers of the Royalist Sir Peter
Leycester occurs a schedule of debts of Peter Leycester the younger
of Nether Tabley, which included a debt of £30, a considerable sum,
to 'Mr. Piggot now schoolemaster at Shrowesbury'. In his will, made
in 1659, Pigott made provision for six of his seven children,
envisaging a portion of at least £100 for each of them, and possible
additions from land he had purchased some years before at Somer-
ford in Cheshire.[36] The connection of the Pigott family with
Northwich was well established and survived the Civil War: his
son, Richard, was curate at Witton from 1663 to 1669, and another
son, Thomas, from 1669 to 1674.

The ushers

The usher or under-master was not mentioned in Deane's statutes, but he had been mentioned in the schedule attached to the deed of feoffment, in which it was laid down that if the profits of the lands exceeded £12 (the master's salary) they should be used at the discretion of the churchwardens for an usher or otherwise for the good of the school. The lack of any statute dealing with the usher meant that his electors, qualifications and functions were all left obscure. The first reference to an usher occurs in the first surviving account, when the payments to master and usher were lumped together; subsequently, in 1580 and 1581, they received £16 between them, and in each year the usher, Gilbert Bradshaw, was given 20*s* 'upon good will'. The master received no such gift and may not have been at the school as long as the usher: certainly a son of Gilbert Bradshaw had been baptised in September 1575. In 1582 the two payments were separated, and Bradshaw received £3; he disappears after 1584, however, and there is no further reference to an usher until 1590, when the feoffees went to 'Mr. Barne of Kinderton'* about obtaining John Ashbrooke to be usher, but with no result. No usher was paid until 1601, when Jeffrey Bramall was paid at the rate of £6 a year but soon left. He was possibly the Geoffrey Bramhall who entered Emmanuel College, Cambridge, as a pensioner in 1596, matriculated in the same year, but took no degree. There followed a candidate whom the bishop apparently rejected, since the accounts record expenses in 1602 'at goinge to my lord bishoppe with Sur Symon Savage when he should have been the usher of the scoole', and two transient ushers, Newton and John Caye.[37] From 1607 to 1613 the name of the usher is not given although payments were regularly made, but he may well have been the 'Ran. Berchenhead' who is named in 1613, and whose wages stood at £8 from 1612, but only £6 (with 20*s* upon good will) in 1616, when a second usher, Thomas Newall, was appointed at a salary of £6. This second appointment may indicate a growth in the school's numbers, but possibly only the increasing age of Thomas Farmer.

Berchenhead and Newall are rather less shadowy figures than their predecessors. Before his appointment Newall had been parish clerk for at least eleven years: an entry in the parish register records for posterity that no register was kept for 1605 and 1606 owing to the negligence of the minister, the clerk, Thomas Newall, and the churchwardens. Newall remained usher and clerk until his death in

* *Cf*. the 1591 account: 'Paid to Mr Baron of Kynderton' the chamber rent.

1626, and he was succeeded as clerk by his fellow usher, Randle Berchenhead or Birchenhead. This combination of the two posts may represent the continuation of a medieval tradition whereby teaching the parish children was among the clerk's duties. Berchenhead's 'good italic hand' and 'some nicely executed Gothic lettering and ornamentation' in the register have been remarked, accomplishments useful in an usher. Berchenhead was another mature usher, being thirty-two in 1613, and he had moreover, another occupation. The family, long settled in Northwich and perhaps related to the gentry family of the same name, were dependants of the Stanley family, and at least as early as 1621 Randle appears to have been the lessee from the Earl of Derby of the Swan Inn, although it may have been managed mainly by his wife, Margaret, mentioned in Farmer's will. Berchenhead had several sons, one of whom was Farmer's godson and another, the famous Sir John Berkenhead, and he himself was a man of standing in the community. At the end of 1633 illness prevented him from keeping the church register for a month, but though not mentioned by name in the school accounts for 1632 and 1633 he may have remained usher until the end of 1633: he died in March 1636.[38]

No new usher was paid until 1638, when 'Mr. Simcocke' had a brief term: he may have been Farmer's godson, Matthew (and probably his pupil), and he was, presumably, also founder's kin. Simcocke was succeeded in 1639 by 'Mr. Harrison', who continued into the 'forties. He was in all probability Jeffrey, the son of Thomas, a substantial Northwich man. Jeffrey Harrison matriculated at Brasenose College, Oxford, at the end of 1638 at the age of nineteen, but took no degree. He became a feoffee in 1641* and in the 'fifties a churchwarden: later, after the Restoration, he played a part of some importance in the school's affairs in getting rid of Thomas Swinton, the master.[39]

There is no contemporary evidence of the usher's function during this early period of the school's history or of the extent to which his teaching was of English or Latin, and as this was later a subject of dispute it would be unwise to draw conclusions from the practice of other schools, which, in any case, varied. All that can be said is that until 1607 the usher's role was very intermittent: serious efforts at procuring a succession of ushers date from the beginning of the seventeenth century, and from 1607 one or more ushers was the rule. If two ushers were perhaps necessitated by Farmer's age, the need for one regular usher can be taken as a sign of an increase in the number of pupils. But whereas some grammar schools had ushers

* Thomas Newall appears also to have been a feoffee and usher at the same time.

with degrees, Witton's ushers had no higher qualification than matriculation at, or admission to, an Oxford or Cambridge college and not always that.

The pupils

The statutes required the master to enter the names of new pupils in 'a rolle of parchment', but although in the first full year for which the accounts survive the feoffees bought a 'Regester boocke', it has unfortunately not survived. The first surviving actual registers date from the end of the eighteenth century, but a solitary list of pupils at the end of seventeenth century was found among the diocesan records. For the period with which this chapter deals we know with certainty the names of only those pupils who went to certain Cambridge colleges which recorded a boy's school* and of the single pupil who received money from Farmer's bequest. The absence of names of schools from Oxford college entrance records is particularly unfortunate, since many Cheshire boys went to Oxford, particularly to Brasenose, a college with strong Lancashire and Cheshire connections, and in addition Christ Church's ecclesiastical patronage at Great Budworth may have drawn boys from the neighbourhood to it. In all, we know with absolute certainty the names of under a dozen pupils in this period of the school's history.† A few more graduate pupils can be suggested with great probability, since in those early years, with the nearest free school ten miles away,‡ most local boys had probably been educated there: such were Thomas Litler, 'generosus', described in Witton parish registers at his death as 'Vire ad modum literatus', who graduated B.A. in 1604 from Queen's College, Oxford, his son Richard, who matriculated at the same college in 1635, and William Bentley, later a dominant school feoffee. Bentley was baptised at Witton Chapel in March 1600; he matriculated at Balliol College, and graduated B.A. in 1623. Although he was not made a Doctor of Medicine at Oxford until 1661 his epitaph of 1680 referred to at least fifty years' practice of the art 'pie, perite, benigne'. In fact he was already licensed as a doctor by 1630, which makes him one of the small number of physicians practising outside London before the Civil War. He was clearly a man of learning, and left at his death a collection of books and manuscripts. The range of Bentley's interests is suggested by a list of books belonging to the Royalist minister of

---

* Even here there are gaps, and one, probably of great significance for Witton, is that the register of admissions to St John's begins only in 1630.
† See the list at the end of this chapter.
‡ This statement was made c. 1650—see Chapter V.

Brereton which he purchased in 1647, when they were sold for the
use of the State. The list included the works of Augustine, Aquinas,
Jerome, Pope Gregory, Tirino (a Jesuit writer), Eadmer's History
(a medieval chronicle), 'Florentine history', Josephus, Apuleius, and
Plutarch's *Ethics*, and the total cost amounted to £8 5*s*.[40]

The grammar schools in their heyday were noted for their mixture
of social grades, and there is no reason to think that Witton was an
exception.* Some variation in the social status of the pupils is
shown among those who went to universities. A few went as 'pen-
sioners', indicating usually that their fathers were men of substance:
they included Benjamin Winnington, who entered Christ's College
in 1627, Samuel Catherall, the son of the rector of Swettenham,
admitted to St John's in 1634, Samuel Wrench, son of Ralph
Wrench, yeoman of Davenham, admitted there in 1638, and John
Norcott (or Northcott), admitted to Christ's in 1646, who was the
son of the minister of West Derby Chapel but had a relation of
substance in Northwich. Thomas Pierson, too, was admitted to
Emmanuel as a pensioner (later becoming a scholar), but this
appears to be a misleading guide to his father's wealth. Pierson's
biographer stated that he was educated at Northwich 'by the care
of his parents and friends', and that at Cambridge he was 'maintained partly by his own industry, partly by exhibitions from others
(his parents' estate being too small to defray such a charge)'. One
of his chief benefactors was the lord of the manor of Nether Whitley,
William Touchet, at whose house he received some of his education.
Most of the boys from Witton, however, went to the university as
sizars or servitors, that is, pupils who did menial tasks while at
college to pay their way: their fathers were described in the college
records as 'yeoman' or 'husbandman'. One such pupil, Richard
Steele, the son of a husbandman of Barthomley, was admitted to
St John's, Cambridge, as sizar to his tutor, 'Mr Wrench', who was
himself an old Witton pupil and a former sizar who had become
a fellow of the college. Wrench was in fact the only holder of
Farmer's exhibition before 1653, and his father had had six payments of 20*s* in 1634–5. Subsequently Wrench was expelled from
his fellowship by the Parliamentarians, becoming chaplain to the
Bishop of Durham. Like the school's founder he remembered the
locality in his will, leaving a bequest of nineteen nobles to nineteen
poor families in Davenham, to be paid out of a rent charge on his
estate of Moulton Lodge there.[41]

Such evidence, confined to boys who went to universities, gives an

---

* Was William Pickmeyre, to whom the feoffees in 1639 gave 13*s* 4*d*
'to buy him a suit of clothes' a poor pupil? *Cf.* the expenditure in 1575 at the
King's School, Chester, on apparel for a pupil. (Burne, *op. cit.*, p. 54.)

unbalanced picture of the school and leaves us ignorant of those who, in the words of an eighteenth-century master, 'annually go out to business'. The law,* the trade and industry of Northwich, and the agriculture of the district must have absorbed many of Witton's pupils. Probably many of the feoffees were educated at the school, and they covered a wide range of local gentry and yeomen, lawyers, tradesmen, salt-makers and artisans. (It is worth noting that Thomas Sudlow, a feoffee who died in 1625, referred in his will to 'all my bookes which are in my clossett'.) In reply to a questionnaire sent out in the 1670s by Christopher Wase of Oxford, Peter Woodnoth, then headmaster, stated that 'most of the gentry of Cheshire have been brought up at Northwich Schoole'. Such a statement does not inspire confidence in his reliability as a witness, but he would hardly have made it if some of the gentry had not been educated there.† Nevertheless, in 1581 the three sons of Ralph Leftwich of Leftwich (outside the chapelry, but adjoining Northwich) were not at their local grammar school but at Shrewsbury School. Evidence about pupils who went into trade is conjectural, but almost certainly these included the sons of the usher, Randle Berchenhead: Randle,‡ who succeeded his father as lessee of the Swan; Thomas, the godson of Farmer, who was described at his burial in St Bride's Church, London, as a 'servante', meaning probably an apprentice; and Roger, who was apprenticed to an apothecary in Chester in 1636. Another likely pupil is John Huett, son of William Huett of Northwich, yeoman (a feoffee and a man of substance), who was apprenticed in February 1642 for ten years to Peter Ince of Chester, stationer, a noted Puritan.[42]

Although originally designed by Deane for boys of the township and also, probably, the chapelry of Witton, by the early seventeenth century the school was taking boys from beyond these narrow limits. Boys whose fathers were of Over Whitley, Weaverham, Swettenham, Davenham, Great Budworth, Barthomley, and Stanthorne (near Middlewich, but in the parish of Davenham), were at the school, and some at least of these, together with Benjamin Winning-

* In 1565 two Northwich men entered the Middle Temple—George, son of George Sudlowe, gent., and Richard, son of William Wrench, gent. (H. A. C. Sturgess, *Register of Admissions to the Middle Temple*, 1, 29.)

† See below, Chapter VII. Woodnoth's reply may be the basis for the statement that Northwich School was favoured for the education of gentlemen's sons, made by Joan Simon, *Education and Society in Tudor England*, p. 363. Mrs Simon was unfortunately not able to cite the source.

‡ The complexities of social status are illustrated by the marriage of Randle, Jr., to Elizabeth, daughter of Richard Harcourt of Wincham, gentleman. Sir Peter Leycester recorded that this Randle was the son of the 'usher of the free-school of Northwich'. (Ormerod, 1, 629.)

ton, who followed Pigott from Halton, must have been 'tablers' or
boarders in the town: the early hour at which school started would
alone have made this necessary. The dispute over eligibility for
Farmer's exhibition suggests that competition from outside the
chapelry existed. There is no contemporary evidence about the
numbers of pupils at the school, but it may perhaps be legitimately
assumed that a figure given thirty years after the Civil War as a
peak in the school's history applies to this obviously prosperous
period, if it has any validity at all. During the 1670s the master
replied to Wase's questionnaire that the school had had '220 scholars
at once'. This may, of course, be an imaginary figure but it may
equally be a high point which had remained part of the school's
traditions: it is noteworthy that the master did not give merely a
round figure of 200. Such a total is certainly high, but it is not
beyond the bounds of possibility. Rochdale School, by its constitution, was not to have more than 150 pupils; 140 pupils were said to
be at Blackburn School in 1557, and 200 at Middleton about 1600,
while at Shrewsbury School four masters taught 400 boys. At a
more general level, the Speaker in the House of Commons in
1563, bewailing the loss of schools in England, spoke of the deprivation caused 'if in every school there had been but an hundred
scholars . . .'.[43]

The most notable of the school's old pupils of this time was Sir
John Birkenhead, long claimed as a pupil by tradition. The discovery
that he was later a feoffee of the school seems to clinch the argument
and remove the element of surmise. Although the absence of an
authentic baptismal entry in the parish register makes it impossible
to prove, there seems little doubt that John Berkenhead was the son
of the usher, Randle Berchenhead. John Berkenhead must have
shown academic aptitude, for in 1634, at the age of seventeen, he
matriculated at Oriel College, Oxford, having entered as a 'servitor'
in 1632. There his skill as a scribe caught the attention of Archbishop Laud, then Chancellor of the university, whose secretary
he became, and through whom he rose. He had gained his B.A.
in January 1637, but in January 1640 Laud, by diploma, caused
him to be created M.A., and by letters commendatory to All Souls'
College secured his election there as a fellow. When the Civil War
began, and Charles I with his army and court came to Oxford, it
was presumably Berkenhead's connection with Laud which led to
his choice as editor of *Mercurius Aulicus*, the Royalist newspaper.
This appeared regularly every week from January 1643 to the
autumn of 1645, when the Royalist cause collapsed, and the editorial
office is thought to have been in Oriel College. C. V. Wedgwood
declares that 'the editor, leader-writer and chief reporter, Sir John

Birkenhead, is the true father of English journalism', and that 'for wit, clarity, compactness and vigour he has rarely been surpassed'. By way of reward he was appointed Whyte's Professor of Moral Philosophy, but he left Oxford soon after the flight of the King in 1646. In 1648 he was ejected from his fellowship and Chair, and spent his time in London and on the Continent. The Restoration brought him full recognition: the degree of D.C.L. at Oxford, election to Parliament in 1661, knighthood in 1662, and in January 1664 the lucrative office of Master of Requests. In addition he was elected a fellow of the new Royal Society, of which he was a founder member. It is not surprising that in 1665 his old school hastened to elect him one of its feoffees.[44]

No other contemporary Witton pupil reached Berkenhead's lasting fame, but at least two pupils of this period were noted in their day and deserve to be recalled. Thomas Pierson (who has been mentioned earlier as a benefactor) was a native of Weaverham, who probably benefited for a few years from Farmer's teaching, and went up to the new Puritan foundation, Emmanuel College, in 1590. No doubt his school can take some of the credit for his being a 'most exact grammarian in Latine, Greeke, and Hebrew'. At Cambridge he became a student of William Perkins, a leading Puritan preacher and scholar; he was ordained in 1598 and returned to Witton as a 'lecturer' or preacher for two years, followed by a further two years as 'lecturer' at Weaverham.* He then returned to Cambridge, where he edited some of Perkins' works, one of which he dedicated to Sir Thomas Holcroft of Vale Royal: he had as co-editor of some of the sermons William Crashaw, father of the poet, Richard. During this time, until 1612, he was household chaplain to Lord St John of Bletso, but was then presented by Sir Robert Harley to the living of Brampton Bryan. He was a staunch Puritan and very active in raising the standard of the clergy in his neighbourhood, but at the same time discreet in his attitude to authority, and showing a tolerant good sense. His biographer relates certain anecdotes of him to this effect: one of his favourite sayings was that of Perkins—'some men hang salvation on so high a pinne that many poore soules can never reach it'. On one occasion, too, being asked to deal with a young gentleman 'wearing his haire extraordinary long', he answered 'let him alone till God renew his heart and then he will reforme his haire himselfe'. He was described by Calamy as 'so famous in his generation', and in his own house he educated many for the university and trained gradu-

---

* In 1602 he was one of several responsible clergymen appointed by the Bishop of Chester to deal with a sick Northwich boy, thought by some to be possessed. (W. Axon, *Cheshire Gleanings*, 1884, pp. 10–11.)

ates for the ministry. This concern for education and preaching is shown in his bequests: apart from his gift of books to the school, he gave several books, including Foxe's *Book of Martyrs* and Perkins' works, to the grandson of his benefactor, William Touchet, and £50 to the preaching minister at Witton Chapel, as well as a capital endowment for a preacher at Nether Whitley Chapel.[45]

Richard Steele, though now scarcely remembered, was another of Witton's most distinguished pupils in his day. He was the son of a husbandman of Barthomley, and one of the number of pupils sent up to St John's College, Cambridge, by Pigott. It is no doubt a sign of the disturbed times that although he matriculated in 1642 he did not take his B.A. until 1650; he took his M.A. in 1656 and was incorporated at Oxford in the same year. He became chaplain of Corpus Christi College there, and from 1650 was vicar of Hanmer, Flintshire. As a strong Presbyterian he was a member of the fourth Shropshire *classis,* and the ordainer of Philip Henry, the noted nonconformist minister. After the Restoration Steele was ejected from his living, but although 'silenced' continued to preach in many places, for which he was charged at the diocesan visitation of 1665. He moved to London and became a leading nonconformist minister there, ordaining Matthew Henry in 1687. Calamy described Steele as 'a very valuable and useful man and a good scholar, a hard student and an excellent preacher'. His fame rested largely on his writings, notably *The Husbandman's Calling* and *The Tradesman's Calling,* the latter perhaps the most important of a whole class of treatises by Dissenters in the Restoration period designed to show tradesmen and others how to serve God in their work or calling. Steele's *The Tradesman's Calling* was cited by R. H. Tawney in his *Religion and the Rise of Capitalism* as evidence of the Puritan ethos in economic matters. Although the purpose of the book was to develop the 'godly' tradesman, exercising 'grace in his calling', it formed in fact 'a manual of practical business technique'. Farming was more intractable as a spiritualised 'calling', and much of Steele's *The Husbandman's Calling* was devoted to exhorting the farmers to be content with their lot, despite heavy rents, high taxes and the oppression of landlords, who would be punished only in the next world. At his death in 1692 Steele, like other Witton pupils, showed a concern for education and left £50 for the endowment of a school at Barthomley, where the children of the Steele family of Claycroft were to be taught free.[46]

These two Witton pupils were representative in two ways of a number of their less eminent fellows who went to the university—in their profession of clergyman and in their Puritan leanings. Nine pupils are known to have been sent to Cambridge when Pigott was

master, and of these nine, six became clergymen: of these clergy
one signed the Presbyterian manifesto of 1648, the *Testimony*, two
others were ejected for nonconformity at the Restoration, and one
probably retired at the time. If we take into account also that
Pigott's Halton pupil became preaching minister at Ormskirk, Pigott
can be seen contributing from the grammar school to that 'kind of
Puritan order of preaching brothers' shaped afterwards in the universities, especially at Cambridge.[47]

Known pupils, 1557–1643, Cambridge University

Thomas Pierson, born at Weaverham *c.* 1570. Adm. pensioner, Emmanuel
   College, January 1590; Scholar; B.A., 1594; M.A., 1597. Ordained 1598.
   'Lecturer' at Witton *c.* 1599–1601. 'Lecturer' at Weaverham *c.* 1601–3.
   Returned to Cambridge and edited Perkins' works. Household chaplain
   to Oliver St. John, Baron of Bletso, until 1612. Rector of Brampton
   Brian, Herefordshire. Married, 1609, widow of Rev. Christopher Harvey
   of Bunbury. Died 1633.
Peter Jackson, son of John, husbandman. Born at Over Whitby [? Whitley]
   Cheshire. School: Northwich. Adm. sizar, Sidney Sussex, 1620. B.A.,
   Christ's, 1624. Perhaps subsequently one of the local curates of that
   name, e.g. Lower Peover, 1636–8; Great Budworth, 1640–2.
Benjamin Winnington, son of Hugh. Born at Cranage. Schools: Goostrey
   (Mr. Vaudrey), Holmes Chapel (Mr. Griffin), Morton Green (Mr.
   Whitehead), Congleton (Mr. Redman), Haulton, Northwich (Mr. Pig-
   gott). Adm. pensioner, Christ's, 1627; B.A., Emmanuel, 1631; M.A.,
   1634. Vicar of Great Burstead, Essex, 1640–1; probably vicar of Bibury,
   Glos., 1641–73; vicar of Laindon Hill, Essex, 1648. Died 1673.
Richard Wrench, son of Randle. Matric. sizar, St. John's, 1627; B.A.,
   1632; M.A., 1635; B.D., 1642. Fellow of St. John's, 1636–46, when
   ejected by the Parliamentarians. Prebendary of Durham, 1645–75; vicar
   of Heighington, 1661; rector of Boldon, Durham, 1665–75; chaplain to
   Bishop Morton. Died 1675, buried in Durham Cathedral.
Samuel Catherall, son of Ralph, rector of Swettenham. Born at Handley.
   School: Northwich (Mr. Piggott) for six years. Adm. pensioner, St.
   John's, 1634, aged sixteen; B.A., 1638; M.A., 1641. Succeeded father as
   rector of Swettenham, 1642; rector of Handley, 1643–84. Signed the
   Presbyterian *Testimony* of 1648.
Thomas Royle, son of John, 'yeoman', of Davenham. Born at Rope,
   Wybunbury. School: Northwich (Mr. Piggot) for four years. Adm.
   sizar, St. John's, 1634, aged sixteen.
William Chrimes, son of Robert, 'yeoman', of Weaverham. Born at
   Weaverham. School: Northwich (Mr. Piggot) for two years. Adm. sizar,
   St. John's, 1637, aged seventeen; B.A., 1641. Probably Ll.B. from St.
   John's, 1652.
Samuel Wrench, son of Ralph, 'yeoman', of Davenham. Born at Daven-
   ham. School: Northwich (Mr. Piggot) for seven years. Adm. pensioner,
   St. John's, 1638, aged seventeen; B.A., 1643; M.A., 1649.

John French, son of John, 'husbandman' (agricolae) of Great Budworth. Born at Great Budworth. School: Northwich (Mr. Piggot) for seven years. Adm. sizar, St. John's, 1639, aged nineteen; B.A., 1643; M.A., 1646. Ejected from Wenvoe, Glam., 1662. Died 1691.

Richard Steele, son of Robert, husbandman of Barthomley. Born at Barthomley. School: Northwich (Mr. Piggot) for two years. Adm. sizar, St. John's, 1642, aged nearly fifteen; Matric. 1642; B.A., 1640; M.A., 1656. Incorporated at Oxford 1656; chaplain of Corpus Christi College, Oxford. Vicar of Hanmer, Flints., 1650–62; a member of the fourth Shropshire *classis*. Ejected from Hanmer 1662, but continued preaching. Became a nonconformist minister in London. Died 1692; buried at St. Bartholomew the Great.

John Norcott, son of William, minister of West Derby Chapel, Walton parish. Born at West Derby, Lancs. School: Northwich under Mr. Piggott. Adm. pensioner, Christ's College, 1646, aged twenty; B.A., 1651. Given in Venn as 'Northcott' or 'Norcott'.

    A John N. was minister of Stanstead St. Margaret, Herts., 1656–62, when he retired.

The lack of any record of schools in Oxford college admission records makes it impossible to prove the admission of Witton pupils there, but several virtual certainties, including Sir John Berkenhead, are mentioned in the text.

V
Civil war: losses and recovery

1. *Northwich in the Civil War*

The original dislocation caused in Northwich by the Civil War is reflected in an entry in the parish register of 1645. 'These three or four years past the names of such as were wedded, baptized, or buried—throw civil wars, flying of ministers and Clarks, feares, distractions and troubles of the tymes were lost and burnt by cavaliers and others of this garrison, that their names could not be collected or found to be inserted and engrossed in this book as formerly.' This perhaps suggests that Northwich had a more disastrous experience in the first Civil War than was the case. The town had not the strategic importance of Nantwich in the campaigns in Cheshire, and consequently did not suffer to anything like the same extent, but it played a part in the swaying fortunes of the fighting. In a petition for financial aid the school feoffees, backed by the deputy-lieutenants of the county, drew attention to the fact that Northwich had been 'garrisond from the beginning of these troubles, and once taken and plundered by the enimy', and a contemporary pamphlet stated that Northwich was especially fortified 'being a markett towne'. From early in 1643 Sir William Brereton, the parliamentary commander, fortified the town, putting, as Malbon says, 'a sufficiente garrison therein whoe fetched in daylie many horses, goods, cattell and prisoners'. A Parliamentarian pamphlet, published in March 1643, stated, 'we have fortified Northwich with trenches, sconces, etc. for the securitie of all those parts, which have been so infected by the [Royalist] Commission of Array, and the Earl of Darbies forces at Warrington, and wee have often sallied out for the clearing of those parts which were most in danger', in particular the house of Mr Brookes of Norton, which was threatened from Halton Castle. It was at Northwich that in March 1643 Captain Spotswood ineffectually attacked Brereton, and from Northwich in the same month that Brereton advanced against Middlewich, and with help from Nantwich defeated Sir Thomas Aston, the Royalist commander who had occupied it. The re-

inforcement of the Royalists at the end of 1643 by troops from
Ireland enabled them to harry Brereton at Middlewich; 'the noise
of this', according to a contemporary pamphlet, 'caused Northwich
to be quit' by the Parliamentarian forces, and a Royalist garrison
was put in. Nantwich remained the only Parliamentarian garrison in
the county, and was besieged by the Irish army, fresh from the
massacre in Barthomley church. The raising of this siege in January
1644 by the combined forces of Sir Thomas Fairfax and Brereton
swayed the fortunes of the county. Northwich was probably evacu-
ated at once by the Royalists: certainly by August 1644 it had a
Parliamentarian garrison again and formed a base for a successful
expedition against the Royalists at Tarvin.[1]

In both 1644 and 1645 Prince Rupert was in Cheshire: in 1644,
marching north to the help of the Earl of Derby and the Marquis of
Newcastle, he bivouacked at Rudheath. After his successes Northwich became one of the very few remaining Parliamentarian garri-
sons. In 1645 Rupert joined his brother, Maurice, in a move to lift
Brereton's siege of Chester, and was so successful that he relieved
Beeston Castle and caused Brereton to retire north temporarily to
Knutsford and Bowdon. The alarm caused by Rupert's activities is
vividly revealed in an incident at Northwich described in a petition
of 1650 from Katharin Stubbs, widow of John Stubbs of Witton.*
She complained to the justices that 'whereas your peticioner haveing
her habitacion without the walls of Northwich in the tyme of the
garrison, and being her house joynd unto the outmost guard, upon
the comeing of Prince Rupert against the towne as the officers and
souldiers within the towne suspected, the officers and gentlemen
within the towne caused fower bayes of her building to be pulled
downe for feare of giveing advantage to the enimye soe that your
poore peticioner sustayned great losses there'. The justices ordered
the treasurer to pay compensation or else to show cause to the
contrary.[2] Northwich thus saw its share of the fighting, and experienced the upheavals of successive occupation by the opposing sides,
but suffered comparatively little.

A peculiarity of the situation in the town was that the lords
of the two chief manors, of Northwich and Witton, were both
Royalist, and both suffered sequestration of their lands by the victori-
ous Parliamentarians. The lands were administered by sequestration
commissioners, among whom were Dr William Bentley and William
Leftwich, both school feoffees, and Thomas Robinson, one of the

---

* Probably the John Stubbs of Witton, who, with others, was responsible
in 1646 for bringing prisoner to Halton Castle Robert Bromfield of Hapsford,
late of Witton, 'delinquent', for failing to make his composition according to
Act of Parliament. (Harl. MSS. 1999, f. 329.)

pre-war Puritan circle round Mather and Pigott. In 1654 Robinson had to seek permission from the central commissioners for the payment out of Lord Derby's estate of a fee for the steward of the town and the costs of dinners for the burgesses at the time of the twice-yearly fairs. The rents of the Venables estates in Witton were also paid over to the commissioners, and not all the efforts of Sir Peter Venables' friend, the antiquarian Elias Ashmole, who spent the summer of 1644 at Kinderton, could get off the baron's sequestration: the Venables, father and son, had to pay a fine of £6,150. Lower down the social scale the son of the former usher of the school, Randle Berkenhead Jr, met with disaster: a letter of the Cheshire County Commissioners to the Committee for the Advance of Money in April 1652, states, 'Berchenhead, of Northwich, was discharged from sequestration as not worth 200*l.*: his estate is only 3*l.* or 4*l.* a year, and his family live partly on charity. He was bailiff to the Earl of Derby, and on Charles Stuart's coming to Northwich,* proclaimed him King, went with the earl to Lancashire, escaped in the rout of Wigan, and is now living in or near London.' The Berkenhead family indeed went through some curious vicissitudes during the Civil War. Sir John Birkenhead's rise and fall have been described, but the career of his younger brother Isaac (born 1622), doubtless also an ex-pupil, was odder. Whereas Randle Jr remained loyal to the Stanleys, Isaac betrayed them. In 1651 he was captured when on the point of sailing to the Isle of Man to plot a rising in Lancashire with the Earl of Derby. He made disclosures to the Parliamentarians in return for which he was clothed at the State's expense and sent to assist in the downfall of the earl, his testimony being thought valuable to Colonel Mackworth, who was to preside at the earl's trial. Later he acted as a spy for the government, and finally was attached to General Robert Venables as adjutant-general in the unfortunate expedition to the West Indies. He died at sea in 1655 on the return voyage.[3]

The appearance of Charles Stuart, the future Charles II, in Cheshire created little stir, and he aroused no support, but Northwich was a key point later in the Interregnum during the rising of Presbyterians and Royalists under Sir George Booth against the government in 1659. The decisive battle, in which Booth was defeated by General John Lambert, took place, after action among the inclosures of Hartford, at Winnington Bridge in August, and on the previous night Booth had lain in Northwich while Lambert lay at Weaverham. After the battle Northwich was occupied by

---

* In August 1651 the Scottish army under Charles II was quartered in Nantwich. (Lysons, II, 314.)

Lambert and the church was used as a prison for 200 of the men
he had captured.

The school in Civil War and Interregnum

Despite these disturbances, which no doubt provided excitement
for the pupils, there is nothing to suggest that Witton School suffered
anything like the school at Weaverham. In 1652 Robert Warburton,
esq., the patron, with the churchwardens and other inhabitants of
Weaverham, petitioned the justices of the peace at Nether Knutsford for an order assessing a ley throughout the whole parish
to repair the schoolhouse, since 'the sayd towne was soe envyed
by the Cavalleere partye that they defaced the sayd schoolehouse
and broke downe both the doores and windowes and otherwise
abused the same breaking the seates in peeces so that it is not fit to
keepe schoole in'. But Witton School was affected in various ways
by the Civil War. A sad loss was that of the school library, for when,
in the 1670s, the master came to answer the query in Wase's questionnaire* about libraries and manuscripts belonging to the school, his
reply was that 'Our librarie was destroyed in the time of war'. There
is no evidence to show how this misfortune happened: the only
light is an entry in the accounts of October 1656 of 11s 4d spent
upon 'our minister, schoolemaster, and our selves for the charge of
horse hire and of our selves in goinge to Winwicke Schoole, and for
the costs of a warrant to make search in that schoole for sundry
bookes heretofore belonginge to Witton Schoole'. No record of the
warrant has been found, and the history of Winwick School is
silent on the matter. Winwick School, refounded in 1616, was under
the patronage of the Royalist Leghs of Lyme, and was one of the
leading schools of Lancashire during the seventeenth century.[4]

The finances

The most serious effect of the Civil War on the school sprang from
the virtual destruction of the Saracen's Head property. When, in
June 1646, ten feoffees surveyed the school lands, they recorded
'Lands lying within the Foregate Street within the City of Chester
containing and being ten roods in length and four in breadth upon
which formerly stood an antient inn house called the Saracen's Head
with two large stables and two kilnes with other necessary buildings,
in all containing fifty and three bays of building, but now all of it
ruined and demolished': no rent was given for it. In the summer of
1651 the feoffees paid to Mr Robinson (presumably Thomas), 'when

* See below, pp. 119–20.

hee came from London', 10s for delivering a petition to Parliament. This was presumably the petition (of which a contemporary signed copy survives) from ten of the feoffees which was counter-signed in confirmation of its truth by the sheriff and four deputy lieutenants of the county.* After describing the Saracen's Head, it continued:

... All belonging to the sayd free schoole of Witton, being the maine subsistence thereof, but of late all of it consumed and burned, together with tables, bedsteds, and other wainscot, by the king and parliament forces, for want of fuell during the siege against the sayd citty. The losses amounting in all to the value of fourteene hundred pownds and upwards. By reason whereof the sayd schoole is lykely to be unsupplyed to the great dammage of the country (there being noe free schoole within ten myles thereof) unlesse some speedy course be taken for supply.

May it please your Honours (the premises considered together with the poverty and extreame pressures of that part of the County, Northwych an adiacent Market towne within sayd the [*sic*] chappelry of the sayd Witton, having bin garrisond from the beginning of these troubles, and once taken, and plundered by the enemy, as allso the necessity of the good education of youth) to allow and appoynt such monyes for repayre of the premisses as your Honours in your wisdomes shall thinke fit and suitable to so pious and charitable a purpose. ...

Although there was some exaggeration in the claims made here, the feoffees had a case and the deputy lieutenants joined in earnestly desiring the speedy granting of the petition. In September 1645 the Parliamentary commanders had stormed the outworks of Chester and made themselves masters of St John's Church, the adjacent lanes, Foregate Street and all the eastern suburbs. The citizens were forced to defend themselves from behind the walls, which ran along the line of the East Gate, Foregate Street being outside them. During the siege thirteen pieces of cannon were placed against the East Gate. By the time the city surrendered in February 1646 Foregate Street had suffered severely, and it is recorded that all the houses were burned to the ground. Despite this, and the care for the King's School shown by the Long Parliament, the feoffees had no response to their petition. In 1657 the school accounts refer to the taking down of part of the Saracen's Head property (Ball's house) and in 1660 the feoffees set about securing timber and stone belonging to the inn. In 1659 they were reduced to collecting 6*d* from four pedlars standing against the Saracen's Head at Midsummer Fair.[5]

Like other landlords and other schools, the feoffees found that the

* The fact that the sheriff was H. Brooke suggests that the petition was drawn up earlier: he was sheriff 1644–47. The deputy lieutenants were G. Booth, John Legh, Thomas Marbury and E. Hyde.

Civil War aggravated their difficulties with tenants. Between 1642
and 1648 the annual rents received amounted to less than a third of
the immediate pre-war total, and unpaid rent totalled nearly £130.
Richard Amion, innholder of the Saracen's Head, owed over four
years' rent to Christmas 1645, amounting to over £72. By 1653
other tenants were well in arrears, some for as much as seven and
ten years. Letters and legal action proved of no avail, and in 1657
the feoffees brought their complaints before a Commission for Pious
Uses. The records of the inquisitions taken at Nether Knutsford in
January 1658 reveal that John Ball owed the feoffees £16 15s 6d for
part of the Saracen's Head and Jane Iliffe owed £6 for part of the
Swan. Further, an earlier inquisition showed that in February 1646
John Johnson had 'inuriously and with strong hand' taken a messuage belonging to the Saracen's Head, refusing to pay rent or yield
possession, depriving the feoffees of £18. The tenants of the minor
properties had also defaulted. Thomas Wood, whose ancestors had
regularly paid their rent of 6s, owed nine years' rent for his holding
at Nether Peover. George Venables of Agden had for sixteen years
detained the annual rent of 3s 4d he owed. The bailiff feoffees laid
out a considerable amount to gain their ends: over £10 was spent
on legal expenses and fees for counsel, while over £4 went on the
feoffees' expenses and more on the cost of entertaining commissioners
and jurors to dinner. The suits took the bailiffs (and on one
occasion the schoolmaster, the hire of whose horse to ride to the
commission court cost 1s) several times to Knutsford, to Congleton
and to Holmes Chapel.

Decrees were issued in July 1657 and January 1658 ordering the
tenants to pay their debts forthwith. The decree concerning George
Venables contained an interesting variation. Decreeing that he
should pay his rent regularly at the messuage in Hartford which he
had inherited, it continued:

in consideration whereof the said Peter Venables and George Lowe, bailiff
feoffees, do offer and are content on the behalf of themselves and of the
succeeding feoffees for the said school That so long as the said messuage in
Hartford shall be the inheritance of the said George Venables and his heirs
and that the said yearly rent of 3s 4d shall be paid there in the manner
aforesaid That the children of such as now are or hereafter shall be tenants
and occupiers thereof and resident upon the same shall be instructed and
taught from time to time at the aforesaid free Grammar School in like
manner and as freely as any children ought to be by the ordinances and
statutes of the same school.

The feoffees had difficulty in securing the payment even after the
commission's decree, for Venables took the case up to London to
the Chancery Court, involving them in further expense. In January

1660, however, he paid his arrears of £3 and £3 costs. Decrees were, as this shows, by no means the end of the matter: of the tenants concerned only Venables of Agden and Thomas Wood obeyed.[6]

Curiously enough, the feoffees had no difficulty with their Larton tenants during the Civil War and Interregnum. Although the Larton rent remained constant at £1 a year throughout, the occasional payments of heriots and, more strikingly, of fines increased the income from this source. In 1653 a new lease was sealed to Alice Warrington, the widow of William, and during the year she paid in instalments a fine of £70, more than half the school's receipts in that year. The school's income from its salt rights kept up reasonably well during the Civil War: in the years between 1642 and 1649 (the accounts of which were lumped together) seventy-six 'peecings of walling' brought in £56 10s. Subsequently the yield from walling varied from £18 in 1656 to £12 in 1657, and £6 in 1659.

The feoffees

The disturbed nature of the years of the Civil War is reflected in the continuation of the two bailiff feoffees of 1641 until halfway through 1649, and the accounts themselves appear to have been made up all at once at the end of the period. In fact from 1641 to 1664 the bailiff feoffees' position revolved among only seven men —William Bentley, William Rowe, Peter Venables, George Lowe, William Leftwich, Jeffrey Harrison and John Sworton, all but one of whom became feoffees in August 1641. As might be expected from the character of the school before the Civil War, a number of the leading feoffees had Parliamentarian or at any rate Puritan leanings: Peter Venables (of Lostock Gralam), for instance, was a member, together with Thomas Robinson of Northwich, of Richard Mather's and Richard Pigott's circle.

The most politically active of the bailiff feoffees was William Leftwich, a feoffee from 1641 to at least 1685: he was a leading lawyer in Northwich who periodically engrossed feoffments and surveys for the school. During the Civil War Leftwich became a sequestration commissioner to administer the lands of Royalists, handling and accounting for sums varying from £295 in 1643 to £784 in 1645 and £1,586 in 1646. His accounts for the State show the same meticulousness which characterises his school accounts for 1653 and 1654, and their contents reveal his powerful position in the community. He was administering (under a committee) the rents of such neighbouring Royalist landowners as Earl Rivers, Lord Cholmondeley, Peter Venables of Kinderton, Lawrence Winnington, Sir Thomas Wilbraham, John Holford of Davenham, and the

Earl of Derby, authorising payments out of Venables' rents for a
new millstone at Witton Mills, and out of Lord Derby's for the
repair of the Court House in Northwich and the purchase of scales
and measures for the Market Lookers there. To him the feoffees
paid 2*s* 9*d* 'for a Cheiffe rent to the State for our scoole wallinge',
presumably the rent due to the Earl of Derby, but never apparently
paid before. Leftwich had, too, more general responsibilities for the
community. In December 1643 he paid Robert Lowe, commissary
for the garrison at Northwich, the charges of waynemen for leading
wood to supply the 'centryes' [sentries] there, and in March 1644,
with the consent of his fellow sequestrators, he paid £5 to Major
Carington 'for the callinge back and continuinge of the Lancashire
souldiers in Northwiche garrison for one night longer for preservacion thereof from the enemy'. Later he paid men who collected
and despatched cheese to the Parliamentarian army besieging
Chester. His accounts for 1646 included payments to several ministers in February 1647 for preaching at Witton Chapel after Richard
Holford had left. Later, in 1654, on the recommendation of Thomas
Robinson, Leftwich was appointed by the sequestration commissioners to assist Robinson in examining witnesses. Robinson described
Leftwich as 'honest and rational', and in the same letter he provided
evidence about his social status. This was substantial but not very
high: Robinson distinguished him on the one hand from 'men of
so high a quality as the justices of the peace of the County' (men
he thought of as 'so far above me') and on the other from 'men of
inferior quality [who] could not afford to take the pains and receive
only their charges'.[7]

In this middling status Leftwich seems to have been representative
of the school feoffees during this century, although there were
variations. George Lowe of Hartford, who was baptised at Witton in
1598 and died, much respected, in 1669, was styled 'gentleman';
William Bentley, the physician, who was a dominant feoffee in this
period (so much so that in 1660, when he was again bailiff, a woman
was paid 2*d* to bring the school chest down from the school to Dr
Bentley's house), was probably above the average in wealth and
position.* He was the son of Richard Bentley, gentleman (probably
of Hulse), who was one of those fined in 1631 for failing to take up
knighthood, and came originally of a Staffordshire family. William
Bentley entered his pedigree at the herald's visitation of 1663, and
incidentally married as his second wife a daughter of George Venables of Agden, the school tenant. No doubt his medical practice

* Bentley's political activity as a Parliamentarian sequestration Commissioner became known to me, too late for inclusion in the text here, from
J. S. Morrill, *Cheshire 1630–1660* (1974), p. 87.

was profitable, and by the end of his life he was of the standing to issue a certificate of fitness for episcopal licensing to practise surgery for a Congleton man. Among his patients was Adam Martindale, the Presbyterian minister at Rostherne from 1649 to 1662: in his autobiography Martindale records that 'Dr. Bentley's physick wrought cleane contrary to his expectations yet it did me apparent good'. When Bentley died in 1680 he was a man of considerable wealth, possessing a mansion house in Northwich and lands in the neighbouring townships. He was also a lender of money, for of the total value of his goods in the inventory of over £1,415 over £1,090 was in debts due by specialty. His care for Witton Chapel is indicated by his legacy of £20 to the preaching minister there, but, perhaps curiously, he left no gift to the school: all his books and manuscripts were left to a nephew, Thomas Barker, to be preserved by him until he had a relation able to make use of them. A bailiff feoffee of lower status was John Sworton, a relation by marriage of Richard Pigott: Margery Pigott's will mentioned a cousin, Anne, wife of John Sworton of Witton. He was a blacksmith, who between 1642 and 1648 was paid for providing iron rods for the school windows. In 1661 Mrs Anne Sworton, widow of John, who died in 1660, was selling wood for carpentry at the school to the feoffees. Sworton's son, John, acted as usher at the school from 1656 to 1659, when he entered St John's College, Cambridge, as a sizar; his father was then described as 'agricola' or 'husbandman', but it is well known that this term covered a variety of occupations.[8]

The school buildings

The confusion occasioned by the Civil Wars was reflected in the accounts from 1642 to early in 1649, and to a much lesser extent from 1649 to early 1653, but after that things returned very much to normal: in February 1653 the feoffees resumed their dinner at the account day, and in 1653 they even gave 6s 8d for a jump cloth* and furniture to it for their messenger, Thomas Malbon. During the 'forties a few necessary repairs were done to the school and the master's chamber, but during the 'fifties the feoffees were especially active in maintaining and repairing the school building: some of this activity was stimulated by the appointment of a new master in 1656. In 1655 slates, bought from Mr Peter Venables, were brought from Lostock Gralam for the school, and moss with which to moss the school slating.† In the next year a considerable amount

* A 'jump' was a kind of short coat worn by men in the seventeenth century.

† This seems to have been a primitive form of insulation: moss was placed between and under the slates.

was spent on repairs and decorations, locks and glazing, including
the setting up of a grate and hob in the school chamber, as well as
a grate for the schoolmaster's chamber, and in 1657 the 'quires' in
the school were mended: the last must surely have been a fairly
frequent occurrence, and figures in the accounts of 1642–9 and
1649–53.

The 'fifties were marked by great improvements to the master's
accommodation. The building of a new house for the master was
begun in 1653, and during the next two decades the feoffees spent
a good deal of money on the two-storeyed thatched house. A
number of vivid details are recorded in the accounts. In 1653 and
1654, during the making of the wattle and daub walls, the feoffees
paid to 'Thomas Rogerson a boy, for himself and another boy,
for ridinge of 2 horses that did tread the said 6 loads of clay' 6d; to
Anne Worsley for three thrave of barley straw to be litter for the
said clay, 6d; and to Thomas Torbocke 'for leadinge of the said 6
loads of clay from Witton bridge to the said new house' 3s. In May
1654 600 of bricks, at 2s 8d per hundred, were brought by John
Barker of Sandiway to the new house to make the chimneys and
hearths. There is good reason to think that this house was built on
the site of the old chamber, but it is difficult to explain two entries in
the accounts for 1657 and 1658 of payments for glazing and
thatching 'Mr. Earle's chamber': in 1658 the schoolmaster was
paid 'for causing Mr. Earle's chamber to be thatched'. It is not
clear what responsibility the schoolmaster had for this 'chamber'
or where it was, since Peter Earle was at that time curate of Witton.
Earle had been involved in discussions with the feoffees about a new
master early in 1656, and he may well have played a part in securing
Thomas Coulton, whose initiative in improvements and repairs is
reflected in the accounts.

The masters and ushers

The grouping together of the accounts from 1642 to early 1649, and
the fact that arrears were sometimes paid after a master had left,
make it impossible to give exact dates for the masters in these
years, but after Pigott left there were several changes, and perhaps
some periods without a master.* The times were disturbed, and
another Cheshire school, Stockport, had the experience of two

---

* The list of masters for this period given in the Charity Commissioners'
report is very inaccurate: Harrison's name is given as Hanmer; Higginson is
put before Guest and his Christian name given as Charles; Liptrott is
omitted altogether.

masters deserting the school without warning between the end of
1644 and Easter 1646. Harrison, the usher, may well have had to
act as a stop-gap after Pigott's departure, but he is not included in
the list of masters given thirty years later in the Wase return.
'Rand. Guest' was master when the survey of school lands was made
in 1646, and his wages of £40 10*s* suggest that he may have been
there for about two years. He can almost certainly be identified with
the Randle Guest who, as a Presbyterian minister, was ordained by
the Manchester 'classis' to the living of Pulford in February 1648 at
the age of forty. He does not appear to have had a degree but was
apparently a man of some learning: the books he mentioned in his
will included some of Greek, and one of his two sons (both of whom
went to Cambridge) was described as 'bred at home'. His successor,
William Liptrott, who was also without a degree (or matriculation),
was duly taken to Chester to be examined by the master of the Free
School, 'Mr Greenhault' (who reappears in the school's history),
there being no bishop. Liptrott was a master of ability who went
on in 1656 to teach at Chester School, where he had a salary of £40,
double that of Witton, and then had a long career at Weston, where
an inscription of 1688 in the church extols his merits as a teacher.
Probably less than a year of Liptrott's lengthy teaching career of
forty-six years was spent at Witton, but the feoffees were in touch
with him in 1656.[9]

Liptrott was followed by Samuel Higginson, whose dates at Witton
are not easily established owing to the confusion of the accounts, but
he appears to have come in 1648. Higginson is difficult to identify
with any certainty. A man of his name, from Chester, matriculated
at Oxford in 1642, while a 'Samuel Higginsonus Anglus' graduated
at Glasgow University in 1648. Little is known of his mastership at
Witton: the only incident recorded in the accounts was a disagreement with the usher, Thomas Nickson. In May 1650 the feoffees
spent 2*s* 'to make the tow [*sic*] masters frends'. One pupil of his,
Robert Farrington, son of a husbandman of Stanthorne, went up to
Cambridge: he matriculated in 1652 at St John's College and
went on to take his B.A. Higginson left Witton probably towards the
end of 1651, and went on to be minister of Sutton and schoolmaster
at Tarvin, and, from 1655, Independent minister at Church
Minshull until his ejection in 1660. Ejection was not, however, the
end of his clerical career, for, like other Puritan ministers in the
north-west, he is found, after the Restoration, at a chapel. For at
least ten years after 1661 he was curate at Peover Chapel. He
retained his connection with Witton school and chapelry, for in
1661 the school's Peover tenant paid his rent to the feoffees through
Higginson, and in 1664 his son, Ralph (Raffe), was baptised at

Witton Chapel.* In 1684 a 'Samuel Higginson, clerk', was elected
a school feoffee and was still active in 1700: Ralph Higginson
later attempted to intervene in the school's affairs.[10]

The next master seems to have come at the beginning of 1652, and
his identity is also rather difficult to establish. He appears in the
accounts at first as 'Mr Hulme' but thereafter as 'John Holme': in
the Wase return he is John Holme, but in the records of St John's
College, where he sent a pupil, 'Mr Hulme'. He was quite probably
John Holme of Kinderton's son, who matriculated at Merton
College, Oxford, in 1634, aged nineteen. Whether or not he was the
minister at Witton Chapel named John Hulme, whose income was
made up in July 1650 from £10 to £60 a year by the enforced payment out of the tithes and profits of Great Budworth rectory
sequestered from the Duke of Richmond, is unknown. Holme
remained at the school until midsummer 1656, and one of the few
definite facts about him is that he sent two pupils to Cambridge—
Samuel Woodward† to Magdalene in 1653 and John Holbrooke,
from Over, to St John's in 1654: Holbrooke had been under him
for two years.[11]

More is definitely known of Thomas Coulton or Colton (sometimes
referred to as Cotton), who was admitted as master in July 1656, and
who gave such satisfaction that in 1657 he was given a gratuity of
£2 by the feoffees, although his salary still remained at £20. The
feoffees seem to have been anxious to obtain Coulton as master: they
went to Knutsford to solicit him to that end, and spent freely on
him and divers other gentlemen 'which did accompany him when
he came to Northwich' on several occasions, including his admission. No examination at Chester is recorded, but Coulton, who had
entered Trinity College, Cambridge, in 1636, had taken his B.A.
degree in 1640. He appears to have been unusual among Witton
masters in having no local connections: although he had lived in
Cheshire since 1647, his brother was a yeoman of Burnsall in Yorkshire. It is likely that Coulton initiated the search in Winwick
School for the lost books of the school: the expedition consisted of
the minister, (Peter Earle), Coulton and the bailiff feoffees. One boy,
who had spent three years under Coulton, went to St John's,
Cambridge, in 1659, and another, taught by him and his successor,
went to Caius College in 1665.

Unfortunately for Witton, Coulton moved on in 1659 to Audlem,
where there was a newly founded school requiring a master learned
in Greek and Latin. Several letters survive relating to Coulton's

---

* A son, Samuel, had been baptised at Church Minshull in 1658, and a
daughter at Northwich in 1654. (Church Minshull Register.)
  † I owe this name to Mr C. D. Rogers.

move to Audlem, and they reveal that he had become unsettled at Witton. His agreement with the Audlem feoffees (chief among whom was Colonel William Massie) was speedily reached and he departed from Witton without giving the required six months' notice. He anticipated the need to pay the £2 stipulated in the statutes: this, 'the price of my redemption', would, he declared, 'lesse trouble mee then the importunitie of some friends for a longer stay', and he appealed to the Audlem feoffees for the discharge of the payment, apologising 'if I be too saucie, pardon mee, modestie is unprofitable to a beggar'. He was recommended to the Audlem feoffees by a testimonial of June 1659 stating that during his residence in Cheshire for the previous twelve years he had 'behaved himself conformably unto the government of this nation, civilly in his conversation, and in his calling painefully, and successfully', and the feoffees there felt themselves fortunate in his learning and godly life. From his point of view the move was a great improvement, since at Audlem he was to have £40 a year 'together with the profit of all those sholars [*sic*] which are not parishioners, soe they exceed not thirty in number', with the proviso that if the school increased 'so that one maister cannot discharge his duty with profit to the poorer sort of children (for which purpose this schoole was chiefely erected)' he should employ an usher to be paid out of the £40. At Audlem he continued his successful teaching career, sending several boys up to St John's College, Cambridge. He died, much respected, in 1681, asking in his will to be buried in the chancel of Audlem church 'near his accustomed seat', and in 1718 a former pupil put up a memorial there to his learned master:

> Archididaschalus meritissimus
> Vir omnimodis Litteris
> Praesertim Humanioribus Instructissimus.[12]

The position of the usher seems to have declined during these years. Berkenhead and Newall had stayed for nearly twenty years and ten years respectively; Jeffrey Harrison, who had come as usher in 1639, continued possibly as usher for three and a half years from 1642 (unless he acted as master for a year or so); Thomas Nickson or Nixon was usher for about five years until his death in 1653, at an annual salary of only £6.

After Nickson's death there were two short-term ushers who had been pupils at the school and who, after two or three years as usher, went up to the university, assisted by Farmer's money. Peter Birkenhead, who went up to Christ Church as a servitor in 1656, had taught in the school for over two years, and John Sworton Jr., son of the feoffee, who was admitted to St John's College, Cambridge,

in July 1659 at the age of eighteen, had been usher for the preceding three years, a 'raw boy' indeed, like a later usher.[13]

The pupils

Nevertheless the school kept up academically during the 'fifties, and
seven boys are known to have gone to the university, three to
Oxford* and four to Cambridge. A particular feature of this decade
was the great use made of Farmer's bequest: four boys were helped
financially out of a total of nine before 1703. None of these pupils
had a particularly distinguished career: two, Sworton and Birkenhead, got no further than matriculation, but the latter, a nephew of
Sir John, profited from his uncle's loyalty to the King. In 1662 he
was granted a Lambeth M.A. and was also presented to a Crown
living. The other two, Thomas Knight and Raphe Nickson, went
further: Knight, at Christ Church, matriculated in 1651, took his
B.A. in 1653 and, aided by Farmer's money, went on to take his
M.A. in 1655, while Nickson went up to Brasenose in 1651 and
took his B.A. in February 1655. Both, incidentally, were entered as
'pleb.' and not as servitors. Four of the seven pupils are known to
have become clergymen.[14]

Known pupils, 1643–60

Cambridge University

Robert Farrington, son of Robert, husbandman (agricolae) of Stanthorne
    (near Middlewich). Born at Stanthorne. Adm. sizar, St. John's College,
    1652, aged eighteen. B.A., 1656.
Samuel Woodward, son of Peter, of Broomhill, Cheshire. Adm. pensioner,
    Magdalene College, 1653, aged twenty. B.A., 1657; M.A. (from St.
    John's), 1662. Incorporated at Oxford, 1663. Vicar of Aldworth, Berks.,
    1659.
John Holbrooke, of Over, son of Ralph, yeoman. Bred at Northwich (Mr.
    Hulme) for two years. Adm. sizar, St. John's College, 1654, aged eigh-
    teen. B.A., 1658; M.A., 1661. Ordained priest, 1663. Probably vicar of
    Titsey, Surrey, 1662–91. Rector of Edgmond, Salop. Three of his sons
    went to Cambridge.
John Sworton, of Witton, son of John, husbandman (agricolae). Bred at
    Witton (Mr. Colton) for three years. Adm. sizar, St. John's College, 1659,
    aged eighteen. Matric. 1660.

* These are known only because they received money from Farmer's
bequest. Another likely Witton pupil at Oxford is Peter Torbocke, admitted
as 'gen.' of Cheshire at Brasenose in 1653: he did not even matriculate. He is
almost certainly the Peter Torbocke who became a school feoffee in 1665, and
he married a sister of another feoffee, Robert Venables.

Oxford University

Thomas Knight. Adm. pleb., Christ Church. Matric. 1651; B.A., 1653; M.A., 1655. One of this name vicar of Wigginhall St. Peter, Norfolk, 1661.

Raphe Nickson. Adm. pleb., Brasenose College. Matric. 1651; B.A., 1655, as 'Nixon'.

Peter Birkenhead. Adm. servitor, Christ Church. Matric. 1656; Lambeth M.A., 1662. Rector of Somercotes St. Peter, Lincs., 1663 and South Somercotes St. Mary, 1672.

VI

Peace-time problems, 1660–1715

Northwich after the Restoration

After the Restoration the school's fortunes were affected by economic changes in Northwich and district, which altered the structure of the salt industry. The most important of these for the school was the 'decay' of the common brine pit during the 1670s, antedating the breakdown at Nantwich by about thirty years. Although serious for the school, it did not, however, mean a decline in prosperity for the Northwich area. By 1681 there were said to be five brine pits outside the old salt borough and only one inside it, and the opening of new brine pits coincided with the discovery of rock salt at Marbury in 1670. Despite competition between brine and rock salt the effect was to bring economic expansion to Northwich, in contrast to Nantwich, where the industry declined. But at Northwich the industry expanded outside the old burghal limits, and this meant that institutions whose prosperity was linked with the old restrictive rights did not share in the new wealth: significantly the curate, John Fishwick, described Northwich in 1717 as 'very populous but very poor'. A similar situation was to be found at Droitwich: the historian of Worcestershire, Nash, recorded that the exploiting of new pits there in 1725 'caused the "old" proprietors to sink in value from £5,000 per annum to practically nothing. Two hundred persons lost all their property and many schools and charities founded on the brine shares, once the safest form of investment, were utterly ruined.'

In Cheshire Macclesfield School found in 1675 that its salt rights in Nantwich had suffered. In Northwich itself Witton Chapel suffered: after the Restoration the augmentation of the curate's stipend out of the tithes of Great Budworth ceased, and the curacy reverted to its customary straits. By 1663 the fruits of the preaching minister's salt rights had dropped to only £2 10s a year. It is scarcely surprising that Peter Earle, who survived from the Interregnum, was said to have left for better preferment. The collapse of the traditional organisation of the salt industry must also have affected the nature of the community within which the school functioned. As at Middlewich, the quasi-burghal status, which had given 'a measure of self-government', was linked with the salt industry in its controlled form, which now disappeared.[1]

These developments in the salt industry provided opportunities which made for a certain insecurity in local society. The career of Ralph Broome, one of the feoffees from 1684 to at least 1728, provides an example.* He was one of the pioneers of the expansion of the industry at the end of the seventeenth century: he bought land in Witton and Leftwich and sank a new brine sheath which failed. In 1705 he became bankrupt and in 1713 was reported to have absconded: his new works and Anderton property were mortgaged to a London goldsmith whose children sold the property in 1717 to John Hewitt and Ralph Livesey, both school feoffees too. E. Hughes, describing the working of the salt tax in the early eighteenth century, lists the Northwich salt proprietors who were indebted to the Crown for salt duty, and traces their subsequent fate. Among the debtors were Thomas Neild Sr., a bailiff feoffee in 1703–5, and Thomas Neild Jr., almost certainly a former pupil: later the former was reported 'dead, worth nothing', while the latter had 'fled'. Similarly Thomas and Ralph Nickson, both feoffees, who (with another) were indebted to the Crown for £2,000 in 1708, were later declared by the law officers to have absconded: this is made more precise by the statement made in 1718 by John Partington, bailiff feoffee, that Thomas Nickson 'falling under misfortunes is gone to one of the Plantacions in America'. The combination of financial opportunity and danger seems to have been particularly marked in this period and throughout the eighteenth century.[2]

While the economic background in the town was changing, there were educational changes in the town itself and in the county. Between 1688 and 1693 there were entries in the Witton parish registers relating to a James Bloore, of Witton, schoolmaster, who was certainly not a master or usher at Witton School and does not appear to have been licensed by the bishop: he may have kept a private school in the town. In the visitation of 1716 besides the name of the Witton master there appears that of Thomas Penny, possibly a relation of James Penny, the vicar of Great Budworth from 1682 to 1694. He too may have been a private schoolmaster or he may have been connected with the charity school founded in Northwich in the late seventeenth or early eighteenth century. A pamphlet on charity schools, published in 1712, recorded that in

---

* In 1712 he was described in a school lease as 'of Northwich, gentleman', but by 1728 he was 'of Middlewich, gentleman'.

Northwich 'a person did lately bequeath a house for a schoolmaster
and £700 for purchasing land to be settled for the teaching of 10
boys to read, write and cast accompts'. Close to Northwich, there
is evidence of a schoolmaster at Hartford named Harper, who sent
a pupil to Cambridge in 1696. He is probably to be identified with
'John Harper de Witton aeditius [sacristan] de Davenham', who was
buried at Witton in March 1698. Hartford was, of course, in Witton
Chapelry, and in 1671 a John Harper was listed as a schoolmaster
in Witton at the ecclesiastical visitation.[3]

In the county generally the second half of the seventeenth
century saw great activity in the foundation or further endowment
of schools, many of them grammar schools, frequently offering
higher salaries than Witton's endowment allowed. Audlem School
has already been mentioned in connection with Coulton's departure.
The foundation of the school at Acton has been attributed to the
parishioners' desire to provide for the nonconforming minister,
Edward Burghall, who was displaced from the living: the curriculum
included Greek and Latin, and the master had a salary of £20 for
teaching ten free boys, and in addition was allowed to take fee-
paying pupils. Lymm already had a school, but in 1698 Sir George
Warburton and William Domville endowed it with lands, and
prescribed a curriculum which certainly included Latin. At Darnhall in 1698 Thomas Lee, with money received from his mother,
Elizabeth Venables,* gave land to maintain a free school for the
children of the inhabitants of Whitegate and Over parishes and
Weaver township. The curriculum was strongly reminiscent of
Witton's: English, Latin and Greek were to be taught, Caesar and
Tully for prose and Virgil and Terence for verse, and no matter was
to be taught out of any author that might hinder godliness.[4]

The feoffees

The foundation of Darnhall School is linked with one of the two
most eminent of the Witton feoffees in this period, Colonel Robert
Venables of Wincham, both stepfather and father-in-law of Thomas
Lee. Robert Venables, bailiff feoffee for 1672–3 and 1678–9, is one
of two feoffees to have had a national reputation. Although
Venables, the son of a small landowner, was born at Antrobus, his
mother† came from Rudheath, and his father had salt rights in
Northwich: it will be remembered that Richard Mather, the Puritan
curate of Witton, had left Venables a book in his will. He rose to

---

* Elizabeth Lee, widow of Thomas Lee, Sr., of Darnhall, married Col.
Robert Venables: Thomas Lee, Jr. (founder of the school), then married a
daughter of Venables by his first wife.
   † She was Ellen, daughter of Richard Simcox.

fame as a high-ranking officer in the Parliamentary army during the Civil War. In 1643, as a captain, he had taken part in the operation against Dirtwich or Foulwich in south Cheshire to damage the saltworks there which supplied the Royalists; in 1645, as a lieutenant-colonel, he was governor of Tarvin, and in the same year was wounded at the siege of Chester. In 1648 he became governor of Liverpool, and from 1649 to 1654 served successfully in Ireland. In 1654 he was sent on an expedition against the Spanish in the West Indies in which he shared the command with Admiral Penn: the badly managed raid was a fiasco, and for his part in it Venables was cashiered and sent to the Tower by Cromwell. Like many fellow Parliamentarians he turned to Royalism in the late 'fifties, and was made governor of Chester by Monk during the moves leading up to the restoration of Charles II, but after the Restoration he went unrewarded and his governorship of Chester was given to Sir Geoffrey Shakerley. Venables continued in his religious beliefs as a nonconformist, and retired into private life, writing a treatise on angling, published in 1662, for which Izaak Walton wrote a complimentary letter as a preface, and buying Wincham in 1668. He became a school feoffee in 1669 and his influence as bailiff feoffee was considerable. He used it in favour of his nonconformist friends, doing much to secure the appointment as master of the son of Adam Martindale, Thomas, who had been tutor to his grandchildren. In May 1679 the accounts of the school record that Colonel Venables freely remitted to the school £1 14s 1d, being part of the £3 3s 6d which he had paid out above the receipts, while his fellow bailiff repaid himself the 29s 5d he had overpaid. Venables was perhaps a dangerous patron for the school: in 1664 he was informed against for involvement in the Yorkshire plot against the monarchy, though the charge was discounted. After 1667 he sheltered the Covenanter, William Veitch, and in 1683 he was presented by a Cheshire grand jury as a supporter of Monmouth and fined. In June 1685 the King ordered the Earl of Derby to discharge him from bail, 'he being aged and having behaved himself very well'.[5]

The other even more notable feoffee of this period was Sir John Berkenhead, whose connection with the school, long a matter of tradition, can now be proved from a list of feoffments. Berkenhead was chosen a feoffee in 1665 at a time when he was reaping the reward of his Royalism: it is ironic that he had as co-feoffees William Leftwich and Robert Venables. How often he came down from London to attend meetings of the feoffees is not known,* but his

* See a letter from Berkenhead to Sir John Crew of Utkinton, of March 1676: 'I hope next long vacation to see Cheshire once before I dye...', quoted in *C.S.*, third series, XII, 39.

appreciation of the plight of the school and chapel of Witton is indicated by an item in his will. In his will, dated 4 December 1679, he announced his intention 'to settle forty pounds a yeare on the minister where I went to schoole and forty pounds a yeare on the schoolmaster there but this is to be settled by deed ...'. He died in debt a few days later, and since all his legacies are said to have been honoured it must be presumed that he never made the necessary arrangements for this benefaction. The difference which such a generous legacy would have made to the school is incalculable.[6]

In 1669 and 1670 several venerable feoffees of the school died in rapid succession: George Lowe of Hartford, Sr., aged about seventy, Richard Hilton of Witton, Sr., aged seventy-one, and Thomas Torbocke of Witton, aged seventy-three. The entries of their burials in the parish register were made with greater formality than hitherto: each was described in Latin as a feoffee of the school, and John Sudlow, who died in 1674, was further styled 'vir admodo honestus'. This ceremonial description was later used of Richard Deane of Shurlach in 1685 and of Peter Torbocke 'generosus' in 1687: it is perhaps to be ascribed chiefly to the filial piety of Thomas Pigott, the son of the former master, who was curate from 1669 to 1674, when he went overseas. All these men were feoffees of long standing, and their deaths made large gaps in the ranks. Indeed, after the death of Richard Deane in 1685 the name of the founder ceased to appear among the feoffees, although in the next year the founder's kin were represented by Thomas Mouldsworth, son of Ellen, the daughter of Richard Deane, gent., said to have been the direct heir at law of the first John Deane.[7]

In the late seventeenth century one member of the Deane family played an active part in the school's affairs. He is referred to always as 'Parson Dayne' or 'Deane'. In 1662 he was responsible for regaining the statutes, which had been taken away by Jeffrey Harrison; in 1669 he surrendered his key to the school chest, which seems to imply that he had been a bailiff feoffee; in May 1671 a meeting of the feoffees was held 'after parson dayne had violently turned the said Usher [Bertles] out of the school'; and in the crisis of 1680, after the sudden death of the schoolmaster, Parson Deane, though not a bailiff feoffee, played a prominent part. His final appearance was in 1684, when he went to represent the school at the Archbishop of York's visitation held at Warrington. It has proved impossible to trace this man or to discover what his relationship was to, or whether he was, perhaps most probably, identical with Richard Deane, who was bailiff feoffee in 1666–7 and 1682–3, but he is to be distinguished from 'Mr. Deane the schoolmaster', Gerard Deane, who taught at the school from 1681 to 1693.

The names of Sudlow and Lowe still survived among the feoffees, but the family of Winnington of Birches had a new representative— Ralph Starkey of Morthwaite, who had acquired the township of Birches by marriage with a co-heiress of the Winnington family. He acted as the feoffees' legal adviser in 1666 and again in 1671, when he was a bailiff feoffee, but despite this connection with Witton School he left 100 marks in his will to Daresbury Free School. The first list of feoffees since the original one of 1557 to give their status (and trades) dates from 1707, when there were four 'gentlemen'— Thomas Mouldsworth of Wincham, Thomas Rowe of Hartford, John Partington of Staple Inn, London, the feoffees' legal adviser and founder's kin, and Ralph Broome, of Northwich. The yeomen were three: Thomas Hewitt of Witton, Ralph Nickson of Northwich, and Thomas Done of Hartford. There were two merchants, John Hewitt and Thomas Nickson; a mercer, Nathaniel Leftwich of Northwich; an ironmonger, Thomas Cheney of Northwich, and an apothecary, John Sudlow, also of Northwich.[8] Later in the century there were to be feoffees of higher status, but at this date they were still local and of middling rank, with some intermarriage. There were some irregularities in the bailiff feoffees' tenure of office early in the eighteenth century: John Hewitt and John Partington held office from 1708 to 1713, and John Sudlow from 1713 to 1717.

The accounts of this period give much more detail than the earlier records, and they enable us to build up a clearer picture of the working of the school. The ceremony of making up the accounts was kept up. Between 1666 and 1688 6*d* was paid almost every year, usually in the spring, to Thomas Barker 'for his attendance upon the feoffees this day and carrying of the School book of accounts to and from the Church'; from 1691 to 1709 the book, and later the chest, were carried by Thomas Malbon, the sexton. £1 or 30*s* was spent each year until 1678 at the making of the accounts, and in 1677 there was a meticulous record of 6*d* for tobacco 'for the feoffees after the accompts were delivered and the dinner ended'. A master of the school at the end of this period stated that the church-wardens never intermeddled in the school affairs except by being present at the making of the accounts and signing them, 'and even in that they have been very slack and remiss of late years since the practice of making entertainments at such time out of the School revenues has been left off sometimes not one Warden appearing thereat...'.[9] This accusation does not appear to be borne out by the records: there were occasional irregularities, as in 1663 and 1664, when only one warden signed the accounts, and there was a bad run of years when in 1684 no signatures appeared and from 1685 to 1687 only one warden signed. The lapse in 1684 probably reflects a quarrel between the wardens and the feoffees, which culminated in the wardens' 'presenting' the feoffees at the Archbishop's visitation for a breach of the statutes.* After 1687, however, two, three and sometimes even four wardens appeared at each account-making, except for 1713, when only one appeared and he was a bailiff feoffee, a dubious occurrence defeating John Deane's system of checks and balances.

The finances

During these years a drastic change took place in the school's income from its salt rights. There was no immediate change after the Restoration. The school piecings were let out in various ways, sometimes all to one man, sometimes divided between several: certain names recurred frequently, particularly those of Houghton and Broome. The rate per piecing varied even in the same year between different tenants but 30s was common. A curious incident relating to the walling occurred in 1663; the accounts recorded the receipt of £9 from William Houghton but noted 'there are other six peeceing due for the last yeare ending at Christmas 1663 which were set to Wm. Houghton for nyne pounds but Mr. Wm. Leftwich obstructed that bargaine and hath himselfe disposed of them and is to answere the schoole for them the sume of 9*li*'. Only £8 was in fact paid by Leftwich, 'the said 6 peecings beinge set only for 8*li*. by order of Mr. Peter Venables Bayliffe above named for noe more'. In 1670 the receipts from walling were £18, but during the 'seventies they tailed off dramatically, and after 1677 they ceased entirely. The school, which at first had had more from walling than from rents, became in the later seventeenth century entirely dependent on rents and interest for its income. The wich house stead or barn, already described in the 1659 accounts as a dwelling house, continued to be let to the Broome family, the rent rising from the original 3s to 6s 8d by 1690 and then to 10s in 1703–5. Between 1710 and 1713 the feoffees managed, at some expense, to end Broome's lease and to re-let what was now described as a house in the Swine Market in 1713 to Peeres Massey, a saddler, on a long lease of three lives at £1 a year. In the rental of 1718 the place is clearly described as 'one small dwelling house, heretofore a wichhouse or salt-house, and after the failing of the brine-pit in Northwich converted to habitacion'.[10]

In Chester the Saracen's Head had declined from its position at the head of the school's rental. In 1661 the feoffees managed to let it for three lives to a tanner who paid £4 a year in rent, but in

* See p. 119.

1671 there was further trouble when a Mr Kinaston tried to claim 'part of the yard and backside' belonging to the Saracen's Head. In the course of a suit between Hugh Moulson, the tenant, and Kinaston in the Portmoot Court aural tradition was invoked, and the feoffees conferred with 'several ancient persons in Chester to know how long they could prove our title to and quiet enjoyment of those lands without any claim made thereunto by any person to this day'. The case was won, but as a precaution in 1674 the feoffees spent several pounds (including £1 9*s* for seventeen dinners and for wine, beer and tobacco for the commissioners and witnesses) on a commission 'for witnesses to be examined and their testimonies kept for perpetual memory' concerning the land belonging to the Saracen's Head. By the end of this period the former inn was described as a messuage with out-buildings, a garden and a tan yard, and there were still two lives of the lease in being.

The income from the Swan property, on the other hand, steadily improved. For most of this period it had two tenants, one of whom eventually paid £9 for part of the Swan and for the close or field adjoining Flookersbrook, called Herkins Well Field, and the other, Alderman William Starkey, who paid £6 11*s* 6*d* for the rest of the Swan and for Ball's Croft, after the school had had trouble with another alderman, William Bennet. Finally, by 1717 the feoffees managed to unite all these properties in the hands of one tenant, Daniel Pickance, innholder of the Golden Talbot, for £17, on another long lease for ninety-nine years (if three lives so long continued) and for seven years after. This lease was made only after an expensive ejectment, distraining and writ of possession against the former tenant, Mrs Smith, who was in considerable arrears, but to whose children, 'when turned out of doors', the feoffees gave 5*s*.

At Larton, Alice Warrington left several daughters, and heriots were paid on their respective deaths, until the farm came to Thomas Urmston in the right of his wife. As this long lease, with its traditionally low rent, drew to a close in the early eighteenth century it is clear that the Larton estate was of cardinal importance in the school's finances. Among the school records there is a proposal, in handwriting connected with John Partington, in the form of a bond for augmenting the school's income: it is not an actual subscription, for no names or amounts are entered. The draft is dated 22 May 1710, and runs:

... Whereas the place of Upper School-master of the ancient Free Grammar School of Witton is now lately become vacant by the death of Mr. Aaron Nichols late Schoolmaster there, and whereas the income of the school now and for diverse years past has been extremely impaired and decayed by accidents and losses whereby there seems a very great difficulty of obtaining a learned, able and well qualified person to accept of the said place in the state as it* is at present XXX Untill the expiration of an antient lease of an estate of considerable yearly value in Larkton in the Parish of West Kirby

A subscription shall be entered into

The situation improved on the death of Mrs Urmston in February 1713, and two years later, in February 1715, the feoffees signed a new and more advantageous agreement with Thomas Urmston. The lease was for only twenty-one years and was at an annual rent of £12, in contrast to the previous £1. There had been a suggestion in November 1714 that the lands in the Wirral might be exchanged for land belonging to John Wilkinson of Chester in the much more convenient Hartford, but nothing came of it.[11]

The feoffees found the school's debtors an increasing nuisance, and there were frequent writs and suits against those who failed to repay borrowed school stock. One debtor was imprisoned in Chester Castle in 1670, and in March 1682 in Kinderton Court the feoffees secured execution on a cupboard of John Harrison's. From 1658 it became the custom for the bailiff feoffees to record in the accounts that there were other debts besides those listed, but because these were thought to be 'desperate' (hopeless) they forbore to set them down. In the accounts of 1706 and 1707 two even of the 'sperate' debts were labelled 'dangerous' and one 'weak'. There were, however, at this date very few alternative methods of investment open to the feoffees. The school was not alone in suffering in this way: Witton Chapel had similar troubles. In 1719 the vicar of Great Budworth reported to Bishop Gastrell on the money belonging to the preacher at Northwich: 'I sent your Lordship word it amounted to sixteen pounds p. ann. and they have had money enough left to them to have answered that, but they have lost so much that now they have but about eight score pounds principal left'.[12] Although the school feoffees improved their lent-out capital from the immediate pre-war total, it never reached the amount at the beginning of the century, and by 1690 it was only £32, apart from Thomas Farmer's £50.

In the second half of the seventeenth century the school's financial position became more and more shaky. The first sign of difficulty was in 1667, when expenditure exceeded receipts by nearly £2; this occurred again in 1676, in spite of a legacy of £10 in the previous year from Robert Stones, a yeoman of Leftwich.† Sir John Berken-

---

* The word 'now' is crossed out at this point.

† Doubtless a former pupil: he was not a feoffee, but in 1687 a Thomas Stones, probably the nephew mentioned in Robert Stones's will, was chosen a feoffee.

head's projected bequest might well have saved the situation, but in May 1679 Colonel Venables remitted part of the excess expenditure in 1678 of over £3 to the school, and in 1679 the feoffees secured the agreement of the master and usher to a reduction of their wages from £20 to £15 and £8 to £6 a year respectively. This reduction took place at a time when the salary of the headmaster at Macclesfield, which in the sixteenth century had been much the same as Witton's—£13 6s 8d compared with £12— had reached £31 8s, and by 1694 had become £60 plus a house, while the usher had £30.[13] The feoffees practised economies in rent collection: for a few years they no longer went to Chester to collect the rent but paid a small sum to John Dewsbury, salter, for bringing them. In entertaining at the account-making they cut down to a few shillings from 1679 to 1687. In spite of this, expenditure in the following decades was usually either just within the bounds of income or exceeded it.

This enforced economy was the more unfortunate as the school was still of a size to require an usher as well as a master. The absence of an usher from 1687 to 1702 was followed by a memorandum in August 1703 signed by six feoffees, affirming the absolute necessity of an usher or under-master, and, since the revenues were insufficient for both head and usher, diverting the interest on Farmer's money to the payment of the usher's wages. Only after the improvement in the lease of the Wirral property were the feoffees able to contemplate returning this interest to its original purpose, and making up the principal, which had been reduced by £8. The feoffees were forced to yet another expedient to secure the usher's wage: on 7 July 1709 they signed an agreement with a Mr Joseph Clough that he should be admitted

writing master for the Free School of Witton to begin teaching on the first schooling day after Easter yearly. And to be obliged to teach six weeks at least and longer if he thinks fit, during which six weeks no schollar of the Free School shall be allowed to learn writing of any other master. And if any schollar be sent to learn of any other master, such schollar to be suspended by the master of the Free School out of his school. And in consideration thereof Mr Clough agrees to pay twenty shillings towards the usher's sallary so long as Alice Urmston in Worrall shall live. And after her decease to have the said writing thear . . .

The further link with the Wirral property is noteworthy.

The financial situation was somewhat improved in 1716 by a legacy from an old pupil who had become a leading citizen of Chester and a benefactor of the Bluecoat School and medical services there. Peter Cotton, gentleman, an attorney who had done business for the feoffees between 1703 and 1705, was descended from the Cottons of Cotton, and, having completed 'a single, sober and religious life', left various benefactions, including £50 to the minister at Witton and £50 to the school, the interest to be used to augment the master's salary. This was an addition to the total of the school's rent, which was given by John Partington in 1718 as £34 9s 4d.[14]

The school buildings

Improvements to the school continued in the 'sixties. In 1660 1s was paid for almost one day's work in 'amendinge the schoolmaster's seat at the upper end of the schoole'; these 'amendments' included setting up a 'close desk', which was subsequently given a 'bend of iron' and a lock and key. In 1664 the feoffees paid 3s 8d for making two desks 'set up in the said schoole' for the scholars there, and in 1671 3s 'for a deske for his [the schoolmaster's] scholars to declaime at in the schoole'. These orations were one of the chief methods of familiarising the older pupils with Latin. 'Not a day in the week should pass', wrote Charles Hoole, master at Rotherham School and a leading educationist of the mid-seventeenth century, 'on which some Declamation, Oration or Theme should not be pronounced about a quarter of an hour before the school is broken up,' and he advocated that 'there should be two standing desks set opposite in the midst of the Schoole, for boyes to stand at, when they pronounce'.[15] A fresh burst of energy on the feoffees' part occurred in 1664 and 1665, and work on the school study, apparently a room off the school chamber, was followed by a good deal of timber work and plastering at the school. Six loads of lime were bought 'to repaire and beautify the schoole and schoolmaster's house', and 12 lb of black were brought from Warrington to colour the posts at the school and the master's house. The workmen were busy for several weeks in 'washing or whiting of the schoole and blacking of the posts'. Large-scale repairs were made to the school in 1710 at a cost of over £28, probably as a prelude to the arrival of a new master.

In 1677 the school had to have a new chimney, and this is a reminder that the school paid the newly imposed hearth tax from January 1663. The tax was levied at a rate of 2s a year on each hearth or stove, and in 1663 the feoffees paid 2s themselves to the constable, and also reimbursed the master for 4s which he had paid. The school's early payment of the tax is interesting, for the definite ruling by the Treasury that the unpopular tax applied to free schools was not given until 1665. After 1663, however, there is no record of any payment until February 1682, in spite of the building

1 A page of the first surviving account book, showing expenditure for the year 1585

The best information I can give of ye free schoole at Northw. is such y^t followeth

1. That Sr John Deane Priest one of ye sons of Lawrence Deane late of Shurlach in ye Parish of Davenham in ye County of Chest. Prebendarie of Lincolne and Parson of great St Bartholomews neere Smithfeild in London was found of ye free Gramr schoole at Northwich in the Township of Witton.

2. That it was founded ab^t ye year 1558.

3. That it was endowed wth twelve pounds p ann. by our found^r wch but since improved notw^thstanding the loss of s^d Dayes of building wch Chest. p... in ye times of war.

4. Mr Jno Farmer was our first Master who continued 40. years and left for ye maintenance of a poor scholar at either Universitye ye Use of fifty pound. 2. Mr Rich. Ligott 3. Rand Guest 4. M^r Jno thrill. Lightfoot 5. Mr Jam: Higinson. 6. Mr John Holme; 7. Mr Tho: Colson. 8. Mr Tho: Swinston. 9. Mr John Greenhalgh: 10. Mr James Steward. 11. Mr Pet: Woodnoth now resid^t.

5. That our Visit^rs are twelve Trustees wch are chosen out of ye neighbouring Townships at the decease of four, and especially out ye Found^rs Kinsmen if Qualified

6. That our Librarie was destroyed in ye time of war.

7. That most of ye Gentry of Cheshire have been brought up at Northw^ch schoole and that we have had 220 scholars at once.

P: Woodnoth sch m^r

11 Peter Woodnoth's reply to Christopher Wase's questionnaire, mid-1670s; in the Wase collection, Bodleian Library

of the new chimney in 1677. From 1682 until 1689 the feoffees paid
6*s* a year regularly for one chimney at the school and two at the
school house, that is, the schoolmaster's house. From 1686 they paid
for a further two chimneys belonging to Catherine Broome, presumably the tenant of the house in the Swine market. The accounts do
not explain the entry in the hearth tax record of 1688–9: 'not
mencioned', Thomas Holford and John Walman in the 'scoolhouse'.
(Was John Walman, perhaps John Woolmer, the usher?)[16]

The improvements to the master's accommodation continued.
In 1665 sanitation was provided at the new house, and in November
1666 the feoffees agreed with the carpenters for building a new
kitchen. The mid-'sixties were indeed a time for smartening up the
school and the master's house: apart from the whitewashing and
blacking of the posts, the master's house was thatched and given
window covers, and a hedge of 800 quick-sets, together with seventy
sycamore plants from Mr Henry Vawdrey of 'Goosetree', were put
round the master's croft or yard. These improvements were no
doubt connected with the feoffees' treating with the master, John
Greenhalgh, in June 1667 'for his stay and continuance' at the
school. The feoffees continued to pay the same rent for the master's
new house to the Baron of Kinderton and, after his death and the
failure of the male line, to Lord Norris (the husband of the daughter
and heiress of Peter Venables of Kinderton) who succeeded his
father as Earl of Abingdon in 1699. Mysteriously, however, the
rent had become in 1712 rent for the 'church house', and there
seems no doubt that this was the same house:* in 1713–14 it was
described as chief rent for the church house and croft. Already in
1703–5 the feoffees had carried out repairs there; in 1708–9 they
paid for thatching, and in 1713 repaired the church house on the
new schoolmaster, 'Mr. Allen's going to dwell there'. They continued to pay the same rent for the church house to George Venables
Vernon, who inherited from his aunt, the Countess of Abingdon, in
1715.

The masters

After the loss of Thomas Coulton in 1659 the feoffees tried to
'moove' 'Mr. Greenhalgh to be our schoolemaster', but failed. They
chose instead Thomas Swinton, at whose election, hiring and institution they spent only a total of 1*s* 2*d*, compared with nearly £1 at his
predecessor's. The difference is indicative of the difference in

* In 1726, in John Partington's accounts, the usher, then in charge of the
school, paid 10*s* rent for the church house and the same in 1727 for the
'schoole house'.

qualification. Thomas Swinton was almost certainly the man of that name from Cheshire who was admitted as a *pleb.* to Brasenose College in 1654 at the age of nineteen: there not only did he not graduate, he did not even matriculate. Swinton most probably came from Knutsford, and had two brothers who were tradesmen there, one a chandler and the other a bookseller, who incidentally left a bequest in his will for a public schoolmaster there. He settled down in Northwich, marrying, in February 1662, Ellen Yarwood of Withington,* but his stay at Witton School was short.[17] It reinforced the nineteenth-century Charity Commissioners' impression that the school had had an undue proportion of such brief tenures, but there was a particular explanation of Swinton's departure.

In 1662 the Act of Uniformity which came into operation on St Bartholomew's day, 24 August, imposed on 'every schoolmaster keeping any public or private school' and having such a post on 1 May 1662 a declaration disclaiming the right to rebel and agreeing to conform to the liturgy of the Church of England 'as it is now by law established'. This declaration was to be made before the bishop, and failure to make it meant loss of office: the operation of this law was the origin of nonconformity in its literal sense. How exactly this process worked at Witton is not very clear, for there was apparently no automatic dismissal. Swinton was paid his salary regularly up to Michaelmas 1663, and in the brief interval before the arrival of the new master, Humfrey Barlow, then still a pupil, was paid 1*s* for 'teaching the schollers when Mr. Swinton left of teaching', presumably as an assistant to the usher. The feoffees, indeed, seem to have had some difficulty in displacing Swinton, for in 1664 they spent £1 in several journeys to Chester to the Consistory Court to present suit against 'Mr. Tho. Swinton our late schoolmaster and to eiect [eject] and remove him from this schoole for his nonconformity which was not effected till sequestration was granted out by the said Court against the said schoole rents'. Jeffrey Harrison was paid by the feoffees 2*s* 6*d* for his charges in going to the court to be examined against Swinton.

The records of the Consistory Court reveal that in July 1663 Swinton was summoned to answer various charges. The most important of these were that he was teaching without a licence and without subscribing as required, and that he had not conformed before the feast of St Bartholomew and yet had continued to teach. In addition he was accused of not having been legally elected to the school, 'but intruded your selfe therin, or at the least were placed ther in the time of warrs by severall disaffected persons to

* The bondsman was John Yarwood of Knutsford, skinner.

the Government as is now established', and of not being statutorily qualified in age or university degree. With the charge was enclosed a copy of the statutes made by Jeffrey Harrison, yeoman, who swore that it was a true copy made by him of 'the originall Statutes that are hanged up in a frame in the free schoole', 'in all parts except one word which he did not very well understand and therefore left a space'. (It seems probable that it was on this occasion that Parson Dayne recovered the statutes from Harrison.) William Rowe of Hartford also gave evidence, and declared that he and another feoffee had opposed Swinton's election. The case was postponed to July 1664, when, because Swinton had left the school, the judge remitted the moneys involved but condemned him to pay £3 within a period of several months. In October 1664 the 'monition' was renewed, but in May 1666 Swinton paid the costs to the judge and registrar and the case was dismissed.[18]

Although Swinton had acted illegally, the case smacks of a local feud, for a few years later, in 1667, Richard Dayne and William Leftwich, the bailiff feoffees, were on good terms with him. Swinton, then living in Chester and described as 'schoolmaster', helped them in having the statutes framed. Furthermore, in February 1668 the feoffees paid him £2 15s for his arrears of wages and towards his expenses in the Consistory Court in the suit 'commenced against him by Mr William Rowe', bailiff, in 1664–5.* Swinton's removal is even more curious in the light of his subsequent career, for in May 1665 a Thomas Swinton (surely the same man) was admitted to teach at the Free School in Chester and subscribed. In 1668 John Wilkins, brother-in-law of Cromwell, became Bishop of Chester and was said to have brought in many nonconforming ministers by his 'soft interpretation of the terms of conformity'. In 1670 a Thomas Swinton was ordained deacon, and priest in 1672: after being curate at Eccleston he was appointed in 1674 to the living of Wallasey. The identification of Swinton, rector of Wallasey, with the schoolmaster seems strongly probable. The rector's son was apprenticed in Chester in 1691, and in the political crisis of Charles II's reign the rector had been suspected of active Whig sympathies. In July 1683, following on the alarm of the Rye House plot, warrants were issued to search for arms in the houses of various Cheshire sympathisers, among them Colonel Venables and Swinton, in whose house arms were found.[19]

After Swinton's eventual departure, one Rycroft 'labored to be' master, but in autumn 1663 the feoffees appointed 'Mr Greene-

---

* The case was in fact an 'office' one in which the judges acted spontaneously, unmoved by any 'promoter', but often after an 'information' or presentment, doubtless laid by Rowe and Harrison.

hough', John Greenhalgh, aged forty-eight, the man whom they had
tried to secure in 1659. (Some problems of identification arise here
too, as there were two men of that name at St John's College,
Cambridge, within a year of each other, both from Bury, though
of differing social status and on different sides in the Civil War.)
The Witton Greenhalgh was the son of a farmer, attended Bolton
School, and went up to St John's as a sizar. After taking his B.A.
in 1636 Greenhalgh appears as curate at Leigh, Lancashire, where in
1642 he signed the Protestation prepared by Pym, the opposition
leader, in defence of the true reformed religion against popery.
He was already teaching by 1645, when a pupil of his at Leigh,
his cousin, James Livesey, entered Christ's College, Cambridge.
It is possible that it was he, and not his Royalist namesake, whom
the Puritan rector of Stockport and the Parliamentarian commander,
Colonel Duckenfield, backed in 1645 for the mastership of Stockport
School, with the unattractive salary of £10.[20]

At least as early as 1648 Greenhalgh was master at Chester School,
where the salary had been augmented in 1646 by £36, and where,
before 1650, he had as a pupil Thomas, the son of General Robert
Venables. Greenhalgh remained at Chester until 1655, when he was
dismissed by the corporation 'owing to complaints of his mis-
demeanours'. What these were is not revealed in the Assembly
Book, but one writer on the King's School states that they consisted
of fidelity to Church and King. It seems likely that Greenhalgh went
to live at Nantwich, where he owned land and where the feoffees
met him in 1659. In 1657 his cousin, James Livesey, had been presented to the living of Great Budworth by Christ Church, and,
holding very moderate Calvinist views and also, presumably, equally
moderate political views, he was able to retain his living after the
Act of Uniformity. His presence nearby may have attracted Greenhalgh to Witton in 1663, and furthermore the feoffees there were
prepared to take trouble for a master described in his burial entry in
Great Budworth parish register as 'clarissimus'—most renowned
or distinguished. In 1665–6 considerable repairs and decorations
were done at the school and the schoolmaster's house, where a new
kitchen was built, and in 1667 the feoffees treated with Greenhalgh
for 'his stay and continuance at the school', and subsequently agreed
to increase his salary by £5 to £25. They prized him, no doubt, for
the degree which distinguished him from several of his predecessors,
and for his learning: at his death he left books valued at the considerable amount of £20 10s to his cousin's son, Humphrey Livesey,
himself a private pupil of a later master of Puritan leanings, Thomas
Martindale. After leaving Witton early in 1669 he seems to have
lived in Great Budworth, where he died in 1674: among his bequests

was 20*s* to Thomas Knight, clerk, of Castle Northwich, almost certainly a former Witton pupil.[21]

With the next master the statutory procedure of examination by the Bishop of Chester was resumed: in 1669 the bailiff feoffees spent 16*s* for three days and nights attending at Chester to have James Steward examined by the bishop, 4*s* on the bishop's chaplain, and 1*s* on the bishop's porter. Furthermore all the feoffees had to sign a certificate to be taken to Chester, concerning the new master.* This is the first record of such an examination since that of Pigott. Steward's subscription, dated 29 September 1669 and signed by him, survives, and is worth quoting in full to show the requirements of conformity.

I James Steward do declare that it is not lawfull upon any pretence whatsoever to take armes against the King, And that I do abhorr that traiterous position of taking armes by his autority [sic] against his person or against those that are commissionated by him. And that I will conforme to the liturgy of the Church of England as it is now by law established. And I do declare that I do hold there lyes no obligacion upon mee or any other person from the oathe commonly call'd the Solemne League & Covenant to endeavour any change or alteracion of government either in Church or State, And that the same was in it self an unlawfull oathe & imposed upon the subjects of this realme against the known lawes & liberties of this kingdome.

Steward was the son of a yeoman of Mobberley who, in his will (proved in 1664), left half his lands to his son James, towards his maintenance in learning. James Steward was indeed quite well provided for, since in addition to this legacy he had £10 out of his father's household goods and £10 which had been left to him by his grandfather: after his mother's death he was to have the other half of his father's lands, paying to his brother John on his majority £60 out of certain fields. He had originally matriculated at Oxford in March 1665, but then moved to Jesus College, Cambridge, where he was a pensioner. Later he became a scholar of the college, took his B.A. in 1669 and his M.A. in 1672, and at the time of his appointment at Witton was twenty-one. He remained at Witton only until 1673, appeared at Rostherne as curate in 1674, and ended as vicar of Dodford, Northamptonshire, from 1679 to 1703.[22]

Peter Woodnoth, the new master, aged about twenty-three, was freshly down from Oxford, where he had been entered as 'pleb.', 'pauper puer' at Christ Church, and had taken his B.A. in 1672. He too was a Cheshire man, being the son of Robert Woodnoth of Acton, and he was licensed at Witton by the bishop in September

---

* Doubtless a nomination certificate similar to that which survives for Aaron Nicholls.

1673, after being taken to Chester by the feoffees for his examination. Within a few years, however, things were clearly not going
well on either side. The accounts for 1678 are followed by two
signed declarations, probably both made in March 1679. The first
(undated), signed by seven feoffees, stated:

Whereas the revenues of the schoole of Witton are much decreased by the
decay of wallinge, and in the late troubles by destroyinge of severall buildings in the City of Chester by fire, insomuch as the wages for the present
masters of the schoole will not amount to the ancient salaries allowed and
paid unto them, now upon mature deliberation taken of the present
incomes of the schoole, and finding the same will not defray the necessary
charges of the same and pay the head-master twenty pounds per annum
and the under-master eight pounds per annum, formerly allowed them,
and yet paid unto them, without subtractinge the stocke of moneys now in
beinge, therefore the head-master doth at present condiscend to accept of
and take fifteene pounds per annum and the under-master sixe pounds
per annum. And to the end that the said masters may be satisfied the
remainder of the defalcations, in case the schoole revenues should be in
any manner advanced, & the profitts thereof encrease to make good theire
present abatements, we whose names are subscribed, Feoffees of the schoole
abovesaid, do hereby condiscend to, & likewise require and desire such
other Feoffees for the time to come that may succeed us, to pay unto the
present Masters of the schoole aforesaid such summes of money as shalbe
due unto them by reason of theire abatements, and that really they shalbe
unpaid of theire severall wages & salaries of twenty pounds and eight
pounds per Annum as aforesaid.

The second declaration was signed by Peter Woodnoth and dated
14 March 1679; it stated:

There beinge this day a meetinge of the Feoffees of the Schoole of Witton,
& some complaints made by them against me of my neglects in officiatinge
the schoole aforesaid, And beinge that noe complaint can positively be
made out against me, nevertheless I do hereby promise & engage, that for
the time to come, if any iust complaint can be made against me for any
neglect, or any other iust fault, not to be done by me as Master of the
schoole aforesaid, to avoid & depart from the schoole aforesaid, (the same
complaint beinge proved against me) at the end of six moneths next after
notice thereof given unto me.

The situation illustrates the warning given in Christopher Wase's
Considerations concerning Free Schools, published in 1678, against
paying schoolmasters inadequate salaries: 'to be abridged in neces-
saries', he wrote, 'must needs discourage labor: and the mind under
daily distraction can less intend its more desirable charge'. Witton
was by no means alone in facing this problem, and there is an
example from the neighbouring county. In 1676 the governors of

Ormskirk Grammar School decided that their master's stipend was
inadequate, and that for the present year he could augment it by
charging for every English scholar 16*d* a quarter, for every Latin
scholar 2*s*, and for every Greek scholar 3*s*. In Cheshire the governors
of Frodsham School in 1678 authorised charges of 2*s* a quarter for
the Latin accidence and 5*s* a quarter for Greek. At Witton this more
controversial solution came much later; for the time being the
feoffees fell back on the easier but discouraging method of reducing
the masters' salaries. Not surprisingly, Peter Woodnoth began to
preach, with, it was thought, a view to leaving the school. This he
did in the late summer of 1679, signing on 15 August a discharge to
the school for any obligation to him under the feoffees' declaration.
His departure seems to have been hurried and to have led to some
dissatisfaction in the town, for in 1684, when the Archbishop of
York carried out a visitation of the diocese of Chester, the churchwardens of Witton presented the school feoffees for 'detaininge 40*s*
from the poore which was forfeited by Mr Woodoth's [sic] goeing
away and for denying to shew the statutes of the schoole or act
according to the statute and for wasting the schoole stocke'. The
relevant statute enacted that six months' notice should be given on
either side (feoffees' or master's) for the departure of the master:
'if a shorter tyme will not serve booth the partyes more convenyently,
And if hee neclect to gyve the said warnying, I will that their shalbe
stayed in the handes of the Feoffees, that have at that tyme the
collecyon of the rentes, of his wageis fourtye shillings, which I will
shalbe gyven to fortye poore people of the said Parisshe of Wytton'.
The feoffees attended the visitation twice, and secured their dismissal.[23]

It is ironic that Peter Woodnoth, who made no visible impression
on the school, should survive in two external records. The second is
the collection of answers to a questionnaire sent out by Christopher
Wase, Architypographer and Superior Bedell of Civil Law at Oxford, who began his investigations into the state of grammar schools
soon after 1671. The queries which he sent out were usually
addressed to the master, and they covered the name of the founder,
the date of the foundation and the method of endowment, the succession of masters '*if at hand*; otherwise such as are in memory to
have been eminent, or authors of any extant work', any university
exhibitions attached to the school, the names of the governors,
patrons and visitors, and finally 'what libraries in them, or in townes
adjoining, with what manuscripts?'. The response from Cheshire
was poor: only four schools replied to Wase—Halton, Macclesfield, Mottram in Longdendale, and Northwich: there was no reply
from Chester, Nantwich or Stockport. Peter Woodnoth, whatever

his other defects, gave a comprehensive if not always strictly accurate account of the school.* In the first answer it is interesting to see that he referred to the free grammar school at Northwich, and then added as an afterthought 'in the township of Witton'. In describing the endowment he declared that the original £12 had been 'since improved notwithstanding the loss of 44 bays of building in Chester in the times of war'. Inaccurately Thomas Farmer was named as 'our first master', but otherwise the list was correct. The feoffees were still chosen 'especially out the Founder's kinsmen if qualifide [sic]'. The library was stated to have been 'destroyed in the time of war', and finally Woodnoth asserted that 'most of the gentry of Cheshire have been brought up at Northwich schoole and that we have had 220 scholars at once'.[24]

Thomas Martindale, who succeeded to the mastership at Michaelmas 1679, and was taken to the bishop for examination in October, is one of the few masters of Witton about whose life and circumstances we have any body of information. His father, Adam Martindale, a noted Cheshire Puritan, who was Presbyterian minister at Rostherne during the Interregnum and schoolmaster at Warrington after his deprivation at the Restoration, left a detailed autobiography which contains a lengthy account of his son's education and career. Thomas Martindale was actually of the statutory age of thirty when he was appointed at Witton. He had been a pupil at Manchester Grammar School, but later had a curious academic career owing to his father's scruples about involving him with the oaths of religious conformity at the universities. He was entered at Trinity College, Cambridge, but came down at once and was sent to Oxford but not entered at a college: he lived in a private house and had tuition from 'a gentleman of Brazenose College'. This arrangement proved unsatisfactory, as the youth was plagued with questions about his position from his fellow students. He was therefore sent for two years to an academy in Worcestershire run by a former fellow of Magdalen College, a famous Oxford preacher ejected at the Restoration, and with him he studied 'the whole bodie of philosophie'. In 1670 Adam Martindale took his son to Glasgow University, where the coercion to take the oaths was not rigorously applied. There he was admitted to the class studying for the M.A.: in seventeen weeks he covered the course and gained the degree. On his return to Cheshire Thomas was provided by his father with a class of young men as private pupils, to instruct in Hebrew and to prepare for the university, and was, according to his father, a very successful teacher: among his pupils were Ephraim Elcock, the future master of Tarvin free school and Humphrey Livesey, the son of James

* See plate II.

Livesey, vicar of Great Budworth. He continued teaching for a year, when his father moved to Millington in 1674, and then himself moved on to be tutor to the grandchildren of 'Colonel' Venables of Wincham.

After this there followed an interlude in London which runs like a contemporary cautionary tale. Failing to secure a chaplaincy to a sea captain of Wapping, because his preaching was 'too high for the seamen—even the captains themselves', Thomas was fortunate in being appointed chief usher at Merchant Taylors' School, in spite of the headmaster's original prejudice against his nonconformist backers. His new situation seems to have raised him above himself, and he began to keep company to which his finances were not equal. 'Being a meere scholar, that was alwayes used to have his cloaths bought and kept in repair for him, and knew not how to buy a paire of gloves, when he came to weare rich cloaths, such as pure Spanish cloath gownes, silk cassockes, and stockings, cloath shoes, and such like and being subject to be cheated by every one he dealt with, and running fast through such costly apparell for want of good looking to; the charge of maintaining himselfe in habit fit for such company was very considerable.' His plans to recoup himself by marrying a rich wife or being presented to a wealthy living fell through: 'at last a rooke tells him of a great fortune at the other end of the towne, a gentlewoman that waited on two young ladies, and makes him beleeve she had 600 pounds to her portion; and if he would seale him a bond of 10 pounds he would help him to obtain her. He did soe, and after paid the money; but never had soe much with her, that I heard of. And now he had done his business, throughly, having himselfe to provide for, and a wife, without a portion, to be maintained like a gentlewoman, and by this foolish marriage rendered himselfe incapable to keepe his schoole.'

He left Merchant Taylors' with a gratuity of £5, and after failing to get employment in London, 'downe he came in a wagon, and his wife with him, in the month of October 1677, in their summer clothes—such as they had worn in London'. Adam Martindale took them in, got his son a fortnightly preaching job and paid his debts. After a while Thomas set up school at Warburton, and was then called to a school at Lymm: here, according to the rector's answers to visitation queries in 1679, he had been 'teaching a public school', 'but whether licensed is not known'. About 1677 he took Anglican orders, but he missed by a short head the office of curate to the vicar of St Oswald's, Chester. He seems, however, to have made a success of his teaching: earlier his father had warned him that he would 'spoile all by measuring others by himselfe: for though learning was both his calling and recreation, he must not think it would be so to them his pupils; and by keeping them so over strictly to it, he would get a name of severity, and deterre youths from coming to him—as it fell out in the event. . . . Now I could prevaile with him to carrie so in his schole as to win the hearts both of his boyes and their parents.' As a result, when he went to Witton from Lymm some of the parents sent their sons after him.

About August 1679, Adam Martindale records, the minister of Northwich wrote to Thomas to supply his place for a day in order to make interest for the schoolmaster's post there, since the existing master (Peter Woodnoth) was neither satisfactory nor satisfied. This minister was John Fishwick, originally of Chorley, and a pupil at Rivington School. His academic career resembled Thomas Martindale's and implies Puritan leanings: he entered St John's College, Cambridge, as a pensioner in 1664, but did not even matriculate; four years later he enrolled at Glasgow University, and although not appearing in the list of 'laureati' there was described in the visitation of 1691 as A.M. of Glasgow. He was appointed curate at Witton in 1675, and remained there until his death in 1718. Thomas, warned by previous experience, asked advice of his father: 'I disswaded him from it, making account that his appearing might make the schoolmaster to prize a place that another sought for, and make his friends bustle for him if he had any. Besides, if he sought for a new place and missed it, the people at Limme would have a lower regard of him; but if without his seeking, he were chosen by the feoffees, (which might easily be his noble friend and mine, colonel Venables, being that yeare Bayliffe-feoffee, that is the chiefe actor, a man of great interest among them, and well acquainted with his abilities,) then the people at Limme would not be so disingenuous as to hinder his advantage . . .' Thomas Martindale entered on his labours at Witton at Michaelmas 1679, keeping on his preacher's place at Warburton.

The move from Lymm represented advancement, and there was, too, the new master's house at Witton: as Adam Martindale put it, 'those few household goods he had at Limme would not suffice here; I therefore gave him some, lent him others, (which proved gift in the event,) and furnished him with money to buy such as I could not spare'. Extra work fell on Thomas owing to the death of the usher and the feoffees' choice of 'a raw boy' to succeed, but 'tablers' —that is, boys from a distance who boarded in the town—began to attend the school; 'diverse more (whereof some were persons of quality) were about to send him their children', and his scholars 'came well on'. The father's hopes, however, were dashed by his son's sudden death of a fever, which had spread in the town and eventually struck him, although 'the school where he dwelt and taught, being upon a little hill by the church, a prettie distance from the towne, was free a good while from the infection'. 'His corpse was accompanied from Witton-schoole (drawne upon the frame of Mr. Venables' coach) to his grave [at Rostherne] with many gentlemen and other fashionable persons, and met with many more out of Rotherston parish, Lymme, Warburton, and North-wych.' James Livesey, vicar of Great Budworth, preached at the funeral, giving him 'the character of *an industrious, learned, and usefull young man,* insinuating that it would be a more easie thing to find a man that could make shift to preach a passable sermon, than one so fitted for a great schoole as he was'. 'But,' concludes Adam Martindale's narration of his son's life, 'all that could not call him againe, nor the teares of his relations and scholars, nor sorrowe of the towne that their schoole suffered a wofull loss, as after it quickly proved, for it is since almost dwindled to nothing.' This account has been given in detail although Thomas Martindale was only at the school for ten months because it provides a rare example of a detailed biography of a Cheshire schoolmaster, even if the Martindale family's circumstances were not entirely typical.[25]

The unfortunate Martindale, who was paid only £15 a year, received his last payment up to the beginning of August: then for a quarter the curate, John Fishwick, acted as master, but a new master seems already to have been hired in September, after several meetings of the feoffees. The new master, who began to teach in January 1681, apparently came from Great Budworth, for the feoffees went over there to meet 'Mr. deane the schoolmaster and Mr. Livesey and severall others', and he may well have been related to 'Parson Deane'. Gerard Deane was a Cheshire man, 'generosus', according to the parish register, and possibly one of the founder's kin. He had been admitted as a sizar at Jesus College, Cambridge, in 1676 at the age of sixteen, took his B.A. degree in 1680, and was licensed by the bishop as master at Witton in July 1681. He established himself quickly in Northwich, marrying, in July 1682, Gracia Hewitt, possibly a relation of Thomas Hewitt, bailiff feoffee for 1680 and 1681: by 1693 he had had eight children, three of whom died in infancy. Deane's tenure of office at Witton, where he too was paid only £15 a year until 1691, when the salary was raised to £20 again, seems to have been unremarkable. Only one pupil of his is known to have gone to a university: George Ward, who held Farmer's exhibition, entered Deane's own college in 1686, but did not proceed to a degree. The dwindling of the school 'almost to nothing' which Adam Martindale, perhaps with paternal partiality, mentioned in his autobiography must refer to Deane's time, since the journal is thought to have been written in 1685, and Martindale died in 1686. One entry in the accounts during Deane's mastership rouses unsatisfied curiosity: it is the payment in 1683 of 6*d* for a flute for the scholars. Later, after 1691, Deane took orders, and he left the school in 1693.[26]

The new master, who first came to the town in June 1693, was almost certainly secured, like Thomas Martindale, by John Fishwick, the curate, since they had been contemporaries at Glasgow University. Aaron Nicholls or Nichols was, most probably, the son of Richard Nichols, baptised at Warrington parish church in 1649. He went up to Glasgow University in 1668, and though, like Fishwick, he is not included in printed lists of 'laureati' there, he too was later described as M.A. In 1674 he was schoolmaster at Warrington, and in 1677 he was at the free grammar school of Liverpool (where he was licensed in December 1676); from there he moved to Farnworth School, where he succeeded James Urmston, who died in 1677. He was probably at Farnworth until his appointment at Witton, and was certainly there in July 1689, when he took the oaths of allegiance to William and Mary after the 'Glorious Revolution'. The certificate of his subscription still survives and was submitted to the bishop at the time of his licensing at Witton, in proof of his loyalty to the régime.

Although Nichols was paid a salary as master at Witton from midsummer 1693, it was not until April 1696 that the feoffees wrote to the Bishop of Chester giving notice of their election of him.* In a letter signed by six feoffees and witnessed by three churchwardens the feoffees presented Nichols, 'Master in Arts', 'whom wee believe to bee throughly qualifyed for the sayd office and imployment both as touchinge his inward qualifications and outward moralls & a fitt person for the funtion [*sic*]'. At the same time a testimonial was sent to the bishop from the inhabitants of Northwich and district.

We the Inhabitants of the Town of Witton, and Northwich, and other neighbouring towns and villages do hereby certifie the Reverend Father in God Nicolas Bishop of Chester that Aaron Nichols, elected Schoolmaster by the joynt consent of the Feofees being Master in Arts, is a person of good morals, conformeable to the Church of England, both for discipline and doctrine, and well affected towards the present government; of whose industry, and sober deportment in his office, as likewise of the eficiency of those Schollers who have been recommended to his tuition, we have hitherto had the happy and succesful experience; and those of us (whose names are likewise subscribed) who have had no children to send

---

* This probationary period may have been usual. *Cf.* Over Whitley School, where, in 1702, the trustees applied for a licence for John Leycester after making 'tryall of him'. (*C.D. Recs.*, EDP 131/9.)

unto him hitherto, doe freely acquiesce in and are fully satisfyed concerning the good opinion and character we hear of him, as touching his piety
and good morality . . .

This statement was signed by Jo. Davie, vicar of Frodsham, and
Stephen Morhall, vicar of Weaverham, by the coroner of Northwich,
John Barker, sen., three chapel wardens, and thirty-two local inhabitants from Davenham, Aston, Shurlach, Shipbrook and Barnton,
as well as Northwich and Witton.* These good reports were accompanied by a submission by Nichols himself, which included a catalogue of the scholars of Witton School, and a list of former pupils
of his who had gone to the university, 'some whereof are ministers
at this day, others who were judged fit for the same, being otherwise
disposed of'. The latter list runs as follows:

Mr. Marsden minister at Prescot.
Mr. Warin one of the Curates at Winwick.
Mr. Holt Chaplain to Lord Killmorrey.
Mr. Charles Penketh.
Mr. Wm. Burtonwood, minister in some part of Ireland.
Mr. Golborn min. in Yorkshire.
Mr. Tho. Heywood.
Mr. Heapie Minister once of Burtonwood.
Mr. Clark. Mr Joshua Platt.
Mr. Pullon now minister at Hail.
Mr. Low, etc.,

Burtonwood, Golborn and Heywood can probably all be identified
as natives of Warrington; the two former went up to Oxford in
1674 and 1673 respectively, while the last was perhaps the Thomas
Heywood licensed as a surgeon at Warrington in 1684. Thomas
Waring, a curate of Ashton in Makerfield in the parish of Winwick
from 1690, was the son of John Waring of Liverpool, and matriculated at Oxford in 1681: he was possibly a link with Nichols'
Liverpool days. Christopher Marsden, who was left in charge at
Prescot from 1693 by the non-resident vicar, had matriculated at
Oxford in 1680, but his school can be traced from the record of
his entry to St John's College, Cambridge, in January 1683, where
it was given as 'Farnworth (Mr. Ormstone)'. Thus, although taught
by Nichols after the death of Urmston (or Ormstone), Marsden
seems to have considered himself primarily a pupil of the older
master. William Pullen A.B. was admitted to the cure of Hale
Chapel in May, 1695, but his school cannot be traced. In spite of
all this favourable documentation, Nichols did not secure a licence
from the bishop until over a year later, in June 1697, when he had

* See plate III.

already been teaching at Witton for four years. Nichols exhibited
his licence at the visitations of 1705 and 1709; it will be noticed
that the licence was specifically related to a particular school, for
he had previously had a licence at Liverpool and presumably also
at Farnworth.[27]

The whole affair of the licensing of Nichols means that, for the
first time in the history of the school, there is in existence a list of
pupils.* The school under Nichols was of a respectable size, about
eighty, but there is little sign of academic achievement: the 'Mr.
Low' listed as a former pupil was doubtless Samuel Lowe, who
went up to Cambridge in June 1696 with a grant from the Farmer
bequest. On his entry at St John's, however, he was described as a
pupil of Mr Harper at Hartford: it is odd that two pupils claimed
by Nichols should in fact be entered as pupils of other teachers.[28]
The terms in which the feoffees made their decision to divert the
Farmer bequest in 1703 to pay the usher imply that no scholar,
poor or otherwise, had recently gone to Oxford or Cambridge or
was likely to do so. Nevertheless there is some sign of activity in
the payment of 6s 8d to Nichols for a dictionary for the school's use
in 1707, and in the provision of two new desks.

The payments of Nichols's salary were pretty irregular at first:
in the accounts for 1694, 1695 and part of 1696 (all lumped together)
he was merely handed the rents paid by the Chester and Wirral
tenants, amounting to £35 14s 10d, while in those for the rest of
1696 to 1698 nothing is recorded except 10s lent to him in 1694
and the payment of over £11 to 'Mr. Nicols and for his use to
severall persons': later, however, the salary settled down at £16 a
year. Nichols's mastership drew to a wretched close: in 1709 the
feoffees were meeting about 'the Master's sickness', and by the
spring of 1710 he was suffering from 'a long and lingering weakness
and infirmity of body . . . whereby he is become unable to attend
the duty of the said school as he ought to do, to the extreme loss
and prejudice of the Scholars thereof, and to the great lessening and
impairing of the said School' as was stated in the articles of agreement between him and the feoffees, drawn up in April, 1710. By
these articles Nichols was to resign and to be allowed £8 a year for
his life, an early example of a pension. The situation must indeed
have reached a desperate stage, but the articles can scarcely have
taken effect (if at all), since Nichols died in May 1710. (During his
last months a 'Mr. Lancaster' received an allowance of 25s, mostly
out of deductions from the masters' salaries.) Nichols's state of
poverty was such that the feoffees paid his funeral expenses of

---

* See the list at the end of this chapter.

£2 16s, even down to the price of the rosemary and of the affidavit that he had been buried in woollen.[29]

For five years after Nichols's death the future looked more hopeful at Witton. The financial position improved and the school had a promising new master, Joseph Allen. In July 1710 the feoffees took him to Chester and the Wirral to show him the school estates, and then bestirred themselves to repair the school and the church house, 'upon Mr. Allen's going to dwell there'. Allen could not be prevailed upon to accept the post without an increase of salary, raised by subscriptions, varying from 5s to £1 a year, from the trustees and many of the inhabitants of the chapelry. Furthermore it later emerged that when he discovered how small the school revenues were he required not only an increase of salary but an engagement by the trustees to use their interest to unite the mastership with the curacy when the latter fell vacant. There is no reason to doubt that this additional salary was paid, but it does not appear in the accounts, which show only £16 a year until midsummer 1713, but from then on £20. Allen, the son of Robert Allen of Betley, Staffordshire, had been at school at Audley, in that county, and had entered Trinity College, Cambridge, as a sub-sizar (the very lowest status of student) in July 1705. He took his B.A. in 1709, and went on to teach at Little Budworth. At the time of his appointment he was twenty-four and unmarried, and thus fulfilled two of Deane's three requirements. Although he caused the feoffees some disquiet in 1712 by his absence, he soon raised the standard of academic achievement, sending three boys from Witton to his own college in 1713 and 1714, and one to St John's in 1715.[30]

It was Witton's loss that after Michaelmas 1715 Allen moved on to Lower Peover, where he was given the mastership of the school founded there in 1710 by Richard Comberbatch, the schoolhouse of which still survives. At first sight it seems strange that a man should go from Northwich to Lower Peover, particularly as the school was not a grammar school like Witton, being designed for the benefit of the poorer inhabitants (those with property of less than £10 a year or holding a farm worth less than £30 a year), whose children were to be instructed in the English language only: furthermore there does not seem to have been a house for the master until 1770. But the attraction undoubtedly lay in the combination of the mastership with the perpetual curacy of Lower Peover chapel, which was given to Allen by the patron, Sir Francis Leicester. Allen had already preached at Witton Chapel occasionally, but the long-lived John Fishwick was still curate there, and this prevented any possible union of the two offices such as had been discussed. In a letter of 1721 Allen later stated that when Sir Francis Leicester

'gave me Peover, he told me he was sorry it was no better, and
that had it been a living of two hundred a year, he wou'd have
given it me before any clergyman he knew'. At Little Peover Allen
married in March 1716 Ann, the daughter of John Comberbach of
Lymm. He did not, however, restrict his teaching to the limited
terms of the foundation, for between 1717 and 1719 he sent half a
dozen pupils to Trinity. Significantly, in his will of 1720 Richard
Comberbatch envisaged the possible encouragement of a Latin
school at his foundation, and the whole episode provides evidence
of the power of a master to mould the character of his school.
Allen's career in this area shows, too, the attractive power of a good
master: while he was at Witton boys had come to him whose fathers
were of Knutsford and Peover. When he moved to Peover he had
one pupil from Flintshire, who went to Trinity and subsequently
became Professor of Anatomy at Cambridge; another was the son
of Thomas Banks of Winstanley, Lancashire, and a third came from
Hulme in Cheshire. Ominously for Witton School, Joseph Tovey,
the son of John Tovey of Northwich, went to Peover under Allen,
and proceeded to Cambridge in 1718. Not surprisingly, Allen moved
from Peover to a larger school. On the recommendation of the
Archbishop of York (formerly Bishop of Chester) he was appointed
headmaster of Macclesfield in May 1720 at a salary of £60 a year,
and continued there until his death in 1745, in spite of accusations
of Jacobitism.[31]

The ushers

From 1659 to 1671 the usher supplied the continuity which the
rapid succession of masters failed to give: John Woolmer seems to
have made something of a career of the ushership, and the feoffees'
appreciation was marked by several gratuities. For two years before
his death he had an assistant usher, Thomas Leftwich, one of the
senior boys, who later went up to Cambridge. Edward Bertles,
another usher of some duration, survived his stormy beginning in
1671, when he was violently turned out of the school by Parson
Dayne, and remained there until his death in 1679, winning from
Adam Martindale the description 'an honest and ingenious young
man'. It is not surprising that Martindale lamented the extra work
which fell upon his son when, after Bertles' death, the feoffees
appointed 'a raw boy', Coulden, as usher. The usher's salary, £8
until 1679, when it was reduced to £6, was not an attraction, and
after the departure of Benjamin Leftwich in 1687 the school was
without an usher until 1702, a situation from which a drastic fall
in numbers might be deduced. At Beverley, in 1670, about fifty

scholars were held to justify the appointment of an usher, but at
Witton about 1696 there were over eighty pupils. The absence of
an usher therefore denoted the falling off not of numbers but of
income, and without doubt of efficiency, since the headmaster had
to struggle with this large number of pupils of very varying ages.
The desperation of the position is shown by the diversion in 1703
of Farmer's money to pay for an usher, who was declared to be
absolutely necessary. The insecurity of the post and its lack of
prospects is indicated by the rapid succession of ushers between
1703 and 1712.

The certain duties of the usher at Witton are not definitely known
at this date. In some schools, besides English and elementary Latin,
the usher taught writing, but commonly it was looked on as an extra
subject to be paid for by a special fee. Sometimes the boys had to
go elsewhere in the town for instruction; sometimes a travelling
scrivener stayed for a few weeks in the year and taught them. At
Witton the first evidence is in the early eighteenth century: in 1706
Joseph Clough, writing master, paid 10s towards the usher's salary,
and in 1707 and 1708 he paid £1, but in 1709 his money was
'abated him on account of the Blackmores teaching'. These were
doubtless rival teachers in the town, and also doubtless the cause of
a written agreement between Clough and the feoffees, drawn up in
July 1709,* whereby the terms of his engagement were stated and
his monopoly assured. The fact that Clough paid for his monopoly
implies that he charged the boys a fee, and it appears that besides
writing he taught casting accounts. In 1710 and 1711 Clough paid
only 10s a year, and after that he disappeared from the school
accounts and had no successor; either the boys were free to go
where they liked, or possibly the usher became responsible for
writing and accounts, as he was at Lymm in 1719.[32]

The pupils

For the first time in the history of the school we have a complete
list of pupils, giving the names of seventy-seven boys, five of whom
were described as 'cu fr' ('cum fratre', 'with brother') making a
total of eighty-two.† The addition of a list of pupils taught by the
master at other schools makes it possible to connect the list with
Aaron Nichols, and to date it about 1696. This links it with the
testimonial to Nichols's teaching ability signed in April 1696 by a
number of local inhabitants, some of whom were fathers of pupils.

* See above, p. 111.
† The divisions in the list presumably represent the forms, the last and
largest being the 'petties'.

Among these were Richard Smalwood of Davenham, Thomas Jackson of Aston, gent., John Amery of Barnton (also one of the borrowers of school stock) and Josiah Lowe, almost certainly to be identified with the man mentioned in a memorandum of 1687 in the parish register: 'that Josiah Lowe, had a child baptised abroad [i.e. elsewhere than in Witton Chapel] and hath not brought it to be registered'. A search of the baptisms recorded in the parish register between 1678 and 1691 for boys who would have been between the ages of six and about eighteen in 1696 makes possible the identification, with tolerable certainty, of half the boys in the list. Only some of the probable fathers' occupations are given in the register, but they form an interesting range which was no doubt typical during much of the school's early history. They include clothier (pannificis), brewer or maltster (brasiatoris), carpenter (fabri-lignarii), shoemaker (galicarii), farmer (agricolae), glover (chirothecary), shopkeeper (propolae), miller (molendarii), druggist (pharmacopolae), and clergyman. Experience has shown that the character of the school and the provenance of its pupils varied with the ability of the master. The picture of Witton School under Nichols is one of a circumscribed community in which the fathers of the boys, the feoffees, the churchwardens, the borrowers of the school money, the providers of the materials for the repair of the school and the craftsmen who did the work mingled and overlapped.[33]

The provenance of his pupils was a matter of some importance to the master. The special concession gained by George Venables in 1659 that the children of his tenants at Hartford should be instructed 'as freely as anie children ought to bee by the ordinances and statutes of the same Schoole' suggests that the freedom was at that time strictly limited. It seems probable that the 'tablers' who came to the school under Thomas Martindale were paying pupils, and that in this way, as probably happened at Stockport, the narrow bounds of the statutory salary were extended. Under Allen there were pupils who came from Wybunbury, Knutsford and Peover, but there were said to have been complaints at this time of the extension of the 'freedom' to all and sundry, an extension difficult to understand, since neither feoffees nor master apparently stood to gain from it.*

The flow of Witton pupils to Oxford and Cambridge during the later decades of the century was somewhat sparser than before: whereas Pigott had sent seven pupils to St John's College, and three had gone there between 1652 and 1660, only one went there afterwards.† This may, of course, represent a switch from one college to

* See Chapter VII.
† Henry Eaton in 1715; two, if Samuel Lowe is included.

another, since headmasters tended to favour a particular college, often their own: Steward and Deane were both of Jesus College, Cambridge, and the latter is known to have sent one pupil there, while Allen sent three boys to his own college. Of those whose careers are known, all became clergymen: James Marbury, the son of the rector of Davenham, who spent five years at Witton under Coulton and Swinton, went to Caius College, Cambridge, as a scholar in 1665, and not to his father's college, Brasenose: after taking his M.A. degree he succeeded his father at Davenham. Thomas Leftwich became a minor canon of Chester Cathedral; George Ward became vicar of Leigh, Lancashire, and Samuel Lowe ended as preacher at Bunbury.[34]

Not all the links, however, were with the established Church and the strictly Anglican-controlled universities. As might be expected, Glasgow University, where Thomas Martindale, John Fishwick and Aaron Nichols had all been students, exerted a pull. Unfortunately the description of English students entering Glasgow at this time was usually confined to 'Anglus' (after the Union 'Anglo-Britannus') with only an occasional mention of their county of origin, but it is known with certainty that Daniel Lowe, 'Anglus-Cestriensis', who went there in 1721, was educated at Witton. He was the son of Joshua, of the Hulse, an Anglican married to a Presbyterian. His family was of the minor gentry and is said to have had special privileges at Witton School, perhaps from some distant association with the foundation. After a successful career at Glasgow,* where he formed friendships with some young English Presbyterians, Lowe was licensed by the Cheshire Classis (the union of Presbyterian and Congregational ministers) at Knutsford in 1725. Subsequently he moved to Norton in Derbyshire and kept a flourishing school where, he recorded, 'I have fitted many for 'prentices and some few for Glasgow, and other places': in fact two of his pupils became High Sheriffs of Derbyshire. Although Lowe is the only certainly known Witton pupil at Glasgow, another graduate may possibly have been educated at the school. John Partington, 'Anglo-Britannus', who entered the university in 1718 and graduated in 1719, was licensed in 1720 as a candidate for the ministry, and later ordained, by the Cheshire Classis; he ministered to a congregation at Northwich until 1724. It has not proved possible to trace any relationship between him and the school feoffee of the same name.[35]

The payments out of Farmer's money in this period raise some interesting points. After John Sworton no payments were made for a few years, but between March 1666 and April 1667 Humphrey Barlow, who, presumably as a senior boy, had been paid 1s for

* His diploma was still preserved in the family in 1916.

teaching when Swinton left, received £4 15*s* 3*d* as 'a poore schollar'
at Dublin. In May 1667, however, a public meeting of the feoffees
was held 'about the deciding of the claime made by Cornet Barlow
for his son Humphrey concerninge Mr Farmer's exhibicion': this
must have been a request for a renewal of payments, which was
granted, and payments of about £3 a year in instalments were
made to Humphrey or his father until 1673. Humphrey Barlow,
the son of Robert Barlow of Leftwich, was admitted as a pensioner
in 1666 to Trinity College, Dublin, became a scholar in 1667, and
took his B.A. degree in 1669, but there is no record of any further
degree. Between 1674 and 1680 payments, also averaging £3 a
year, were regularly made to 'Mr. William Leftwich' (probably
actually a feoffee at the time) for his son, Thomas, a student at
Emmanuel College, Cambridge, who did not, apparently, take a
degree.* He was ordained deacon in 1677 and priest in 1679 by
the Bishop of Chester, and subsequently was curate at Shotwick in
1691, and a minor canon of Chester Cathedral. On what grounds
Thomas qualified for the grant is not very clear, for William Leftwich was a man of standing in local society (and incidentally had
had a loan of £7 from the Farmer money, which he had repaid by
1676), but possibly his son was the only Witton boy then at a university and he had previously helped the usher in teaching. There are
signs of difficulties with the borrowers to whom Farmer's money was
lent out, but from 1685 to 1689 regular payments of £3 a year were
made to George Ward for his son, George, a sizar at Jesus College,
Cambridge. Ward did not matriculate or graduate, but was ordained
priest by the Bishop of Chester in 1689; in 1691 he was at Eccleston,
Lancashire, and from 1696 was vicar of Leigh. Again, the grant to
George Ward was made only after a public meeting of the feoffees
in December 1685 'at Betty Nickson's house' (i.e. an inn) 'concerninge yonge George Wards having of m^r Farmers exhibition as a
poore scholar'. During Ward's tenure of the grant the feoffees were
forced to take about £11 out of Farmer's money for general purposes, and to put out a bond owing to the school in order to raise
money for the scholar.

It is the more ironic that the next payments of Farmer's money
—£20 between 1696 and 1699—were made to Samuel Lowe at
Cambridge. In 1696 Samuel Lowe, the son of John Lowe, gent.,
was described in the records of St John's College, where he went
as a pensioner, as 'born at Harford [*sic*] . . . bred at Harford under
Mr Harper'. John Lowe, the son of George Lowe of Hartford, a
former feoffee of the school, was a man of substance who had

---

* A Thomas Leftwich appears at the visitation of 1674 as schoolmaster at
Weaverham. (*C.D. Recs.*, EDV 2/7, f. 5v.)

settled at Winnington, and in 1694, together with others, bought a moiety of the manor of Hartford. (It is not clear whether he was the same as, or related to, the John Lowe who was a feoffee from 1678 and was the sole accounting bailiff feoffee when Samuel received his payments.) It must be assumed that Samuel Lowe had spent some time at Witton before going on to Harper, and possibly some of the special privileges mentioned in connection with Daniel Lowe may have operated in his case. Samuel Lowe had, in fact, a reputable academic career: he went on to take an M.A., and from 1705 to 1711 was a fellow of his college. He eventually became a preacher at Bunbury in 1717 until his death in 1760, and was followed at St John's by a son. He was the last recorded (and probably in fact the last) pupil of Witton School to benefit from the generosity of Thomas Farmer.[36]

Of the day-to-day life of the pupils in the school during these years there is little trace, but under Swinton there is the first record of some festivity at the breaking up before Christmas. In 1659 the feoffees gave 1s 6d 'to the schollers that acted at breaking off the Schoole at Chrismas', and this provides the only evidence of a school play being given at Witton. Plays were favoured by progressive masters, since they helped the boys to speak Latin well. Shrewsbury School was famous for its plays, but they were also put on in smaller schools. The statutes of Sandwich School actually provided 'at every Christmas time, if the master do think meet, to have one comedy or tragedy of chaste matter in Latin to be played, the parts to be divided to as many scholars as may be, and to be learned at vacant times', and nearer home, at Nantwich School, five boys acted at Christmas time in 1692. Just after the Restoration, indeed, before the period of financial stringency set in, the Witton feoffees seem to have been in an expansive mood. During the 'sixties pupils coming to the school saw constant improvements: work on the school study, new 'sills' at the school, plastering and painting to 'beautify' the school and the master's house, and the building of a kitchen and making of a garden for the master. In 1667, too, the newly engrossed copy of the statutes, in a new frame of wood, coloured and with two lids or covers, was brought to the school. Old traditions seem to have been observed more strictly too, for although by 1660 (according to Hoole) many schools were abandoning the old schoolboys' custom of barring out the master, it is in these years that the Witton feoffees recorded their encouragement of it at the Christmas breaking-up. Possibly the custom had been forbidden under Puritan rule as it was at Leicester Grammar School. In December 1661 3s 4d was 'given to and spent on' the scholars at their breaking up; in 1664 the feoffees spent 5s at the barring out of the master, and in December 1667 they spent 5*s* at the barring out and gave 3*s* to the head scholars. The feoffees' financial straits later in the century no doubt explain the absence of any further encouragement of the custom, but even in the neighbourhood there are signs that opinion was changing: when in 1698 statutes in many ways similar to Witton's were laid down for Darnhall School, the 'barring, bolting or locking out of the school' of the master by the scholars was forbidden on pain of expulsion.[37]

Known pupils, 1660–1726

1. *A Catalogue of the Schollars of Witton School**

Thomas Fishwick†
Robert Low
Thomas Jackson, cum frat.
Richd Smalwood
Wm Eaton, cum frat.
John Richardson
John Pickering
John Geffreys
Thomas Barlow

Thomas Nield
John Sudlow
John Burton
John Holland
Wm Plumly
Richd Yearsley
Wm Higgison
Walter Welding
Tho. Whitlow

John Goodwin
Robt Fishwick
John Eaton
John Baker
Tho. Hewit
Richd Dixon
John Linsdey†
John Harper

Robt Lamb
Sam Whitlow
Robt Hewit
Peter Eaton

Edwd Heesom
John Wildow
Georg Rogerson
John Worral
Ralph Rogerson
John Freer
John Shaw
George Miller
John Miller
John Roberts
Christ. Steeven
Isaac Woods
George Elloms
Peter Barker
Sam. Leicester
Peter Bagaley, cum fr.
Wm Low
John Cook
Charles Jackson
Charles Lindsey
George Barker
James Dorton
Henry Lamb, cum fr.
George cum Johanne Green
Wm Burroughs
Tho. Carter
Richd Amery
Richard Sutton
Edwd Rowlinson
Joseph Cubborn
Richard Hewes
Samuel Stones

* *C.D. Recs.*, EDP 305/11. Undated but *c.* 1696. The arrangement of the names has been kept in order to indicate the forms.   † *Cum frat* struck out.

Richd Ditchfield
Tho. cum Roger Gorse
Georgius cum Johanne Dakin
Tho. Eaton
Joseph Jackson
John et Sam. Tivie
Tho. Seamon
John Beckett
Tho. Lee cum fratre
John Ditchfield
Robert Ridgway

2. *At universities*

Cambridge University

James Marbury, son of James, rector of Davenham. Five years at North-wich School under 'Cotton' and Swinton. Adm. Caius College, scholar, 1665; B.A., 1668; M.A., 1672. Rector of Davenham, 1681–1725. Vicar of Over, 1680.

Thomas Leftwich, son of William. Farmer grants, 1674–80. Emmanuel College. Ordained deacon, 1677; priest, 1679. Curate of Shotwick, 1691–6. Minor Canon of Chester Cathedral.

George Ward, son of George. Adm. sizar, Jesus College, 1686. Ordained priest, 1689. At Eccleston, Lancs. 1691. Vicar of Leigh, 1696–1733.

Samuel Lowe, son of John, gent., of Winnington. Adm. pensioner, St. John's College, 1696. Born at Hartford. School: Hartford (Mr. Harper). B.A., 1700; M.A., 1703; Fellow, 1705–11. Ordained priest, 1703. Preacher at Bunbury, 1717–60.

Peter Mainwaring, son of Peter, lawyer, of Wybunbury. School: North-wich (Mr. Allen). Adm. sizar, Trinity College, 1713; scholar, 1715; B.A., 1717; M.A., 1720.

Thomas Barrow, son of William, of Peover. School: Northwich (Mr. Allen). Adm. sub-sizar, Trinity College, 1713; B.A., 1717; M.A., 1720. Ordained deacon, 1717.

John Bertles, son of Edward, of Knutsford. School: Northwich (Mr Allen). Adm. sub-sizar, Trinity College, 1714; sizar, 1715. Did not matriculate or graduate.

Henry Eaton, son of Henry; born in Cheshire; bred at Northwich. Adm. sizar, St. John's College, 1715. B.A., 1719.

Trinity College, Dublin

Humphrey Barlow, son of Robert. Born Leftwich *c.* 1649. Pupil of Green-halgh. Adm. pensioner, January 1666; Scholar, 1667; B.A., 1669.

Glasgow University

Daniel Lowe, fourth son of Joshua, of the Hulse, an Anglican married to a nonconformist. Born 1699. Entered Glasgow University, 1721; M.A.,

1723. Licensed at Knutsford by Cheshire Classis, 1725. He later kept a
school.

3. *Other known pupils*

Peter Cotton, descended from the Cottons of Cotton. His father had
bought a messuage in Witton or Northwich. He himself was an attorney
in Chester.

VII

Controversy: the Finlow case, 1715-27

Much about the running of the school in its first century and a half remains uncertain, but, as a result of lawsuits arising out of deep divisions in the local community, a shaft of light now illuminates many of these earlier obscurities. Not only do these controversies provide welcome evidence about the school in the later seventeenth and early eighteenth centuries, but they raise most of the problems which were to vex the school in the next century and a half. The legal disputes in this period reveal that the controversial points which were to bring about the downfall of the foundation, as hitherto known, in the middle of the nineteenth century were already in existence. The Finlow lawsuits were the first of the three major legal disputes which injured Witton School educationally as well as financially.

Even before the actual disputes arose, some of the feoffees had felt in Allen's time a certain disquiet about some aspects of the conduct of the school. Various pieces of evidence suggest that the moving spirits in this re-thinking were John Partington and, to a lesser extent, John Hewitt: both were elected feoffees in 1707, and it is symbolic of these new brooms sweeping clean that Deane's letter of August 1561 was found in 1708, 'at the bottom of the school chest', by Partington, then bailiff feoffee, after only a year as feoffee. Financially the feoffees felt that their predecessors had not made the most of the school properties, leasing them for three lives at ancient rents. They themselves improved the Larton rent from £1 a year to £12, but considered this to be the limit, 'the same being very poor ground though of a pretty large extent And the building extream old and decayed'. To this more rational rent policy belongs the suggestion in 1714, which came to nothing, to exchange the more distant Larton property for land in Hartford. The rents at Peover and Agden (or more properly Hartford) were not capable of improvement, since they were merely chief rents and the school did not own the lands themselves. The Saracen's Head property was of only limited value, since the feoffees after the Civil War had been

unable to afford to rebuild out of the school revenues. The more
recent feoffees had, however, done their best, and after 1719, when
the last life in the lease ended, they refused to accept the low offers
made and insisted on a tenancy at will. They had indeed doubled the
school rents by comparison with those of the 1680s, and in order
to encourage a master with adequate qualifications they agreed to
pay over to him the residue of the rents (after repairs), out of which
he was to pay an usher. During the lawsuit the feoffees defended
their practice by referring to various recent legal decisions about,
for example, university fellowships, where the fall in the value of
money and the increase in the value of land had been taken into
account: the increased income beyond the original fixed amount
had been awarded to the holder, or, alternatively, the holder had
been allowed to hold another preferment at the same time, in spite of
an original prohibition.[1]

When Allen was master, and possibly stimulated by him, various
feoffees realised that 'several errors and mistakes had been for a
long time committed' in the management of the trust. Stricter
scrutiny arrested 'the indolent pursuit of the steps of predecessors'.
The most prejudicial to the school and its standing were, first, the
'sufferance of an universal freedom from all parts of the world (even
from America)'* whereby for an entrance fee of 4*d* and 1*d* a year
afterwards the school was burdened with remote scholars to the
prejudice of neighbouring families; and, second, 'admitting English
to be taught whereby many were sent in Primmers (if not hornbooks) not in expectation of learning so much as to keep 'em out
of harms way or doing mischief at home'. (This, it must be remembered, was an *ex parte* statement in a dispute.[2])

The teaching of English was felt to be a hindrance to the classics
scholars and a discouragement to a master of academic education.
At Frodsham School a complaint by the master that the attendance
of children unable to spell hindered the teaching of those who could
read English and of the Latin scholars led to an order in 1694 that
no parents should send children unable to read in the Testament.
Deane had made no provision for the teaching of any subjects
besides the classics, mainly Latin. Some grammar schools in their
foundation made special arrangements for teaching subjects such
as writing, ciphering or doing accounts, and for elementary instruction in reading. Other grammar schools—St Paul's and Merchant
Taylors' in the lead, but followed by some smaller schools—required
pupils to read perfectly and to write legibly before admission. John
Brinsley, the famous educationist, writing in 1612, held it a hind-

* Possibly this refers to the children of Thomas Nickson, who had fled to
Pennsylvania for financial reasons.

rance to the attention which should be given to 'our Grammar scholars' to have to teach ABC: 'the very little children in a town, in most country towns which are of any bigness, would require a whole man, of themselves, to be always hearing, posing and following them'. For many country grammar schools, however, it was a counsel of perfection that children should be required to be able to read and write before they were admitted, and, as Brinsley recognised, the task of elementary instruction by the grammar schools had to be 'borne with patience and wisdom, as a heavy burden'.[3]

These anxieties led the majority of the feoffees to decide to lay the school statutes, with a list of queries, before the Bishop of Chester, who was considered to be the proper Visitor of the school, for his direction. Sudden calls to London prevented the bishop, Sir William Dawes, from keeping his appointments to deal with the matter in 1713 and 1714, and he was subsequently translated to the Archbishopric of York in 1714. His successor doubtless had more urgent business to deal with at first in his new diocese, so that it was not until August 1718 that Bishop Gastrell had the evidence before him and 'gave his resolution . . . thereupon in his own handwriting'. Neither the original of the feoffees' queries nor that of the bishop's decision survives in either the school or the diocesan records, but copies of both were submitted as evidence in the later lawsuit, and are of such interest that they are reproduced in full.[4] The queries show signs of a legal mind at work, doubtless that of the dominant feoffee, John Partington (of Staples Inn, London), anxious to resolve every ambiguity in the foundation documents and to have a ruling even on long-established practice. The queries were not wholly legalistic, however; the attempt to vary school hours according to the season was very practical.

1. Whether it be a school universally free to all persons,—Or but to the parishioners of Witton Chapelry—Or only to the single Township of Witton,—Or barely to the founder's relations:—And if it be not free in generall:—(as it has been esteemed to be for above eighty years last past, and for ought we can find to the contrary ever since the foundation,)—Whether the Master by his own authority may & ought to refuse or expell such as have not a freedom,—or who else may do it?

2. Whether any Scholar ought to be admitted or taught in English, or if he be not in the Accidence, altho' he be 6 years of age:—And whether all English scholars,—(Who for ought we know have been taught ever since the school was founded, we are sure for above eighty years,) are to be expelled,—And by whom?

3. Whether the right of election or presentation of a Master be not in all the Parishioners of Witton Chapelry, in conjunction with the feoffees,—And not in the feoffees alone,— (tho' the practice for above

eighty years has gone along with thcm alone, and perhaps from the
founder's death,)—And whether the choice of a Master by them alone
be justifyable & valid?

4. Whether it be essentially necessary, that the Schoolmaster of Chester,
and the Parishioners of the Chapelry do joyn with the feoffees in
admission of a Master, If it be; the charge will imp* his sallary very
much, And we don't find it has been practised these eighty years, if
ever?

5. Whether the right of appointment of an usher,—And of the disposition
of the surplus of the school-rents, after payment of twelve pounds per
annum to the Master for his sallary, be not solely in the Wardens of
Witton Chapelry,—Who doubtless were meant by the founder, tho' he
stiles 'em Church-wardens of Northwich,—for in strictness, there being
no such Church as Northwich Church, there can be no such Churchwardens, for the true stile is, the Parochial Chapel of St. Helen in
Witton, whereof Northwich is only one quarter, division or member
out of four, every one whereof yearly elects one Warden, severall of
whom are very often farmers, shopkeepers, & artificers, And 'twill be
great difficulty & expence to get 'em all to meet together on any
business:—And whether the trustees taking upon them—or the Master
upon him,—to put in an Usher,—or the trustees to dispose of the
surplus of the rents,—be not contrary to the foundation: And whether
the Bayliff-feoffees can justify, or ought to pay the Master above
twelve pounds per annum, or even that,—But whatever he receives,
whether that or more; should be conveyed to him thro' the hands of
the Wardens,—Tho' it can't be learn't that at any time for above
one hundred & thirty years last past, they have ever medled either
with the surplus or that sallary,—Or the Parishoners in naming an
usher;—But for that space of time, and probably always before; all has
been done the feoffees only, [sic] or as to the Usher joyntly with the
Master.—And by whome; And for what causes an Usher may be
displaced?

6. Whether a person married,—or one who is not a graduate of Oxford
or Cambridge;—Or under thirty years of age;—may not now be
chosen & admitted Master, learning being vastly improved in much
younger persons, and yet no graduates, since the founder's time;—And
it being very difficult to get a person so qualifyed into a school of so
small a revenue; Or whether a graduate of any other University be
qualifyed,—Or if a Master marry after admission, whether he ought
to be discharged,—Or whether rather the injunction of celibacy in this
case as well as in the clergy, ought not to be esteemed as utterly
abolished since the establishment of the Reformation?

7. Whether frequent preaching be allowable in a Master in holy orders
which some have before; & some take after admission: It being urged

* To 'imp' is to 'add to', strictly, but the *O.E.D.* notes a usage based on
a misunderstanding of the hawking term, and meaning to 'clip'.

by many parents of scholars, & other parishioners, to be an occasion of his absence from, & neglect of the school: And whether in his absence; the usher's teaching the upper scholars, be a sufficient provision that they be taught, supposing the Usher to be fully qualified for it, (which he rarely is,)—seeing the lower scholars may, and very probably must be much neglected thereby: And how, and by whom such neglects (when happening,) are to be reformed:—And by whom a Master may be removed upon just cause appearing?

8. What construction is to be made of the sixth Article of the Statutes, to reconcile—recreation, with reasonable occasions, & urgent business?

9.*Whether the direction,—that the Chatechism (which is wrote Catechisma in the Latin,) shall be read in the school,—and then the Accidence;—does not amount to an indication of the founder's intention that an English Catechism should be taught, And by inference from thence an English Primmer. (tho' the Statutes are only, to use it in the Church—And some select parts of it to be said (not taught) in the school,) for it seems preposterous to suppose; that a Latin catechism should be appointed to be taught before some knowledge of the tongue which is initiated with the Accidence,—And yet it would be much better for the school, if there was no English Scholar in it?

10. Whether a scholar, tho' in Latin, ought to be admitted, if he be under six years of age:—And all under that age now in the school, to be expelled,—And whether by the Master or the trustees, or whom else?

11. Whether the Scholars may be allowed to break up sooner than a week before Christmas & Easter, or at Whitsuntide at all,—the Statutes only appointing the two former festivalls: Yet it has been accustomed for above eighty years, and perhaps from the originall foundation, or founder's death, to break up at Whitsuntide; and much earlier at Christmas & Easter?

12. How far, and how much of the article;—Of Prayers & Prayer-time;—now since the Reformation ought strictly to be observed:—And in regard many scholars come daily a great way out of the country, (As the freedom is now admitted at large;)—whether the Master may not alter the statute—hours of coming to, & going from school, (which are seven in the Morning, & five in the evening thorough the year,) to more commodious times, viz.,—from the tenth of February to the tenth of April, And from the tenth of August to the tenth of October, (being about the equinoctialls,) at the statute hours of seven & five: from the tenth of Aprill to the tenth of August, (being the midst of summer,) to come at six & go at five,—And from the tenth of October

---

* In the margin of each query there are references to the relevant parts of the foundation deeds, and here there is also a reference to 'Dr. Nichols Coment: in Prec. Commun.', i.e. William Nicholls's 'Comment on the Book of Common Prayer', published in 1710.

to the tenth of February, (being the depth of winter,) to come at eight
& go at four?

13. Whether Easter day, & Easter Eve, be not the days meant by Jesus Day,
& Jesus Eve, or what other days are meant thereby?

14. Whether the two Bayliff-Feoffees who are to go out, have any vote in
the election of the succeeding two.—(which has been long practiced,
even so long back as memory can reach,)—Or only the rest, & the
Wardens,—And whether the Wardens votes be essentiall,—for it can't
be remembred that they ever did vote,—And whether the Bayliff-
Feoffees are not strictly bound to accompt yearly,—tho' we don't find
any have for these one hundred & thirty years, but only when they go
out:—And if there be an absolute necessity for the Wardens to concern themselves in the trust,—(which few or none have or will, &
many of 'em utterly unfitt for it,)—Can they,—And how, be compelled
to it?

Answers to Quaeres proposed in relation to Witton School

1. I take the School to be free only to the Township of Witton, Town of
Northwich, & kindred of the founder. The freedom may by a favourable construction be extended to the whole Chapelry, but no farther.

2. No Scholar ought to be admitted under six years of age; It was not the
intention of the founder that the Master of this school should teach
English: And he may refuse to admitt any English Scholar.

3. The Master ought to be chosen, & admitted by the Bishop of Chester
or else by the School-master of the Free School of Chester: this being
the last signification of the Founder's will in his letter dated Aug.
30.An.1561.

4. It is necessary upon the choice of every Master that the School-master
of Chester should be desired to be present at his admission.

5. The right of appointing an usher is not placed in any person by the
Founder, and therefore it most properly belongs to the Master. By
Churchwardens, & Churchwardens of Northwich is certainly meant the
Wardens of the Church or Chapel of Witton. Those two feoffees who
are called Bayliff-Feoffees are to receive the rents, pay the Master his
sallary, and account yearly to the other Feoffees & the Churchwardens
of Witton according to the directions given Stat. 16 & Lett. Art. 7.

6. The person to be chosen Master ought to be unmarried at the time of
his choice, And a graduate of Oxford or Cambridge, and thirty years
of age, if a person so qualifyed can be found, If a Master marrys after
admission I do not see which way he can be discharged, the founder
having given no order or direction in this matter.

7. The Master may be in Holy Orders, and preach, and perform all the
other dutys of a Minister on Sundays & Holydays without any incon-

veniency to his school. And no usher should be taken in who is not fit
to teach the upper schollars. The Master must have a license from
the Bishop and cannot be removed but upon just cause shewn to the
said Bishop, and according to the common methods of proceedings in
such cases.

8. The Master is to be allowed thirty days absence absolutely for recreation or business as he shall see fit.

9. An English Catechism & particularly the Church Catechism ought to
be learnt by all the scholars & repeated in the school to the Master. By
English Primmer is now to be understood the Book of Common Prayer
which every boy ought to bring to Church with him.

10. As to the admission of English Scholars, and such as are under six
years of age: no such should be admitted for the future; but those
that are already in the school may be suffered to stay there.

11. The Scholars should break up a week before Xmas and Easter & no
sooner, and they may be allowed to break up at Whitsuntide; there
being no order to the contrary, and that season being to be recconed
among the holydays upon which by Stat. 12, they are allowed to
refresh themselves.

12. Some short prayer should be said in the school 3. times a day, vizt. at
7. when the scholars first meet in the morning, And at 11. & 5. when
they are dismissed, which hours of meeting & being dismissed should
be kept, the Master having no power to alter them.

13. By Jesus Day I believe is meant Christmas Day.

14. The Bayliff-Feoffees are to be chosen by all the other Feoffees, except
those two who are removed from that office; and the Wardens whose
votes are as necessary as the others. The Bayliff-Feoffees are obliged
to accompt yearly. If the Wardens are unwilling to be concerned in
the trust, there is no need of compelling them, it will be sufficient in
that case for the Bayliff-Feoffees to be chosen by the rest only, And to
accompt to them only without the Wardens.

Certain of the bishop's judgements were extremely relevant as
evidence in the nineteenth-century Chancery suit between Charles
Hand, the master, and the feoffees, particularly those relating to the
'freedom' of the school, the appointment of the usher, and the
teaching of English. Presumably Hand was unaware of their
existence. The feoffees' solicitors certainly knew of the Finlow
case, since they had copies made of a number of the documents
involved, one of which recited the bishop's replies, but possibly they
did not find this particular document, of which there is no copy
in the school records: it would in any case have been very inapposite
for their clients, though the evidence of the practice of the school
in the *Quaeres* might have encouraged them.

Some of the queries are especially interesting for the light they throw on the past history of the school, or at least what the feoffees about 1718 believed to have been the practice of the previous eighty years. They believed that the school's 'freedom' had been unrestricted, possibly since the foundation, in itself a remarkable state of affairs, and at variance with the implication of the concession to George Venables in 1658. There is a strong contrast with the school at Audlem, where the freedom was restricted to the parishioners, and that at Acton where it was even further limited, to ten boys. Furthermore, the feoffees were sure that there had been English scholars at the school for more than eighty years, taking it back before the Civil War, and as a corollary to this they admitted that the usher was rarely qualified to teach the upper or classical scholars. The bishop stood out for all the requirements for a master laid down by John Deane—age, degree and celibacy (at least on appointment)—'if a person so qualifyed can be found', and also for an usher 'fit to teach the upper scholars', but he could not, of course, solve the school's financial problems, which made his direction a counsel of perfection. The school's problems had thus been aired before the actual crisis occurred.

After Allen's departure before Christmas 1715 the usher, Thomas Finlow, was promoted to the mastership despite his meagre qualifications. The foffees' certificate to the bishop of his election and the promise to submit him for examination, signed by nine of them and dated January 1716, described him only as 'Gentleman', 'whom we take and believe to be a true and sincere member of the Church of England, As by Law established', though they later maintained that he had 'the character of a good scholar'. This attachment to the Church of England was further proved by the accompanying sacrament certificate required under the Test Act of 1673—a piece of parchment signed by Robert Baxter, minister,* and the churchwardens of Great Budworth, certifying that Finlow 'upon the Lord's Day commonly call'd Sunday, being the first day of January 1715 [i.e. 1715/16] imediately after Divine Service and Sermon, did in the Parish Church aforesaid receive the Sacrament of the Lord's Supper according to the usage of the Church of England'. These attestations served to secure the approval of the bishop and Charles Henchman, the master of the Free School at Chester, and a licence from the bishop.[5]

In his subsequent vindication of himself Finlow maintained that 'for these four score or very many years now last past no master could be gotten for this school who was a graduate of Oxford or Cambridge and thirty years of age and unmarried but he would

* Presumably the curate, since Charles Henchman was vicar from 1700.

III Certificate of recommendation of Aaron Nichols to the Bishop of Chester, 1696, with some of the signatures; from the Chester diocesan records in the Cheshire County Record Office

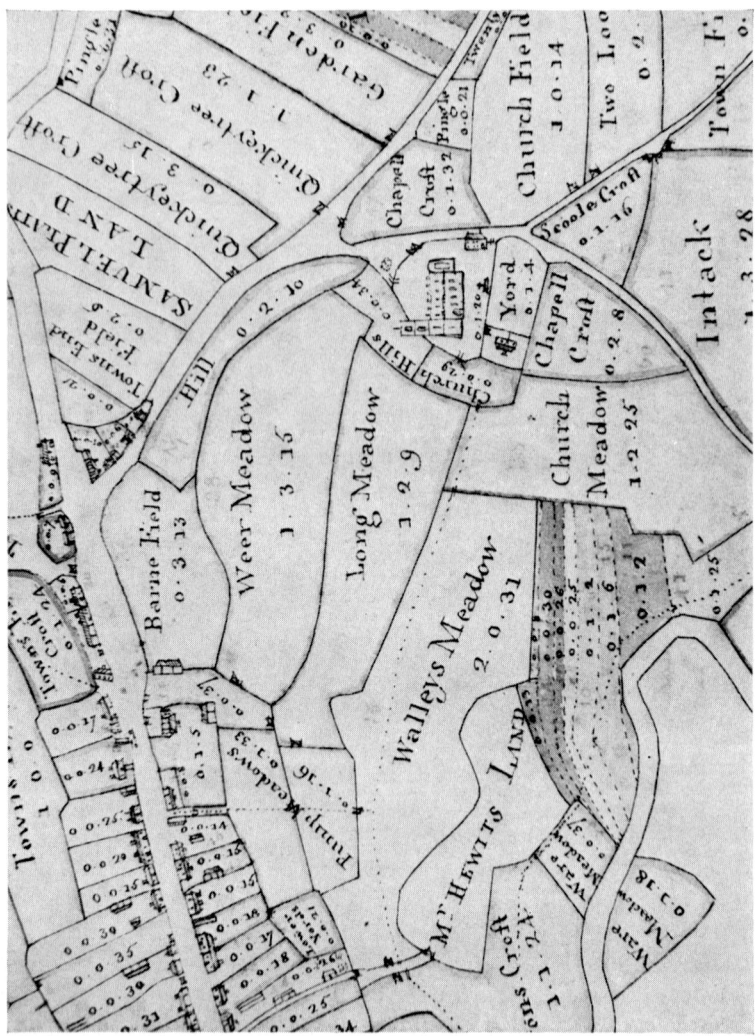

IV Witton Chapel and the first school: detail from a map of the manor of Witton, 1721 (attested copy, 1829), in the Brunner Library, Northwich. For a discussion of this map and the site of the first school see appendix IV

have been wanting in some or one of those qualifications'. Unlike Allen, however, Finlow was lacking in the academic qualifications, and even on his own showing they were thin. The son of Thomas Finlow of Congleton, he was at school at Macclesfield, and entered Trinity College, Cambridge, Allen's college, on 29 March 1714, at the age of twenty as a sub-sizar: there he neither matriculated nor graduated. In his own words he 'had been a considerable time entered in Trinity College Cambridge and had kept several terms there and had been there resident every time he went thither by the space of a month and upwards and once was there above three months together'.[6] Since he was being paid as usher at Witton from Michaelmas 1712, these terms must have been fitted into his teaching year, and indeed after he became master the feoffees gave him leave to go up to Cambridge. The accounts contain regular payments to Finlow as master from Michaelmas 1715 to Lady Day 1718, at the rate of £16 a year, with a further payment of £1 15s 5d out of Peter Cotton's bequest.

Finlow later stated that at his appointment promises were made of a union of the curacy and the mastership at Witton in the event of a vacancy at the chapel: in the meantime he preached there occasionally in 1716 and 1717.[7] The situation changed completely at the end of 1718 with the death, after forty-three years at the chapel, of the aged curate, John Fishwick, which touched off a feud in Northwich society. According to Finlow, when Fishwick was grown 'very ancient and weak and low of voice' many of the inhabitants of the chapelry asked Finlow to officiate, and proposed to secure an allowance for him from Fishwick. Failing in this, they then sought to raise the sum by subscription, and for about two months before Fishwick's death in December 1718 Finlow officiated at the chapel, but without any payment. He was then, so he affirmed, backed for the curacy by 'the far greatest part of the Gentlemen and of the most sufficient persons of estates and ability in the chapelry', and for at least a fortnight no rival appeared. Then, however, 'some few' of the parishioners encouraged Robert Horrobin to stand. Horrobin had been curate at Great Budworth in 1704, had moved on to be curate at Warrington, but was at the time without a place. At a public election by popular vote in Witton Chapel he was elected preaching minister or curate,* but his candidature met with opposition from the vicar of Great Budworth, the influential Charles Henchman, master of the King's School, Chester, prebendary of Chester Cathedral and rector of Alderley as well.[8]

Henchman opposed the churchwardens' claim that the parish-

---

* According to Horrobin he had a majority above eight times as many as Finlow. (*C.D. Recs.*, EDP 305/5.)

ioners had the right to choose the curate in a case in the Consistory Court at Chester. It is undoubtedly for this case that a paper still in the diocesan records entitled 'The Inhabitants of Witton, Case that Witton Chapel is a Parochiall Chapell within Great Budworth Parish' was produced. This argued that the inhabitants had 'time out of mind' elected their own minister, whom the bishop had then licensed, and produced evidence from John Maddock, aged eighty-four, who had been a chapel warden over sixty years earlier, and had been present at the elections of Thomas Pigott and Fishwick. Henchman, they claimed, was pretending to a right not claimed by any of his predecessors at Budworth, 'wherefore Mr. Henchman is supposed to have more judgment or greater pride' than them. Bishop Gastrell declared for Henchman and licensed Finlow as curate at Witton in August 1719—a significant date in the history of the chapel, since it marked the end of the parishioners' voice in choosing their minister.* In 1811 the curate, answering a questionnaire from the bishop, stated that Witton's curates, or rather occasional ministers, were furnished from Great Budworth 'till such a time as a Subscription was entered into by the Inhabitants of the Chapelry towards the maintenance of a resident and what was then termed preaching Minister'. The communal support represented by salt rights had dwindled by 1663 to £2 10s, and by about 1720 the surplice fees, Easter dues and the rent of a poor cottage in Northwich were all the certain provision for the minister, and the financial basis of the parishioners' rights had thus decayed. These rights had been exercised in association with the right of the Barons of Kinderton, and it may be significant that the choice of curate on Fishwick's death was the first to be made after the ending of the male line of Venables of Kinderton in 1679, and indeed after the death of the direct female heir, the Countess of Abingdon, in 1715. The chapel wardens were said by their opponents to have brought a Bill in the Exchequer Court in Chester against Finlow and Henchman in the name of Horrobin, which for lack of substance never came to a hearing.[9]

Finlow had thus incurred the hostility of a vocal section of opinion in Northwich and Witton, led by one of the chapel wardens, Ralph Higginson, the son of Samuel Higginson, clerk, a former master. It was later said that Finlow's enemies, having failed to dislodge him from the curacy, turned their attention to the school. It was Finlow's misfortune that just at the time of the crisis in the chapelry, between Michaelmas and Christmas 1718, his usher, John Simcock, a man of twenty-three, left to become master of a school

---

* An attempt was made to revive it in 1739–40, but without success. (Weston, *N.P.C.*, p. 47.)

near Neston. Simcock, though born at Middlewich, had been at Finlow's old school, Macclesfield, and, like Finlow, was entered at a Cambridge college. Unlike Finlow, however, Simcock matriculated in 1717 (the year of his admission), although he went no further: he was nevertheless more highly qualified than the master, and was held by the feoffees to be fitted to teach the highest scholars in the school in Finlow's absence. After the loss of Simcock the position deteriorated further: Thomas Finlow had to look after the whole school, 'wherein have been most commonly if not constantly . . . about sixty scholars or upwards', with only the help of his brother George, the upper or head scholar, most reliably estimated to have been fifteen or sixteen. Finlow was said by his defenders to take care of the Latin and Greek scholars, while his brother was 'chiefly if not wholly employed in hearing the pettys or English scholars', without any title or salary or 'allowance to give correction'. It was clearly an unsatisfactory situation, which Finlow's opponents made the most of, accusing him of being absent sometimes four days in a week, while he claimed only to have left the school to his brother on one day when he went to a friend's funeral twelve miles away.[10]

This irregular position was ended when Finlow (according to himself, as soon as he could) secured Thomas Cottrell as usher. He recommended him to the bishop as a 'person of orthodox principles and good morals': no other qualifications were put forward, but Cottrell was thereupon licensed by the bishop in August 1719, a licence which he exhibited at the visitation of 1725.[11] Finlow had thus regularised the position, but only after almost a year. Ralph Higginson of Hartford and his associates, the chapel wardens, put forward in October 1719 an alternative candidate as usher, Thomas Wright, 'a determined* Bachellor of Arts of Hart Hall Oxford'. Their proposal came too late, and, thwarted in a direct intervention in the school's affairs, they took the battle into the law courts. They gained the support of sixty or seventy people in the chapelry, including three of the feoffees, (Nathaniel Leftwich, Ralph Nickson and Thomas Done) and with this financial backing instigated a suit against Finlow and the feoffees in the Exchequer Court at Chester in December 1719. They had indeed a legitimate case in that Finlow patently did not fulfil the statutory requirements about age and degree, but they bolstered their case by dubious statements that Finlow was related to some of the feoffees (later he was said to be only a friend), that the feoffees had

---

* I.e. already a B.A. 'Determination' was the name of certain disputations (in which the candidate resolved a question, *determinare quaestionem*, or maintained a thesis) which completed the taking of the degree of B.A.

dcnied that Deane founded the school or made statutes, and that there were gifts of considerable yearly values which made up the schoolmaster's £12 to 'a considerable income for a country school'.[12]

The relators'* charges against Finlow as master were of negligence and absence, failing to teach the statutory authors, refusing to admit children of inhabitants of the age of six if their parents were poor or if he disliked them, and causing the decay of the school, since various inhabitants had to send their sons to other grammar schools. The charges against the feoffees (especially Partington) were primarily of failing to consult the wardens in the appointment of the master and usher and in the disposal of the surplus over £12, failing to account financially to them, and, of course, appointing an unqualified master. The relators were above all anxious to assert the wardens' 'rights' mentioned in the foundation documents, particularly their 'right' to use the surplus income to pay an usher. According to the defendants, Higginson and his party were actuated by spite against Finlow for his victory over the curacy, and were bent on ousting him from the school or, failing that, either on reducing his salary to the statutory £12 or so ruining the school by the costs of the suit that his post would be of little value. They also accused the relators of designs on the school's curriculum; of wishing to use the revenue over £12 to pay an usher 'who they will oblige to teach English in the said school or if they cannot bring that to bear, that they will apply it for his teaching of English scholars in some other place in the said chapelry'. This, they maintained, would be the end of Witton School, which was, in their view, intended as a grammar school and for the teaching of Latin and Greek and the learned languages. It seems that there may have been matters of principle as well as of personality at issue, but the defendants were not in a strong position, having appointed an academically unqualified master.

Finlow counter-attacked by bringing a cross-suit against his accusers in the same court,[13] but he also rebutted the charges of negligence and claimed to have taught all 'the most celebrated and usual' of the prescribed authors, though he had omitted some as not being in use in other schools. His arguments about his qualifications were feeble, consisting chiefly in the contention that 'young gentlemen and other persons who have not taken any degree or been of any University are better qualified to teach a Grammar School and are greater critics in the Latin and Greek Languages and the Classic authors now at one or two and twenty than most in the universities in that age were at four or five and thirty years old'. Both he

* A relator was one who supplied materials for an information by the Attorney General.

and the feoffees, however, had a valid point when they emphasised the difficulty of getting a strictly qualified master for the salary
offered at Witton. The feoffees were doubtful whether there had
been an Oxford or Cambridge graduate for sixty or eighty years
before Allen, though they admitted that there had been Glasgow
graduates: but in this they were exaggerating and ignoring such
masters as Greenhalgh, Steward, Woodnoth and Gerard Deane.
They repeated the arguments used to the bishop earlier on the
master's salary. The wardens' claim to interfere they denied, except
in restricted matters such as making the accounts and admitting the
master, and they argued that the rights given to them in the
schedule and the statutes had been superseded by the arrangements in Deane's later letter. On one thing, nevertheless, both
accusers and defenders agreed: for whatever reason, whether malice
or justifiable indignation, some parents had sent their boys to school
elsewhere,* notwithstanding Finlow's assertion that there were
'now as many or more scholars than when Mr. Allen left it'.[14]

Worse was to follow, for Finlow did not stay the course of litigation long, dying in November 1720 at the age of about twenty-six.[15]
In spite of the legal processes set in motion, seven of the feoffees, on
the direction of the Bishop of Chester, met on 1 December 1720 to
choose a new master. John Partington's description of the proceedings in a letter of 12 December to the bishop reveals strikingly the
pitch which the local conflict had reached. Partington reported that,
by four votes to three, the trustees had chosen as master the Rev.
Thomas Spencer, then master at Lymm and curate of a mediety
there. Spencer had all three required qualifications, being over
thirty, a graduate of Cambridge, and unmarried, to the extent of
being a widower. His opponent, Thomas Wright, who had figured
in the competition for the ushership, was under thirty and married.
There is a hint of some other, possibly political, division involved
when Partington reminded Bishop Gastrell that Wright had been
'Capt. Warburton's Chaplain last year at Winington', and that his
interest was supported 'by that party'. On Partington's showing,
Wright's supporters descended to a low trick, temporarily winning
over one of his four opponents by bribery: the feoffee, Ralph
Broome, of Middlewich, was instructed to say that 'he was obliged
to it by a gentleman who was Mr. Wright's friend to whom he was
engaged by many strong tyes', but it emerged on the morning of
the meeting that 'the gentleman who had such a powerfull
influence was a noat under Mr. Wright's hand, and all of his own
writing, except the testimonial and witness, for paying him ten
guineas'. When the plot fell through, it caused 'a strange surprise

* E.g. John Tovey, who sent his son to Allen at Peover.

and mortification to Mr. Wright and his friends, particularly to
your Lordship's old acquaintances Mr. Higginson, who demanded
the votes of all the inhabitants (of whom he had mustered up a
considerable body) to be taken'. When Partington refused this,
Higginson made threats, and the prospect of a further lawsuit
alarmed Spencer, who was 'of a pacific temper' and reluctant to
enter upon such a controversial post. Higginson even went to
Chester to enter a *caveat* against the granting of a licence to
Spencer, but in the event Spencer remained at Lymm until 1753,
and is known to have sent two boys to St John's College, Cambridge,
during the 1720s.[16] The matter of the curacy was settled soon after
Finlow's death with the appointment of William Bradshaw on the
nomination of the vicar of Great Budworth, but the school's affairs
were not settled so quickly, and the usher, Thomas Cottrell, had
the entire burden of some sixty pupils at very varying stages. In 1724
he was reduced to appealing to the Exchequer Court for payment
of the arrears of his salary.[17]

It might have been thought that with the death of Finlow the lawsuits would have stopped and the school would have returned to
normal, but the feoffees were also defendants and the legal mills
continued to grind. Objections and technical insufficiencies delayed
the case until October 1721, when, to save expense, since it concerned a charity, it was referred to two arbitrators, John Williams
of Chester and Edward Blundell of Prescott, who before June 1722
were to file their award, which the court would then confirm unless
good cause was shown to the contrary. For nearly a year the arbitrators did nothing, partly owing to the illness of Williams, and the
school was going downhill 'to the great loss and detriment as well
for the persons inhabiting in the said neighbourhood as others and
their children'. The court, therefore, in September 1722, while
extending the time for arbitration, took the stop-gap measure of
appointing Charles Cholmondeley of Vale Royal to nominate a
master, at a salary of £20, to act until the hearing of the case. A
temporary post of unpredictable duration at such a salary was
hardly very attractive, and six months later (in February 1723) it
emerged that neither the arbitrators (one of whom, Blundell, had
died) nor Cholmondeley had acted. Partington refused to agree to
the continuation of the arbitration; Cholmondeley was urged to
appoint; and the various parties to the case were required to complete their Bills and Answers. By June 1724 the relators, acting on
permission given over two years before, had at last amended their
Bill by including the Bishop of Chester as a defendant, but had
failed to serve him with a proper letter. It is scarcely surprising after
this rather suspect dilatoriness (attributed by the defendants to loss

of financial backing) to find that on the death of Bishop Gastrell in 1725 the relators were advised by their counsel not to proceed further with the case. In February 1726 the court ordered the case to be dismissed, the defendants discharged from any further attendance at the court, and that, as the case was to settle a charity, no costs were to be paid by either party.[18] The whole conflict had ended inconclusively; not one of the problems ventilated in the course of the suits had been solved, and to this barren end a good seven years of the school's life had been sacrificed.

VIII

Mid-eighteenth-century developments, 1727–86

Northwich in the eighteenth century

This was a century of economic expansion for Northwich and its immediate neighbourhood. In 1721, after a struggle lasting more than twenty years, the Weaver Navigation Act had been passed by Parliament and the promoters were free to implement its proposals for making the Weaver navigable from Frodsham Bridge to Winsford, and Witton Brook as far as Witton Bridge. The recording of boats, cargoes and tolls began in 1732, and by the 'fifties the Navigation was beginning to show a substantial profit. Numerous locks had been made by 1742 and the river was navigable to Winsford, but after 1760 large outlays on repairs were necessary, which had to be met by borrowing. Among the subscribers to Navigation loans between 1760 and 1762 were a number of men who figure in the school's history: Jonathan Brayne of Northwich (on a large scale), Sir Peter Leicester and Joseph Hadfield of Tabley, clerk. Further borrowing of over £10,000 was required in 1779, much of which came from salt proprietors and others of Northwich, among them Peter Bradburne, Thomas Marshall, William Thearsby, surgeon, and John Furey, merchant, of Winnington, all but one feoffees. By 1787 all the money had been repaid, for in spite of competition after 1778 from the new Trent–Mersey canal, the Weaver Navigation was producing by the 'nineties a remarkably increased yield of tonnage dues which reflected the expansion of the salt industry. Between 1747 and 1777 shipments of rock salt down river were almost quadrupled and white salt shipments almost doubled. In 1810 it was said that the quantity of salt made at Northwich had doubled in the last ten years, and that there were ten or twelve rock salt pits worked in the neighbourhood in the townships of Witton, Marston and Wincham.[1]

This expansion had repercussions on the general prosperity of the town: 'the market', according to the same author, 'has of late years become very considerable in consequence of the increased population occasioned by the extension of the salt trade'. The fairs in

August and September lasted nearly a fortnight each, and among their commodities were Yorkshire and Manchester goods. A description of the chapelry in 1778 singled out for mention 'several merchants and tradesmen of independent fortunes', and in 1811 they figured as 'opulent merchants and proprietors of salt works', living in 'modern' houses. In 1787 W. Tunnicliffe, land surveyor, in his *Topographical Survey of Cheshire*, listed seven principal merchants in Northwich, of whom three were school feoffees: they were Peter Bancroft, John Blackburn, John Cheshire, Richard Kent and John Mort, merchants and salt proprietors, and Edward Lowe and Thomas Marshall, merchants.[2] There is evidence, too, of the expansion of the local population. The census of 1801 recorded 859 families in Witton chapelry, an increase on the 831 families reported to the bishop by the curate in 1778. Reliable comparisons are possible after 1801: in 1801 the population of the chapelry was 4,376 (including 1,531 in Witton and 1,338 in Northwich); in 1811 the total was 5,194 (1,966 in Witton and 1,382 in Northwich), and by 1821 the total was 6,181 (2,405 in Witton and 1,490 in Northwich). As early as 1775 Thomas Marshall, a school feoffee, had built his New Street houses, the earliest example in Northwich of tightly packed industrial housing.[3]

The school thus had as its background an expanding community, but a certain financial instability continued to be a feature of the area, doubtless as an accompaniment of the expansion of the salt industry. Since charity money was still lent out on bond to individuals for much of this period, the instability had its effects on the prosperity of charitable institutions. The churchwardens of Great Budworth, who lent £400 from the 'Poor's stock', and the trustees of the school there who lent £100 to the Weaver Navigation were fortunate in their investment, but individual borrowers were less reliable. The churchwardens and schoolmaster of Church Minshull had recourse to law in 1725 to recover £100, the loss of which was allegedly due to the bankruptcy of Ralph Broom and the death, insolvent, of Thomas Neild. Thomas Farmer's money was the most vulnerable of Witton School's assets: as early as 1725 the feoffees declared that most of the principal had been lost many years earlier by bad securities on small loans, and that 'the greater part of the remainder is or lately has been very hazardous'. Farmer's legacy finally disappeared when 'a Mr Livesay,* who died insolvent in 1746 gott the money and no part of it was ever repaid'.[4]

* Probably Robert Livesey of Northwich, esq., a school feoffee. Witton parish register records the burial on 1 April 1746 of Robert 'Livesley' of Northwich, 'Counseler at Law', and in a new school feoffment of 7 April the last-named of the dead trustees was Robert Livesey, gentleman.

The school was not alone in suffering in this way. When in 1836 the Charity Commissioners investigated the charities of Northwich and district they listed a number of 'lost charities'. A book of accounts relating to benefactions to the poor of the chapelry of Witton and for the benefit of the preaching minister had come to light in 1830, after having been missing for many years. The Charity Commissioners commented, 'the abstraction of this book from the parish chest, accompanied or followed, by the total loss of the charity money, which appears by the accounts to have been lent on bond to different persons in the town and neighbourhood, is a circumstance calculated to excite suspicion of gross misconduct'.

One of the great collapses which reduced the charity money of the chapelry was that of John Barrow, a school feoffee, in the middle of the century. He owned land, mines and salt springs in Wincham, Pickmere, Northwich and Witton, but was decreed bankrupt in 1767 with debts of £16,000. Among his creditors were Lord Vernon, Sir Peter Warburton, the Rev. John Eccles and other names connected with the school such as Hewitt, Chantler, Cheney and Done. Ralph Higginson, merchant, of Northwich, a school feoffee from 1746, was involved in bankruptcy in 1750, while the same fate befell the prominent Northwich family of Mort-Wakefield in 1803, when its members were unable to pay the enormous salt taxes within the stipulated time: John Mort (from 1784) and Jonadab Mort (from 1793) were both school feoffees. A later bankruptcy which critically affected the school was that of Thomas Chantler, feoffee from 1793 and treasurer of the Weaver trustees from the same year.[5]

Various changes took place in this century among the local manorial lords. The manor of Northwich was sold in 1784 by the Earl of Derby to John Mort, one of the principal merchants and salt proprietors and the former lessee from the earl of the market tolls. It passed by marriage to Thomas Wakefield of Witton and from him to a Liverpool banker named Heywood. The manor of Winnington had passed from the Warburtons by the marriage, in 1765, of an heiress to Richard Pennant, who had done much to develop the slate trade of Wales. He had been M.P. for Liverpool, and in 1783 was created Lord Penrhyn: he was indeed, as the curate recorded in his return of 1778, 'the most considerable person resident in the Chapelry', and, not unnaturally, became in 1767 a school feoffee. After his death in 1808 his widow sold the manor to Sir John Stanley of Alderley, who resided there only occasionally. The most important change, however, from the school's point of view was in the manor of Witton. It had passed after the death of the Countess of Abingdon in 1715 to the Vernons of Sudbury in Derbyshire, connections by marriage of the Venables, but in 1757 George Venables Vernon, later Lord Vernon, sold it to Sir Peter Leicester of Tabley. Combining the lordship of the manor with the patronage of Witton Chapel, the Leicesters (later the Fleming Leicesters) exercised considerable influence in the district until the great sale of their property, including the advowson, in 1828.[6]

The Leicester influence was particularly marked in the chapel, so closely connected with the school. The vicar of Great Budworth did not retain his control long. In 1722, in return for an augmentation of the living, Mr Vernon of Middlewich, who paid £200 into Queen Anne's Bounty Office, secured the patronage from the vicar and the Dean and Chapter of Christ Church, and it subsequently passed to the Leicesters. In 1768 Sir Peter Leicester presented Joseph Hadfield to the curacy of the chapel, and the Leicester influence at Witton was reinforced when Joseph's brother, William, was appointed schoolmaster in 1770.* Although in 1770 Joseph Hadfield had advanced a further £200 to entitle Witton Chapel to a second bounty, the cure was still by no means a good one. The curate's stipend in 1778 averaged only about £45 a year, and there was still no parsonage house. It is not surprising that in the later eighteenth and early nineteenth centuries the incumbent held a living elsewhere and put in an assistant curate. In 1771 Joseph Hadfield was presented to the living of Knutsford by Samuel Egerton, but he reported to the bishop in 1778 that his brother, who did no other clerical duty, acted as curate at Witton, receiving from him a salary of £35 or £36 a year. The extent of the Leicester influence in Witton was revealed at the death of Joseph Hadfield in 1785. At Tabley House there is a copy signed by William Cragg of minutes of conditions under which the livings of Peover and Witton Chapels were given:

4 December 1785 Memorandum that I was present by and did hear Mr. Tomkinson of Bostock in the Breakfast room at Tabley tell the Revd. Mr. Steel of Peover that Sir John Leicester had nominated and given him the living of Peover Chappel—during pleasure. That Sir John had a friend in contemplation and that he might want it in 4–5 or 6 years . . .

5 December I was present by and did hear Mr. Tomkinson deliver to the Revd. Mr. Hadfield (at the Crown Inn in Northwich) the living of Witton Chappel upon the same terms as Peover Chappel is above mentioned to be given to Mr. Steel. That Mr. Hadfield accepted it with kindness and gratitude and said he wou'd resign it whenever Sir John Leicester required him.

* According to Weston (*N.P.C.*, p. 75), Joseph Hadfield married into the Leicester family.

There followed in rapid succession the death of William Hadfield in 1786 after his appointment of a curate of whom the bishop disapproved, the bishop's nomination of a curate through a misunderstanding, and a fresh nomination on the Leicesters' instructions. In 1787 a new incumbent, John Torre, M.A., was presented by Sir John Fleming Leicester; by 1811 he resided elsewhere, near Beverley, and put in a curate, George Okell, who competed with a curate at Great Budworth, similarly placed, for the fees for solemnising marriages.[7]

Meanwhile the nonconformist elements in the chapelry, which had figured largely in the seventeenth-century history of the school, declined socially and numerically. The Presbyterian meeting house, established in 1722,* where John Partington had ministered, was still in existence in 1778, and there were then said to be 'a few Presbyterians', 'but none of fortune or consequence'. The meeting had apparently broken up about 1759, and for a time the Wesleyans used the chapel, but the succession of Presbyterian ministers was resumed, and under Job Wilson (1795–1838) there was some revival. A new chapel was opened in 1806, and in 1811 forty-five families of the chapelry were reported by the curate as 'embracing Calvinistic doctrines'. These, however, were stationary in numbers while the Methodists were on the increase. In 1778 the Methodists, including also none of fortune or consequence, were said to attend the church almost as constantly as the conventicle, but there was already a Meeting House in the town, in the township of Leftwich and strictly in the parish of Davenham. By 1811 there were 124 families converted to Methodism of the 'Westlian' persuasion, as Okell wrote it, and a Methodist Sunday School with 653 children.[8]

The second school and the ordained master

The school returned to normal in 1727 with the installation of a new master, Samuel Harrison, in a ceremony which marked the reconciliation between the feoffees and the churchwardens: in the accounts of the latter, one warden recorded 9d spent at John Jeffrye's 'after wee with the feoffees had given Mr. Harrison possession of the school'. None of the problems had been solved, but a letter to the bishop and schoolmaster of Chester from eight of the nine surviving trustees (dated 9 September 1727) reveals the nature of the compromise over the letter of the statutes. The feoffees

* Witton parish registers refer to children being baptised there in 1723, 1725 and 1728.

with most humble thanks and great alacrity and joy after near seven years vacancy, do hereby, so far as in us lyes, testify our approbation of the Reverend Mr Samuel Harrison to be Master . . . entirely relying upon it for our security against objections and for our future guide, that in regard he stands recommended by your Lordship, it is your Lordship's judgment that the qualification required by the founder's statutes, of the person to be admitted Master to be then thirty years of age at the least, may now be dispensed with, in consideration of the great difference there is in learning betwixt the present age and that of the founder.[9]

It is inconceivable that the feoffees did not start their records of accounts afresh at this time. They may even have begun to record minutes, for very rough notes of a meeting in August 1765 survive. But, whatever records were kept between 1727 and 1784, all trace of them had disappeared as early as 1811, and only discontinuous pieces of evidence survive for that half-century. The rapid succession of masters in the middle of the century, on which the record is fullest, gives a rather unsatisfactory picture of the school's condition, but this is somewhat counter-balanced by the evidence of vitality shown in the erection of a new school building about 1747. The dominant feoffee for twenty years, John Partington, survived until 1729. During the 'thirties and 'forties Sir George Warburton of Arley and George Venables Vernon of Sudbury were among the feoffees, but the management of the school seems to have lain with a group of men in Northwich and district. Prominent among them were Ralph Barrow and John Done in the 'forties, and John Barrow in the 'fifties and 'sixties. Jonathan Brayne, clerk to the Weaver trustees and treasurer of the tonnage dues from 1761, and his son, Thomas Ives Brayne, who succeeded him in 1767, were also to the fore in the school management. At the end of this period there is some evidence of rivalry between the school feoffees and the lord of Witton Manor, Sir John Fleming Leicester. In February 1786 a memorandum taken from William Hadfield, curate and master at Witton, included the statement that 'he has great reason to think that Mr. Brayne [Thomas Ives Brayne] and the feoffees of the School wish to get the sole power of the management of it into their hands and also the nomination of the Church*'.[10]

Relations between the school and the lord of the manor were strained soon after Sir Peter Leicester acquired the property. In his account of the school properties in 1718 John Partington had pointed out that the master's house, garden and croft were held of the Baron of Kinderton's heirs only by courtesy and without any

---

* The memorandum has 'the School' written above 'the Church' but the words are crossed out.

deed or lease. In 1765 the feoffees learned that Sir Peter Leicester was insisting on his sole right to the school house croft, and intending to serve ejectments immediately to recover possession. In their legally hopeless position the feoffees decided to submit to Sir Peter's generosity. This generosity seems to have been only limited, for Sir Peter gave part of the croft (on which no building is mentioned) to enlarge the chapel yard, leasing the remainder to the feoffees in 1766 for twenty-one years, solely for the benefit of the headmaster. In 1790 Sir Peter's son, Sir John Fleming Leicester, leased to the trustees the remainder of the croft, about a quarter of an acre, lying on the south side of the chapel yard, for use as a garden by the headmaster, who already held it. The lease was for twenty-one years, but the needs of the churchyard again took precedence over those of the school, for in 1802–3 Sir John presented the garden to the chapelry to enlarge the graveyard. A few years later the inhabitants of the chapelry compensated the trustees by a payment of just over £50, and they in turn gave the headmaster about £35 for the loss of his fruit trees.[11]

The school was indeed paying the price of its traditional site close to the chapel, and the position was not improved when a new school building was put up about 1747.* This seems to be a welcome sign of vitality and of local interest in the school, but unfortunately there is scarcely any contemporary record of it. Only a nineteenth-century copy, said to be of the original order of the feoffees and churchwardens for completing the school, exists. The original, though not included in any schedule of school papers before 1834, was apparently discovered in the school muniment chest during a search for material to support the trustees' case in their legal battle with Charles Hand, and was sworn to as evidence in the Chancery case in 1846. According to this document, dated 31 March 1747, the old school had 'by length of time become quite ruinous and decayed', and had been taken down about three years earlier 'in order to be rebuilt'. The inhabitants of the chapelry had raised over £100 and the rebuilding had already begun when it was found that another £80 was needed. Since there was 'now no regular Master belonging to the said school', the chapel wardens and the school feoffees empowered the bailiff feoffees, Ralph Barrow and John Done, to use the school's income for the next two years to complete the building. Confirmation of the genuineness of

---

* There is no basis for the date 1723, which appears on an incised stone outside the present school. The usually accurate Weston was curiously uncertain about the date of rebuilding: he gave 1723 in his history of the parish church (1908) and 1760 in his booklet on the school (1885). The date 1717 was also put forward.

this document comes from the only surviving contemporary evidence, a bond signed by Barton Shuttleworth when he was appointed master in April 1748.* By it Shuttleworth agreed to forego any income accruing to the school for the year ending Lady Day 1749, and in return was allowed to charge fees. The school revenue for that period was to be used to meet the charges incurred by the bailiff feoffees under the order of 1747 to finish the school.[12]

The new school was a stone's throw from the east end of the chapel, on the south side, facing inwards to the churchyard as shown in the Twemlow drawing.† There is some doubt as to whether or not it was on the same site as the original school, and this problem is discussed in appendix IV. Subsequently the school formed part of the eastern boundary of the churchyard, but later enlargements of the churchyard make it uncertain whether the school was originally inside or outside.[13] A drawing, made probably not long before the second school was pulled down in 1869, shows it to have been a pleasant, dignified building of brick with stone quoins, with four large round-topped windows on the ground floor facing west, four square-topped windows above, and a door with a round-headed pediment over which was an empty niche.‡

Since most of the school records for the mid-eighteenth century concern the appointment of masters, the succession can be traced in some detail. Samuel Harrison, who was appointed in 1727, was almost certainly the son of William Harrison of Lyme (Lymm), who graduated from Wadham College, Oxford, at the age of about twenty-three in 1727. He had probably been a pupil of Thomas Spencer at Lymm, and may well have been the master at Lymm Grammar School from 1755 to 1763. If not already in orders (he was described as 'Reverend' by the feoffees and as 'clericus' at the visitation of 1728), he was certainly so by 1733, when at the visitation he produced his 'letters of orders of priesthood' dated 2 August 1731. In 1733, too, he exhibited his licence from the bishop, of September 1727, to 'teach the rudiments of grammar and other good authors'. The only light thrown on Harrison in the school papers reveals disagreement between him and the feoffees: in September 1741, as a result of 'diverse complaints ... made to the said feoffees of irregularityes' committed by him, he entered into a bond of £100 with two of the feoffees (Ralph Barrow and Ralph Cheney, ironmonger, of Northwich) that as long as he was

* Both the order and Shuttleworth's bond have the same error about the founder: in each 'Sir John Dean' appears as 'Knight'.

† See plate V. A photograph in Weston, *N.P.C.*, p. 51, shows the levelling of the site of the second school after its demolition.

‡ See plate VII(*a*).

master he would observe the rules and statutes of the school dili-
gently. The agreement was short-lived, for on 30 October 'the major
part of the feoffees' issued a declaration that

> by negligence and continued remisness (after several admonitions) of the
> Reverend Samuel Harrison, clerk, in not attending his duty as Master of
> the said school and otherwise and for several irregularitys by him com-
> itted contrary to and in breach and contempt of the several statutes, rules
> and orders of the said Free Grammar School . . . We the said feoffees have
> thought it our duty and absolutely necessary to remove the said Samuel
> Harrison from being schoolmaster of the said school.

It is possible that Harrison's shortcomings were connected with
his acting as assistant at Witton Chapel: entries in the parish register
for 1739 were signed by him describing himself as 'curate'.[14]

In their statement, which was sent to the bishop, the feoffees
announced their election of the Rev. Samuel Williamson, late of
Brasenose College, and then of Comberbach, as a person well
qualified according to the statutes. Williamson, the son of John
Williamson of Liverpool, had become an M.A. of Oxford in 1734 at
the age of about twenty-three, so that he was of the statutory age.
On his appointment he bound himself in the sum of £200, that if
he accepted any ecclesiastical preferment with a cure of souls he
would, if so required by the majority of the feoffees, quit the school
within three months. This practice, whereby the master gave security
for his obedience to the regulations, was a device to enable the
governors to expel him if necessary from what was often a freehold
office. At Macclesfield School in 1745 the master gave bonds in the
sum of £5,000, while at Lymm in 1700 and Congleton in 1709 the
sum was £100. By spring 1747, Williamson had apparently left,
perhaps already embarking on the clerical career which made him
rector of Great Barrowby in 1754.[15]

In March 1748 the feoffees were advertising in the Chester newspaper *Adam's Weekly Courant* for a master who was to be a
graduate. The certain profits of the post were said to be £50
a year, besides perquisites, and the feoffees were to meet at the
Angel in Northwich to receive proposals. Details of four candidates
survive, giving their qualifications and recommendations. Richard
Smith of Wellington, aged twenty-three and an Oxford undergraduate twelve months short of being entitled to his degree, was
recommended by the schoolmaster of Newport, on whose sole
recommendation, so the memorandum stated, the head schoolmaster
of Derby had been chosen. But the feoffees did not accept this
testimonial from a master who was described by Boswell as 'a very
diligent good teacher, at the time in high reputation'. (Dr Johnson's

father had applied to the master, Samuel Lea, to have his son admitted as a scholar and assistant at his school, but unsuccessfully, and in later life Lea used to recall that 'he was *very near* having that great man for his scholar'.) Samuel Bardsley, B.A., of University College, Oxford, also twenty-three, was recommended by the Master and Fellows, and had certificates from various clergymen and John Eccles, M.A., Fellow of Brasenose College, was also recommended by his college. But the successful candidate was Barton Shuttleworth, the son of a Middlesex vintner. He had been educated at Rochdale, and was a pensioner and B.A., of St John's College, Cambridge, aged twenty-five, and with a lengthy list of backers, including the vicar of Rochdale.

To all four candidates the feoffees had put forward three proposals: that the school debt should be discharged out of the first profits of the school; that the master was to give a bond to the feoffees for good behaviour and observance of the statutes; and finally that he was to keep an usher to teach English scholars and to allow him £10 a year, 'as usual', such an usher being approved by the majority of the feoffees. All four candidates agreed to these conditions, and Shuttleworth signed 'I chearfully agree'. In April 1748 his bond for £500, beautifully written, was drawn up: oddly it described Sir John Deane as 'Knight', suggesting a real lapse of local tradition* and that the feoffees who confessed, during the Finlow case, that if ever they had read the statutes they 'did not well regard or take much notice of the purport and contents thereof' were not alone. (The error also appears in the bonds of several later masters—Eccles, Jones, Hadfield and Litler.) By way of compensation for foregoing the school's profits for nearly a year to pay for the new building Shuttleworth was to be allowed to charge 'the usuall rates' for teaching Latin scholars until 25 March 1749, a real departure from the terms of the foundation. After that date he was to keep an usher to teach the English scholars 'as of late hath been accustomed'. In spite of the new school building Shuttleworth did not remain long at Witton: indeed, he may not even have been officially installed, for the only evidence for his mastership is the bond, which was conditional on his proving qualified. Later he too followed a clerical career: in 1771 Barton Shuttleworth, A.B., was ordained and licensed, on the nomination of the vicar of Rochdale, to the curacy of Langs.[16]

According to Shuttleworth's bond the usher had to be approved by the feoffees and was paid his £10 by them. Although the usher had probably taught English for a century, the bond is the first formal assertion that this was his function. Williamson's bond had

* Harrison's bond of 1741 correctly described him as 'priest'.

not contained this provision, and the bishop had earlier declared
that no usher should be appointed who was not fit to teach the
upper (that is, classical) scholars. The question arises whether the
parishioners' contribution to the building of the new school had
some connection with this specific requirement. Thomas Cottrell,
the usher chosen by Finlow and responsible for the school during
the lawsuit, did not die until 1739, apparently still in office. No
successor is known from contemporary records until James Boyer,
about 1778, but in 1826 the Rev. George Leigh, then aged eighty-
one, deposed that in his childhood his father was writing-master
at the school, teaching writing and accounts: he himself, when
older, helped his father by teaching reading to the pupils. Leigh Sr.'*
would thus have been teaching in the 'fifties.[17]

The next two masters after Shuttleworth also had brief careers at
Witton. In November 1750 John Eccles of Peover, clerk, signed a
bond similar to Shuttleworth's. Eccles was of local origin, being
the son of Samuel Eccles of Great Budworth; he had been an
applicant at the previous vacancy, and had been presented in 1748
to the curacy of Lower Peover by Sir Peter Leicester. Several papers
relating to Eccles's appointment survive: his nomination of 20
November 1750 was signed by seven of the feoffees, and was sent
to the bishop with a testimonial, signed by the vicar of Great Budworth, the assistant curate of Witton and three others, testifying that
'since his residence amongst us, viz., for two years and upwards,'
Eccles had led 'a pious, sober and regular life'. Finally the master
of the Free School at Chester certified that he found Eccles qualified
to teach 'grammatical and classical learning'. Eccles soon returned
to Brasenose College (of which he was a fellow when appointed at
Witton) and from 1756 was Junior Bursar, moving on eventually
to a college living.[18]

Fresh candidates were under consideration in 1754: among them
were John Tench, a Cambridge B.A. of over thirty, and Henry
Mayer, aged only twenty, who was a year off his degree at Oxford.
The successful candidate was Tench, the son of John Tench of
Nantwich, and educated under Samuel Lea of Newport, Shropshire.
Six feoffees nominated Tench to the bishop in April 1754, and in
the same month the minister of Little Budworth and two inhabitants
of Acton and Nantwich wrote to testify to his ability to teach a
grammar school and to his being well affected to 'our present constitution in Church and State'. (The relevance of this is underlined
by an entry in the Witton churchwardens' accounts recording that

---

* He may have been George Leigh of Northwich, stationer, whose daughter
was baptised at Witton in May 1754 (Par. Reg.): a later writing master, John
Dawson, was a printer.

the church books were buried when the 'rebels' came through Cheshire under the Young Pretender.) Benjamin Nicholls, the Chester schoolmaster, certified that Tench was capable of teaching at Witton Grammar School, and in May 1754 he was licensed by the bishop. The feoffees had made the usual proposals to both candidates: both had agreed, but Tench had added a further pledge— 'I do hereby promise and agree not to officiate or perform any duty as a clergyman in any church or chapel (Sundays and holidays excepted) or engage in any other employment repugnant to the vocation of a schoolmaster'.*[19] This promise focuses attention on a very real problem of schools in this period—that of the ordained master.

After John Bretchgirdle the curacy and the mastership at Witton diverged, though school and chapel were close neighbours. The masters before the Civil War were not, as far as is known, in holy orders: certainly neither Farmer nor Pigott, the two outstanding masters, seems to have been.† One or two of the masters during the Civil War and Interregnum may have been in orders while they were at the school, and certainly several were in later life, but after the Restoration the majority of masters ended as clergymen, and it is with Peter Woodnoth, the master who had to accept a reduction of salary, that the conflict between the roles of clergyman and schoolmaster first appears. The Finlow case touched partly on this, and especially on the master's relation to the curacy of the chapel.

Some schools were more lenient to the ordained master than others. At Sandbach, since the master's salary was inadequate, he often combined this post with that of the curate. At Stockport one of the most successful masters, the Rev. Joseph Dale, master from 1703 to 1752, held concurrently with his mastership the curacy of Chorlton Chapel, of Birch Chapel, of Denton Chapel (at £20 a year), and later, at £40 a year, the curacy of Stockport Church. At Rivington about 1788 the governors used the prospect of a 'curacy in the neighbourhood where duty on Sunday only is required' as an inducement to candidates, and at Winwick many of the masters were occasional curates of the parish, although in the early nineteenth century the school suffered from a master who neglected it in favour of his living of Burtonwood. At Macclesfield the position was precisely stated in the regulations of 1745. If the headmaster was presented to a living of £100 a year and inducted there, he was

* The wording of the statute.
† Cf. Joan Simon, 'Post-Restoration developments', in B. Simon, *Education in Leicestershire, 1540–1940*, p. 51: '... in the earlier seventeenth century there had been a marked trend towards the establishment of teaching as a profession distinct from the Church.'

to resign the school; further, he was not to officiate as curate or
preacher in Macclesfield Church or to do any church offices for the
minister there within school hours, except administering the sacrament to a sick person or private baptism of a child in danger of
death, and then only in the absence of the minister. However, if he
officiated in any chapel out of Macclesfield or on Sundays occasionally exchanged with the Macclesfield minister it was not to be
accounted a breach of this article.[20]

For whatever cause, John Tench resigned from Witton less than
a year after his appointment: he did not, however, desert the teaching profession, for in 1762 he was licensed to the free school of
Davenham, but there he was able to act as curate to the rector.[21]
In April 1755 the feoffees nominated the runner-up at the previous
election, Henry Mayer, who had a Latin testimonial from the Master
and Fellows of Brasenose, among them John Eccles. Mayer, the son
of a Macclesfield gentleman,* had gained his B.A. degree in 1755
at the age of about twenty-one. Although he settled as licensed
master at Witton and seems to have married a daughter of one of
the feoffees, John Jeffreys, he retained his ambitions at Oxford,
and was also ordained in 1757. In March 1758 the clerk to the
governors of Macclesfield School was writing to Lord Fauconberg
(a descendant of the founder of Brasenose) to urge Mayer's claims
to a fellowship, said to be appropriated to those born in Prestbury
parish, which had been given to 'a Cantabrigian and a meer stranger
to the colledge', Egerton Leigh. Mayer's appeal to the Visitor of
the college was successful, and in July 1758 the Visitor ordered his
reception as a fellow. He seems to have held this fellowship concurrently with his post at Witton, where he was recorded as master
at the Visitations of 1760 (when he exhibited his licence) and 1766.
The claims of his college asserted themselves, however: in 1768–9
he was Vice-principal and in the next year Junior Bursar.[22]

Mayer was succeeded in October 1767 by Thomas Jones, B.A.,
of Jesus College, Oxford, who had been second master at Macclesfield School for two years. In the first recorded use of testimonials
at that school he had been recommended, as to his learning and
morals, by the head librarian of the Bodleian and Principal of Jesus
College, who had 'intrusted him with the care of the Bodleian
Library'. The Macclesfield governors recommended him to the
Witton feoffees as able and well qualified. Jones is noteworthy at
Witton only because his licence to teach there survives among the
school records, the only master's licence in existence. The presence
of such licences in school archives is unusual, for they were the

* Henry's brother, Peter, was under-master at Macclesfield School. (Robson,
op. cit., p. 185.)

property of the masters, but Jones's probably came into the hands of the feoffees as a result of a clause in his bond. His own bond does not exist, but it was doubtless similar to those of previous masters. Williamson's bond was to be cancelled and he released from financial obligation if, on taking any spiritual preferment with cure of souls (and so required by the majority of the feoffees), he quitted the school and surrendered his licence so that another master could be appointed. Tench agreed to a proposal that on any considerable neglect of his duty he would quit and deliver up his licence on three months' notice. (Licences usually related to teaching in a particular school; though sometimes valid for any part of a diocese, they were not personal licences to teach anywhere.) Thomas Jones's licence of 21 December 1767, signed and sealed by Edmund, Bishop of Chester, authorised him to teach children in the free school of Witton 'grammar, writing and arithmetick, and effectually instruct them in the same and all other lawful and useful learning'. The wording corresponds with that of the licence of the master at Nantwich Grammar School in 1733, who was to teach 'grammar, writing and arithmetick', but it is doubtful how much it reveals of the curriculum at Witton, since the document was a printed form with the name inserted. Thomas Jones was privately ordained by the bishop in August 1768 and remained at Witton only until 1770. By 1778 he had been appointed by the vicar of Great Budworth to the cures of Little Leigh and Aston.[23]

It is with the appointment of the next master, after advertisements in the *Chester Courant,* that the school emerges somewhat from the obscurity of this half-century of sparse evidence. No list of candidates survives, only the usual proposals signed by William Hadfield, the new master, and his bond of £500 to John Done and Thomas Ives Brayne to keep an usher to teach English, not to have a deputy, and to observe the statutes, 'which statutes are deposited in the school chest and have been perused by William Hadfield'. William Hadfield, younger brother of Joseph Hadfield, was the son of a clergyman of Mellor, and had been a pupil at Manchester Grammar School from 1762. He entered St John's College, Cambridge, in 1767 as a sizar, became a scholar, and matriculated in 1768, but proceeded no further. He is said to have been 'commonly called "Count Hatfield", a Manchester fop, and is still remembered as being the first gentleman who, at least in this part of the country, wore a white hat'. There is little doubt that the Leicester influence secured him the mastership, and he remained compliant to it: in February 1786, when several people had applied to be assistant in the church and school, Hadfield was reported as saying that 'none are fixed upon nor will he do it without Lady L's or Sir John's appro-

bation'. Hadfield married Anne Pownall, whose family had been
resident in the chapelry for generations; she was the daughter of
Robert Pownall, gent., of Witton, the Weaver Navigation engineer
and a school feoffee from 1772 to his death in 1780.[24]

William Hadfield was appointed to a school which was reported
to the curate in 1778 to be endowed with lands 'to a considerable
amount',* all of which were held on long leases for £52 a year,
except for Larton, 'which falling out of lease at Ladyday next is
expected to be a considerable addition to the salary'. In 1778, with
the usher, James Boyer, he had in the school fifty to sixty boys, who
were instructed in Greek, Latin, English, writing and accompts.
A few years later, in September 1785, both the headmaster and the
usher, Christopher Smith, made returns of the names of their
scholars, the first list of pupils since Aaron Nichols's.†

William Hadfield's return gave the names of ten boys under him,
together with the classical books they were studying. It is of some
interest that one pupil under the headmaster, an occasional scholar,
was studying English only. The usher, Christopher Smith, had
twenty-seven pupils: three were doing writing and accompts, of
whom one was also under Hadfield; fifteen were 'Writers', of whom
four were under Hadfield; and nine were 'Readers'. The usher's
pupils were thus nearly three times the number of the headmaster's,
but the latter kept a general oversight over the school: he reported
to the feoffees that his 'daily business' included 'my attension [*sic*]
to the Lower Boys'. According to two pupils at this time, giving
evidence fifty years later, the master and usher both taught in the
lower school room. The total number had dropped considerably
from the fifty to sixty of 1778, but fluctuations were common at this
period in all schools.

Of Hadfield's scholars William Bradburne, the son of Peter Bradburne, merchant, of Northwich, went as a pensioner in July 1785
to Trinity College, Cambridge, where he matriculated but proceeded no further, and John Walker, son of Thomas Walker of Little
Budworth, went there also as a pensioner, but took his B.A. degree
in 1790 and his M.A. in 1793. No other pupils went to Trinity,
and it is tempting to speculate that the Leicester influence may have
been at work again: two of Sir Peter Leicester's sons went to Trinity,
John Fleming in 1781 and Henry Augustus in 1783.[25] Some fifty
years later William Hadfield's son, Robert Pownall Hadfield, gave
evidence about the state of the school in his father's time and immediately after, and stated that 'when I went to the school both the

* The words also used in a description in the *London Magazine* in 1750,
quoted in Calvert, *op. cit.*, p. 81.
† See the lists at the end of this chapter.

upper and the lower school was open to all classes' and that 'children of all classes did attend from the gentleman's to the poorest labourer's child without any complaint being made on that account'. He further testified that, but for the free education at the school, neither he nor his brothers could have been educated after their father's death. Another witness, John Barnes, a pupil of the usher in 1785, also stated that at least a dozen pupils were sons of flatmen, or persons navigating barges or boats on the Weaver. But there were signs that some Northwich people were looking beyond the local school for their sons' education. In 1741 Thomas, son of Robert Hewitt of Northwich, entered Trinity College, Cambridge, from Beverley School, Yorkshire, at that time undergoing a revival under John Clarke. Several local boys appear in the register of Manchester Grammar School: in 1756 the son of Charles Lyon, Supervisor of the Salt Office at Winsford; in 1761 John, son of the late Walter Antrobus, physician, of Northwich, a school feoffee (described as an 'apothecary') in 1754; in 1761, too, Jonadab, the son of John Mort, salt works proprietor at Northwich and later a school feoffee, and in 1779, Peter, son of Thomas Ravenscroft of Leftwich Hall. In 1790 Alfred Hadfield, who had been at Witton, was removed to Manchester School, which was, however, his father's old school.*[26]

Certainly by 1778, and probably soon after he became master, William Hadfield, who was ordained priest in 1772, acted as his brother's assistant curate at Witton Chapel. After Joseph's death in November 1785 Sir John Leicester handed over the curacy to William on a temporary basis, but he did not live long to enjoy it, dying in April 1786. His double office would undoubtedly have led to objections by the feoffees. When, in April 1786, they put forward proposals to candidates they added to those of 1770 a clause 'That whoever is appointed shall not on any account accept of the living or Curacy of Witton Chapel or anywise officiate or do duty at the said chapel without licence and consent of the majority of the feoffees ... in writing under their hands for that purpose'. The minutes of the feoffees' meeting on 13 April show that they deliberately inserted this clause which limited a master's prospects, although in 1800 they gave the master leave to do occasional duty at Witton Chapel in the absence of a curate. The feoffees, though in the interests of the school, were thus barring one way in which a master could increase his salary.[27]

* Possibly some of these boys had their early education at Witton. Dr John Latham of Bradwall, an eminent physician and Physician Extraordinary to the Prince of Wales in 1795, was said to have been a pupil. (Peter Barker's affidavit, Hand case.) His school is usually given as Manchester, but he did not enter there until he was about twelve, in 1774.

1. Return of Scholars under Rev. Mr Hadfield 15 September 1785

ACCOUNT OF CLASSICAL SCHOLARS IN WITTON SCHOOL UNDER
THE IMMEDIATE CARE OF WM. HADFIELD

Wm. Bradburn, reading Xenophon, and Horace, and translating Knox's
Essays, with miscellaneous Exercises in Prose and Verse, in English
and in Latin.

John Walker, reading the same, saving that he translates from the
Pantheon,† and privately at times reads Virgil at home.

Barnett Hough, reading Cornelius Nepos, and translates from Garretson's
Exercises.

Wm. Beaman, in Sententia and the same Exercise.

Thos. Mort, in the same.

John Wrench, in the same.

Alfred* and Edwin Hadfield, in their Syntaxis, and writing Verbs.

Samuel Hardy, an occasional scholar, in Bishop Lowth's English Grammar,
and Milton's *Paradise Lost*.

William Warton in the Accidence.

This with my attention [*sic*] to the lower boys is the daily business of
your Humble Servant, W. Hadfield.

2. Mr Smith the Usher's Return of Scholars, 15 September 1785

Writing and Accompts

> Richard Weston
> Robert Clare
> John Wrench

Writers

> Wm. Beaman
> Thomas Mort
> Alfred Hadfield
> Edwin Hadfield
> Wm. Warton
> John Edge
> Samuel Edge
> John Heywood
> Thomas Weston
> Mark Ronorth
> Geo. Ranorth
> John Barnes

* Alfred Hadfield was later reputed to be a good classical scholar: he
was a frequent contributor to the *Gentleman's Magazine*. (*Manchester School
Register*, II, 176–7.)

† Andrew Tooke's handbook of classical mythology.

Joseph Oldham
Samuel Stanway
Charles Hadfield

Readers

Thomas Higginson
Richard Chantler
James Weston
Wm. Edge
Wm. Houghton
Wm. Hall
Edward Richardson
James Heywood
Robert Hadfield

IX

Growing problems, 1786-1823

The late eighteenth century and the early nineteenth were a severe testing time for the old endowed grammar schools: some declined into little more than primary schools, some were reduced to very small numbers of classical scholars, while a few trace back to this period their rise out of the ranks of local grammar schools to become non-local 'public schools' giving a classical education. Yet others emerged from tension and controversy with a curriculum broadened beyond the classical requirements of their original foundation, and capable of attracting strong local support. One fundamental problem for the old foundations was that of finance: the revenues of many endowed schools were still based largely on sixteenth-century money values. Sometimes their financial straits were met by allowing the master to charge for teaching subjects not specifically mentioned in the foundation, thus avoiding any legal objection to the practice. Another common method was for the master to take in boarders and to charge them accordingly: indeed, masters of decayed endowed schools sometimes used their office to create private boarding schools of their own.

The other main point of stress and debate in this period lay in the curriculum of endowed grammar schools. Many old schools, like Witton, made specific provision only for the teaching of classical languages and literature, particularly Latin, but this restriction was at variance both with the practice of the numerous and successful private schools and academies which had been founded to meet the contemporary educational demands, and with the current of reforming opinion. Criticism of the purely classical curriculum had been voiced in the seventeenth century, most notably in Locke's writings. It gained force in the eighteenth century, and came into the sphere of politics, when the *Edinburgh Review* championed the inclusion of modern studies—languages, geography and mathematics—and when, in 1821, Henry Brougham introduced, unsuccessfully, a Bill to allow English, writing and accounts to be included in the curriculum of grammar schools.

The Radical criticism gained force from certain legal decisions given by Lord Eldon, the Lord Chancellor. The most famous of these concerned Leeds Grammar School. At this school the governors attributed the decline in numbers in the 1790s to the inadequacy of the curriculum for a town like Leeds, and proposed to appoint masters to teach writing and accounts, French, and other foreign languages, but the headmaster disagreed and the dispute was taken to law. A first report by a Master in Chancery in 1797 was favourable to the proposed innovation, declaring that nothing in the endowment excluded the teaching of any useful learning, but further dissension resulted in a judgement by Lord Eldon, based partly on Dr Johnson's definition of a grammar school as an institution 'for teaching grammatically the learned languages'. This new scheme, Eldon held, was 'to promote the benefits of the merchants of Leeds' by teaching their clerks modern languages, and not to teach the poor inhabitants English, and it was a clear contravention of the founder's intentions. Subsequent decisions by Eldon maintained this attitude, and though he may not have been quite the obstacle to reform that he has been considered, since he was prepared to see modern subjects introduced if strictly subordinate to classical ones, nevertheless modifications of the curriculum were likely to be difficult if the matter actually came to law at this time. The legal position did not change until the Endowed Grammar Schools Act of 1840.

It would, however, be misleading to visualise all old grammar schools as strictly confined to the classical education laid down in their foundations. The kind of complaints which localities made, for instance at Harrow, when a grammar school was becoming a non-local boarding school concentrating on the classics, were met in part by the practice of less prosperous endowed schools. A pamphlet of 1818 estimated that of 500 grammar schools at work, 120 taught 'every variety of subject', fifty-six of them taught 'English' subjects only, and in eighty parents were allowed to choose between an 'English' and a classical course of studies. Two processes were at work here: a genuine modification of the curriculum to provide teaching in mathematics and modern languages, but also, sometimes, a decline of teaching, often to an elementary level of instruction in reading, writing and arithmetic. Hull and Beverley grammar schools at this time broadened their teaching in relation to public demand, neither being bound by statutes to the classical curriculum. Among the Cheshire grammar schools, one of them, Macclesfield, in 1762 made provision for the introduction of writing, accounts, mathematics and French. The teaching of writing and accounts was not in itself unusual, the teaching of French more so, but what distinguished Macclesfield in the late eighteenth century was that in

1774 the governors secured a private Act of Parliament authorising
these innovations and thereby forestalling any legal objections such
as arose at Leeds. At Stockport the headmaster from 1793 to 1829,
Elkanah Hoyle, had stretched the school out of its original mould.
Although by the foundation the school was to be free of charge to
all the children of Stockport who cared to come, in 1826 Hoyle
stated that 'he had hardly any free boys in the School, though
admission had never been refused to any claiming to come in free'.
His charges were six guineas a year, and these were 'sanctioned
[he said] by the Corporation and the inhabitants of Stockport upon
his introducing a more enlarged scale of education than that required by the Founder': this was in a town 'in which there are
many cotton manufactories of considerable importance, and very
populous'. Thus two of the Cheshire grammar schools in manu-
facturing towns had made provision for broader curricula, and at
Stockport the 'freedom' of the school had been circumvented,
partly, it seems, as a result of lack of demand. The developments at
Witton must be seen against this general background.[1]

The finances

A reorganisation in 1784 provides an opportunity to survey the
state of the school and its property. In that year the feoffees began
a new minute book and account book, ordered a survey of the school
property, a schedule of the school papers and a strong oak chest in
which to keep them. In 1785 they received the first of a series of
lists from the headmaster and usher of the scholars in the school,
and altogether their activities were more businesslike for a time.
The twelve feoffees in 1784 were as follows: Lord Penrhyn, Sir
John Fleming Leicester, William Brooke, John Mort, Thomas
Marshall, John Cheshire, John Barker, John Hunt, John Cheney,
John Furey, Thomas Ives Brayne and William Thearsby; the bailiff
feoffees chosen in that year were Thomas Marshall and Thomas
Ives Brayne. They represented a wealthy and influential section of
local society, and many of them were engaged in the salt industry
and trade, notably John Cheshire of Hartford Hall, John Mort,
John Hunt, John Furey and Thomas Marshall.

Information is most readily available about Thomas Marshall,
and his family is the subject of an informative article by a former
pupil of the school, Mr D. A. Iredale. This Thomas Marshall, the
second of the name, had succeeded his father as the head of the
largest salt shippers in Northwich in 1772, the year in which he
became a school feoffee: by the time of his death in 1797 he
estimated his estates and works to be worth £50,000. Under his two

sons, John and Thomas (both pupils and subsequently feoffees of the school), the firm became the largest and wealthiest industrial company in central Cheshire. The two Thomases were driving personalities, and the younger declared his belief, in 1818, that he was the largest proprietor in rock and white salt in the kingdom: he played an all-important role in organising the salt industry. Ties of marriage and business linked the Marshalls with two other school feoffees; the younger Thomas married a daughter of William Thearsby, an exceptionally wealthy Northwich surgeon, while the Braynes had served the Marshalls as attorneys from at least 1734.

In 1793, after the deaths of five of the feoffees, including Thomas Ives Brayne, new feoffees were appointed, among them Jonadab Mort, the lessee of the school land in Northwich, Thomas Barker and Thomas Chantler. Braynes and Chantlers worked as the oldest of Northwich's firms of attorneys, and both Thomas Ives Brayne and Thomas Chantler were treasurers to the Weaver trustees: indeed, the connections between the two sets of trustees, school and Navigation, were such that on occasion the meetings of the school feoffees were held at the Navigation Office. Even closer ties united the feoffees after 1811: those named in the feoffment of that year included two Marshalls, two Barkers and two Chantlers.[2]

Although outside observers were still repeating the description of the school as well endowed, the school's financial position was not very happy. The total income from rents in 1786 was £83 9s 4d, and practically the whole of this went on the master's and the usher's salaries, so that the feoffees worked on a narrow margin. The Peover chief rent was still at 6s and that in Hartford at 3s 4d, although from about 1717 to 1789 it was not paid for lack of application by the trustees, and in spite of a resolution to exact it in 1789 there is no record of payment afterwards. The Saracen's Head site, leased in 1728 to Gabriel Wettenhall, a notable barrister, for £10 a year on a very long lease of three lives and fifty-three years, now contained 'three good houses with iron palasades', which he had built there about 1730, and which William Hadfield estimated to be let for over £100. The lease was not due to expire until 1831, but in 1799 the feoffees, having lost the counterpart of the original lease, tried to claim that it was for only twenty-one years after the last life. In protest Lord Vernon wrote to Lord Penrhyn on behalf of his sister, who had inherited the property, and the affair subsided after reference to arbitration. (The £47 paid to Chantler in 1800 for business done for the school doubtless referred to this.) The Swan property was let in 1754 on another long lease, three lives and ten years, at £20 a year; William Hadfield thought these buildings possibly worth £100 a year. The Swan produced a windfall in 1796,

when the daughter of the lessee paid £150 to have her life put into
the lease; the feoffees invested the money in Consolidated 3 per cent
annuities, the first investment in government funds, and the first
departure from the old method of lending to individuals. What had
once been a major source of income, the wich house, was now
'a plot of land in the Swine Market Street': the house which had
been there in 1718 had disappeared, and, according to Hadfield in
1786, a man who had intended to build there had 'failed in his
circumstances and it hath for this 10 years back lain waste'. In 1786
it was let to Jonadab Mort for £3 a year on a very long lease of the
kind criticised by the feoffees at the beginning of the century.[3]

The Larton estate had, however, improved considerably with
the years. Whereas in 1778, just before the lease fell in, it was held
to be let much under its real value at £21, in 1785 George Day
was paying £50 a year on a lease with seven years to run, and in
1798 the feoffees accepted £66 a year on an eleven-year lease.
(Furthermore, in 1785 George Day paid £50 as a forfeiture for
over-tilling his estate contrary to his covenant, and the feoffees
decided to put this out at interest and accumulate a fund for new
farm buildings.) Agricultural land had proved a more profitable
source of income than town property, though this may have been
Witton's peculiar misfortune, for Macclesfield School's property in
Chester appreciated in value between 1736 and 1774, when several
leases fell in. Even Larton had its problems, for the farmhouse
buildings were in a bad state, and in 1811 the feoffees went so far
as to have a plan and estimate for a new farm house. Moreover,
while the French Revolutionary and Napoleonic wars were a
boom period for agricultural landlords, immediately after the end
of the war there was a sharp drop in profits. In 1816 the feoffees
had to inform candidates for the mastership that 'the present stipend
for the head Master can only be for the present £80 per annum
clear: it has been for several years past £100, but the estate in
possession is reduced in value in consequence of the present low
price of landed produce'. Ormerod was informed in 1817 by John
Barker that the school's income was only £114 7s, whereas a few
years before it had been £149 7s. In August 1818 the trustees
decided that in view of a new enclosure near Larton and the
necessary repairs there, which had led to a considerable debt, the
headmaster's salary would have to be reduced to £60 and the under-
master's to £15. In 1819 the masters' salaries were discontinued
entirely until certain outstanding debts had been paid.[4]

The finances of the school were further complicated by the
conduct of Thomas Chantler, who acted as bailiff feoffee with
Thomas Marshall from 1793 to 1797, and as sole bailiff feoffee

(after Marshall's death) from 1797 to 1811. This was not in accord
with John Deane's rules; and furthermore, from 1785 to 1806 no
churchwardens were present at the making of the accounts, which
were passed by the feoffees themselves at a public meeting; after
1806 not even this formality was observed, and the bailiff feoffee
carried on without surveillance. Between March 1806 and January
1811 there were no meetings of feoffees at all, and by 1811 seven of
them were dead and their places unfilled: there was clearly no
interest in the management of the school. In January 1811, however,
new feoffees were chosen, among them John and Thomas Marshall,
John Barker of Witton, Thomas Chantler Jr and William Twemlow
of Winnington, surgeon.* The feoffees reacted strongly to Chantler's
behaviour, especially when he ordered the school's tenants to pay
their rents to him alone, at a time when he was bankrupt. In May
1811 the feoffees elected two new bailiff feoffees, called on Chantler
to make up his accounts, and recorded their disapproval of his
disrespect to them in not having consulted them for several years
on the school business. They were forced in August 1811 to initiate
a suit in Chancery against Chantler to compel him to hand over his
accounts, the money in his hands and the school's books and deeds.
In order to have money in hand for the expenses of the suit the
headmaster and usher were deprived of their salaries but given leave
'to make a reasonable charge for the instruction of boys in Grammar
until it shall be convenient to order otherwise'. From 1811 to 1816,
as a result of the Chantler affair, the school's finances were under
the direction of the Court of Chancery and the minute book was not
used. The Chantler case had a disastrous effect on the school's
financial position, for in October 1816 the feoffees had to sell stock
to the value of £260 12s 6d in order to pay their legal representatives over £300. They had thus lost their reserves, and the next few
years showed the crippling effect of the case.[5]

The school and its site

The school, meanwhile, as befitted a comparatively new building,
was in a good state, shown in the periodic reports of John Johnson,
inspector and manager for the Weaver trustees. The occasional
glazing needed explains the school rule that 'if any boy *breaks* a
window, or does any other *wilful* damage, he shall *pay* for it; and
after reasonable time being allowed for the repair, if it be not done,
he shall be excluded the School till satisfaction be made'. In 1816,
in printed proposals for candidates for the mastership, the feoffees

* Twemlow's pride in the office of feoffee is revealed in the inscription on
the engraving showing the church and school. See plate v.

described it as 'an excellent school, two stories high 43 feet in length and 20 feet in breadth well lighted and in good repair; the situation near the Parochial Chapel of Witton is elevated, healthy'. The situation may have been healthy, but the school's closeness to the chapel had other disadvantages besides the loss of the headmaster's garden to the churchyard. In 1807 the churchwardens' accounts recorded 8s paid for someone to attend the church while the schoolboys were breaking up at Christmas, to prevent abuses. Doubtless the boys were often a nuisance in the churchyard, but they do not seem to have had anywhere else to play. It is incidentally from the early nineteenth century that the evidence dates of what was probably an old marriage custom involving the Witton School boys.* Weston recorded a card dated 5 October 1830 which ran 'It being an ancient custom with the scholars of this school (whenever a respectable marriage takes place at this church) humbly to solicit from the new married couple what is termed Garter-Money, or the Brides-Garters—we hope we shall not offend, by following up the old rule', and there is further evidence of this custom during the Hand case.

The school was also being hemmed in by the churchyard. Through the churchyard there ran an ancient pathway, which in 1814 the vestry decided to close, making a new foot road round the church on land provided by Sir John Fleming Leicester. The decision may have been connected with an entry in the wardens' accounts of 1813 of expenses to keep 'the rabble out of the churchyard on Sunday nights', but it affected the school closely. The main door of the school faced west on to the churchyard, but the vestry meeting resolved that the pathways through the chapel yard should be carried on the outside of it, 'as also that leading to the school the door way of which to be placed on the eastern side of the said school' (that is, facing outwards), at the expense of the chapelry and in a way sanctioned by the trustees. Three years later, however, another vestry meeting recorded that the wardens had diverted the way into the north end of the school, in a manner 'which does not meet the ideas of this meeting and in particular it has been objected to by the Bailiff Feoffees of the School as being inconvenient to them'. In 1825 the new master found that the main door of the school was unusable except by opening large iron gates, the key of which was in the possession of the churchwardens.[6]

---

* *Cf.* Lancaster Grammar School, where, by ancient custom thought to date from pre-Reformation times, the six senior boys had wedding money, possibly in origin a payment for their attendance as acolytes. (A. L. Murray, *The Royal Grammar School, Lancaster*, p. 107.)

The headmaster's department—pupils and curriculum

On the death of William Hadfield the feoffees appointed as head-master Robert Litler, a native of Northwich and very probably educated at the school, as he was the son of Peter Litler of Northwich and descended from the Litlers of Wallerscote in Edisbury Hundred. Litler had matriculated at Brasenose College, but had not proceeded to a degree, and when appointed at the age of twenty-five he was already in orders. He had testimonials to his good scholarship and ability to teach a grammar school and to his 'sober life and con-versation' from three vicars in the diocese of Lichfield, and was nominated by the feoffees and licensed by the bishop in 1788. At the time of his appointment the feoffees approved rules for the scholars, to be printed and hung in the school 'for the preservation of discip-line and regularity, and the avoiding of punishments'.* Three copies of these rules survive and were, incidentally, printed by J. Dawson of Northwich, the usher. They run as follows:

I. Every boy shall appear at school precisely at SIX o'clock in *summer* and at EIGHT in winter; and for every morning in the week that he is *absent* from school at prayers, he shall have a task of *ten* lines, to be got the succeeding night; and if absent *more* than once in one week, an addition of *five* lines to be made to his former task; for not getting of which he *shall be punished.*

II. For the proper support of *neatness* and *decency* every boy shall come clean washed and combed, and for every *breach* of this rule he shall have a task to be got the succeeding night.

III. Every boy shall be provided with pens, ink and such books as are usually read in his class, or be sent home till they be provided.

IV. If any one absent himself from school without *leave* from the Master, or a *note* from his friends; for the first offence he shall be admonished and have a *task*, for the second shall be *severely* punished, and for the third be expelled as an example.

V. He that tells a *lie, swears, steals*, or is guilty of *profane* or *debauched* language, shall for the first offence be admonished and have a task, for the second be severely whipped, and for the third *expelled*.

VI. If any boy *breaks* a window, or does any other *wilful* damage, he shall *pay* for it; and after reasonable time being allowed for the repair, if it be not done, he shall be *excluded* the school till satisfaction be made.

* See plate VI. In December 1832, during their dispute with the master, Charles Hand, the feoffees ordered that the rules observed in the time of Hadfield and Litler should be enforced and copies printed. These copies, many of which survive, vary in minor details from the original rules, e.g. 7 a.m., not 6 a.m., was the time for summer attendance, the boys were to be decently dressed, the trustees were to give the prizes.

vii. Every boy that is *idle* and *talkative* in school-hours shall be spoke to *once* or *twice*, and if persisting, have a task, and for not getting it be corrected accordingly.

viii. Two impositors shall be chosen by weekly rotation, whose office shall be to keep the keys, acquaint the Master when coals are wanting, and see that the school be kept clean; for every omission of his duty he shall be *punished*.

ix. That justice may be impartially distributed, and to prevent all groundless complaints of severity: if any boy pleads *not* guilty to any of the above rules he shall be tried by *five* of his school-fellows, and condemned or acquitted by their determination.*

x. And to *encourage* dilligence *two books* will be given every Christmas by the Master to the *two* boys who, in their several classes, have behaved *best* and made the *greatest* improvement in learning.

xi. Lastly, that no one may plead ignorance or *expect* indulgences that cannot be impartially allowed: these rules shall be read over by the Master four times in the year, at the commencement of every quarter, and *no* one shall be *admitted into* this school who *will not* submit to be *governed* by them.[7]

Although lists of the names of scholars under the usher survive for the last decade of the century, there are no lists of the headmaster's pupils, only their numbers in the Minute Book. In 1789 the headmaster had twenty boys; in 1790 twelve, in 1791 fifteen, in 1796 fifteen and in 1806 twenty-two, when the usher had forty-six. By chance we know a little of the history of one pupil under Litler—the eminent engineer, Eaton Hodgkinson. Hodgkinson was born at Anderton in 1789, and lost his father, 'a respectable farmer', at the age of six. His mother, to meet the wishes of an uncle, a clergyman who designed the boy for the university and Church, sent him to Northwich Grammar School, where he studied the rudiments of Latin, Greek and Hebrew under the immediate supervision of the headmaster, Robert Litler. A memoir of Hodgkinson, written in 1865, states that 'to the severe treatment which he here received, his cousin, Mrs. Thompson, attributed the nervous tremor of his hands and speech which continued with him through life and was a serious impediment to his success'. The Rev. Robert Litler, like many of his more famous contemporaries, was, it appears, a severe disciplinarian, trying to flog lessons into boys who could not learn. Hodgkinson, without any aptitude for languages, was thrashed severely, and in consequence removed by his mother from Witton

---

* This is quite at variance with Deane's statute on discipline, by which the pupils were subject to the master's correction: 'which correcion shalbe alwaies referred to the discression of the schoolemaister and not to the opynyon and mynd of the schollers . . .'.

School and sent to a private school in Northwich run by a Mr
Shaw, 'a gentleman of superior mathematical attainments and
possessing great tact in teaching and in the general management of
boys'.* Here Hodgkinson finished his education, and when in 1811
his family moved to Salford he became a pupil of John Dalton,
and went on to a distinguished career, ending as Professor of
Mechanical Engineering at University College, London. Among
other achievements he was responsible for calculations essential to
the design of Robert Stephenson's Conway and Britannia tubular
bridges.†[8]

Hodgkinson himself was an exceptional man, but the history of his
'education' at Witton has a more general bearing. Northwich was a
town with industrial interests, and Shaw's school was clearly a local
example of the characteristic eighteenth-century school which arose
to meet the demand of the commercial middle class for a 'useful'
education, not adequately provided by the grammar schools, in
subjects such as English, mathematics, surveying, navigation and
accounts. There is one specific piece of evidence of modernisation of
the curriculum at Witton, although there is no indication as to
whether it concerned the master's or the usher's department. In
1799 the feoffees purchased for the school, at the considerable cost
of over £7, a pair of globes.[9] Globes seem to have been a sign of
up-to-date teaching: they appear in the curricula of academies and
private schools and in the reformed curriculum at Macclesfield.
Moreover, the advanced Dr Joseph Priestley gave lectures to adults
at Nantwich on scientific subjects such as 'the use of the globes'.

Hodgkinson's career shows the grammar school's loss of a pupil
to a local private school, but the school was also failing to attract
even some of the feoffees' sons, who went instead to public schools.
The rapid improvement of coach travel in these years encouraged
the sending of boys to boarding schools, and in describing the town
in 1816 the feoffees stated that 'a mail coach runs daily through
Northwich from London to Liverpool, by way of Leicester, and
there are several other coaches daily, by which persons at reasonable
charges may be conveyed to every part of the kingdom'. College
admission records provide evidence of Witton School's loss. Joah
Furey, the son of John Furey of Witton, salt proprietor and school

* Mathematical schools did not have to be licensed, so that there is no
mention of Shaw's school in the diocesan records. (See W. E. Tate, 'The
episcopal licensing of schoolmasters in England', *Church Quarterly Review*,
CLVII, p. 429.)

† It is unfortunate that we do not know where Robert Pownall (1710–80),
civil engineer to the Weaver Navigation, was educated: his plan for making
Witton Brook navigable won the approval of James Brindley. He became a
feoffee of the school, and it seems very likely that he was educated there.

feoffee, entered King's College, Cambridge, in 1794 as a scholar
from Eton, later becoming a fellow and vice-provost. In 1820
Thomas Marshall, the son of the feoffee and former Witton pupil,
Thomas Marshall of Hartford Cottage, Northwich, entered St
John's College, Cambridge, as a pensioner from Rugby School, and
John Wakefield Mort, the son of the feoffee, John Mort of Northwich, was admitted, also as a pensioner, from Shrewsbury School.
Some feoffees, however, notably the Barkers, were faithful to the
school. Nicholas Carlisle, who carried out a survey of grammar
schools published in 1818, stated that most of the ten day-scholars
to whom the headmaster, William Whitworth, was expected to teach
the Latin and Greek languages only, were sons of the trustees: the
list of pupils in December 1817 has only two pupils marked 'free'
out of a total of ten.[10]

The decline of the master's school

The position of the headmaster deteriorated from 1811, when he
and the usher were deprived of their salaries and allowed to make a
'reasonable charge' for instruction. The master, Robert Litler, and
the usher, Thomas Johnson, left at about the same time in 1812,
Litler becoming curate of Goostrey in 1814. A new usher, Robert
Hayward, was appointed in the summer of 1812 and remained at
the school as usher for eleven years, but there was a rapid succession
of headmasters. The feoffees had difficulty in securing a suitably
qualified master, and had to accept John* Robinson Winstanley
who, though twenty-eight, was in his own words 'not exactly a
graduate of the University of Oxford, but I have been nearly 7
years a Member of St. Alban Hall. I have still 3 more terms to keep
after which I shall be entitled to the degree of A.M.' Winstanley's
slow progress in taking a degree was the result of his holding teaching posts 'in some of the most respectable schools in the South of
England'. Significantly, in his letter to the bailiff feoffees he expressed his hopes of a curacy, and his willingness to be ordained if

* The christian name of this master has been a source of much difficulty.
In a list of 1836 and in Weston's he appears as 'Thomas', but no Thomas
Winstanley of the right date appears in the records of St Alban Hall, Oxford,
where (according to Winstanley in a letter to the feoffees) he had been, and
of which his uncle was head. A John Winstanley from Liverpool matriculated
at St Alban Hall in 1803, and his age fits with that which Winstanley gave
to the feoffees, though not with his time at the hall. Winstanley wrote to the
feoffees in 1812 from Liverpool, but his signed initials could be either 'J.R.'
or 'T.R.'. However, affidavits in the Chantler case and by Robert Hayward in
the later Hand case give him as 'John Robinson', and a printed subscription
list of 1813 for the Northwich National School includes the 'Rev. J. R.
Winstanley', so that on balance this seems to be the correct name.

there was a church to be had in the neighbourhood. By the end of July 1813, however, Winstanley was anxious to resign his post. Reading between the lines of proposals he made later with a view to returning, some of the causes of his dissatisfaction appear: his appointment was only temporary; as an ordained master he was irked by the restrictions on clerical duty, although he apparently did Sunday duty at Davenham; the trustees did not support him by sending their own sons to the school, and, above all, relations with the usher were impossible. Winstanley's successor, the Rev. Frederic Gwynne, though academically well qualified, was also on a temporary basis, and neither was licensed by the bishop. Gwynne, after a roving undergraduate career at Christ's, St John's and Jesus colleges, Cambridge, took his B.A. degree in 1807, being seventh Wrangler, and his M.A. in 1815. By the end of 1815 he had left Witton, where he had about twenty-five pupils, to become headmaster of Beverley Grammar School, and he died in 1816.[11]

During the vacancy (in which Edward Allen taught briefly at the school) the feoffees countered an attempt by the Bishop of Chester to intervene in the choice of master, asserting that the school was not a corporation with a seal and a Visitor, who might be the bishop, but a charitable trust in a general sense under the King, acting through the Lord Chancellor. The feoffees had such a large number of applicants from their advertisements in the Liverpool, Chester, Oxford and Cambridge papers that they produced a printed sheet of information about the school and proposals to candidates. On the management of the school the feoffees stated that the school hours were to be from seven to twelve in the morning (with an hour for breakfast) and two to five during the summer months, and from eight to eleven and one to four in the winter months; holidays, apart from half-days on Wednesday and Saturday, were to be four weeks each at midsummer and Christmas and three days each at Shrovetide and Easter. Greek and Latin were to be taught free of charge to all boys over six who came to the school, and only the Eton Grammar* was to be used, but charges for other branches of education were to be fixed by the trustees. In discipline, the master had to undertake not to beat the boys 'improperly or immoderately'. The feoffees could only offer a salary of £80, but they held out the prospect of an increase of £100 in 1830 on the expiry of one lease, and of a further increase of £100 on the expiry of another lease ten years after the deaths of two elderly ladies. In the meantime, though they forbade the master to hold a church living, they allowed him to do Sunday duty. Equally, though they could not offer a house for the master,

---

* See Chapter III, p. 40.

they were willing for him to have boarders, and pointed out that the
number of boys who had been taught Greek and Latin at the school
for the past thirty years had never exceeded thirty-six and seldom
amounted to twenty-five, thus, presumably, allowing time for
boarders. These conditions were accepted by William Whitworth
(from Newbury), who had no degree, nor even residence at a university; he had a testimonial from the master of Bolton School, was
examined by the bishop and schoolmaster of Chester, and appointed
in August 1816.[12]

Two commonly used methods were thus in use at Witton to increase the master's income: allowing him to take boarders and allowing him to charge for subjects other than classics. It is not known if
Whitworth had any boarders, but he received four guineas a year
for each pupil. Three lists of pupils survive, one of which is given
at the end of this chapter. In June 1817 Whitworth had fourteen
pupils and in December ten (of whom two were free): the curriculum was almost wholly classical, although in two of the lists English
composition and geography appear. Later, giving evidence in the
Hand case, a former pupil stated that Whitworth also taught mathematics. Whitworth, however, did not give satisfaction: in March
1818 the feoffees had to investigate a complaint by a parent of two
of the boys that he had chastised them 'otherwise than by the cane',
thereby contravening the conditions of his appointment. Whitworth
admitted the fact, but denied that it had been 'to the injury of the
boys', and, after much discussion, renewed his undertakings. After
this incident the feoffees, wishing to attract more pupils, issued an
advertisement to inform the public that the school was a Free
Grammar School—that is, free for the teaching of Greek and Latin
to boys over six—but by 1819 they were instituting an inquiry into
'why so few boys as 7 attend', and deciding to take measures to
make the school as useful to the public as possible. The financial
circumstances gave little ground for hope: having reduced the
masters' salaries in 1818, the feoffees discontinued them entirely in
1819. It is hardly surprising that Whitworth resigned in the same
year. The continuity of the classical school was broken by the
feoffees' decision not to appoint a successor for several months,
there being no funds to pay his salary. In fact, not only was no
headmaster appointed by them but between August 1819 and
February 1821 the feoffees held no meetings. Not until June 1821
did Litler secure his arrears due from over ten years before, and the
feoffees feel able to inform headmasters of public schools that the
vacancy would be filled at midsummer.[18]

The rise of the usher and the English school

This break in the classical school was not, however, paralleled in the usher's department, and the years from 1786 to 1823 were in fact a critical period in the relations between the two departments. The contemporary dissatisfaction with the grammar school curriculum was met in some degree at Witton by the practice of the usher's department. When the post of usher was advertised in 1796, for instance, the governors required someone who 'can teach the English language grammatically, write the different hands neatly and correctly, capable of teaching Arithmetic in all branches, Mensuration and Geometry, Merchants' Accounts and Book-keeping etc. in the modern and most approved methods'. Applicants had to submit specimens of their handwriting.[14]

Between 1785 and 1797 nine lists of the usher's pupils exist; there are two for 1817 and one each for 1821 and 1822. In 1785 the list was divided into three sections: three doing 'Writing and Accompts', fifteen 'writers' and nine 'readers'. In 1791 the pupils' studies were more exactly described: two were doing 'Merchants' Accounts', two 'Mensuration', three 'Vulgar Fractions', four 'Arithmetic', nine reading and writing, and seventeen, whose subject was not given, were presumably 'readers'. From 1785 to 1795 the numbers varied from twenty-seven to forty-seven and were usually two or three times more than the headmaster's pupils. A change of usher in 1796 may have led to a drop to thirteen, rising to only nineteen in 1797, but by 1806 the number was up to forty-six. In 1817 the usher had about forty pupils, of whom seven were also under the headmaster, but in 1822 there were only thirty-one.

An interesting feature of the lists is that Dawson's in 1790 and 1791, contain a number of girls' names: in 1790 there were seven of them, all described as 'Miss'. In 1791 there were ten girls: Miss Barlow for arithmetic, Miss Pickering, Miss J. Stubbs, Miss M. Deakin, Miss Gresswell, Mary Clarke and Maria Dale for writing, and three others, Elizabeth and Nancy Worthen and Hannah Dawson (possibly the usher's daughter) presumably for reading. In the later lists of 1817 there are no girls, and in those of 1821 and 1822 only four and three respectively. During the controversy of the 1830s the feoffees asserted that tradespeople and farmers 'and even those in higher stations, have always been accustomed to send their children, both girls and boys, to the usher of Witton school'. The girls were taught by Dawson in a separate room on the upper floor, previously the library, where a few books and the globes were kept. Witton was not alone in this: at Rivington in Lancashire, for example, between 1615 and 1617 there had been a handful of girls,

though none afterwards until 1678. In 1827, however, there were
ten girls under the master, and generally speaking just over a quarter
of the pupils under the usher and the writing master were girls; local
feeling had wished for their attendance at the school for two
centuries and so the custom had remained. There is also some
evidence that during the mastership of Elkanah Hoyle at Stockport
Grammar School, from 1792 to 1829, a class of girls was taught
there.[15]

The gradual separation of the usher's department from that of the
headmaster, and the emancipation of the usher from the master's
control, can be traced between 1776 and 1823. During the
nineteenth-century Chancery case several former ushers gave
evidence of the usage of the school. The earliest was John Davies,
usher or rather teacher of English, writing, reading and arithmetic,
from 1776 to 1781.* He testified that the master, William Hadfield,
occasionally gave him directions as to his teaching and also inspected
his pupils' writing and account books; furthermore, Davies received
his salary from the headmaster and no other payment, the charge to
Davies's pupils of 7s 6d a quarter for writing and arithmetic being
made by the headmaster for his own benefit. Occasionally, in
Hadfield's absence, and at his request, he taught junior pupils of the
headmaster elementary Latin. The links were still close between the
two departments, and a curious incident about the appointment of
an usher in 1785, recalled by Hadfield's son, Robert Pownall Hadfield, emphasises this. The candidate known to be favoured by
Hadfield was John Dawson, a printer, and the boys appeared at
school wearing favours in their hats announcing 'Dawson for
ever'. Dawson was, in fact appointed at a salary of £10, with an
extra £5 a year if the headmaster recommended him for his care
and attention. Dawson remained usher for ten years, most of them
in Litler's time: he deposed in 1826 that his stipend of £10 was for
teaching English reading, but that he made his own terms with
parents for teaching writing and accounts, according to him, as his
predecessors had done. By his time, if not a few years earlier, the
usher was teaching in the upper schoolroom and the master
below.†

From 1803 to 1812 Thomas Johnson, the usher or English master,
taught no Latin or Greek and had nothing to do with the master's

---

* These are the dates given by John Davies in evidence when he was aged
seventy-nine: it is not clear how they are to be reconciled with the report to
the Bishop in 1778 that the usher was James Boyer (see p. 166).

† This was certainly so in Litler's time, but the practice under Hadfield
apparently varied: Davies said he taught in the upper room, but Smith,
according to a pupil (Samuel Edge), taught in the same room as Hadfield.

boys, except that most of them were sent for two hours a day to learn writing and arithmetic from him. On his showing the master did not control the usher in his teaching and only examined the usher's pupils twice a year in the Church catechism: occasionally, however, he chastised the usher's boys for making a noise on the stairs. Admission to the usher's department was in the hands of the usher himself (although he borrowed the book of rules from the master for the parents to sign), and he made charges for his own benefit of 5*s* a quarter for writing, 7*s* 6*d* for common arithmetic, and 10*s* 6*d* for mensuration and the higher branches of arithmetic.

The seal was set on the division in the time of Robert Hayward, usher from 1812 to 1823, not surprisingly, since it was a time of vacancies and short masterships in the other department. The master then never examined the usher's boys, and they were admitted without any form on application to the usher and payment of 2*s* 6*d* to him: the only exception to this was that Winstanley, when headmaster, had remonstrated with Hayward and claimed the right to admit the boys. By 1818, according to Carlisle, the usher had the right to charge 20*s* a year for reading and writing, and an additional 20*s* for cyphering, book-keeping and mathematics.* Furthermore, the two schools, the usher's and the headmaster's, were entirely distinct from each other: 'neither has the headmaster any connection or concern whatsoever with the other school'. This kind of separation could be paralleled at other grammar schools: at Rivington, for example, the division had become more marked towards the end of the eighteenth century, and in 1827 it was accepted by the headmaster as traditional.[16]

The much greater numbers of the usher's school and its continued functioning under Hayward while Headmasters Winstanley, Gwynne, Allen and Whitworth came and went, and during the complete vacancy in the mastership from 1819 to 1823, led to the domination of the school by the 'English' school. Class distinctions seem to have aggravated the division between the two departments: twenty years later two of Whitworth's pupils testified that they had been forbidden to speak to the usher's boys as being 'of a humbler class of life'.[17]

Vivid contemporary evidence appears in letters to John Barker, a bailiff feoffee, written by Winstanley, the former master, in 1819, when he was considering applying for the mastership on a permanent basis. Basing his opinion on his personal experience at Witton a few years earlier, Winstanley wrote, 'I am sure as long as the

---

* Hayward's charges, according to his deposition, were 7*s* 6*d* a quarter for writing and 10*s* 6*d* for writing and arithmetic.

English School continues to be held in the same building I could not conscientiously advise you to send your boys to the school, perhaps the same master is there (Mr Hayward) and of all persons he would not like me there, for I kept both him and his myrmidons in such excellent order, that they must have found it quite delightful after my departure.'* Winstanley put forward a series of conditions on which he would undertake the mastership, of which the *sine qua non* was the dismissal of the usher, who had his English school in the upper room of the school above the room where the master taught, 'for', he wrote, 'if the salary were 500£ a year, he [Mr Winstanley] could not, either in justice to himself or the respectable part of the people, undertake the school, for it is as absurd to suppose that the School could flourish under the present circumstances as to imagine that the doctrines of the established Church would do so, if a *Methodist Preacher*, with his disciples, were to occupy (every Sunday) the galleries of *Witton Church*'. Winstanley's views on the Methodists can be paralleled by his political views. He took care to reassure Barker that he highly approved of 'the spirited conduct of the Manchester Magistrates', that is, at Peterloo. 'I think,' he continued, 'that the education of the lower orders of society, does not make them better Christians, and certainly renders them worse subjects; but the Established Church is compelled to teach them to read etc. for if they were not educated in the principles of their forefathers, they would be educated in those of the Methodists.'

Winstanley' proposals were that the usher should be dismissed ('and he can keep a private-school in the town which will answer every purpose') and that the headmaster should have both salaries and find his own assistant. English, Latin and Greek languages were to be taught, and in addition, 'as it is intended to render the School as respectable as possible, that no boys be allowed to come ... but such as can pay at least 1 Guinea p. quarter, for the necessary accompaniments of a classical education, such as Geography, History, Rhetoric, Elocution etc.'. This payment was to be in addition to a guinea entrance fee, while boys living outside the chapelry of Witton were to be charged double at least. Winstanley suggested that if the usher did not wish to run a private school 'those of his boys who don't like to pay the sum of 1 Guinea p. quarter for the usual accompaniments of an *English-classical* education will be best placed by their parents under the tuition of the Parish Clerk'. Although in the end Winstanley withdrew his application because

* There is an interesting comment in Winstanley's letter of 25 September 1819: 'I should presume that the "National School" has taken off a great number of the "Radicals" and that they are there properly drilled in their duty to their "Church and King".'

his fiancée did not wish him to run a 'free grammar school and specially in the north of England', his criticisms of the school and his suggested reforms are revealing, and show that the later crisis involving Charles Hand was but the culmination of a process.[18]

It was for a school in this state of division that the feoffees were trying to find a master in 1821. Almost a year after they had started they were still applying to heads of public schools for recommendations, but later in 1822 they advertised in the Chester, Macclesfield, Oxford, Cambridge and London papers. As a result they had thirty applicants, including Robert Litler's son and Edward Allen, then at Newark but formerly at Witton between Gwynne and Whitworth. He showed some insight into the situation by insisting that the unanimous support of the trustees would be necessary for the efficient conduct of the school, and by dissociating himself from 'any feeling towards anyone connected with the school in which the indiscretion of Mr Whitworth may have involved him'. He further expressed the hope, in a letter to John Marshall, of establishing a respectable school 'on a method which will exhibit the mildness and emulation of the New System without rejecting the Eton Grammar and other acknowledged excellencies of the Old System'. Allen, who in any case had no degree, withdrew, and the feoffees' choice, a fateful one in the history of the school, fell on Charles Hand.

Hand was the son of Samuel Hand, described in 1816 as of Holywell, Flintshire, but formerly an exciseman in the Northwich area and an active Methodist there. Charles Hand had spent five years at Witton School under Litler, and this entitled him to a preference. The following years had been spent at Dr Davies's school at Macclesfield (the grammar school) and at Oxford, where he matriculated at Jesus College in 1816, at the age of nineteen, and took his B.A. degree in 1821. He had been appointed by his college to the mastership of Abergavenny School and was already in holy orders. Curiously, in his letter of application Hand stated that he was an M.A. of Oxford, and this the unsuccessful candidates were told by the trustees. In December 1822 Hand wrote accepting the mastership: 'to the regulations I feel no inclination to object'. After some delay he arrived in Northwich at the end of February 1823, when he was nominated (correctly as a B.A.) to the bishop by the feoffees and was licensed in August 1823, a late example of an episcopal licence. He arrived at a time when it was not clear what the school's function in the community would be, and after a very unsatisfactory decade. With his installation a completely new personality entered on the scene and precipitated dramatic consequences by attempting to cut the Gordian knot of statute, usage and local demand.[19]

1. *Scholars in Dawson's department, October 1791*

Thompson	⎫
Tomkinson Jno	⎬ Merchants' Accounts
Warburton	Mensuration
Holland Edwd	D^o
Atherton	Vulgar Fractions
Hadfield Charles	D^o
Pickering	D^o
Ellis	Arithmetic V
Banton	D^o
Alcock	D^o
Tomkinson Rich^d	D^o

Holland W^m
Stanway
Hough
Moore
Barlow Matthew }Reading and Writing
Weedall W^m
Stokes
Jackson
Dawson

Barlow Jno
Hadfield Jno
Deakin W^m
Alcock Peter
Weedall Jno
Horton Thos   Girls
Perry
Markland   Miss Barlow   Arithmetic
Horton Rich^d   Miss Pickering   ⎫
Penketh   Miss J. Stubbs   ⎪
Oldham   Miss M. Deakin   ⎬ Writing
Deakin   Miss Gresswell   ⎪
Aston   Mary Clarke   ⎪
Cooke   Maria Dale   ⎭
Deakin   Eliz. Worthen
Chantler   Nancy Worthen
Green   Hannah Dawson

2. *Return of Scholars in the Head Master's Department of Witton School, 17 June 1817*

| Master Parry | Homer's Iliad. Xenophon's Cyropaedia. Sallust's Jugurthine War. Ellis's Shorter Exercises. Neilson's Greek Exercises. English and Latin Composition. |
| – Simon | |

| – Myers | Greek Testament. Horace. Virgil's Aeneid. Ellis's Shorter Exercises. English and Latin Prose. |

– Cliffe	
– Price	Virgil's Eclogues. Caesar's Commentaries.
– T. Simon	Clarke's Exercises. Eton Greek Grammar.
– Coates	

| – Barker | Phaedrus's Fables. Eutropius.* Eton Exempla |
| – P. Barker | Minora. Eton Latin Grammar. |

| – T. Harvey | Collectanea Latina. Eton Latin Grammar. |
| – Wakefield | |

– T. Wakefield	
– H. Parry	Eton Latin Grammar. Valpy's Vocabulary.
– Jos^h Meek	

* A simpler classical historian who first came into regular use in schools in the eighteenth century.

X

Crisis and breakdown, 1823-57

During these years John Deane's foundation proved unworkable according to the rules laid down by him at its institution. The causes of this breakdown lay partly in a clash of personalities which brought the crisis to a head, but the unsatisfactory state of the school during the previous decade showed that the causes lay deeper. Certain difficulties were inherent in the foundation itself, and some lay in the actual wording of the foundation documents, which may have benefited from the 'godlye and discrete advise of the learned', as Deane asserted, but seem to have lacked rigorous legal inspection. Deane himself was apparently aware of another danger inherent in the nature of his foundation. The oversight of the bishop and schoolmaster of Chester was intended to counteract the dangers of parochialism, but it seems probable that the circle of feoffees, with its bias towards Deane's own relations and its self-electing character, was too narrowly local and restricted. Other problems which Witton shared with similar foundations lay in the economic development of the institution. The nature of the original property may have been partly responsible: it included an inn already described as ancient in 1606, land at Larton said to be 'very poor ground tho' of a pretty large extent', and chief rents which apparently could not be raised, where the school did not own the property itself. The misfortunes of the Civil War in Chester and the decline of the old brine production in Northwich were partly responsible, but there was also unenterprising management. The whole resulted in an income inadequate for the various demands of upkeep and salaries.

Furthermore—and this problem could not be solved by reference to the original documents—the norm of education had changed since the sixteenth century, when a classical education represented the training useful to literate men, and Deane's school, if run strictly on the lines laid down by him, was not meeting the educational demands of parents in the neighbourhood. Between 1801 and 1851 the population in the Northwich area doubled, and in 1867

there were 10,000 people within a radius of a mile from Witton
School.[1] The population of the chapelry of Witton was described by
the school feoffees' solicitor, Thomas Ives Brayne Hostage, in 1846
as consisting mainly of labourers, farmers, tradesmen, mechanics,
shopkeepers, salt refiners, and others chiefly engaged in trade.* He
further testified that 'there are not as I believe a dozen persons of
independent property resident with the chapelry whose means of
livelihood do not arise from one or other of the above occupations
or trades with the exception of a few solicitors medical men and
clergy'. A too narrowly vocational training for trade, which
perhaps would have satisfied many parents, was not the function
of the grammar school, but there was room for a broadening of the
curriculum; James Deane, for instance, a surgeon and a man of
some standing in the town, was opposed to the running of the
school solely as a grammar school for the learned languages, because
boys attending it 'would be in great measure precluded from acquir-
ing an English education'. The National School, set up in 1813,
catered for the education of 'the poor' in large numbers—195 boys
and 101 girls in 1825, rising to a thousand in the 1860s. In 1815 the
curate reported that there were in the chapelry twenty-eight day
schools, including the grammar school and the National School,
educating 504 boys and 525 girls; with the exception of those two,
all were private schools in dwelling houses, the majority probably
petty schools.[2] The chief problem in the area, as in so many places,
was the provision of a suitable, and also an acceptable, education for
the 'middle class', a great concern of contemporary educational
reformers.

The school remodelled

When Charles Hand arrived in Northwich in 1823 as headmaster
of Witton School he was twenty-six, a young man whose character-
istics are suggested by the words used in his obituary, written by an
admirer—'earnest', 'high sense of justice', 'integrity', 'severe
discipline', 'upright'. It is difficult to gauge his scholastic ability,
but in his retirement (according to the obituary) he spent his leisure
studying the classics and the Greek Testament, and he had several
works published, including a pamphlet on slavery and 'a learned
argument' on the scriptural basis of papal authority. He came to
a post which offered only £60 a year, but with a promise of £300
when two leases fell in in 1830 and 1831, and in fact he was paid

* The end of the salt duties in 1825 deprived the collectors of employment;
according to Hand, when he was a pupil at the school, a third of the boys
were sons of salt excisemen.

£100 from the start. He bound himself, as previous masters had
done, to employ an usher to teach English scholars, if required to do
so by the feoffees. He had been at the school just over six months,
when the usher, still Robert Hayward, with whom Winstanley had
had disagreements, complained that Hand had corrected his boys,
and accused him of wishing to 'annihilate' the English school. This
seems, indeed, to have been Hand's intention, for on 19 September
1823 he submitted to the feoffees a series of propositions:

1. That the Grammar School has not flourished.
2. That an adequate cause for its depression exists in the circumstances
   of the English School attached to it.
3. That such an appendage is subversive of the well-being of a grammar
   school, and contrary as well to the original constitution of Witton School
   as to the universal example of similar establishments.
4. That by it pupils are kept from the grammar-school, and the friends of
   those in the school have already, in some instances, expressed their
   regret that its members are exposed to the contagion of boys of the
   worst principles and lowest habits, whose conversation is corrupt alike
   in matter and style.
5. That whilst the present English school in various ways deteriorates and
   suppresses the grammar-school, it is attended with no advantageous
   results whatever.
6. That it be therefore abolished.
7. That the grammar-school, receiving universally such boys as, according
   to the intention of the founder, shall be presented for instruction in the
   languages of Greece and Rome, etc., shall be open also for the occasional admission of select pupils to receive an exclusively English
   education.

After some delay the feoffees met early in October to consider
these propositions, and also the 'propriety' of fixing the number of
boys to be taught free by the headmaster for his salary. Eight feoffees
were present, and Sir John Fleming Leicester apparently sent a
resolution by a clergyman named Gee recommending the feoffees to
support Hand 'in the situation to which they have chosen him', and
to make rules answering to the original purpose of the foundation:
'being originally founded as a *Grammar* School, the formation of
an *English* School ought to be subordinated to the original Institution'. This proposition was very reasonable, and might have led to
some such arrangement as existed at Macclesfield. The feoffees
adopted a fresh scheme for the school, and ordered Hayward* to
cease to attend as usher. Under the new arrangement the headmaster
was to teach grammar in English, Latin and Greek free to twenty

---

* Hayward had earlier (26 September) announced that he would discontinue his attendance because of Hand's 'insolence'. (*School Recs.*, box E,
bundle 1.)

boys, nominated by the feoffees as foundation boys. In addition the feoffees authorised fees: boys not on the foundation were to be charged for the same subjects a guinea a quarter, while all boys at the school were to make smaller quarterly payments for writing and accounts. Two weeks later the school was put under the sole direction of the headmaster. The arrangement had obvious similarities to that suggested by Winstanley in 1819.[3]

Hand clearly intended to make this admittedly 'much neglected' foundation into a profitable and socially respectable establishment. Alterations at the school were sanctioned by the feoffees: in 1824 they ordered the conversion of the school cellar into a dwelling, presumably for a caretaker, and in 1828 authorised two new windows for the schoolroom. Boarders now came to the school, lodging both in Hand's house and in the town. (There was no official master's house, and the feoffees refused a suggestion in 1829 by the tenant of the Saracen's Head that he should provide a house in Witton for the master, which the feoffees would take in exchange for the property in Chester which he rented.) The master was also to resume his place in the community: in June 1824 the feoffees resolved that a pew in Witton Chapel should be bought for £50 for the use of the master: Hand's own master, Robert Litler, had had his own pew for a time, but in 1795 the pew had been leased out by the feoffees.

There are signs that Hand stood on his rights in relation to the curate and wardens of Witton Chapel. A copy of a long letter from him to the Bishop of Chester in October 1825 reveals a sad deterioration in relations between the school and the chapel, once so intimately connected. The site of the school was partly responsible. As we have seen, during the alterations to the churchyard paths in 1814 the way into the school was to have been moved to the east side of the building, leading off the new way round the chapel yard, but in fact, as the feoffees had complained in 1817, the wardens had diverted the way into the north end of the school. Probably owing to the decay of the school nothing was done to meet the feoffees' complaint, so that on his arrival Hand found that the main door of the school was unusable except by opening large iron gates, the key of which was in the wardens' possession. He accepted the situation until 1825, when, so he said, the curate acquired a close off the chapel yard and had a cow driven regularly along the new narrow footpath used by the scholars. As Hand pedantically phrased it, the curves of the path were so abrupt that they 'allow a person to come in contact with the horns of the cow without the least notice'. Hand threw down the iron fence which made the approach to the school awkward, and although the outcome of his appeal to the bishop is not known, he was clearly prepared to take on the curate and the wardens single-handed. He had a sharp eye, too, to the profits of the school estates. In 1827, writing to John Barker, he pointed out that the Larton tenant in his letter had originally intended offering a larger rent but had altered the figure. Hand was for holding him strictly to his covenant about repairs, and his offer to go over to Larton himself was accepted by the feoffees in 1828.[4]

Hand apparently had some success with his experiment. Whereas when Hayward was usher Hand had had only three pupils, in 1825 he had in his charge twenty boys (in his words, 'young gentlemen'), double the number under Whitworth, and in 1832 there were still eighteen. The trustees themselves later admitted that there was a considerable number of paying pupils. Hand's pupils in 1825 included three Barkers, one Hadfield (the son of John Hadfield, surgeon, of Middlewich), who went on to Caius College, a boy from Liverpool, who boarded in the town, and the son of a gentleman of Holywell, Hand's own town, who went on to his own college, Jesus College, Oxford.* (It may be recalled that in 1819 Winstanley told John Barker that he could not advise him to send his boys to the school while the usher's school remained.†) The parents who later gave evidence for Hand were satisfied with his teaching, if not especially enthusiastic, but he seems to have had a reputation for severity in punishment, and two witnesses who had been free scholars accused him of bias against them. Similar charges of bias against free boys occur at other schools at this time, including Stockport. The Charity Commissioners who investigated the administration of John Deane's endowment in 1836 were forthright in denouncing what they called 'this most improper system', namely the imposition of fees and limitation of free scholars, and according to them the trustees nominated only two boys to be taught free in eight years. Witton School was thereby coming close to the state of Malpas Grammar School, where for forty years the headmaster, John Vaughan, carried on a flourishing school (including some pupils who came by the Eastham packet from Liverpool) 'without the incumbrance of any free boys'. John Deane's school was thus being made an instrument of social discrimination contrary to the foundation, even if in its curriculum it now approximated more closely to the founder's rules. Although later, in the course of a legal battle, Hand championed the narrowest definition of a

* See the list at the end of this chapter.
† Hand's relations with Barker in 1825 were very good: in a letter to Barker of 1 February 1825 he referred to 'the many and great kindnesses you have conferr'd upon me'. (*School Recs.*, box D.)

grammar school as a place for teaching classical languages, in fact English and also geography were taught under him, and, when there was an usher, writing and arithmetic. Ushers came and went spasmodically: there were four between 1824 and 1832, mostly living in Hand's house, and paid by him.[5]

Discontent and conflict

Not unnaturally this educational policy caused discontent in the chapelry, and in November 1826 a vestry meeting was called to restore the school to 'its primitive and legitimate regulations'. What these were in the meeting's view is shown by the following resolutions passed by over seventy parishioners:

1. That from time immemorial the free grammar school of Witton, in the County of Chester, having been supplied by the feoffees of the said school, and the wardens of the parochial chapelry of Witton aforesaid, with an assistant master to instruct in reading (gratis) the children of the parishioners admitted to the same, thereby enabling the classic master the better to attend to the duties of his department: and the inhabitants at the present day, taking more especially into consideration the great increase of population, being fully convinced of the utility and necessity for preserving such regulations as aforesaid, do earnestly request the said feoffees and churchwardens to proceed without delay to the nomination and appointment of an assistant master, as before time, under the like injunctions, privileges, salaries and stipulations as those by which his predecessors have been appointed.
2. That the intention of the Founder and the usage at the aforesaid school having confined the benefits thereof as relates to the admission of the Scholars, to the children of the parish only (the Founder's kin excepted) and that boarders whether in the Master's house or in any other are exempted as prejudicial to the tuition of the children of the parishioners it is hereby Resolved that none of the latter description, viz. boarders from other parishes be admitted.
3. Resolved that in conformity to Statute the sixteenth of the Founder the Bailiff Feoffees being therein required to make up their Accounts and produce the same to the other Feoffees and to the Church wardens for the time being of Witton aforesaid on Christmas Eve annually it is hereby requested that the said Statute be punctually observed.[6]

Hayward's dismissal had not only left a gap in the provision of education in the district, but in particular had deprived the parents of free instruction in reading for their children. The hostility of the inhabitants to boarders was understandable, but it was an obstacle to one method of improving the school's financial position.

This local hostility may have weighed with the feoffees, although they took no action to comply with the parishioners' request for an usher for several years, and only after a breach with Hand had already arisen. This breach arose out of financial disagreements: a promise had been made to Hand on his appointment, and had indeed been included in the circular advertising the post,* that when the Chester leases fell in his salary would be raised to £300. In fact the lease of the Saracen's Head property was surrendered before its time, and when it was re-let in 1825 at £75 a year the master's salary was raised to £150. Both Hand and the trustees knew that the Swan lease was to expire in January 1830, when he could expect his increase. Relations deteriorated in 1829. Hand had embarked on repairs and alterations to the school beyond those authorised by the trustees—four windows instead of two and wainscoting to replace the plain boarding in the schoolroom, and in January 1830 the trustees disclaimed responsibility and protested their inability to pay. When the Swan lease fell in, the trustees put the property in the hands of a house agent, who improved the rent by over £100, increasing the school's total rental to about £270, but they refused to raise Hand's salary, claiming that the extra income should be used to pay an usher and for repairs: the Charity Commissioners later reported the Swan extremely decayed through age. As early as October 1830 the feoffees proposed to take legal advice as to the disposal of the surplus: whether they were bound to pay over the increase to Hand or had the right to appoint an usher.[7]

As a result of their counsel's advice the feoffees in the autumn of 1831 rescinded their resolution of 1823, which he had described as 'very unadvised', and subsequently did their best to conceal the fact that they themselves had authorised Hand's management of the school and the imposition of fees.† From July 1831 they took care to head their minutes 'Witton Free Grammar School' and not, as formerly, 'Witton School' or simply 'the trustees', and they ordered the printing of copies of the foundation and statutes. In response to the feoffees' recourse to legal advice, Hand threatened to take proceedings against them in the Court of Chancery, and although the threat was not put into force until January 1834 the situation was full of uncertainty, so much so that the churchwardens refused to co-operate with the feoffees in the appointment of the usher for fear of being involved in a lawsuit. In 1831 both feoffees and master were casting about for legal precedents in their favour: Hand cited a decision relating to Thetford School, while the feoffees pinned their hopes on that relating to Ashby de la Zouch, where the Lord

* One candidate, Robert Wilkinson, had wisely asked if there was to be a bond assuring the master of the increase. (*School Recs.*, box A.)

† See especially their calculatedly misleading reply to the enquiry by the Secretary of State. (Minute Book, 25 November 1833.)

Chancellor had decided that 'the school was not for the instruction in the learned languages *only* but for instruction in the minor branches of Science, "Juvenes pueros infantes et parvilos [*sic*]" being mentioned in the foundation Act—persons too young to be taught Latin and nothing but Latin'. The feoffees' counsel, however, dismissed this case as irrelevant to Witton, which was intended to be strictly a grammar school, with a strictly subordinate usher's department, and he rejected the feoffees' anachronistic argument that, since Deane had, by his will, left 10s a year to his *poor scholars*, 'it is not to be supposed but he intended useful knowledge to be taught'. Hand, blaming the 'recklessness, illegality and perfidy' of his opponents for forcing him into legal action, maintained that 'an usher in Sir John Deane's foundation would be a subsidiary teacher of the Latin and Greek languages', and that the only way of settling a point 'involving the essential character of the institution' was by reference to the Lord Chancellor. Financial disputes had thus led on to a debate on matters of principle, and by the middle of 1831 feeling on both sides was very bitter.[8]

In June 1832 the feoffees appointed as usher, at £20 a year, Thomas Jones, who in 1830 had opened a school at Macclesfield to educate 'a limited number of Ladies and Gentlemen', and had formerly been Classical Assistant at 'Mr Magnus' Academy, Foden Bank'. He had, incidentally, been educated at a Dissenting college in Carmarthen, where he claimed to have learned Latin, Greek and Hebrew. With the appointment of the usher the dispute passed beyond words to actions, and what the Charity Commissioners called the 'squabbles (for they scarcely deserve a more dignified name) between the headmaster and the trustees' took on a more disreputable colour. Hand at first denied the usher access through the outer door which led to both the upper and lower storeys, but after the feoffees had changed the lock, they circulated in the town, in August 1832, printed handbills (placarded on the church door, according to Hand) to advertise the opening of the usher's department. The advertisement was carefully worded: 'the usher now attends daily for the purpose of performing his duty as usher or under-master'. 'Boys of six years of age and upwards, residing in the parochial chapelry of Witton, will be taught grammar free; writing, accounts and other branches of education are to be paid for.' The language whose grammar was to be taught was not specified. Hand later maintained that Jones taught only the elements of the learned languages to two or three children, and was ignorant of them, and that the children were not sent for the purpose of receiving classical instruction. The trustees replied that Jones taught the Latin grammar and the elements of the learned languages, as in their belief he was competent to do, but they did not conceal that his true function was to teach English grammar, reading, writing and arithmetic.

For a few months there was a lull: while Hand taught his classical scholars, to the number of eighteen at midsummer 1832, in the lower schoolroom, the usher had pupils numbering at one time over 120 (the vast majority boys) in the upper room and overflowing into the library. In his complaint to Chancery Hand asserted that many of these children were under six; that some of them had neither shoes, stockings nor shirts; that a great number of them wore clogs, and that Jones was quite unable to control them.* In February 1833 his complaint to the feoffees was met by an order for sawdust to be put on the school stairs, and an injunction to Jones to control his pupils. It may be observed that 120 pupils were vastly more than previous ushers had taught; the total had been usually in the forties. (Jones claimed that he had eighty to ninety pupils at first, and subsequently fifty.) Meanwhile Hand's classical scholars declined by midsummer to eleven, and fell still lower: according to the trustees, the removal of scholars from his school (among whom were Thomas Cheshire, William Worthington and two sons of John Barker) was due to dissatisfaction with him, but Hand himself ascribed the loss to the nuisance of the upper school. By March 1833 Hand had revoked his undertaking not to obstruct the usher, and declared his immediate intention of resorting to Chancery: early in August he barricaded the school door against Jones and his pupils. The trustees, who in March 1833 declared they were not justified in paying the headmaster's salary,† were embarking late in 1833 on an action against Hand for obstruction. In February 1835 they recognised defeat on one front when they discontinued the usher's salary until the school should be reopened to him, and ended their Minute Book with the statement 'There are now no Scholars at the School'. An attempt was made to reopen in the next year. In February 1836 Jones was required to give notice of his school being open for the teaching of grammar, but in October he was discharged from his post after Christmas 1836.[9]

Such was the dismal state of John Deane's school when the Charity Commissioners arrived in April 1836 to investigate the management of the foundation. They found, as they said in their

---

* A point in dispute between witnesses was whether Jones's pupils were of a lower class than the pupils of former ushers. Years later, in 1870, Weston was told by William Holland, sexton of Witton and a pupil under Jones, that the scholars were the roughest lot of youths who were ever brought together. (Weston, Notebook No. 6.)

† In 1832 Hand had refused to sign a receipt lest his case for an increase should be prejudiced. (*C.C.R.*)

report, a woman occupying the lower part of the school to give information, but not only were there no scholars but no applications for admission either. As the commissioners observed, it was 'deeply to be regretted that so respectable an endowment should have been placed in such a situation as to be injurious rather than beneficial to the inhabitants of the chapelry'. Since the dispute between Hand and the trustees was *sub judice* at the time, the commissioners did not comment on the issues involved, but they deplored the 'dissension and party spirit' in the populous community. They also speculated as to whether the poor relations between the master and the trustees might not have originated in the constitution of the school laid down by its founder. Studying the list of masters, they observed that over a period of eighty-five years (out of the school's 278) there had been twenty-five masters, whose respective stays had averaged only three years and eight months. The list given by the commissioners was in fact rather inaccurate, both in names and dates, and their statement that none of these masters died in office is untrue. They ignored the fact that Swinton was deprived under the Act of Uniformity and that Fishwick was merely a *locum tenens*, nor did they make allowance for the disturbed period of the Civil War. Nevertheless the commissioners had put their finger on a recurring weakness in the history of the school from the late seventeenth century onwards, the period of decaying finances. The commissioners were inclined to suspect that 'the close contact of the masters with the trustees (who have always been selected from among the inhabitants of the chapelry*) must have led to misunderstandings, and created local and personal prejudices', and they were able to quote Deane's own letter of 1561 to show the early existence of local dissension. The Charity Commissioners closed their report on Witton School with the hope that the proceedings then pending in Chancery might 'have the effect of placing the charity on such a basis as will secure a full enjoyment of the advantages intended for the inhabitants of Witton by its pious founder'.[10]

The resort to law

The dispute between Hand and the feoffees entered at the beginning of 1834 the labyrinth of the Court of Chancery. This was the Chancery evoked by Dickens in *Bleak House*. The famous passage

---

* It is, perhaps, relevant to note here the death in 1827 of Sir John Fleming Leicester (first Lord de Tabley), who, as a feoffee of the school, had supported Hand in 1823: his death left the circle of feoffees entirely local. The de Tabley influence in Witton was lessened by the sale of the advowson in 1828.

at the beginning of the novel conjures up imaginatively the windings of a Chancery case:

Never can there come fog too thick, never can there come mud and mire too deep, to assort with the groping and floundering condition which this High Court of Chancery, most pestilent of hoary sinners, holds, this day, in the sight of heaven and earth.... On such an afternoon, some score of members of the High Court of Chancery bar ought to be—as here they are —mistily engaged in one of the ten thousand stages of an endless cause, tripping one another up on slippery precedents, groping knee-deep in technicalities, running their goat-hair and horse-hair warded heads against walls of words, and making a pretence of equity with serious faces, as players might. On such an afternoon, the various solicitors in the cause, some two or three of whom have inherited it from their fathers, who made a fortune by it, ought to be—as are they not?—ranged in a line, in a long matted well (but you might look in vain for Truth at the bottom of it), between the registrar's red table and the silk gowns, with bills, cross-bills, answers, rejoinders, injunctions, affidavits, issues, references to masters, masters' reports, mountains of costly nonsense piled before them.

Dickens's picture of Chancery proceedings was scarcely exaggerated: delay was by this date built into the Chancery system at every one of the numerous stages of its proceedings. By their very nature they were cumbersome and dilatory, producing mountains of documents, since all the proceedings were now in writing. The Witton School suit experienced almost to the full the delays of which the Chancery system was capable.

The case of the Attorney General, at the relation of Charles Hand *v.* John Barker and his fellow trustees ate over twenty years out of the life of the school. It absorbed a crippling proportion of the school's income, made inroads on its capital, and can have profited nobody in the community of Witton and Northwich except the solicitors who managed the trustees' case. The community as a whole suffered from the divisions arising out of the case, for local feeling ran high.* The effects penetrated through all the layers of society: in support of their statements Hand and the trustees brought sworn evidence from sixty-four and thirty-one witnesses respectively. Former ushers, former scholars (several aged eleven and twelve, and one, aged sixteen, then at Manchester Grammar School) and parents of scholars testified during 1836 to the merits and demerits of Hand or of Jones. The parents' occupations ran from 'esquire of Leftwich', gentleman' of Hartford or of Winnington, solicitor of Northwich, through all the various tradesmen and shopkeepers—bookseller, mercer, innkeeper, hatter, saddler, cord-

* Echoes of it were still heard when Hand's death was reported in the *Northwich and Winsford Guardian* of 13 September 1873.

wainer, blacksmith—to 'navigator', flatman employed by the navigation, bricksetter and labourer.[11]

The effects of the case on the opportunities for education in the neighbourhood must have been disrupting: where did the 112 boys and eleven girls* who had been under Jones, and the much smaller number under Hand, get their education? Of those who had been under Hand, two were removed to be sent to school away from home; a solicitor sent his son to Shrewsbury School; William Stelfox of Hartford, gent., sent his son to a private school at Hartford kept subsequently by Thomas Jones himself. There is very little evidence about the education of Jones's pupils. Two fathers, a hatter and a nailmaker, sent their sons to fee-paying schools, but another, a bricksetter, could not afford this. Hand produced as witnesses two private schoolmasters and the master of the National School to testify to the number of schools for reading, writing and arithmetic within a mile of the grammar school. Besides the National School, where the charge was a penny a week, there were seven private schools, of which four had existed when the usher's school was opened; these schools mostly varied in size from thirty to fifty, though one, Edward Rothwell's, averaged sixty to eighty, and their charges varied from 4s or 5s to 15s a quarter.[12]

At a fairly early stage in the Chancery case signs of public disquiet were shown in a resolution passed at a vestry meeting in January 1839. The vestry asked that the suit should be referred to the Bishop of Chester for arbitration. Hand was agreeable to this, but the feoffees, advised by their lawyers, declined to answer the suggestion until the churchwardens had been made parties to the suit. When this was done, the churchwardens, also under legal advice, declined the proposed arbitration. Thus ended the possibility of an early conclusion to the dispute. Public concern was not confined to Northwich and district, for a note on the school highly critical of the feoffees appeared in the *Chester Courant* of 8 October 1839. The writer, after describing the origin of the school, summarised the object of 'this admirable foundation, which is very similar to St Paul's School', as 'to give a liberal education at a moderate expense to all who might choose a profession, more particularly the Church, and to be a benefit for ever to the neighbourhood where the founder was born'. The original endowment was described as 'for the time' 'very munificent', and had it been well managed 'for the use limited by the founder' it could have been worth £1,000 a year at the present time. After describing the Chancery case, on the master's prayer to have the feoffees dismissed for mismanagement, the article underlined the fact that

* Figures given by Hand.

this was the third time the school's affairs had been in Chancery, and that each time a lawyer had been one of the bailiff feoffees. The article provoked an indignant but unspecific letter from the bailiff trustees denouncing it as a 'tissue of falsehoods', and asserting their willingness to satisfy any enquirer as to the true state of affairs. The next number of the *Courant* included a repetition of the feoffees' letter and an aggressive letter from 'A. Hand' proposing a meeting between the writer of the article and the bailiff trustees at the school, at which 'A. Hand' would prove the article substantially correct.[13]

The arguments

The differences between Hand and the trustees can be summarised under three headings. The first consisted of different interpretations of the historical evidence about the nature of the school and its curriculum and about the financial arrangements, particularly the relation between the total revenue and the master's salary. The second lay in differences of opinion about the course of events from the appointment of Hand, and the third, and more constructive, part was the submission of different schemes for the future management of the school for the decision of the Court of Chancery.

On the first point Hand argued that until the previous fifty or sixty years—that is, up to about 1770 or 1780—the school, as founded by John Deane, had been 'exclusively conducted as a grammar school', but that during the last fifty or sixty years the trustees had appointed ushers to teach English reading, writing and arithmetic. The admission of children to be taught the three Rs and not the elements of the learned languages was, in Hand's view, contrary to the nature and objects of the foundation and against the school's laws and statutes. The trustees, in their answer, were anxious to prove from the accounts going back to 1577* that there had always been an usher, paid by themselves and not by the churchwardens. They cited the case in the Chester Exchequer Court in 1717 which, they held, (inaccurately) turned on the two questions—by whom an usher should be appointed, the headmaster or the trustees, and whether or not he should teach English. The case had ended in mutual consent, and subsequently the appointment of an usher was resumed, and continued without a break. They countered Hand's arguments that the master had formerly lodged in,

---

* The feoffees were somewhat inaccurate about these dates. Elizabeth I's regnal year ran from 17 November to 16 November, so that 11 October, 20 Elizabeth, the first date in the account book, was 11 October 1578, since 20 Elizabeth ran from 17 November 1577 to 16 November 1578.

and always controlled, the upper storey of the school, by tracing the building back to 1747 and maintaining that the lower storey, 'as defendants believe', had always been used by the headmaster and the upper storey by the usher, 'in which it has been customary for a period long before the reach of living memory' for him to teach English grammar free, and writing and accounts for a small fee. The trustees reinforced their views on the curriculum of the school by producing the episcopal licence given to Thomas Jones, the eighteenth-century master, empowering him to teach not only grammar but writing and arithmetic. The trustees disclaimed knowledge as to whether 'from the time of the death of Sir John Dean the school was conducted exclusively as a grammar school for the teaching of the learned languages'. Admitting that, as Hand claimed, there were other schools in Witton 'such as Sunday schools and National schools', they asserted that 'tradespeople and farmers will not send their children to them, whereas such persons, and even those in higher stations, have always been accustomed to send their children, both girls and boys, to the usher of Witton School'. (They curiously omitted to take into account the private schools.) It will be seen that while Hand's case rested on the letter of the foundation documents, especially the statutes, the trustees' case was founded on alleged traditional practice going back 'long before the reach of living memory', and on a belief that the teaching of English grammar, reading, writing and arithmetic was 'not contrary to the spirit of the original foundation'.

On the financial side Hand asserted that until fifty or sixty years ago the whole of the revenues, originally £12, after payments for repairs, had been paid over to the headmaster, but that since then part had been allotted to the usher. The trustees contradicted by insisting that at the time of the foundation the revenues exceeded £12, and that after the master's salary had been paid a fund was accumulated out of the surplus. Not until within the last fifty or sixty years were the whole revenues of the school, after repairs, handed over to the master: on the contrary, £10 to £20 a year had usually been paid to the master as a remuneration for teaching 'an indefinite number of boys'. Here the trustees' account seems to agree more with the evidence of the account books.

When it came to the course of recent events Hand's chief charges concerned the trustees' management of the property and their attitude to him over the promised increase of his salary to £300, and the 'unauthorised' appointment of an usher to teach English and the three Rs. Hand charged the trustees with allowing houses and property belonging to the school to fall into disrepair without adequate compensation from the tenants. Furthermore he accused the bailiff feoffees of having wrongly been in office for ten instead of two years, and made allegations that, with one exception, all the trustees were related to, or connected with, either John Barker or the deceased bailiff feoffee, John Marshall. The 'information' demanded an account from the trustees of the management of the property, payment for what Hand had spent on repairs at the school, and also the arrears of his salary at £300 a year from January 1830. The trustees explained their failure to pay the promised increase of salary (which they did not deny) by 'the depreciated state of landed property, and the expense of necessary repairs'. Denying the accusation of mismanagement, they pointed out that part of the Chester property consisted of two ancient houses and twelve old cottages apparently built centuries ago, which had become 'what builders call spent'. They had begun an action against the tenant for dilapidations, but being advised to compromise, they had accepted a sum fixed by a respectable builder as compensation. Admitting that the new lease of the Swan property had raised the yield by over £100, they had thought it should be used for repairs and to pay an usher. They defended the lengthy tenure of office of the two bailiff feoffees as an old custom, 'because it was desirable that such office should be held by men of business', and counter-attacked by describing the alterations carried out by Hand at the school as 'mere ornamental and quite unnecessary' as well as unauthorised. The usher's appointment they justified on the scores of tradition and public demand.

For the future Hand demanded a complete change of trustees, that the school should be conducted 'altogether as a grammar school', and that a new scheme of management should be settled by one of the Masters of Chancery. The trustees submitted to the judgement of the court the question of the future curriculum and management of the school. The exact nature of the school in the future did not arise in the case until much later when detailed schemes were submitted by several parties. [14]

In January 1834 the trustees were informed of a subpoena summoning them to appear in the Court of Chancery to answer a Bill of complaint, and in June they swore to the answer drawn up by their solicitor. Only one thing in the Chancery case was settled briskly, at least for the time being, and that was the question of Hand's salary. As early as October 1835 the Vice-chancellor ordered that the trustees should pay Hand £600 for his salary to Michaelmas 1835, and from then a salary of £150 a year: they were to continue this payment until the hearing of the cause. The trustees were thus saddled with this payment although the school was not functioning, and in addition they were paying large sums to their solicitor during the 'thirties. They had to pay these sums out of estates which, for whatever reason, were presenting more and more problems. Larton Farm was the most difficult: as early as 1811 the trustees had paid for a plan and estimate for a new farmhouse, but nothing had come of it and the deterioration had continued. In 1835 the new tenant threatened to quit unless his rent was reduced, and the Charity Commissioners recorded that 'the farmhouse and buildings are in a state of considerable decay'. After the expiry of a twenty-one year lease of the Saracen's Head property in 1846 the trustees discovered that the tenant had failed to prevent the building of part of the Commercial Hall on the school's land. At the Swan property the trustees had difficulties over regaining compensation for dilapidations in 1830. At Ball's Croft a sub-tenant was quarrying stone without any authority and after the end of the lease. The land in Northwich, the site of the original *salina*, was bringing in its £3 a year, but the chief rents in Peover and Agden were either lost or on the way to being so: at Peover in 1844 the tenant denied his liability to pay, and at Agden the rent had not been paid for over forty years.[15]

As the Chancery case progressed, if that is the correct word, the number of trustees was steadily diminished by death. As early as 1833 there had been only eight trustees living, but Hand's attitude to the last election inhibited the trustees from making up their number. In 1836 Thomas Chantler, the son, died, and Thomas Marshall, elected bailiff feoffee in 1833, was incapacitated by ill-health and had to be replaced by William Twemlow. By March 1841 John Barker, the leading trustee, had died. As bailiff feoffee since 1818 he had held the school books and documents, and when in August 1841 his son sent to the trustees the Witton School chest, with the school papers, the trustees recorded their opinion in the Minute Book that 'from the deranged state in which it has been represented to us the affairs of the late Mr. Barker have been left and from the confused state of the school accounts' it was desirable to call in an accountant to discover what was due to the school from Barker's estate. Although nearly £100 was due, the school obtained only just over £50, a dividend of 11*s* in the pound. By 1843 Twemlow had died, only three trustees survived and during almost all the meetings from 1846 to 1848 only James Royds was present: from 1848 to 1851 no meeting of the trustees was held.[16]

Delays, decree and debates

After the trustees had put in their answer there was some delay until the end of 1836, when the witnesses were examined in the town.

but a more serious cause of delay was the trustees' objection, raised
before the Lord Chancellor in December 1838 and January 1839,
that the churchwardens should have been made parties to the suit.
Eventually the Lord Chancellor decided in their favour, and this
meant that Hand had to amend his Bill; as the trustees' agent wrote,
'he will almost have to begin *de novo*'.[17] Apart from this, much of
the demoralising delay seems to have been due to Hand: in 1840,
five years after the original order in the case, the trustees moved
that the suit should be dismissed for want of prosecution by the
plaintiff, Hand, but this was refused when he gave assurances that
he would speed matters. Much later the trustees attributed the delay
principally to Hand's 'pecuniary inability' to carry on proceedings.
The trustees had their own financial difficulties. They were committed to paying Hand's salary until the case was heard, but in
October 1841 they were in debt to their counsel and unable to pay
Hand's salary of the previous year. They therefore gave notice to
Hand to prosecute the suit within three months or they would
withhold his salary or move the court to suspend the order (for its
payment) until the re-hearing. A final attempt at an adjustment of
the suit failed, and the case came at last before the Vice-chancellor in
1844. By a decree of 25 June the school was declared to be a free
grammar school (though without mention of the usher), and certain
parts of the suit charging the trustees with misconduct and neglect
of the school's property were dismissed, but without prejudice to
the question of costs.* The chief points at issue were then referred
to one of the Masters in Chancery: these were a survey of the
school property and the settling of what was due to Hand as salary
and as repayment for cost of repairs; the making up of the number
of trustees to the proper total of twelve; and, most important of
all, the settling of a proper scheme for the future management of the
trust in accordance with the feoffment, rules, statutes, Deane's
letter and, in addition, the recent Act of Parliament regulating
grammar schools. This Act, passed in 1840, empowered trustees of
endowed grammar schools to extend the curriculum beyond the
narrow limits laid down at the foundation.[18]

The reference to the Master began a new cycle in the affair, for
procedure before the Chancery Masters was almost inconceivably
dilatory. More affidavits had to be sworn by the parties; in March
1845 the trustees approved a scheme for the future management of
the trust and the school, and in December 1846 a survey of the
properties was ordered. The Master had in fact three different
schemes before him, put forward by Hand, the trustees and the

---

* Later Hand was required to bear the costs of this part of the Bill. (*The
Times* law report, 1 May 1852.)

churchwardens, and these contained significant variations. The chief aim of the current wardens (among whom was Thomas Richard Barker, son of John Barker) was to make the most, and more, of the references to them in Deane's foundation documents, and to set themselves up beside the trustees in the choice of master and usher. They were anxious, too, to restrict the choice of trustees to residents in the chapelry, and the privilege of free education at the school to the founder's kin and boys resident within the chapelry. The trustees, in their scheme, were with the wardens as far as the freedom of the school went but they were strongly opposed to the residence qualification for trustees. In a marginal note on the wardens' scheme the trustees objected that there were 'few such persons [i.e. residents within the chapelry] who either from station, property or intelligence would be proper trustees and free from the imputation of jobbing': if residence was demanded they wished the property qualification to be raised. (They had in 1846 suggested nine names to complete their number, and these included Lord de Tabley, James Hugh Smith Barry and the Rt. Hon. Edward John Stanley.) The churchwardens' views played little part, however, since the Master decided that they had no power to introduce a scheme, so that the conflict of views lay between Hand and the trustees.

Hand's scheme was more traditional, and clung to the details of the statutes: it retained examination of a new master by the bishop and schoolmaster of Chester and preference for the founder's kin or an ex-pupil in the choice of master. Further it insisted that, to remove a master, the trustees should apply either to the bishop or to the Court of Chancery. Hand wished to restrict the freedom of the school to the much narrower limits of the *township* instead of the chapelry of Witton, holding to the words of the deed of feoffment, that the school was 'for the good instruction of boys within the township of Witton near Northwich': scholars from outside the township were to pay tuition fees set by the master. Hand also stood by the classical and religious ideals expressed by Deane: he wished the master to teach the Latin and Greek tongues, authors and composition, the boys to 'serve God in the school' twice (Deane had said thrice) daily; and he laid down in minute detail the passages from the Bible to be read. He mentioned no other subjects, and made no provision for an usher. The founder's kinsfolk were to be preferred as trustees if they were Church of England communicants.

The trustees disagreed with Hand, of course, on the matters of the size of the master's salary, the procedure for removing him, and his role in managing the school, but their most significant differences were on the curriculum and the freedom of the school; on both of these the Master, Sir George Rose, seems to have been sympathetic

to them. As far as the 'freedom' was concerned, Rose was bound by
the words in the feoffment 'villa' and 'juxta Northwich', so the
trustees took pains to point out the powers given by Deane to the
'churchwardens of Northwich', and their solicitor swore to a paper
which he had found after a search among the school records showing
that the inhabitants of the *chapelry* had contributed £100 to the
new school building put up about 1747.* Furthermore, they produced statements from four 'old boys' of the school, two yeoman,
one 'gentleman', and one salt proprietor, whose ages ranged from
fifty-nine to seventy-four, proving that the school had existed for
the benefit of boys from all the townships of the chapelry, and not
only Witton. In general, too, the trustees emphasised the small number of houses in Witton, compared with Northwich and the other
townships. The trustees wished the curriculum to consist of Latin
and Greek, but also mathematics, geography, general history, and
other branches of literature 'requisite or proper to qualify scholars
for the learned professions and for trade and mercantile business':
these subjects were to be taught by the master while the usher taught
reading, writing and accounts, the rudiments of Latin, history and
geography. The trustees were told that the Chancery Master was
disposed to extend the teaching as much as possible, but that he
was doubtful if he could insert mathematics; he thought, however,
that the phrase 'all branches of a liberal Education so as to qualify
the scholars for the learned professions ... etc.' would answer the
purpose. By way of reinforcing their case the trustees' solicitor
gave evidence of the dominance of the salt industry in the area. This
seems to be the first sign of the trustees' desire for a more modern
education, as distinct from elementary instruction by the usher.[19]

The report of the Chancery Master

The Master, Sir George Rose, produced his report in March 1850,
after considering all the various school documents, statements of
facts, and schemes laid before him. Rose reviewed the foundation
deeds and the original school properties, almost all of which (the
exception being Agden) were still in the possession of the trustees
and brought in £366 gross, annual rent (£266 net). He named ten
new trustees to fill up the trust, including Lord Stanley of Alderley,
Rowland Egerton Warburton of Arley Hall, Lee Porcher Towns-
hend† of Wincham Hall, the Rev. Richard Greenall,‡ Rural Dean,

* See Chapter VIII, pp. 158–9.
† Descended from Thomas Lee of Darnhall; see Chapter VI, p. 104.
‡ Son of Peter Greenall, esq., of Warrington, who had bought the advowson
of Witton at the sale of the manor of Witton in 1828. (Weston, *N.P.C.*, p. 75.)

WITTON CHAPEL AND SCHOOL,

Presented to this Work by Wm Twemlow Esqre   Surgeon of Hatherton & Northwich

He married 1794 Mary Anne   only Child of Peter and Mary

kering of Hartford and Grandaughter   of Thomas and Mary (Venables)

Beswick of Winnington   He also served the Office of one

of the Trustees of this School   for upwards of Twenty Years

TENEO TENVERE MAJORES

Drawn by J Twemlow Esqr & Engraved   by J Pigot & Son Manchester

v Witton Chapel and the second school, from an early nineteenth-century
engraving after J. Twemlow, in Chester Public Library

R U L E S

To be obſerved by the

Scholars *of the* Free-Grammar-School

O F

W I T T O N,

For the Preſervation *of* Diſcipline, *and* Regularity, *and the avoiding-*
of Puniſhments.

I.

EVERY Boy ſhall appear at School preciſely at SIX o'Clock in *Summer*, and at EIGHT in *Winter*; and for every Morning in the Week, that he is *abſent* from School at Prayers, he ſhall have a Taſk of *ten* Lines, to be got the ſucceeding Night; and if abſent *more* than once in one Week, an addition of *five* Lines to be made to his former Taſk; for not getting of which, he *ſhall be puniſhed*.

II.

FOR the proper ſupport of *Neatneſs* and *Decency*, every Boy ſhall come clean waſhed and combed; and for every *Breach* of this Rule, he ſhall have a Taſk to be got the ſucceeding Night.

III.

EVERY Boy ſhall be provided with Pens, Ink, and ſuch Books as are uſually read in his Claſs, or be ſent Home till they be provided.

IV.

IF any one abſent himſelf from School, without *leave* from the Maſter or a *Note* from his Friends; for the firſt Offence, he ſhall be admoniſhed, and have a *Taſk*; for the ſecond, ſhall be *ſeverely* puniſhed; and for the third be *expelled*, as an Example.

V.

HE that tells a *Lie*, *ſwears*, *ſteals*, or is guilty of *profane* or *debauched* Language, ſhall for the firſt Offence, be *admoniſhed* and have a *Taſk*; for the ſecond be *ſeverely* whipped; and for the third *expelled*.

VI.

IF any Boy *breaks* a Window, or does any other *wilful* Damage, he ſhall *pay* for it; and after reaſonable Time being allowed for the Repair, if it be not done, he ſhall be *excluded* the School till Satisfaction be made.

VII.

EVERY Boy that is *idle* and *talkative*, in School-Hours, ſhall be ſpoke to *once* or *twice*; and if perſiſting, have a *Taſk*, and for not getting it be corrected accordingly.

VIII.

Two Impoſitors ſhall be choſen, by weekly Rotation, whoſe Office ſhall be to keep the Keys, acquaint the Maſter when Coals are wanting, and ſee that the School be kept clean; for every Omiſſion of his Duty, he ſhall be *puniſhed*.

IX.

THAT Juſtice may be impartially diſtributed, and to prevent all groundleſs Complaints of Severity; if any Boy pleads *not* guilty to any of the above Rules, he ſhall be tried by *five* of his School-Fellows, and condemned or acquitted by their Determination.

X.

AND, to *encourage* Diligence, *two Books* will be given, every Chriſtmas, by the Maſter, to the *two* Boys, who, in their ſeveral Claſſes, have behaved *beſt*, and made the *greateſt* Improvement in Learning.

XI.

LASTLY, that no one may *plead* Ignorance, or *expect* Indulgences, that cannot be impartially allowed; theſe Rules ſhall be read over, by the Maſter four Times in the Year, at the commencement of every Quarter; and *no* one ſhall be *admitted into* this School, who *will not* ſubmit to be *governed* by them.

29th of July 1786.　We approve of the above Rules.

Penrhyn,	*John Mort*,	*W. Brooke*,	*John Barker*,	*John Furey*,	{ *Tho. Marſhall*, }
J. F. Leiceſter,	*John Cheſhire*,	*W. Thearſby*,	*John Hunt*,	*John Cheney*	{ *Tho. Ives Brayne*, } Bailiff-Feoffees

together with the curate of Witton. He settled the matter of Hand's salary, deciding that the schoolmaster was entitled to only £12 a year out of the school revenues, but that £150 a year was proper to have been allowed him for his salary from 1830 to the hearing of the cause, under the decision of 1835. The most important part of the report, however, was the sixth schedule, which contained his scheme for the future running of the school. He required that as soon as the trustees had the funds they should build a new farm at Larton and put their other properties into repair, but that this should not delay, beyond three years, the payment of a salary of £150 to the headmaster: until then it was to be £60. On the 'freedom' of the school he came down in favour of extending it to the whole of the inhabitants of the chapelry, who were to pay only 4d for admission. On the curriculum, too, he favoured the trustees' views, and included besides classics the subjects they had advocated: the usher was to teach the rudiments of Latin as well as English subjects. Rose had laid down that the school was to be run by an usher as well as a master (scholars were not to be admitted to the usher's school under six, or to the master's under eight), but until the master's salary reached £150 the trustees were not obliged to appoint an usher. The qualifications for future trustees represented a compromise: they were to be either inhabitants of the chapelry of a certain wealth, or non-residents owning freehold property in the chapelry to a certain value or having a certain financial standing. Otherwise the report consisted of details of the running of the school, though these were fairly generally treated.[20]

The Master's report was confirmed by an order of the Court of Chancery in June 1851, but this was not the end of the affair. Although the new trustees* appointed under the order met in September 1851 and elected as bailiff feoffees Lee Porcher Townshend and the Rev. Richard Greenall, who was to play an important role in the school's later history, the new scheme of management did not come into force. The aim of the new trustees was to bring the suit to as speedy an end as possible, but objections to the Master's scheme, almost amounting to a reopening of the case, seem to have been raised by Hand, and the question of costs was yet to be settled. The Attorney General put forward a new scheme, which modified the Master's scheme in various ways. The trustees, though in general approving of the plan, disagreed with it strongly on certain points, some of greater significance than others. The old question recurred as to whether there should be a preference for boys from the *township* of Witton: the trustees opposed this on

* 'Persons of rank and high respectability'. (*The Times*, law report, 11 February 1853.)

the ground that Witton township had only about 2,500 inhabitants
out of a total of 10,000 in the whole chapelry: they particularly
did not wish the special reduced capitation fee of 10s 6d to apply
only to the township boys. They raised objections, too, to required
teaching of the Church catechism and to religious instruction
according to Anglican doctrines, on the ground that it would
lessen the usefulness of the school, since a large proportion of the
local inhabitants were Dissenters. Their other chief objections
were financial: that the proposed salaries of the master and usher,
and the retiring allowance for Hand, were too high in view of the
state of the school's property.[21]

The Vice-chancellor's order and the close of the case

The trustees were unsuccessful in their objections, for when the case
came before the court again, in February 1853, Vice-chancellor
Stuart (hearing one of his first cases)* replaced the Master's scheme
by a fresh one, closely following the Attorney General's. The
trustees' conduct was regulated in much greater detail than in the
Master's scheme,† and the removal of a headmaster was to be subject
to an appeal to the Bishop of Chester. There was a more explicit
emphasis on religion: both masters were to be Anglicans, the headmaster in holy orders, sacred as well as general history was to be
taught, and specifically Anglican instruction was included. The
headmaster's and usher's salaries were fixed at £120 and £60 a year,
but each was allowed to take a certain number of boarders (who,
however, must be taught in common with the other boys) and to
receive a proportion of the capitation fees. These were fixed at a
guinea a quarter for boys from outside the township of Witton but
10s 6d for boys of the township, unless they were learning only
Latin and Greek, when they entered free, a tenuous link with the
original foundation. The pupils were to be drawn from the
chapelry, and only if not enough boys from there attended were
the trustees to admit boys from outside; but, if numbers pressed even
within the chapelry, preference was to go to Witton *township* boys.
The trustees were empowered to engage masters, to whom the boys
would pay fees, to teach modern languages, drawing and other
subjects outside the regular courses. There were arrangements for
an annual examination and prizes, and for the eventual formation
of a library. One of the immediate problems was settled when Hand

---

* W. S. Holdsworth, *A History of English Law*, XIII, 439, described
Stuart as 'not a strong judge'; 'his decisions were often reversed'.

† Though the new farm at Larton and the other repairs were not specified,
as in the Master's report.

was given leave to retire, if he so chose, within the next six months, with a retirement allowance of £80 a year.[22]

The two surviving trustees were ordered by the Vice-chancellor to pay out of the balance of £837 9s 8d, which was reckoned to remain in their hands, £300 to Hand in arrears of salary. Further, they were to pay those costs of the suit which were a charge on the charity property. If these could not be met out of the residue and current income they were to be raised by a mortgage on the school's property. The amount of the costs had still to be settled by the Taxing Master, and this proved to be a lengthy business. These directions dismayed the trustees to such an extent that three of them tendered their resignation, and all feared that the new scheme would be unworkable because of the liabilities it imposed. They considered an appeal to the Lords Justices of Appeal, but on the advice of their legal advisers did not embark on it: since their existing financial obligations were unknown, it was thought unwise to incur others. The years slipped by in the untangling of legal knots relating to the conveyance of the property to the new trustees, and particularly to the determination of the costs payable by the trustees. Hand had actually resigned the mastership in July 1853, and a year later was living in Wales and, according to his legal agent, was starving: this at any rate was said in his plea for payment of his allowance. True to form, Hand's representative delayed sending in his client's costs until some time after the trustees had submitted theirs, and not until July 1855 had the trustees got before them the total bill of costs in the suit:

Costs of Hand taxed* at	£1160	15s	8d
Costs of Attorney General at	78	17s	2d
Costs of churchwardens at	73	2s	2d
	£1312	15s	0d
Arrears of Hand's salary	526	5s	0d
	£1839	0s	0d

To meet this the trustees had only £1,090 18s 10d due to the trust from James Royds, the one surviving old trustee. Several years would be needed to pay off this sum, particularly as there were in addition Hand's retiring allowance of £80 a year, solicitors' bills, and the dilapidations of the buildings at Larton farm to be covered, as well as any current expenses. The new trustees insisted that they would not execute the deed of their appointment until the suit was dismissed. In fact, after lengthy discussions the trustees' legal repre-

* I.e. assessed.

sentatives reached the conclusion that there was no need for a formal dismissal, as the suit had 'died a natural death'. The trustees executed their deed in July 1856, by which time the bulk of the costs had been paid out of the balance, and the Vice-chancellor had authorised them to sell two fields in Chester to raise the remainder. The sale of these two fields in Chester, part of the Swan property, one for £130 and the other for £905, marked the first inroads into John Deane's original endowment. The sale, however, put the trustees in a position to propose opening the school, 'on or about 25 March 1857', on the basis of the new scheme of management and curriculum. They were able to advertise for a headmaster, and to write to training schools at Cirencester, Chester, Battersea, St Mark's Chelsea and Cheltenham about an under-master. The opening of a new phase in the history of the school may be found in the minutes of the trustees of 3 January 1857, when the Rev. Henry Linthwaite, M.A., of Cambridge was chosen as headmaster at a salary of £120 with a proportion of the capitation fees.[23]

Retrospect

It remains to ask what was the significance of Hand's mastership at Witton and of the whole tedious expensive business of the Chancery case. One view was expressed by John Weston, a trustee of the school from 1874, in his booklet on the school first published by order of the governors in 1885. Weston wrote of these events, 'the times had changed: the privilege of the few who desired their sons to receive a classical education was considered the right of the many, and the persistence of the one who stood firm on the lines laid down by the founder [Hand], and who aimed thereby to make this school rank with the great schools of the land, was finally overruled'.[24] This was, no doubt, how Hand himself saw it, and before we dismiss it as unrealistic at this date we should remember the amazing powers of recovery shown by schools, and the remarkable transformations made by outstanding headmasters in this period. However, apart from the qualities needed in the master himself, two conditions seem to have been needed for such recoveries, either operating singly or together. A school had to have numerous boarders or strong support from its local community. Possibly for a time Witton School could have attracted boarders, but it is unlikely that, with the increasing industrialisation of Northwich during the nineteenth century, they would have continued to come in sufficient numbers.* Furthermore,

---

* Helsby, in 1882, referred to 'the sometimes dense smoke of the town'. (Ormerod, III, 162.)

the school itself was later said to be in a bad and possibly an unhealthy position, close to an overcrowded churchyard, and it lacked an official master's house. As far as the community's support went, it seems to have been given chiefly to the usher's department of the school.

The school's misfortune was the gradual separation which had grown up between the master's and the usher's departments, resulting virtually in two schools, of which the 'English' school was the popular and dominant one. From the parishioners' point of view all was well so long as the two were allowed to co-exist: the vestry of 1826 was quite prepared for the headmaster to devote his energies to the classical scholars provided that an usher was appointed to relieve him of the burden of dealing with the rest of the pupils. But the experience of the previous decade had shown the strains of coexistence, and with Hayward as usher an *impasse* had been reached and the English school was undermining the primary function of the school. A reorganisation of some kind was clearly overdue,* and if, after 1823, Hand had re-formed the English school under an usher of his own choosing the fate of the school might have been happier. Such a reform was not, however, in keeping with his conception of the school.

Hand's views were correct in theory, in that the original grammar school pattern was that the usher grounded the pupils in the Latin accidence, laying the foundations on which the master built, but it is apparent from early schoolmasters' writings that, from the start, many children came to grammar schools without a proper training in English. Some could not even read their native language well, so that before the usher could start them in Latin grammar he had to improve their English reading and grammar. Some grammar schools, even as early as the sixteenth century, actually made this part of the usher's duty; others, Warrington and Manchester grammar schools among them, arranged for a senior pupil to teach English reading and grammar. Unless some such provision was made, it is easy to see how the usher's function in a grammar school in a small country town could imperceptibly move over to the teaching solely of English subjects. At Witton this had certainly happened by the late eighteenth century, and probably earlier: certainly from the mid-seventeenth century English was taught at the school, even if the usher still had classical duties, and at the beginning of the eighteenth century complaints had been made that children were sent for elementary instruction in English, 'in

* Carlisle noted in 1818 that 'all innovations of the statutes, it is said, are likely to be abolished'.

Primmers (if not Hornbooks)'. By his stand on principle Hand was undermining the *modus vivendi* which had enabled the school to survive in the critical eighteenth century, but he was entirely right in taking a stand against the independence of the English school. Whatever qualifications may be made that English was taught in classical grammar schools,* there is not the least doubt that English should have been subordinate to the school's chief business.

On the other hand, although in practice Hand had included some English and geography in his curriculum, in his scheme for the future conduct of the school he stood out for a classical education with the addition of religious instruction. (The master's duty should be 'to teach the boys coming to the said school the Latin and Greek tongues and for that purpose to read with and explain to them the classical authors of Greece and Rome and to exercise them in Greek and Latin composition . . .'.) This was at a time when Lord Eldon's word was no longer law, since the Grammar Schools Act of 1840 had empowered trustees to broaden curricula. Hand was thus moving counter to a very strong current of opinion, and even among his own witnesses three out of four who gave an opinion were against the conduct of the school solely as a grammar school for the learned languages. The one who favoured it based his view partly on social considerations: that 'if so conducted the school would be more respectable and better adapted for the education of the class of children for whom it seems to have been intended by the founder'. (It was this parent who removed his son from Witton and sent him to Shrewsbury, then a flourishing public school, although when Samuel Butler became headmaster in 1798 it was reputed to have had only one pupil on the roll.) Even the schools in Cheshire and Lancashire classified by the Taunton Commission in 1869 as 'classical' had adopted some sort of compromise curriculum: the most successful were those where the teaching of classics went on side by side with the efficient teaching of commercial subjects. Where the parents saw that commercial subjects were not sacrificed to the classics, they did not object to the classical instruction which kept open lines of communication with the traditional liberal education.

There is, however, curiously little evidence of a desire in Northwich and district in the early decades of the nineteenth century for an advanced modern education, including mathematics and modern

---

* Replying to a query, in 1762, from Macclesfield School governors as to whether modern languages, writing and accounts could be taught in the existing foundation, the Attorney General said they could not: 'That description [Grammar School] comprehends no more than reading the mother tongue and teaching the learned languages.' (Wilson, p. 330.)

languages.* The concern expressed by the parishioners in 1826 had been for the free teaching of reading: by contrast, the would-be reformers of Leeds Grammar School had wished to *exclude* the teaching of writing.[25] Hand's offence was not so much to deny the inhabitants a modern education for their children as to deprive them of an elementary education, to some extent free, which yet had the status of belonging to the old grammar school. As for the trustees, their actions in relation to Hand showed, to say the least, a marked lack of consistency. In backing Hand in his alterations in 1823 they presumably either underestimated or ignored local opinion, but it is less easy to understand the kind of management which advertised an ultimate salary of £300 without considering whether the property would bear it.†

No doubt some modernisation of the curriculum would have come to Witton School in any case after the 1840 Act, though probably not until after Hand's death, but the course of events meant that it came after a resort to law, an unsatisfactory method of solving an educational problem. The scheme of 1859 by which Warrington Grammar School was governed was described by a Schools Commissioner in 1869 as, 'like most Chancery schemes', 'very far from perfection', and the Witton scheme was described by Weston as a compromise which failed to satisfy either party. The suit worsened the school's financial position, itself one of the roots of the crisis, saddling it not only with the costs of the suit but with a substantial retiring allowance to Hand. The Vice-chancellor, in 1853, at the final hearing of the case, declared that the active litigation, which had continued from 1834 to 1853, 'had consumed hundreds of pounds of the funds of the charity in costs in a manner most unnecessary and disgraceful'. Furthermore the affair had undermined the confidence of the neighbourhood in the school. Something was done towards restoring this by widening the circle of trustees and choosing leading and respected local figures, but these were chosen as individuals and not on any representative basis. The

---

* *Cf.* James Bryce's report on Blackburn Free Grammar School: 'Their [the parents'] objection to Latin does not arise from a desire to see something else substituted for it in a scheme of liberal education—natural science for instance or modern history: it is to a liberal education itself that they object, seeing no profit in anything but writing and arithmetic.' (*S.I.C.*, XVII, 171.)

† Weston, strongly pro-Hand, believed that John Barker's desire for a classical education for his sons was the reason for attracting 'a superior master' to Witton, but that when that purpose no longer existed the school's future was unimportant and Hand's 'uprightness' gave offence. (Notebook No. 6.) This is evidence at the very least of the strength of feeling generated by the case.

lapse of the school for some twenty years* had, however, broken the chain of sons following fathers as pupils, and such a tradition could be rebuilt only slowly.[26]

Charles Hand's scholars, Christmas 1825

THE NAMES OF THE YOUNG GENTLEMEN IN WITTON SCHOOL IN THE
HALF-YEAR BEGINNING AT MIDSUMMER 1825†

Adams, John
Barker, Charles Frederick ⎫
Barker, Thomas Richard   ⎬ (sons of John Barker)
Barker, William Fairclough ⎭
Bellyse, Richard Baker
Brady, Edward Clarke
Brady, Robert Henry
Coates, Henry Frederick
Deane, Charles Kilshaw (son of James, of Northwich, gent., who took his son away from Witton School to send him to a school away from home and where more boys attended. C. K. Deane matric. Queen's College, Oxford, 1836, aged nineteen. He became vicar of Over.)
Ellson, Thomas Dobell
Hadfield, William (son of John, surgeon, of Middlewich. Admitted pensioner, Caius College, Cambridge, 1825, aged sixteen.)
Hammond, James
Highfield, Thomas
Holbrook, John
McNeile, Robert (? son of Robert McNeill; born at Liverpool; admitted pensioner, Trinity College, Cambridge, 1835. School given as Royal Liverpool Institution.)
Reynolds, George (son of Mr. William Reynolds of Liverpool; lodged with Jane Pennington; at Witton School for a year or more.)
Saxon, John Siddeley (son of George, solicitor, of Northwich; after six years at Witton went on to Shrewsbury School.)
Speakman, John
Speakman, Thomas
Williamson, George James (son of William, of Holywell, Co. Flint, gent. Matric. Jesus College, Oxford, 1829, aged seventeen.)

---

* In 1853 it was stated before the Vice-chancellor that there were no scholars at the school, and that for a great many years past there had never been more than a few, and sometimes none at all. (*The Times* law report, 11 February 1853.)

† *School Recs.*, box E, bundle 1.

XI

New schemes and new buildings, 1857–1908

Changing Northwich

Two events in the early 1870s symbolised the changes which were taking place in the neighbourhood. In 1873 Ludwig Mond and John Tomlinson Brunner purchased Winnington Hall from Lord Stanley of Alderley and established in its grounds their alkali works based on the new ammonia–soda process. A few years earlier, in 1870, the Northwich local board had purchased the manorial rights of Northwich.

The change at Winnington Hall was one aspect of a major development in Cheshire in the later nineteenth century—the emergence of the chemical industry, centred in the county on Runcorn and Northwich. The Brunner Mond works were planted round what has been described as 'a tumbledown manor house', said in 1860 to have been 'pleasantly situated amongst some delightfully picturesque and romantic scenery', and occupied from about 1850 to 1868 by a boarding school for young ladies. Mond and Brunner took up residence in the hall, and the works came into production in 1874; after setbacks in that year, prosperity set in from 1875. In 1885 the works were described as the largest of the kind in the world, and their output increased at a remarkable rate: in 1898 it was nine times and in 1908 fourteen times that of 1881. The establishment of such an enterprise, employing in 1896 nearly 3,000 and in 1902 nearly 4,000 workmen, only a mile and a half from Northwich could not fail to affect the social environment of the school. The additions to Ormerod's original descriptions of 1819 made by Helsby in 1882 show the great changes in the size and character of Northwich and its surrounding townships in the previous twenty or more years. By 1901 the population of the parish of St Helen's, Witton, was over 13,000, and that of Northwich urban district and township over 17,000.[1]

While one manorial lord gave way to industry, the rights of the other were acquired by a statutory local authority based on the representative principle. This principle permeated the localities

during the second half of the nineteenth century. Local Boards, the
forerunners of the urban and rural district councils, were set up
under Acts of 1848 and 1858; those at Witton and Northwich were
set up in 1863 and were amalgamated in 1875. In 1888 the County
Councils were created, and the centuries-long rule of the J.P.s in
Quarter Sessions was replaced by that of elected representatives:
one such councillor was Algernon Fletcher (a Liberal and Nonconformist), the son of a salt proprietor and educated at Witton and
Mill Hill Schools. Contests for the County Councils ran in part on
denominational lines: in 1889 at Davenham, George Slater opposed
Colonel France-Hayhurst to secure some representation for Nonconformists.[2]

Even before the County Council was set up the status of Northwich had changed, for in 1885 it became a parliamentary constituency distinct from the county. Local party associations were active.
In 1880 the Northwich and Weaverham Conservative Association
was inaugurated, with Christopher Kay (salt manufacturer and
subsequently chairman of the school governors), C. J. Hughes (a
former pupil), and W. H. Verdin as prominent members. On the
other side, the activity of the Unitarian John Brunner was outstanding: from 1880 he was reported as an enthusiastic member of
the Northwich Liberal Association, and by 1885 he was said to have
contributed nearly £1,000 to the funds of the Mid-Cheshire Liberal
Association.

Unlike his partner, Mond, Brunner entered fully into the public
affairs of the locality. In 1877 he was elected a member of Northwich Local Board and showed himself a generous benefactor to the
town: though a Nonconformist he contributed £300 to the restoration of Witton Church, and in 1885 he presented Northwich with
a public library. In 1885 he became a J.P. and was elected member
for the newly created parliamentary constituency of Northwich: his
friend, Algernon Fletcher, became his agent. Brunner's Liberal—
and later, Home Rule—views, together with his determined
campaigns to secure legislation for brine subsidence compensation
and the reform of the Weaver Navigation Trust, brought him into
conflict with salt manufacturers such as the Verdins and Christopher
Kay, and with representatives of county families such as Colonel
France-Hayhurst, chairman of the old Weaver trustees. His call for
disestablishment roused strong opposition in the 1885 election from
the local Anglican clergy: the denominational feeling was shown in
1891, when Canon France-Hayhurst (a long-standing governor of
Witton School) denied Brunner (also a governor) the use of Davenham National School for a Liberal meeting. From 1885 to 1910
(with the exception of the Home Rule election of 1886) Brunner

represented Northwich, though not without bitter contests.³ To the economic influence of the firm of Brunner Mond in the area was joined the personal drive and public interests of Brunner himself. The school thus evolved in this period against the background of an expanding and a more politically conscious community, at a time when more and more subjects, including education, were coming within the ambit of legislation and of central and local administration.

The working of the Vice-chancellor's scheme, 1857–74

It remained now to be seen if Witton Grammar School could be restored to a position of value in the community under the Vice-chancellor's scheme, which represented a compromise between the intentions of the founder and newer educational ideas. The scheme retained the Anglican character of the school,* the original preference for boys of Witton chapelry and even township, and the classical part of the curriculum, Greek as well as Latin. Modern languages, like drawing, were an extra subject for which separate fees were to be charged. How those responsible saw the school is shown by the advertisement for it in *Morris's Cheshire Directory* (1874): Witton School, it stated, was founded to provide an education similar to that of the great schools and in accordance with the principles of the Church of England.

The new trustees administered the school's property under the close supervision of the Charity Commissioners, though not without some criticism that the lands were let in private at rents below what they would have fetched by public competition.⁴ Some of the property was sold in this period: Ball's Croft in 1861, and the site of the original share of the wichhouse in Northwich in 1874 to the Northwich Local Board, which was building a new Market Hall extending over the site. The chief properties, in Chester and Larton, were, however, retained. In 1873 Fearon (the Assistant Commissioner of the Endowed Schools Commission who inspected the school) reported that the clerk to the trustees had advised them to sell the Chester property, which was 'both distant and of a kind which must involve expense of management', but that they had declined to do so, since property in Chester was rising greatly in value. Indeed, in December 1882 the trustees resolved unanimously that the Chester property should not be sold.⁵

To follow the history of the property to the end of the century: in

---

* In 1867 four out of seven trustees were Anglican clergymen. (*S.I.C.*, xvii, 107.)

1892 A. F. Leach (an Assistant Charity Commissioner inspecting the school) reported that there had been considerable expenditure on repairs at Chester, and that the houses were old and possibly needed rebuilding. He thought the school governors more solicitous to improve the estate than the school building. Larton, after what was described by the Schools Enquiry Commissioner in his report of 1869 as 'a perhaps necessary but very large expenditure on improvements of part of the estates' (referring to the building of a new farmhouse there) drew no comment in later enquiries. In 1885 and 1899 the rent was £110 a year, and in 1892 it was said to show no likelihood of increase.[6]

Despite the drain of a pension of £80 a year to Charles Hand, who did not die until 1873, the school's financial position in the late nineteenth century compared favourably with that of other Cheshire endowed schools. In 1864, of twenty-three secondary schools in Cheshire, five were considered classical and had endowments of an average net annual value of £322, ten, including Witton, were considered semi-classical and had an average of £75, and eight (excluding Macclesfield Modern School, founded only in 1838) were non-classical and had £65. Witton School, with a net annual value of £337, was second only to Macclesfield School. Its gross income of £450 in 1864 had risen to £490 in 1873 and to over £639 by 1892.[7]

The new headmaster was Henry Linthwaite,* a Cambridge M.A. aged about thirty-four in 1857, who had been headmaster from 1848 to 1851 of Hawarden Grammar School, whence he brought testimonials from Gladstone's brother-in-law, Sir Stephen Glynne. From 1848 he had been in holy orders, and had been curate of West Walton in Norfolk, where he had also taught the sons of the vicar, Demetrius Calliphronas. One of these sons followed Linthwaite to Witton, as a boarder, for George Constantine Calliphronas is listed by Weston as a distinguished pupil who had his early education at the school. He became Senior Wrangler at Cambridge in 1874, but he had gone on from Witton in 1865 to Felsted School, of which he later became a governor. Boarders at Witton seem (temporarily) to

---

* A mildly satirical but also sentimental book, *Tales of a Grammar School* by John William Reed (n.d. but preface dated 1864), of which there is a copy in the Brunner Library, seems to refer to the school, under the pseudonym 'Arley Grammar School', in the time of Linthwaite (the headmaster's name is the 'Rev. Henry Lightwood'). It is impossible, however, to place the story at any particular date: there are echoes of Charles Hand's time, e.g. the theft of the plaque from Farmer's tombstone. In the book 'Arley' boys are said to have played cricket but to have had to use the public cricket ground two miles away because the rector would not allow the headmaster to have any of the several fields he owned near the school.

have disappeared by the mid-'sixties, and the lack of an official
master's house was discouraging.[8]

All was not well with the school under the new scheme, and this
was revealed when R. S. Wright made his investigation under the
last of the great trio of mid-Victorian commissions of enquiry, the
Taunton Commission, appointed in December 1864 to cover
grammar schools. At Witton Wright found that eleven boys 'imperfectly represented the poorer class which the founder appears to
have intended to benefit amongst others', and thirty-four boys, who
paid, still more imperfectly represented the other classes in a population of over 10,000 within a radius of a mile of the school.[9] He was
particularly concerned about this second category, since they had
not the educational provision which the National Schools made for
the poor. Wright tried to obtain some accurate statistics of the
number of middle-class boys between eight and sixteen in Cheshire,
but only half the schoolmasters sent answers, and only Witton and
Bunbury provided information purporting to be complete. Witton,
in 1866, was estimated to have 269 £15 (or more) householders,
with an estimated number of 100 such boys: of these, forty were in
the grammar school, thirty in a private commercial school, and
seven in schools 'of a national kind'.[10]

As to the education given in the school, Wright found that no
part of the instruction tested was either thorough or advanced, and
that whereas the Vice-chancellor's scheme laid down a variety of
subjects, including Greek and Latin, designed to prepare boys
for the universities and learned professions as well as for trade, in
fact the subjects taught hardly went beyond those of ordinary
National Schools, with the exception of some French, a little Euclid
and a very little Latin, and were not so accurately known as in
them. Only the French was up to the average of good commercial
schools. No boys had gone to the university within the last five years.

Wright, however, recognised that there were factors at work
which hindered the school's progress, and he did not lay all the
blame on either the masters or the parents. Indeed, he thought that
if the school commanded the confidence of the neighbourhood,
pupils would not be lacking even at much higher fees. The chief
hindrances were the bad position and facilities of the schoolhouse
(by an overcrowded churchyard and lacking classrooms, a playground and a residence for the master) and the dissatisfaction of
the headmaster with the trustees and with his position. Furthermore,
Wright considered it desirable that there should be a greater number
of townsmen on the governing body. These three themes emerged in
the decade between the enquiry and the introduction of a new
scheme for the school in 1874.

Fundamentally, Linthwaite was dissatisfied and resentful about his financial position. Wright thought that he should either receive a sufficient salary from the endowment, in which case he would work more cheerfully under the trustees, or he should be left to make his income by pushing the school. As it was he had a salary he considered inadequate, and the arrangement under the Vice-chancellor's scheme, whereby he was given a share of the surplus income remaining after repairs and expenses had been covered, was calculated to cause friction between him and the trustees. (It is not without significance that Weston recorded that Linthwaite thought that Hand had been 'vilely treated'.) Linthwaite not only protested to the trustees about their expenditure on the property but also complained unsuccessfully to the Charity Commissioners in 1865. From 1865 to 1872, though not every year, the Minute Book records the periodic distribution of two-thirds of half the surplus income to Linthwaite. In 1857 he was allowed £4 10s for a clock, maps and other items, but his request, in 1867, for a library was turned down by the trustees, and only in 1871 was £3 granted for the purchase of books for a library.[11]

The site of the school became the subject of urgent discussion in 1866. The churchyard was full and the parishioners wished to extend it rather than have a distant cemetery, such as the Nonconformists were said to favour. The most convenient site for extending the churchyard was blocked by the position of the parsonage house on the south side, so an extension on the other side of the road opposite the school (Church Road) was proposed. But the site of the school itself was much more attractive, and it was easy to point out that for a school it was unhealthy, surrounded, as it was, on three sides by the churchyard. The trustees alleged that Linthwaite had previously complained of this nuisance, but, faced with expenditure on removing the school which would diminish the masters' share of the surplus income, he championed the old building in defiance of the trustees, as did local inhabitants and parents of scholars. The trustees applied to the Charity Commissioners for permission to sell the site and remove the school (though at first to no specified site) at an estimated cost of £250 for rebuilding on the same plan with existing materials, and reinforced their argument with the consequent acquisition of a playground, which Linthwaite himself admitted would be a benefit of moving.* The commissioners, however, felt that this gain would not justify such an expenditure entirely at the cost of the charity itself.

---

* The trustees had tried, without success, in 1857 to acquire neighbouring land for a playground. (Minute Book, 18 July 1857.)

During 1867 (at the end of which year the churchyard was to be compulsorily closed) the *impasse* was resolved in two ways: the parishioners undertook to enlarge the churchyard and to remove the school without any expense to the charity estate, and Archdeacon Greenall, the owner of the advowson of Witton and a school governor, generously offered to give a site for the school opposite the churchyard and to pay any extra expenses of the removal above the £250 to be paid by the parishioners. (According to Weston, however, he would not *sell* any additional land to the school.) The trustees' gratitude was endorsed by the Charity Commissioners' sanction, and plans were submitted by Archdeacon Greenall. These drew some minor and one major criticism from Linthwaite—the absence of the spacious playground which was one of the reasons for removal: he thought it was 'almost indispensable' that the school should be built on a site of about one acre.[12]

In the event the school suffered a blow in the sudden death of Archdeacon Greenall in November 1867. His trustees were not empowered to give the land for the new school, though in fact they sold it to the school trustees for the very moderate price of £25. Mrs Greenall expressed a wish to carry out her husband's intentions and offered a sum not exceeding £400 (no limit had been mentioned by the archdeacon). She actually contributed nearly £391, which, together with the parish's £250, covered the expense of building the new school, which was opened on 1 October 1869. Some modifications were made by Mrs Greenall in the plans submitted by her husband, and according to Weston the building was carried out 'on a greatly reduced plan'.[13]

The third school, an undistinguished brick building* accommodating seventy boys,[14] stood on the eastern side of Church Road, practically opposite the site of its predecessor: subsequently it became the Church Institute and is now Council offices. Its three schoolrooms were described in 1873 as 'cheerful and well supplied with furniture', but there was only a very small playground. The trustees were anxious to add a playground and to build a house for the headmaster to hold boarders, and from 1869 the acquisition of a site from Greenall's trustees, who were laying out the adjoining land for development, was under consideration. In the end the large master's house (now Council offices) was not built until 1878, at what seems the very high cost of £2,700, and by then the school had also acquired a good adjoining recreation ground.[15] By 1878, therefore, the school was, physically, reasonably well placed.

* See plate vii(*b*).

The new scheme, 1874

The most important development for Witton School, as for so many grammar schools in the late nineteenth century, was the reorganisation of the school under the Endowed Schools Act of 1869. This Act, the result of the Schools Enquiry Commission, set up three commissioners, empowered to remodel educational trusts, no longer by legalistic or mainly financial criteria, but in order to improve the standard of education and to fit a school for the needs of the locality and into a national system.* This provision for direct (and unsolicited) intervention by a central authority introduced a totally new factor into the local situation. The effect in the Northwich area was shown in an application to the commissioners in 1871 by the Witton Local Board for representation on the governing body of the school, an application previously rejected by the trustees on the ground that they could not add to the trustees until the number was reduced to seven. The overworked commissioners could hold out no immediate prospect of devising a new scheme of management for Witton School, since they were fully occupied with other counties.[16]

The school's turn came sooner than might have been expected. The resignation of Linthwaite, in May 1872, to take up a living in Co. Durham, hastened matters, for in advertising the post the trustees had to state that the school would come under the 1869 Act, and they therefore approached the commissioners for guidance.[17] While disclaiming any prejudgement of the issue, the commissioners nevertheless hinted that the 'wants of the locality' would indicate the preparation of boys for professional and commercial pursuits rather than for the universities, and a curriculum including Latin, natural science and one or more modern languages. The need to make up the number of trustees, subject under the 1869 Act to the consent of the Committee of Council on Education, precipitated a visit from one of the assistant commissioners, D. R. Fearon, with a view to preparing a new scheme.

This prospect promised a settlement of certain arguments about the management and nature of the school which had been aired from the mid-'sixties, and which echoed past disputes in the school's history. Two in particular catch the ear, and were, as always, interrelated: the claims of the immediate locality for preference and the debate on the appropriate curriculum, classical or non-classical. Already, in 1866, when new trustees were being appointed, a considerable number of the inhabitants of Witton chapelry, with

* By 1874, when their powers were transferred to the Charity Commissioners, the Endowed Schools Commissioners had seen the realisation of 235 schemes. (B. Simon, ed., *Education in Leicestershire, 1540–1940*, p. 151.)

John Weston as a prime mover and including five members of the Local Boards of Witton and Northwich, had protested to the Charity Commissioners about the number of existing and proposed trustees who lived outside the township and chapelry (though the Vice-chancellor's scheme allowed them to live within five miles of the chapelry), and against the exclusion of those 'who are chiefly interested', according to the founder's intent. Significantly, they objected to the entire control being in the hands of neighbouring gentry and clergy, to the exclusion of the trading men of the chapelry, whose sons were sent to the school. The Charity Commissioners had replied in 1867 deprecating the restriction of Deane's intentions to the township and also the appointment of parents of pupils to the governing body. Furthermore, they held that the school intended by the Vice-chancellor's scheme was 'a classical school of a high order' and therefore best in the hands of those with such an education.[18]

When the post of headmaster was advertised, local inhabitants again expressed their views in a memorial to the trustees in June 1872.[19] They assumed that under a new scheme the headmaster would no longer have to be in holy orders or a graduate of Oxford or Cambridge,* and that the school would have to become either a 'high classical establishment' or 'more popular and less classical than now'. They urged the provisional appointment as headmaster of the second master, George Tweedy, believing him to be 'fully competent to give the highest instruction ever required or likely to be wanted in the school'. Tweedy, who had been educated at a commercial school in Burnham, Norfolk, and had passed examinations of the College of Preceptors and first class in London matriculation (testifying to his classical acquirements), expressed his opinion to Fearon that to make Latin optional in both upper and lower schools would be 'very acceptable to the parents and most beneficial to the school generally'. If Latin were made compulsory in the lower school, he held that the numbers would fall, especially if a private school were opened—doubtless a veiled threat.

Fearon made his inspection in September 1873, interviewing the masters and various local people, as well as having a discussion with the trustees. The trustees were anxious for religious instruction to be according to the Church of England (though with a conscience clause); they thought boarders important, and wished the working of the school in two departments to continue, though they were prepared to change 'Classical' and 'English' to 'Senior' and 'Junior'. They agreed on the level of fees, but had some differences

* The former assumption was correct, being embodied in the 1869 Act.

about the claims of boys from Witton township, where they thought
there would be 'some excitement' if the fees were raised above 10s 6d
a quarter. As to the secular instruction, they approved of a 'Second
Grade'* scheme, such as that for Wallasey School, and thought all
mention of Greek might be omitted—too late they had second
thoughts on this. The new headmaster, the Rev. J. F. Rounthwaite
(with whom the trustees declared themselves well satisfied), wished,
on the contrary, to keep Greek in the senior department, where
he had four boys learning it. Tweedy, since he had been appointed
under the Vice-chancellor's scheme, was in a protected position, and
Rounthwaite feared that if his income were reduced he would leave
and set up a rival school, thereby much impairing the grammar
school. Care was taken in the new scheme to safeguard both
Tweedy's position and his salary.

After going through all its stages the new scheme for the
management of the school was formally approved by the Queen in
Council in October 1874, and it provided the framework (only
slightly altered in 1895) for the running of the school until 1910.[20]
Compared with the Vice-chancellor's scheme, it represented a more
decisive break with the original foundation. In the government of
the school the new scheme introduced the representative principle:
of the twelve governors, five were to be representative (three elected
by Witton Local Board and two by Northwich Local Board) and
seven co-optative. There was some modification of the Anglican
nature of the foundation—the jurisdiction of the Bishop of Chester
in licensing the master was abolished, as was the master's right of
appeal to the bishop, if dismissed. The master no longer had to be
in holy orders (nor, incidentally, thirty years old), but he had still
to be an Anglican, and the religious instruction was still to be
according to the Church of England, though with a conscience
clause.

The curriculum, designed now for 'a liberal and practical education', was altered so that the extra subjects (modern languages,
drawing and music) for which separate fees had had to be paid
were now part of the regular teaching. Greek was dropped and
natural science and political economy were introduced. The qualifications of pupils and the fees paid were rationalised: there was
to be no difference of fees because of place of birth or residence,
and the school was to be open to all boys living with parents, near
relatives, etc., or in an authorised boarding house. (The school was
still envisaged as a boarding school, and the second master was
also allowed to take boarders.) If numbers pressed, however, boys

* I.e. a school where boys would stay to the age of sixteen, and where the
curriculum was geared to 'practical use in business'. (*S.I.C.*, 1, 20.)

of Witton chapelry or Northwich township still had first claim. Admission was to be by examination, with an entrance fee of not more than £2, and fees were eventually fixed by the governors at £4 in the junior and £8 in the senior department, within the limits of £3 and £10 laid down in the scheme.* The governors were empowered to grant partial or total exemption from fees on merit, and half of such exhibitions were to be competed for first by boys from public elementary schools in the local townships. Here was a step towards integrating the school into an educational system conceived as a whole.

Hopes and disappointments under two clerical headmasters, 1874–1903

With a new building and a new scheme, the school seemed set fair. The headmaster appointed in 1872, the Rev. J. F. Rounthwaite, a Cambridge M.A., had held several curacies in Lancashire and Cheshire before coming to Witton. He remained there for ten years before becoming an S.P.G. missionary in Canada, where he died suddenly in 1883. His obituary described him as 'quiet and unassuming', and he does not seem to have left any great impress on the school. (A point of minor interest is that in 1872 he raised the question of a school uniform, at the least a 'college cap', with the governors.) He himself felt that the governors were unappreciative of his efforts. He faced a problem common to most Cheshire schools— the failure of boys to stay long enough in the upper school. In 1877 there were four boarders and fifty-one day scholars, of whom seven were over fifteen and under seventeen and only one over seventeen. (This was an improvement on the position in 1873, when out of forty-three boys only three were over fifteen and none was over sixteen.) In October 1881, however, the governors asked Rounthwaite the cause of the decrease in numbers, particularly in the upper school, where there were only twelve scholars. Soon afterwards, in March 1882, Rounthwaite sent in his resignation.[21] This gave the governors the opportunity of appointing as headmaster the man to whom they had originally offered the post in 1872, the Rev. Arthur Charles Whitley, for whom the chairman of the governors, Canon Blencowe, the incumbent of Witton, gave his casting vote.[22]

* An interesting discussion in Witton Local Board was reported in the *Northwich Guardian*, 4 October 1873. A minimum fee of eight guineas was suggested, to keep the upper school 'more select'. An opponent claimed that some who could not afford so much were equally respectable, and the suggestion that such boys could compete for free places was countered by 'But Englishmen would rather pay for their own education than let any one else do so for them'.

Whitley had been educated at St Paul's School and at Corpus Christi College, Cambridge, where he gained the degree of M.A. From 1863 he was in priest's orders and had had various teaching posts, the last of which was at Scarborough, where he was also curate. He appears to have been a more forceful personality than Rounthwaite, and he remained at Witton until his death in 1903. Whitley was the son of a 'fervid evangelical vicar' and his brother was a bishop in India. He himself was a friend, from their schooldays, of Sir John Stainer, and had a strong musical bent: he composed a number of song settings, including the school song, *Floreat Wittona.** This is but one indication, among several, that he cultivated the school's traditions and esprit de corps;† about 1887 an Old Boys' Club was formed and in 1893 the school's pupils presented to St Bartholomew's Church, Smithfield, a plaque to the memory of the founder. (In 1885 John Weston had produced his booklet on the school's history, and during the 'nineties the governors took to referring to the school as 'Sir John Deane's', although it was still officially 'Witton' Grammar School.) There were signs, too, that the standing of the school in the local community was improving: in 1885, at the opening of the Brunner Free Library, the master and scholars walked in the procession, and at the banquet the chairman of the Local Board described the school as 'really an honour to the town'.[23]

Whitley's impact on the school is indicated by his report to the governors in January 1884 that the school was not large enough for the number of pupils. The new school building had been designed to take seventy boys, but the numbers in 1883, 1884 and 1885 were eighty-one, seventy-eight and ninety-one, and in 1888 actually rose to 110. A proposal to enlarge the school had been postponed in April 1883, but in response to Whitley's report the governors decided to invite a public subscription, since the school's funds were exhausted by ordinary expenses. In fact in 1886, an upper storey was added without trenching on the school's resources. The extension enabled the school to accommodate 130–140 pupils and was commemorated by an incised stone which now stands outside the school. More significant than the increase in the total numbers was the steady increase in the number of boys in the upper school, so that from 1889 to 1892 the upper school actually exceeded the lower school in size. This may have been partly due to the declining reputation of the second master, Tweedy, who was described by the trustees in 1892 as somewhat old-fashioned and once very popular as a teacher in the days before the Education Act of 1870.[24]

* A copy is to be found in the Brunner Library in *Cheshire Miscellanea*, p. 105.   † Whitley also encouraged cricket.

Some of the growth in the upper school was, however, attributable to Whitley's positive policy of trying to weld the upper and lower schools together. How far the old early nineteenth-century tradition of a break between the lower and upper schools was perpetuated even under the 1874 scheme is shown by Whitley's evidence to A. F. Leach in 1892, that when he came the two departments were regarded as absolutely separate, and that as a matter of course boys left the junior department at fourteen and never thought of ascending to the upper school. In some degree Whitley altered this by introducing Algebra, Euclid and Latin into the two upper forms of the lower school,* thereby providing a basis for progress and some continuity of curriculum, but his efforts were frustrated by Tweedy's protected position. (The importance of such efforts is shown in the history of Manchester Grammar School: the making of Latin compulsory in the unreformed lower or English school by Walker, the headmaster appointed in 1859, has been called a 'bold decision', which welded the school together and laid the foundation of its academic achievement.) After Leach had inspected the school,† the Charity Commissioners recommended to the governors the abolition of the distinction between senior and junior departments and their combined management by the headmaster, with no differentiation of fees, except (if any) by the age of the pupils. To the governors' regret Leach failed to recommend the pensioning off of Tweedy, but this was achieved in 1897, when Tweedy, then aged sixty-eight, was given a pension of £105 a year.[25]

The obituary of Whitley in the *Northwich Guardian* spoke of his 'delight to point out' on the honours boards on the walls of the upper school 'those who had become clergymen, doctors, lawyers and distinguished public servants'. Certainly, during his time the school register records a number of boys who went on from the school to universities, in particular to Owens College, Manchester: this was a contrast to the Schools Enquiry Commission report that no boys had gone to a university in the five years before 1866. At the annual prize distribution in 1887 Whitley appealed for the establishment of one or two scholarships to maintain at the universities boys whose parents found the expense too great, and this plea was reinforced by a recommendation of the Charity Commissioners to the governors in 1892. It seems to have borne fruit, for in 1893 Walter Deakin, son of a widow, left to go to Owens College with a Governors'

* The governors had provided in Rounthwaite's time for the teaching of elementary Latin in the lower school 'where required'. (Minute Book, 20 January 1875.)

† In 1887 the Charity Commissioners had instituted a systematic inspection of all schools with schemes under the Endowed Schools Act.

Scholarship of £20—the nineteenth-century equivalent of Thomas Farmer's money. The School was, incidentally, very successful in gaining scholarships to Christ's Hospital, open to those who had spent two years at an endowed grammar school.* A curious defect in the school's academic arrangements was, however, noted by Leach in 1892. Instead of using a recognised body such as the Oxford and Cambridge Schools Examination Board, the school used a neighbouring clergyman to examine the work of the pupils. This was changed by 1899, when the Cambridge and Oxford Local examinations were taken.[26]

Widespread teaching of science was a major aim of educational reformers of the period, and from 1859 the Department of Science and Art at South Kensington had made grants for science and art classes on a payment by results basis. Some science was taught at Witton by 1874, and in 1890 the school was in receipt of grants from South Kensington of £13 10s for teaching twenty-eight boys science and £20 8s 1d for teaching forty-five boys art. In 1889 the Technical Instruction Act gave local authorities the power to make grants to encourage science teaching. In July 1891 the school governors decided to apply for affiliation with the Department of Science and Art, influenced by an understanding that the Northwich Local Board (later the Urban District Council) would make a grant of £50 towards the increased expenditure involved. This grant was made from 1892, but in 1893 a report to the County Technical Instruction Committee stated that the only subject taught at Witton under the South Kensington regulations was elementary drawing.[27] In 1885 there was a science master, but in 1892 Leach noted that the science master was without qualifications. By 1897 a science teacher approved by the Department of Science and Art had been appointed, but the chemistry teaching was still purely theoretical and there was no provision for practical work. Before 1892 Whitley had pressed the governors in vain for a chemical laboratory, and the lack of such a laboratory was one of the defects pointed out in that year by the Charity Commissioners. They suggested that the governors could get some help from external sources such as the Cheshire County Council. The governors apparently explored this in 1893 and agreed to accept two county council representatives on the governing body, but in the event no grant beyond that already made by the Local Board was forthcoming.[28]

The need for a laboratory at the school became even more urgent with the establishment, under the Urban District Council, of the new Verdin Technical Schools at Leftwich. Sir Joseph Verdin's trust

* Numbers of boys left to go on to other schools. (School Reg.)

fund had originally been designed to make unnecessary the passage of a parliamentary Compensation Act by providing compensation for sufferers from subsidence due to brine pumping. After the passage of the Act in 1891 the fund was diverted to public causes, including implementing the Technical Instruction Act. In 1892 the Witton School governors had some hopes of taking advantage of the trust scheme themselves, but these came to nothing. To celebrate the Diamond Jubilee the Verdin Technical Schools were built on a lavish scale out of the fund on a site in London Road and were opened by the Duchess of Westminster in July 1897: they were to provide a sound liberal and practical education in mathematics, physics, English subjects, French, chemistry, drawing, etc., at £4 a year. That the school governors feared the competition of the new schools, if opened as day schools, is shown by a letter they sent to the Urban District Council in October 1896, proposing that for a rental of £100 a year the school at Witton should be transferred to the new buildings for use between 9 a.m. and 5 p.m. Not surprisingly the suggestion failed and the Urban District Council decided to open the Technical Schools as an Organised Science Day School under South Kensington. Spurred on, no doubt, by these developments, the chairman of the school governors, Christopher Kay of Davenham Hall, celebrated the Diamond Jubilee by building at his own expense a chemical laboratory for twelve students for the school. By 1898 the laboratory had been inspected by the Department of Science and Art, and in 1899 improvements were made in the teaching to meet the department's criticisms. The Board of Education inspector in 1904 described the laboratory as well lighted and ventilated but too small, and the science teaching, up to the advent of a new master, as inefficient.[29]

Despite improvements the number of pupils at the school fell off seriously, reaching thirty-eight in 1897 and forty-two in 1899; it rose in 1902, though only to seventy. The drop in fees was serious, and the governors in 1898 were greatly disturbed. Various explanations were put forward. Even as early as 1892 Leach had reported that a technical school, lately established in Northwich, was thought to have had an adverse effect on the grammar school, and this five years before the building of the Verdin schools. Moreover, the physical circumstances of the school were a handicap. Whereas in 1878 the site of the school had been a good one and there was a good recreation ground, by 1892 a large number of small dwellings 'of the artizan type' had been built all round the school and a new cemetery opposite it. The governors had, inexplicably, let the recreation ground be swallowed up in buildings, making no effort to buy the land. (They later dropped an attempt to lease land in 1898 because the rent asked was too high.) As a result the site had become 'a very bad one' and not at all attractive to boarders, whose numbers had fallen from fourteen to four, so that 'the great master's house' represented a great deal of unproductive capital and its erection had been a drag upon the funds.* Leach was puzzled by the governors' willingness to spend money on repairs to the school property but not on the school itself. He thought that with the existing endowment,† it would have been far better, rather than making additions to the school (as in 1886), to have built an entirely new building on a new and ample site. He sensed a certain want of energy in the governing body, though the governors attended well and seemed 'desirous of efficiency'. Following Leach's report, the Charity Commissioners recommended the governors to consider selling or leasing the existing building and removing the school to a more open site.[30]

There were other, less tangible causes of the school's failure to prosper. Searching for these, a committee of the governors in 1897 thought it necessary to spend a considerable sum on refurnishing the school in order to restore the confidence of the inhabitants in it: they attributed the unwillingness of parents to let their sons compete for Brunner scholarships to the fact that 'there is hardly an Elementary School in the district so badly furnished'. In 1899 the failure of the elementary schools to 'feed' the grammar school was still a matter of concern to the governors, and Whitley was asked to explain the grammar school's claim on them and to write a paragraph in the parish magazine on the subject. Even the clerk to the governors admitted that 'there is a strong feeling in the town against sending boys there', and, from outside, an official report on the school to the County Technical Instruction Committee in 1899 referred to 'a strong prejudice against this school in Northwich', though it could see no reason for it, and observed, 'if such prejudice could be removed, this school might be largely increased and become a centre for really good work'.[31]

A turning point?

Whitley died in 1903, and was succeeded by a non-clerical head-master, the first since the end of the Hand case. Herbert Russell Wright was the grandson of the Principal of Lancing Grammar School and two of his brothers were also schoolmasters. He himself,

---

* The debt of £1,500 incurred was due to be paid off by 1903.

† Figures of Cheshire schools' endowments given in the Bryce Commission's report of 1895 show Witton with a gross income of £575, Macclesfield £1,594, Stockport £451, Nantwich and Acton £102 and Lymm £138.

after taking a degree at Cambridge, taught at Berlitz schools in Germany and at his old school, St Edward's, Oxford.[32] The Board of Education inspector in 1904 observed that Russell Wright's previous experience had been in boarding schools of a class different from Witton, and that his teaching was chiefly confined to the classics, but he had two (an insufficient number) very capable assistant masters who took science and mathematics and modern languages and literary subjects respectively. Indeed, the inspector, while thinking that the school had not in the past been in a very efficient state, seemed to think the organisation under the new headmaster promising. However, if the school were to become 'the regular Secondary School of the district' it would have to make more provision for natural science teaching.

The inspector's report, which followed closely on the arrival of Russell Wright, concluded with some very significant comments of the utmost importance for the school's future. It was understood, he said, that Sir John Brunner proposed to give a large sum of money to found a school for secondary education for boys and girls. The new school might be established separately from the grammar school or in conjunction with it. If a separate school with low fees and offering a modern scientific education was set up, there was no doubt that the greater number of boys who would have gone to the grammar school would be diverted from it. In this event the old school would have to be carried on as a high-class school for boys wanting a good grammar school education, and the district was not thickly populated enough for this to be likely to succeed: in consequence, the use of the endowment to the district would be largely lost. On the other hand, the union of the old endowment of John Deane and the new one of Sir John Brunner would make possible a secondary school which, in buildings and education, should reach a very high level of efficiency, not only in newer subjects like science but in the older subjects of a literary education. The additional endowment would pay for the additional numbers and higher qualifications of staff, 'which make all the difference in the tone and style of a school'. Possibly a few boys who now attended the grammar school might leave, but they could be catered for, perhaps, at Knutsford, which seemed more suited for a first-grade school, educating boys to the age of eighteen or nineteen. The decision as to how Brunner's scheme should be put into effect was crucial: 'if the two schools exist side by side it is to be feared that neither will have a sufficient number of pupils or be able to expend a sum on salaries of teachers which would enable it to do first-rate work'.[33] The welfare of the school depended on the addition to the endowment of the Tudor priest of that of the new industrial baronet.

Sir John Brunner, the County Council and the school

John Tomlinson Brunner, created a baronet in 1895, was to be the
second great benefactor of Witton Grammar School, and his wealth,
like that of the founder (though to a much greater extent) was based
on the local salt. Brunner, as the son of a schoolmaster, at whose
private school in Liverpool he had been educated,* took a lasting
interest in education in the area, producing a small handbook on
Public Education in Cheshire in 1890 with T. E. Ellis, M.P., and
another edition in 1896 with J. Lawrence Hammond. In 1886 his
firm set up the Winnington Schools, and in 1898 he himself gave
new schools to Barnton: over Barnton School the strong views he
held, as a Liberal and a Unitarian, brought him into conflict with the
Bishop of Chester. Brunner was particularly concerned about the
advancement of technical and commercial instruction.[34]

Brunner's connection with Witton School began in 1881, when
he offered £50 to provide scholarships to the school as envisaged in
the 1874 scheme: a syllabus for an examination for these scholarships was adopted by the governing body in April 1884. The six
Brunner scholarships were for two-year periods and paid half the
fees: though occasionally given to boys from the lower school, they
were mostly won by boys from local elementary schools, and between
1888 and 1892, of the twenty-four Brunner scholars, only five were
from the lower school. The earliest Brunner scholar mentioned in the
school register (1876–1909) was Frederic William Anker, the son of
a coachman, who was a pupil from 1880 to 1887; another was
Thomas Albert Starkey, the son of a weighman and a pupil from
1883 to 1888, who subsequently became Professor of Hygiene at
McGill University.[35] The last Brunner scholars were admitted to the
school in 1903, but the disconcerting lack of candidates for the
scholarships has already been mentioned.

In October 1883 Brunner was the representative governor appointed by the Northwich Local Board to sit on the school's governing body, and from 1885 he was re-elected a co-optative member and
became vice-chairman. Not until 1907 did he become chairman, on
the death of Christopher Kay, chairman from 1895. The absence of
a Minute Book from 1884 to 1910 unfortunately makes it impossible
to trace Brunner's part in the management of the school in any
detail. His early generosity to the school was continued when he
gave £100 towards enlarging the building,† and in 1891, when he

---

* John Weston was a fellow pupil. (*Northwich and Winsford Chronicle*, 22
July 1885.)

† Mond gave £100 to the funds of the grammar school. (*Northwich and
Winsford Chronicle*, 22 July 1885.)

bought and presented to it a small property in Chester adjoining the school property and of importance to its development. At the time of Leach's report of 1892 Brunner's interest in the school was such that the Charity Commissioners thought it advisable to communicate with him separately.[36]

Brunner's interest in education extended to the education of girls, and this forms another strand in the history of the school. In 1890 the Northwich High School for Girls was founded under the management of a company of shareholders: the building in which the school was held was leased from Dr Mond, and Brunner endowed ten scholarships a year. For a decade the school flourished, increasing in numbers from forty-three in 1890 to eighty-five in 1892 and praised as well conducted and giving a sound education. Not until 1902 did the numbers drop below sixty, but they fell off to thirty-seven in 1904, and the decline was attributed partly to the admission of girls holding county scholarships. By 1904 the school was in financial difficulties, and the governors were anxious to hand over the management to the County Education Committee. The school had already had a County Council grant from 1894 and this had risen to £125 a year in 1903–4: management by the county would make possible application for recognition by the Board of Education as a Secondary School and, in consequence, a higher grant. The county agreed to take over the management and financial responsibility of the school from October 1904, the Education Committee appointing a majority of the governing body, whose first meeting took place in January 1905.[37]

At the time of the county's take-over of the Girls' School it was known that Sir John Brunner was about to build a school in Northwich which would practically supersede the existing Girls' High School. The Higher Education Sub-committee of the County Education Committee reported in October 1904 that the exact character of this school had not yet been defined, 'whether for Boys and Girls or Girls alone'. A letter from Brunner to the sub-committee, read in November 1904, referred to his intention to build a school for girls as soon as the winter was over, and stated his own preference for a dual school for boys and girls, but his unwillingness to force the hand of the sub-committee. He was, therefore, willing to build a central hall at first and to add the boys' wing later, when asked to do so by the committee.[38]

This suggestion naturally raised the whole question of the relationship between Brunner's proposed foundation and the old endowed grammar school of Witton. The situation was summed up by A. Dufton, a Board of Education inspector, in some 'Notes on towns in Cheshire where developments in secondary education are in pro-

gress', written at the end of 1903. He referred to the difficult position
in Northwich owing to friction between Sir John Brunner and the
other governors of the grammar school, in origin (he thought)
'possibly partly political and partly religious'. Some of the grammar
school governors, he knew, were determined to keep the school as a
Church foundation, but Brunner had 'made up *his* mind': 'he has
finally come to the conclusion that it will never be possible to make
the Grammar School into such a school as he thinks Northwich
requires and he has decided to make a new start'. (The official history
of the first fifty years of Brunner Mond & Co. presumably reflected
Brunner's views pretty accurately when its author described the
grammar school's curriculum as one which 'more befitted its age
than the requirements of modern times'.) As early as this date
Brunner proposed to buy ten acres of land adjoining the Verdin
Technical Schools and to erect a school for both boys and girls,
spending £20,000 on it and then handing it over to the town as a
gift. Dufton saw clearly that this prospect would be the end of the
old grammar school (a pity, he felt, 'even if it is a poor one'), since
Northwich from its size and social structure could not support two
schools and needed 'a cheap intermediate school' such as Brunner
would provide. Dufton's view of the governors' attitude was confirmed in an interview between them and the board's inspectors at
the end of the school inspection in February 1904. A draft report
among the school records refers to the governors' unanimity in their
desire to carry on the school under the existing scheme and to their
belief that Brunner would decline to give his help under that scheme
which maintained the character of the school.[39]

Between 1903, when the rift between Brunner and the grammar
school governing body seemed absolute, and November 1907, when
he was arranging the terms of transfer of the new building to the
Witton School, a change had occurred in his attitude.[40] There is no
direct evidence of what actually influenced him, but these were years
of change at the grammar school itself and also of the extension of
the influence and powers both of the Board of Education, set up in
1899, and of the County Council, which was first brought into the
field of secondary education under the Technical Instruction Act of
1889 and then officially constituted the local education authority by
the Education Act of 1902.

From the early 1890s Witton Grammar School was gradually
brought into a relationship with the County Council, though its
financial position was not such as to make it so dependent as Lymm
and Nantwich schools became. In the county authority's view
Witton's endowments were considerable, but they were perhaps
more apparent than real. Although the value of the Chester property

was rising in 1904, the benefit for the school was, as yet, in the future. The report of the 1914 school inspection confirmed this: that property was in need of extensive repairs, constituting a serious financial burden. In general it was unlikely that the school would have any material help from its property for the next twenty years.[41]

As early as 1893 there was a county scholar at the school, under the amending Act of 1891, whereby County Councils were permitted to found scholarships at schools approved by them. In 1904 there were eleven county scholars as well as five Brunner scholars out of a total of fifty-six pupils. In his report of 1892 to the Charity Commisisoners Leach had recommended that two representatives of the County Council should be substituted for two of the co-optative governors, and in 1895 the 1874 scheme was modified so that the representative governors were increased from five to eight (five from the Northwich Urban District Council, two from the County Council and one from the Victoria University of Manchester) and the co-optative ones correspondingly reduced from seven to four. Indirectly, the establishment of the Verdin Technical Schools brought Witton School into closer contact with the County Council. Having become directly responsible for the provision of technical education in the new schools, Northwich Urban District Council in 1898 withdrew its annual grant of £50 made for that purpose to the grammar school. The school governors appealed for help first to the Department of Science and Art, and then, in March 1899, at the instigation of Sir John Brunner, to the County Council. Following a report on the school, the County's Technical Instruction Committee was recommended to make a grant of £50 a year to the school for the year ending 31 March 1900: this was renewed annually and raised, by 1904, to £60. A more drastic step was apparently put before the school governors in June 1903. Printed notices exist among the school records of a proposed meeting of the governors to be held on 15 June to consider a motion, to be moved by Brunner or one of his supporters, offering to transfer to the County Council 'the whole of our undertaking'. The meeting was held, but clearly nothing came of it, and the absence of a minute book deprives us of any further light on the matter.[42]

Another link with the county lay in the use of Witton Grammar School (like Northwich High School for Girls) as a pupil teacher centre from 1904. By this system boys and girls who were apprenticed to teach at elementary schools spent a period as pupils at a secondary school. In November 1904 the governors of Witton School offered to take the existing number of pupil teachers (nine, for whom £125 a year was paid to the school), and the offer was accepted by the Administrative Sub-committee for Education for Northwich and District. This system, however, did not work entirely well in Cheshire, and in May 1908 the pupil teacher centre at Witton was closed, by which the school was, according to the headmaster, reduced by a whole form of twenty lads.[43]

Connections were also established with the new Board of Education. Late in 1903 Dufton stated that the Witton governors proposed to apply for recognition by the board under Scheme B, and at their request the school was inspected by the board's inspectors in February 1904. The governors were urged on by the County's Higher Education Sub-committee, and from August 1905 the school was in receipt of grants under the Board of Education's regulations for secondary schools and was put on the list of schools recognised for the school year 1905–6. Indeed, following inspections in 1905 and 1906, the board sent a report to the Local Education Authority that Sir John Deane's Grammar School,* Witton, was 'now a very promising school', that the numbers had shown a considerable increase, and that there had been a decided improvement in educational efficiency: with adequate financial resources a high rank for the school might be assured. Certainly, between 1903 and 1907, under Russell Wright, the number of pupils more than doubled, reaching 115. Besides his care of the academic side, Russell Wright took a keen interest in athletics: *The Wittonian*, begun in 1904, reported the school's games and sports, including the formation of the boat club in 1905.[44]

While the school was improving its educational standing the County Council, newly constituted the Local Education Authority, was seeking to extend its authority over endowed secondary schools. A strong party in the council was anxious that all secondary schools should be handed over to it, a policy on which the Board of Education exercised a braking influence. Early in 1904 a conference between the Board's representatives and the county authorities met to discuss relations between the endowed grammar schools (of which Nantwich was then in the forefront of discussion) and the L.E.A., from which some of them received substantial financial help. Despite persuasions from the Board, the county stuck to its viewpoint and the Higher Education Sub-committee unanimously passed a resolution, later confirmed by the Education Committee:

That where a Grammar or other Secondary School is unable to efficiently carry out its work without a large contribution from the County funds, this Committee is of opinion that the School should be transferred to the County Education Committee to be administered by a Local Sub-Committee for the district appointed by the Education Committee.

* The name under which it was 'recognised' by the Board of Education; 'Witton Grammar School', however, was still in use even in official records.

The county asked the Board if it would be prepared, on application, so to alter the present scheme of a grammar or endowed school as to bring about this object, and to consent to the existing endowments being made available towards the erection and maintenance of such schools under the control of the Education Committee. Eventually, after a deputation from Cheshire, which included Sir John Brunner, had seen Sir William Anson, the parliamentary secretary to the Board, the Board agreed to amend the scheme of any endowed secondary school aided by the L.E.A. on receiving a sufficient application from the governing body, so as to provide for the appointment of a majority of the governors by the L.E.A. A copy of the Board's decision was to be sent to all aided schools in the county, one of which was Sir John Deane's School.[45]

Between 1904 and 1907 a great deal of discussion at the local level (particularly in the County Education Committee's Sub-committee for Higher Education) and correspondence with the Board of Education took place about Cheshire's proposed County Scheme of Management for Secondary Schools and the overall provision of secondary education in the county in accordance with the needs of different districts. Although invited to take part in a conference to consider the provision of secondary schools in the Northwich district in December 1904 (after Brunner had made his proposals for a school), the governors of Witton School declined, on the grounds that they should be given full details of proposed building and maintaining of secondary schools in the town before a conference with the County Education Committee could usefully be held. In December 1904 the Higher Education Sub-committee came out in favour of having boys as well as girls at Brunner's new school, but left it to the Administrative Sub-committee to give an opinion as to its size and whether it should be mixed or dual. As far as the Northwich area was concerned, the outcome of the discussions was that in February 1906 the County Education Committee adopted the recommendation of its Higher Education Sub-committee that what was needed and should be provided (where not in existence), and aided by the County Council at an estimated cost in capitation grants of £650, was a mixed school for boys and girls of 200 pupils.[46]

Although Witton Grammar School was recognised by the Board of Education, and thus eligible to receive grants for 1905–6, the board informed the L.E.A. in 1906 that this did not guarantee continued recognition, which depended on the development of the L.E.A.'s plans. With the introduction of revised regulations by the Board, effective from August 1907, the situation changed. Under these regulations, to be eligible for public aid, schools had to conform to new conditions of freedom from denominational restrictions,

of representative local control and of accessibility to all classes by
means of a certain proportion of scholarships. Witton was affected
particularly by two requirements: no catechism or formulary distinctive of any particular religious denomination was to be taught
except in certain defined cases, and the scheme under which the
school was governed must not require any member of the teaching
staff to belong to any particular denomination.* Failure to comply
with the new regulations meant failure to gain increased grants to
be given by the Board. The school's 1874 scheme, even as revised in
1895, still contained the survival from the original foundation of
religious requirements: these had been defined in the scheme as
religious instruction in accordance with the doctrines of the Church
of England (though with a conscience clause) and the headmaster's
membership of the Church of England.† In October 1907 the
governors resolved on an application to the L.E.A., asking the
Education Committee to inform the Board that the school was
needed as part of the secondary school provision for the area, and
that, in consequence, these conditions 'might be waived with advantage in view of the educational needs of the area'. The regulations
included provision for waivers of this kind if recommended by the
L.E.A. and granted by the Board, but the county refused to advise
the Board to grant 'the exceptional treatment' asked for by the
governors.[47]

This, then, was the background to Sir John Brunner's ultimate
decision, taken by November 1907, to give a new building and site to
Sir John Deane's Grammar School. In consideration of this
decision the County Education Committee resolved in March 1908
that the local character of the endowment of the school ought to be
preserved. By April 1908 the new school was already in course of
erection, and in July the Education Committee approved the
transfer of the Northwich Girls' High School to the new building
under the management, as a dual school, of the governing body of
Sir John Deane's and under a reconstituted scheme sanctioned by
the Board of Education.[48] It is clear that Brunner's gift and the
county's approval were contingent on the acceptance of the new
scheme of management, which was under discussion from 1908 and
was finally passed by the King in Council in May 1910.

The school moved into the new building, the nucleus of the
present one, in September 1908, with seventy-five boys, but it was

* Lymm School had the same problem over the appointment of a headmaster in 1906. See Kay, pp. 130–2.

† Even the powers given to the Charity Commissioners to make new
schemes were subject, under the 1895 scheme, to the provision that the
religious instruction to be given should always be Anglican.

VII (*a*) The second school, from a drawing (probably mid-nineteenth-century) by J. F. Drinkwater, in the Brunner Library, Northwich

VII (*b*) The third school (left) and the headmaster's house

VIII (*overleaf*) The fourth and present school: an aerial view showing the extensive site and work in progress on Riversdale Meadow, 1960
Airviews (*Manchester*) *Ltd*

under a new headmaster. In 1906 Russell Wright had unfortunately been found to be suffering from phthisis. He was given prolonged leave until May 1907, when he returned to Northwich and tried to take up his duties again, but the effort was too much and in July 1907 he died at Cheltenham at the early age of thirty-four.* His death at this particular moment meant the virtual coincidence of three changes which marked a completely new start for the school. They were a new building on a fine site, a new scheme of management, one of the features of which was the addition of a girls' department to the boys' school, and the appointment of a new headmaster, F. C. Weedon,† who at once gained the approval of the Board of Education inspectors.[49]

* A plaque in Northwich parish church commemorates him.
† L. Gledhill acted as headmaster in the interim, and his name appears in the 1907–8 list of secondary schools recognised as efficient by the Board of Education.

XII

Twentieth-century developments

by L. A. Hopkins

The site of the new building was, and indeed remains, a fine one. Situated on the south of the town, it is bounded on its western side by farmland. The headmaster's house, Riversdale, had been built in the previous century, but was not part of the original six acres of Sir John Brunner's gift: nor was Riversdale Meadow, running down to the river Weaver in front of the school. Clearly the site offered opportunities for development—opportunities which were taken during the next half century of the school's history, so that by the 1960s some twenty-seven acres of playing field had been developed. The new building could not perhaps claim architectural distinction; but its warm red Ruabon brick faced with mellow Bath stone gives it a pleasant appearance. Internally, the architects—Powles & King —had planned for a dual school, the western side for boys and the eastern side for girls. The most attractive feature is the assembly hall, with a fine oak balcony running down one side. The carvings and embellishments of this timberwork appear to have been inspired by some of the work in Gawsworth Church—although no doubt the architects also had in mind the style of the period of the school's original foundation. Certainly the change to this new building from the old cramped quarters of the 1869 school made a great impression on the minds of those boys who transferred to it. Several of them have spoken of the feeling of space and freedom which the new building and estate engendered.

Circumstances thus favoured a new start on a more prosperous period in the school's history. Two years were indeed to pass by before the new scheme of government could be put into effect. During those two years two virtually distinct groups occupied the new building. Although a joint assembly was held at the beginning of the day, boys and girls were segregated for the rest of the time. Miss A. G. Pierce was regarded by her 115 girls and their parents as headmistress. Fees were frequently paid to her, notices of withdrawal were sent to her, and certainly for two years a separate organisation for the affairs of the High School continued to function with Mr E. M. Cross as its secretary.[1] Weedon makes no reference to girls in his reports to the governors until 13 July 1910.[2] Although the President of the Board of Education, Walter Runciman, visited the school on 23 September 1909 and presented the governors with a print of the new scheme—now handsomely preserved in a red vellum folder—this new scheme could not take legal effect until it had been approved by the King in Council on 31 May 1910. That approval having been given, the governors appointed[3] Weedon as Principal and Headmaster, and Miss Pierce as Headmistress. From then onwards Sir John Deane's Grammar School for Boys and Girls could move ahead under a unified control, although the dichotomy implicit in the 1910 scheme characterised the school's organisation under Weedon and his successor.

Frank Charles Weedon had been appointed headmaster of Witton Grammar School in January 1908. He was a Londoner, although his father was a graduate of Christ's College, Cambridge. After attending Colnbrook Ely School he went for two years' teacher's training at St Mark's Training College, Chelsea. In 1890 he was fortunate, as a non-graduate, to be appointed to the staff of Alleyn's School, Dulwich. He attended lectures in physics at King's College, University of London, and initiated the teaching of physics at Alleyn's.[4] In 1903 the then headmaster of Alleyn's, H. B. Baker, M.A., F.R.S., left the school to become Lee's Reader in Chemistry at Christ Church, Oxford. Weedon left with him—no doubt under and with his influence—and matriculated at Christ Church in 1903. Unfortunately there is a gap in the Christ Church tutors' books during the period 1851–1906,[5] so it is impossible to know what special circumstances led the college to accept an undergraduate of the age of thirty-nine, married and with a young son. In 1907 Weedon proceeded to the degree of B.Sc.—an unusual but quite regular Oxford award—his subject being physics. Thus, at the time when Witton Grammar School needed a new headmaster, Weedon was available: an Oxford graduate with some fifteen years of teaching experience—most of it in a good school. Local opinion has it that he was Brunner's candidate: a scientist to implement Brunner's plans for a new direction for the school. However that may be, Weedon took control as Principal in June 1910.

As already indicated, the 1910 scheme regarded the school as a dual establishment, clause 16 saying quite clearly that 'there shall be separate departments for boys and girls'. However, a later clause, No. 24, goes on to say that 'the School as a whole shall be under one Head, who shall exercise a general supervision over both departments, and shall be called the Principal . . . The Principal may

be the Head Master of the Boys' Department.' There can be little
doubt that the contemporary local view of this 'merger' of the
two schools was that there was no intention that boys and girls
should be united in one 'mixed' school in which curriculum and
teaching were unified. A separate organisation was maintained:
girls' classes were kept separate from boys' classes—rigidly separate
below the sixth form, and it was some years before a viable sixth
form in the current sense was established.* Weedon was a strict
disciplinarian who discouraged friendships between boys and girls.
Probably he did not believe in co-education. The divisive clauses
of the 1910 scheme undoubtedly stamped a definite character on
the school and helped to engender an antagonism to genuine
co-education that was still strongly apparent in the 1950s. Clearly,
problems of organisation were bound to occur in these circumstances. For example, Weedon reported on 21 November 1911 that
the board were corresponding separately with Miss Pierce.[6] On the
retirement of Miss Pierce in 1928, the governors wrote to the Board
of Education asking for Clauses 16 and 24 of the scheme to be
amended by the abolition of the terms 'Principal' and 'Headmistress'. This the board refused to do,[7] pointing out that the Principal was Head, and that Miss Pierce virtually occupied the
position of Chief Assistant Mistress, and was paid a salary as such.
It is interesting to note that the governors' minutes contain no
reference to a 'Headmistress' after 1928 and, when Weedon's retirement became imminent in 1929, it was resolved 'to leave the
appointment of a Senior Mistress until the new Headmaster takes
up his duties'.[8] Weedon's successor, C. F. A. Keeble, was appointed
as Headmaster and abhorred the title of Principal.

Some space has been devoted to this particular aspect of the 1910
scheme because it had such a powerful influence on the character of
the school for the next half-century. There are of course other
important parts of the scheme. The 1874 scheme, amended in 1895,
referred to in the previous chapter, provided for the first time
county representatives to the governing body: true, only two out of
a total of twelve, but still a new principle had been introduced. The
end of the nineteenth century had seen important legislation, in 1888
and 1894, by which the modern framework of local government was
set up; and it was to be expected that education, ultimately to become
the biggest spender in local government, should increasingly fall
under the control of county councils and the county boroughs. The
1910 scheme dramatically increased the representation of Cheshire

* The fees lists for the spring term 1911—two separate lists marked 'Girls'
Department' and 'Boys' Department'—show only eight girls and fifteen
boys in the sixth. Five of the boys were under sixteen.

County Council by giving it ten out of a total of sixteen members. Five were to be appointed by the Northwich Urban District Council and one by Manchester University. At least two of the county, and one of the Northwich, members were to be women. Presumably the omission of any representatives from Northwich Rural District Council is a relic of Sir John Deane's original preference for the 'chapelry of Witton'. Indeed, Clause 38 of this 1910 scheme states specifically that preference must continue to be given to boys and girls resident within 'the said chapelry or the township of North-wich as constituted in October 1874'. In point of fact more pupils entered the school from the Rural Council's area than from North-wich itself; and the new scheme of 1947, and the 1967 scheme for the reconstituting of the Estates Governing Body, both recognised the justice of giving representation to the Rural District.

The stronger connection with Cheshire County Council indicated by the 1910 scheme foreshadowed problems of finance over the next thirty or forty years. The school's status was grant-aided, and in the future a considerable part of its revenue was to come from public funds, viz. the Board of Education and the County Council. The county local authority paid fees and bursaries for several boys and girls; in addition it made an annual grant which in the year 1910[9] was approximately equal to that from the Board of Education, at £582 7s 6d. Income from endowment that year was £772 8s 10d; pupils' fees were £773 4s 6d. With care and economy these three sources of income were just about sufficient to meet the day-to-day running costs of the school. But as time went by the governors were to find themselves in some financial difficulty when the need arose for financing new projects. To whom could they turn, other than either the county or the board? And clearly the county would be willing to provide more finance only if it exercised greater control of the affairs of the school. This was to be one of the recurrent problems during the period 1910–44.

The 1910 scheme gave the governors powers if they wished to run a boarding department. No doubt individual masters had from time to time taken a few pupils as boarders; but, although the head-master's house in Church Road was occasionally used for boarders, there was never at any period of the school's history a fully consti-tuted boarding school establishment in the accepted sense. Nor did the governors after 1910 make any official arrangement to organise one. C. F. A. Keeble did accommodate a few boys in Riversdale for a short period when his two sons were in the school. But this was a purely private venture on his part, and the highest total was twelve.

The scheme also empowered the governors to admit pupils from the age of eight. A preparatory department was established from the beginning and was a flourishing institution, finally killed by the reorganisation after the 1944 Act. The argument for doing this was quite simply an egalitarian one: some parents were able to buy privilege and to secure the admission of son or daughter to the main school through paying fees. This issue is now dead; but hundreds of people in mid-Cheshire would have argued in favour of a preparatory department. Admission to the school was to be by an examination under the direction of the Principal.[10] One of the problems which arose was that many parents delayed their application for admission until their children were approaching the end of their career in the local elementary schools. The governors found it necessary to advertise[11] that preference would be given to candidates under the age of twelve, since children who joined after that age found themselves behind in much of the school work. But as the school became more securely established over the next few years, the demand for places exceeded the number available. There were always members of the public who alleged that not sufficient free places were being made available:[12] the cry of 'privilege' was always calculated to incite emotion, alarm and criticism. By the scheme the governors were committed to a minimum of 5 per cent of free places out of their total admissions.[13] The records show that every year this minimum was always very considerably exceeded. In particular it is worthy of comment that the children in the Preparatory Department performed very well in the competitive examinations for free places on the county list. No doubt individual injustice or deprivation did take place from time to time; but, in terms of 'social justice', the school admission registers show that a large number of boys and girls joined the school from the ordinary homes of Northwich.

The admission register, analysed for the years 1910, 1921 and 1937, gives the following results; the pupils are classified by their fathers' occupations according to these categories: A, professional; B, lower middle (e.g. shops and farms); C, skilled working class; D, unskilled working class.

	1910	1921	1937
Total admissions:	50	63	84
Category A	8	6	6
B	27	19	37
C	12	23	27
D	3	15	14
Free places	19	28	37

These figures would appear to support the conclusion that the admission clauses of the 1910 scheme undoubtedly very largely carried out the original intentions of the school's sixteenth-century founder in securing good education for children of humble origin in the Northwich area. That some children who could have derived profit from attending the school were denied the opportunity could not be fairly blamed on the school and its administration; more would have been admitted had public funds made more places available. By the 1920s Sir John Deane's was the largest grammar school in Cheshire—larger than the schools in more populous areas such as Crewe, Altrincham and Sale, and the Wirral. Northwich did indeed owe a debt of gratitude to Sir John Deane and Sir John Brunner.

Another matter which arose quite quickly out of the new scheme was the vexed question of religious instruction. The previous chapter has mentioned Brunner's views and their conflict with those of his fellow governors on the old board. From 1910, if the scheme were to be scrupulously observed, religious instruction in the school was to be in accordance with 'the principles of the Christian faith', but 'no catechism or formulary distinctive may be taught'.[14] A parent or guardian could indeed request, in writing, that his child be instructed according to a particular denomination; but the governors needed to comply with this only if they thought fit. The cost of such special instruction had to be borne out of endowment funds and not public grants. From time to time parents wrote in to ask for Anglican instruction and, in fact, a petition from parents was handed in, asking for their children to be instructed in the Prayer Book of the Church of England. As early as July 1910 Weedon told the governors that he and Miss Pierce were prepared to give Anglican instruction out of school hours; and in the management committee (a sub-committee of the governing body) on 26 July 1910 Mr Roscoe Brunner proposed that distinctive religious instruction should be given. Such a proposal from Sir John's son may appear a little surprising; but his motion was defeated. Canon Binney raised the matter in September 1910, but it was referred back. Weedon gave the management committee a full résumé of his syllabus,[15] which was approved, Brunner once again being baulked in his effort to get denominational instruction. At the annual general meeting of the full governing body, held in February 1911, Canon Binney spoke strongly about the disappointment caused among Church people by the school's religious syllabus, and a lengthy debate followed. Binney's proposal that Anglican instruction should be given in school hours and paid for out of school funds was only narrowly defeated. It was agreed that parents should be sent a circular, asking for their wishes. The result was interesting:

	C. of E.	Undenominational	R.C.
Boys	58	53	3
Girls	71	47	3

It is not surprising to find that, after this, the Roman Catholic priest Father Cregan approached the school to ask for instruction to be given by a Roman Catholic member of staff. The governors passed Canon Binney's resolution that this should be done; but the issue did not come to a head because the request was not made by parents, as required by both the regulations of the Board of Education and the provisions of the scheme. Indeed, there is no further reference to this contentious matter in the governors' minutes; and it must be assumed that these old religious controversies, dating as they do back to the period of English history when the school was founded, died down as a result of practical compromise in the day-to-day running of the school. It is perhaps worth while to reflect that future controversies over religious education are more likely to be waged not over denominational issues but on the basic consideration as to whether any kind of religious instruction should properly be given as part of the curriculum of a school dependent on public funds.

One further point of interest must be mentioned before this matter of religious is left. It is noteworthy that, whereas the 1874 scheme specifically requires the headmaster to be an Anglican, this qualification is omitted in 1910.

So, with a new scheme, new buildings, and the powerful support of a strong governing body, Weedon set out to organise his new 'dual' school. Physically a small man, he possessed a firm, perhaps even a ruthless, character. He set himself specific objectives, and laid down clearly the means by which he meant to attain them. He was undisputed master of his school community. Although always careful to inform his governors of his actions, in practice he appointed and dismissed his own staff. The surprising fact is that only once did a member of staff—a mistress—invoke the aid of her professional association, who secured her an interview with the governing body[16] on the grounds that she had been unfairly treated by Weedon. But the Principal was supported, and the lady went. Generally a man of few words, and somewhat brusque of manner, Weedon nevertheless secured the respect of his staff, who followed his leadership because his objectives were clear and his own professional standards were extremely high. He controlled rigorously the material he expected to be taught, and the methods by which it was imparted to the pupils. He compiled an 'Organisation File', known to the teaching staff as 'The Black Book'—no doubt because of the colour of its cover—and this compilation was in the common rooms for staff to study and to follow. A copy has survived, and makes interesting reading for those concerned with theories of teaching method. He was always zealous to promote esprit de corps, a school spirit. Thus he wrote, 'Form Ms are asked to explain once a term that it is a privilege to be a member of S.J.D.G.S. (see Historical Note on School Prospectus), and that this privilege entails certain responsibilities.' Emphasising the importance of good manners, correct dress, respect for school officers, and care for school property, he went on to advise that 'Pupils should be occasionally reminded of distinctions of former pupils, winners of the Royal Humane Society's Certificate* and those who have laid down their lives in the Great War'. Similarly, of games he said, 'The object of School Games is not the production of skilful athletes, but the training in Form-spirit, loyalty to leaders and to one another, punctuality, cheerful endurance, mastery of detail and the 100 per cent effort.' 'Games,' he goes on to say, 'are an important part of English education.' Unlike his successor, he had no distinguished record as a games player; his own preference was for skating and tennis—neither of which is a 'team' game. But school games flourished during his headmastership.

To return to his 'Organisation File'. Probably his approach to teaching method is best exemplified by his notes on English. He wrote:

The TEACHING must be positive and according to plan. This should be revealed by an inspection of the English manuscript books . . . VERSE WRITING should be frequent and should be imitation of patterns. Pupils should be trained to see that excellent English is not necessarily sentimental, and that the IDEAS of an essay are distinct from their EXPRESSION. As a rule, it is well to mark an essay solely on the technical skill in the composition —ignoring the accuracy or other value of the subject matter. The English of the School being generally weak, a mark exceeding 7 should be given rarely.

The same approach is seen in every subject. Orderliness, industry, organisation, accuracy—these are the key themes. All work must be carefully marked. 'All work,' he wrote, 'Homework or Classwork, which does not reveal painstaking effort should be marked B and

* This is a reference to the tragedy of 29 January 1917. A party of pupils and staff, including Weedon, were skating on Riversdale pond when the ice broke and twenty-one girls fell into the water. Two were drowned. The courage of the rescuers was reported to the Royal Humane Society, who awarded certificates to Mr F. C. Weedon (headmaster), Mr L. Jeans, Mr F. T. A. Leeson, Mr R. G. Mitchell, Mr G. Newall. A plaque in the hall commemorates this.

repeated in detention.' Precise instructions were given on marking, summarised thus:

1. Mark Home lessons with figures.
2. Give a repetition test on every home work and give numerical marks for the test.
3. Give numerical marks for every school lesson . . .
6. Prevent cheating by good discipline.

It is easy today to criticise this rigorous and authoritarian approach, but the success of Weedon's methods in terms of examination results was undeniable. It must also be remembered that he inherited two schools whose standards were not high. As stated in the previous chapter, the revival of the boys' school under Russell Wright was cut short by his ill health and untimely death, whilst the Northwich High School had been unfavourably regarded by the Board of Education inspectors in their inspection of 1909.* Of the boys' school, Weedon in his report to the governors[17] in 1908 referred to 'the great slackness which pervaded the School'; the boys were 'not unruly but indifferent and idle'. The work was 'slovenly', and the masters 'not skilled teachers'. He went on to say 'there will be a stiff task here'. Two years later[18] he wrote to the governors, 'My ambition is that this School shall be to an ordinary secondary school what Oxford—or Cambridge—is to Manchester.' Although the phrase may strike the reader as grandiloquent, it would be an error to deny Weedon's earnest devotion, his zealous commitment, to what he interpreted as the best interests of the foundation he served. Certainly he rapidly won the generous approval of His Majesty's Inspectors, who, in their inspection of 1914, gave him high commendation. Amongst the points raised in this report was the shortage of accommodation, and the Board urged the governors to increase the size of the school and add to the building.[19] By 1910 the numbers had risen to 212—110 girls and 102 boys; and in the summer term of 1914 the figure of 300 (150 boys and 150 girls) was reached. This was the theoretical maximum of the new building, and it was exceeded the following September, when the roll was 149 girls and 163 boys. But the outbreak of the Great War in the previous August made the provision of more accommodation most unlikely. The school therefore embarked on a period of some physical discomfort: already in September 1914[20] the music room and library were taken over as classrooms. How frequently does this pattern repeat itself in the history of English education! A new

---

* It is interesting that the board should have inspected the girls' department separately. This insistence by the board on two separate establishments is referred to earlier.

school is built, the new amenities are praised—and within a year or two everything is overcrowded and out of date, and the school authorities find themselves committed to a policy of make do and mend. More, however, will be said about problems of accommodation and finance later on; at the moment the academic and social progress of the school for the remainder of Weedon's reign must be considered.

It would be tedious to record details of the school's academic successes, in terms of examination results. That these results soon achieved a high standard, comparing favourably with those of similar schools in Cheshire and elsewhere, is hardly surprising in the light of what has been said about the thoroughness of Weedon's organisation. One or two examples must suffice. In 1915 eight out of the eleven boys who were entered for the Oxford Senior Locals secured first-class honours; one boy was the top boy in higher mathematics, and another in physics. The same year saw the award of an open scholarship in mathematics at Sidney Sussex College, Cambridge. Such awards were not infrequently gained over the next fifty years. The important point here is that the marked improvement of the school's academic life from 1910 onwards meant that large numbers of boys and girls proceeded to the universities; by the 1960s the average became of the order of twenty-five to thirty per annum. Thus the historic role of the sixteenth-century grammar school was revived and strengthened. Northwich boys and girls were fortunate in that the school had funds available to give grants to pupils proceeding to the university.

The quality of a school's life is influenced by many factors, of which examination success is but one. The grammar schools of the twentieth century made strenuous efforts to achieve 'tone', a word frequently used by inspectors, administrators and headmasters but whose meaning is difficult to define. Basically it is probably fair to say that most of these schools set out consciously to imitate the public schools—many of whose 'traditions' were very much younger than some imitators realised. Many 'traditions' and 'customs' are, of course, devised and practised in order to establish the unique identity of the institution and to strengthen the loyalty and devotion of its members. One obvious practice is the adoption of an official school uniform, with distinctive badges and colours. A group photograph of the school taken about 1900 shows most of the boys wearing dark clothing; the jackets, however, are not of standard design, though many of them are of the 'Norfolk' style. All boys are wearing an 'Eton' collar, but no standard school tie, of an official design and colour, was being worn. As early as 1905, however, the present school colours—dark and light blue—were worn for games: striped

jerseys for the Second XI, but quartered for the First XI. The school
cap, bearing a silver badge with 'W.G.S' engraved on it, was dark
blue with light blue stripes running down the seams of the panels,
and the summer straw hat sported a dark and light blue ribbon.*
These colours were carried into the new school and were ultimately
also worn by the girls. Weedon wrote to his governors:

Formerly some girls were not suitably dressed, and foolish finery was not
entirely absent. The Lady Governors strengthened the determination of the
Head Mistress, and the girls now dress as is usual in Girls' High Schools
—plainly and usefully. It transpired that many of them felt that they were
not members of the Grammar School, because they were not allowed to
wear the Grammar School colours—Oxford and Cambridge blue. That
disability has been removed. It was formerly a matter of complaint that the
girls were compelled to sport the political colours of the Liberal Party.
It was not true . . . ; the girls' colours were navy and old gold and were
borrowed by Miss Abbott† from Newnham College, Cambridge.[21]

It is noteworthy that two years passed before the girls were allowed
to wear Grammar School colours! Although the prospectus of 1919,
under the heading of dress, mentions only 'the regulation School
Cap or Ribbon' as compulsory, yet school discipline over the next
fifty years insisted more and more on the wearing of correct school
uniform; and Keeble (Weedon's successor) introduced special blazers
and ties for games colours.

Even as late as 1939, however, there is no firm insistence on a
standard school uniform. Keeble's prospectus of that year says,
'Provided that boys are tidy no hard and fast rules are laid down as
to every-day dress, but for those in the Middle School, there is no
better costume than a sports coat or blazer (with pull-over in cold
weather) with grey flannel trousers.' A later paragraph is interesting,
as revealing so much of the outlook Keeble brought with him—
'Though the School cap is the regulation wear for every-day, it is
pointed out that a cap is not the correct wear for Divine Service or
formal occasions, and every boy should wear the regulation straw-
hat (speckled black and white with School band) at such times.
Prefects, sub-prefects, VI Form and "Colours" are allowed to wear
white hats instead of speckled.' The inference from the prospectus is
that the regulations for girls' dress were more rigid.

All schools like to have their own distinctive badge. Weedon
appears to have devised the one still in use in consultation with the
churchwardens of the Church of St Bartholomew the Great, West
Smithfield, during the course of 1910. He decided on a quartered

---

* Details given by Dr Frank Towers, who joined the school in 1905.
† The headmistress of Northwich High School for Girls, 1903–6.

shield. Two quarters carried the arms of Rahere, the founder of St Bartholomew's, one quarter the arms of Cheshire, and the fourth quarter the arms of Sir John Brunner. For those interested in heraldry, the description given by the churchwardens in correspondence with Weedon may be quoted:

'Quarterings
1 and 4. (Arms of the Priory of St. Bartholomew the Great) Gules, two lions passant guardant or, in chief two ducal coronets of the same.
    2. (Arms of Sir John Brunner)
       Gules, on the base of a stone hexagon fountain p/or, a rose of the first barbed and seeded of the second; in the chief two mullets of six points or
    3. (Cheshire)
       Azure, three garbs or.'

Technically speaking, there are heraldic objections to be made to this coat of arms, since it is a mixture of the personal and the institutional. Thus Sir John Brunner's coat carries the red hand of Ulster, which all baronets (save those of Nova Scotia) are entitled to display as a personal augmentation. The school badge has never been submitted to the College of Heralds. However, Weedon presented it to the governors' meeting in September 1910,[22] and it has remained unchanged since then.

The house system—an obvious imitation of the public schools—was introduced and became a convenient device for organising and encouraging games. In Weedon's day houses were decided on a territorial basis, according to a pupil's place of domicile; but Keeble introduced the present four-house system—School, Brunner, Deane, Wilbraham—three of which were named after distinguished people associated with the school. The compulsory wearing of house ties by boys and girls was inaugurated at the same time.

Out-of-class activities form a good pointer to the social and educational vitality of a school. Both Weedon and Keeble fostered music and games: in the case of Keeble, games more effectively because of his interests in the playing fields and in securing the building of a gymnasium. However, more will be said later about games in Keeble's day.

It is indeed time to write more directly about Keeble's headmastership. Weedon retired in 1929, and the governors appointed Cyril Francis Allan Keeble as his successor. Keeble's education had been at the Leys School and St John's College, Cambridge, where he was a Classical Exhibitioner. His early teaching experience had been chiefly in the public school sector, and he had three years' experience as headmaster of a small grammar school in Leicestershire. From the beginning of his headmastership it was clear that his

outlook and philosophy of education—a phrase about which he
would have had some doubts—were, like his experience, quite
different from Weedon's. He had little sympathy with Weedon's
'Black Book'. His temperament was more outgoing, and he imparted
a zest for life and enjoyment. 'His arrival', said one of his senior
staff, 'was like a breath of fresh air'. The impression one gets of
Weedon is that he rarely smiled. Keeble on the other hand seems to
have brought a tremendous sense of fun—though woe betide those
who offended against his canons of etiquette and good behaviour.
He represented the ethos of the public school—an ethos which in
practice is often less stuffy, orthodox and repressive than it appears
to those who have had no experience of it. It would be true to say
that he would have dearly loved to make Sir John Deane's into a
minor public school. He wrote to the governors in June 1937, 'To
make this school co-educational would be the beginning of the end.
It suffered and must suffer from the mistaken policy of 1907. High
School and Grammar School should never have been amalgamated
in as much as that amalgamation finally robbed the Grammar School
of any chance of attaining minor Public School status.'[23] His attitudes
and actions sometimes earned a not altogether deserved criticism
of being tinctured with social snobbery. He dearly loved the school,
and wished to preserve its independence from the local authority
—a desire thwarted by finance and by the Act of 1944. The rejec-
tion by the Minister of Education, Ellen Wilkinson, of the school's
application for direct grant status in 1945 was a sore blow to him.

Before the important issues which faced the school over the next
twenty-one years are discussed, it will perhaps be more convenient
to deal with matters which, although less important, made a more
immediate impact on the pupils and staff of the school. Keeble gave
a fresh impetus to the games of the school. On the boys' side (Keeble
always referred to the 'boys' side' and the 'girls' side') the traditional
games had been cricket and rowing in the summer, and Association
football in the winter. One of the first things he did was to change
the winter game to rugby football. This action provoked opposition
and criticism. Mid-Cheshire is a stronghold of Association football,
and for the leading school in the area to abandon it caused much
comment. Many of the old boys opposed the change, and it is likely
that the Old Wittonians' Association suffered greatly as a result of
it. The change was made at the same time at King's School, Macclesfield. It is fair to say that both schools developed a very high standard
of rugby football, and that Cheshire county fifteens at all levels
have derived considerable strength from these sources of recruitment.
School rowing also received fresh encouragement, and embarked on
a new era of success. Crews began to travel much further afield.

Cricket was encouraged by the provision of better wickets and more skilled coaching. The girls' games, too, prospered; the winter hockey became very strong, with steady successes in inter-school tournaments. Keeble set out deliberately to foster games and social activities, and took particular care to develop a strong prefectorial system on both 'sides'.

Many of his pupils will recall with pleasure his contribution to school music. He had a considerable skill in writing light-hearted operettas; and these gave to many boys and girls their first introduction to stage experience. The orchestral traditions of the Weedon era were maintained; but, as in Weedon's day, the orchestra was strengthened considerably by the addition of instrumentalists from outside the school. School music and drama were helped by the provision of new stage facilities, useful in their day but now replaced by a more efficient steel 'fit-up'.

Keeble himself regarded the late 'thirties, the period just before the war, as the golden time of his reign. Even so, there were serious problems facing the school. A general inspection by His Majesty's Inspectors of Schools in the summer of 1937 revealed considerable shortcomings in staffing, equipment, accommodation and courses of study. Not all the criticisms were justified or fair; but it was clear that improvements had to be made: and, of course, additional building, equipment and staffing would mean money. Where could the governors turn? Five years previously, in 1932, they had discussed the building of a gymnasium, three classrooms and an art room at an estimated cost of £7,500. The governors were in a cleft stick. If they sold property—supposing the Board of Education allowed this—they would reduce the income necessary for the day-to-day running of the school; if they borrowed, then their current needs would be crippled by repayments and interest charges. That they were most reluctant to turn to the county is abundantly clear from correspondence between the clerk and the board. In a letter dated October 1931[24] the clerk accused Cheshire County Council in round terms. 'For many years [they] have starved this School and only within the last three years have they made the reason for this apparent. One or two members of the County Committee . . . have pressed the Governors to hand the School over to the County . . . As a result of reduced grants from the County, there has been an increasing overdraft in the School Account reaching the peak point in September 1930 amounting to £3,494 7s 10d.' The governors realised that the county would be reluctant to make grants for buildings which would immediately become the property of the governors, and that increased income from the county would inevitably lead to greater control by the county. They struggled hard to maintain independence. In 1934 they modified their building scheme and built a gymnasium with changing rooms, deferring the art room and classrooms. The gymnasium cost £3,480; this was paid for by the sale of investments and accumulated endowment income. The Board, through the Charity Commissioners, insisted on a sinking fund for the recovery of the used capital. Thus this building venture reduced for some years the income available from endowment.

The report of His Majesty's Inspectors in 1937 underlined the need for further building. Whence was the money to come? The school accounts (as opposed to the endowment account) for the year 1936–7 showed an income of £11,999 and payments of £12,654 —a deficit of £655. The main sources of the income were: fees, £5,613; Board of Education grant, £4,453; Cheshire County Council grant, £1,500; other sources—chiefly sale of books—£433. The governors believed that a major charge on endowment income would always be the maintenance of the school property, which was chiefly located in Chester, and were not prepared to use more capital for building. Indeed, it was difficult to see how they could. Both in 1936 and in 1937 there were considerable overdrafts at the bank. Thus two events coincided to bring the school to a point of financial crisis—shortage of money and a need for considerable expenditure on additional school buildings. The governors had no option but to turn to the county for financial assistance.

Joint meetings between representatives of the two sides had indeed been taking place during 1936, without any positive result. There were suggestions that the school should make similar arrangements with the county to those agreed by Lymm Grammar School. Briefly, the Lymm governors had agreed that the direct grant from the Board should be paid to the county instead of the school. The county then gave greater financial assistance to Lymm, but also secured greater control of the school's affairs. This 'Lymm' scheme was discussed by the governors at a special general meeting in December 1936,[25] and they resolved to ask the county to send the Director to a meeting to examine the whole matter with them. The Director (F. F. Potter) and the County Treasurer (V. Williams) attended a meeting in January 1937. The Director stated that the county were prepared to help the governors in their present financial difficulties and estimated it would 'cost the County £3,000 a year to put the school straight'. He then outlined in detail the conditions which the county would impose. There were sixteen all told.[26] The most important referred to rigid financial control—including the endowment account: 'they would', he said 'be much firmer about these matters'. Staffing, too, would be controlled. In subsequent correspondence the Director's conditions increased to twenty, and included two which the governors were bound to reject—that all communications regarding any alterations in the property of the endowment would be submitted through the Director to the Board of Education and that all other communications to the Board would go through the Director. The governors also resisted a proposal that the county would, in effect, assume control of all staffing arrangements. In May the County Treasurer presented a long memorandum to the Secondary Schools Inter-sub-committee. In it he analysed the financial situation of the school. He estimated that placing the school on the 'Lymm basis' would cost the county at least £2,875 per annum—after deduction of the board's grant—as well as paying an unknown amount on past deficits. He pointed out that the county could finance the proposed extensions without changing the position of the school by adopting the 'Lymm basis'.

A lengthier version of the Treasurer's memorandum was referred to the governors on 30 June 1937. A covering letter from the Director said that if the governors accepted its principles, the county would 'relieve the School in their present financial emergency, in both the matter of the existing overdraft and of the proposed extensions'. The governors accepted the main points. In effect, the position arrived at could be summarised thus:

1. The school was to be conducted under the original scheme dated 31 May 1910 and to continue to receive its grant direct from the Board.
2. The school must furnish detailed annual estimates, with full explanations, to the county. No excess expenditure was to be incurred without previous county approval. The credit balance in excess of £300 on the school endowment account was to be transferred to the school account.
3. The county were to be consulted on all staff changes, and no changes to be made without previous county approval; but the governors were to be left free regarding personnel.
4. The county to approve the advertisement and terms of appointment of the headmaster, and to reserve the right to reject an unsuitable appointment.

In writing to the Director to tell him that the governors had accepted the county proposals, the clerk (A. W. Chambers) said, 'I understand that a desire has been expressed that bygones should be bygones, with which I cordially agree.' The sentence conceals rather than reveals the large degree of emotions and passion, even of hostility and acrimony, which had emerged during the previous months. Keeble in particular bitterly resented the growth of the county's power, and wrote in considerable irritation to the clerk about the Treasurer's detailed enquiries on such financial matters as telephone costs. However, the governors received substantial financial advantage from the new arrangement. The county's annual contribution was raised immediately from £1,500 to £2,000, and a payment of £1,520 was also made towards the governors' overdraft. The way was now clear to the building of the new extensions on the east end of the school: and these were to be paid for by the county. Even so, although architect's plans had been in being since 1935, there were still long delays in the completion of the work. At one point, owing to the outbreak of war in September 1939, it appeared that the project would be postponed. Whitehead, the builder who had been awarded the contract, withdrew in May 1939 and Messrs Appleton accepted it. The work was not completed until 1941.

These events of 1937 have been dealt with in some detail because they foreshadow the basic problems met in the next important crisis concerning the status of the school. This arose out of the Education Act of 1944. Following the passing of that Act, the newly constituted Ministry of Education issued on 15 December 1944 administrative memorandum No. 19. This document indicated that the governors should make proposals to the Minister concerning the future status of the school. The memorandum contained the ominous sentence: 'The Governors of any school, in respect of which an application is made for an Order directing that it shall be an Aided School, will be required to show that they are able and willing to defray the expenses which would fall to be borne by them under Section 15 (3) (a) of the Act.' The governors had already resolved[27] to meet the Director of Education and A. J. Gooch, H.M.I., to discuss the future of the school. Mr Gooch addressed the governors' meeting on 12 September on the implications of the Act, and the governors deferred any decision pending the issue of Ministry regulations. Memorandum 19 now gave them the spur to work out definite proposals. The inspector made it quite clear to the governors that, in his opinion, they would have difficulty in making out a strong case for the school becoming a Scheme 'A' school, a status similar to direct grant; he thought there would be financial difficulties, and also that the L.E.A. would press for the abolition of fees—thus making the financial position even more difficult. In March 1945 the Ministry issued Circular 32, dealing with direct-grant grammar schools. This documents made it clear that direct-grant conditions were to be revised, and with such revision the number of schools in receipt of direct grant would be altered—and the implication was that the number would be reduced. An important clause in the circular indicated that the Minister would expect governors to state how 'they propose to meet the expenses of the School and the cost of any repairs, alterations or improvements to premises that may be necessary'. In May His Majesty's Inspector discussed the matter with Keeble and the clerk (E. P. Thomas).[28] He stated the Minister would need to be satisfied on three points—finance, the position of the L.E.A., and the 'extent to which the School can claim to be differentiated from other Schools in the area in tradition, character and catchment area'. Mr Gooch added that he thought 'tradition was the strong card'. The governors decided to press ahead, and on 17 May 1945 passed a resolution[29] 'That every effort be made to continue the School as a Direct Grant Grammar School'. The Finance Inter-sub-committee, under the chairmanship of the Rev. A. W. Maitland Wood, got down to work, and on 26 June 1945 an application was sent to the Ministry, together with a statement of an estimated average yearly income and expenditure over a ten-year period based on an assumed average of 480 pupils. This estimate makes interesting reading, and is worth reproducing:

Income	£	*Expenditure*	£
Canteen	2,380	Administration	820
Endowment	1,400	Books and stationery	900
Fees (£25 a head)	12,000	Canteen	3,500
Ministry grant	7,680	Examinations	200
		Extensions	1,500
		Fuel, light, cleaning	1,400
		Furniture, fittings	100
		Rates, taxes	960
		Repairs and grounds	700
		Staff	13,330
	23,460		23,410

The Governors admitted that a fee of £25 was double the existing fee, and proposed a scale of graded fees based on weekly income. On the matter of financing proposed building extensions, they said they would raise a fifty-year loan of £35,000, on an annual cost of £1,421. They also pointed out that, since the 1937 arrangements worked out with the county, the cost of each pupil to the county had been only £5 5s a year—hoping that this argument would meet county opposition to the application. The governors proposed to offer at least 50 per cent of the entry to the county, the remaining places being filled by tests of which the common entrance examination would be the basis. They stated that the results of this selection would be open to the L.E.A. They also pointed out that pupils from the Northwich area were regularly attending two county grammar schools less than nine miles away. On the matter of 'tradition', the Governors wrote:

Sir John Deane's Grammar School is one of the four Ancient Grammar Schools of the County of Chester, was founded in 1557 by a deed of gift of a Northwich man ... The three others (The King's Schools of Chester and Macclesfield and Stockport [Grammar] School) are also seeking to continue as Direct Grant Schools and the long association of these ancient foundations should ... be maintained; moreover they have equal rights in the Elizabeth Dobson Exhibitions* awarded annually, and in the last six years largely to pupils of Sir John Deane's.

Reference was also made to the academic successes of the school, although the number of pupils going on to Oxford and Cambridge was called 'a recent increase'. The governors can certainly be praised for having presented their case in the best possible manner. Naturally, their application met with a mixture of support and disapproval from local public opinion, the particular point of criticism from the egalitarians inevitably centring on the charging of fees. It will be remembered that a Labour government swept the country in the general election of that year, with an overwhelming majority of 186. The nation was in a reforming, idealistic, liberalising mood, looking for a 'fairer' society emerging from the troubles of the war just ended. Clearly this was a bad time in history to be putting forward proposals which appeared to support the right and ability of some members of the community to buy social and economic privilege through a fee-paying system of education. The new Minister, Miss Ellen Wilkinson, was of all people the least likely to condone anything that smacked of social privilege. On 7 December the blow fell.[30] A letter from the Ministry rejected the application. It was of little consolation to the governors that scores of similar applications were rejected at the same time.

The governors quickly appointed a special committee[31] to consider the next move, and this met on 3 January 1946. Three courses were open, namely to apply for recognition either as an aided, or as a controlled, or as a maintained school. The last course was quickly rejected. The overriding difficulty with the first course was the old *bête noir* of finance. Aided status would mean that the governors would have to meet half the cost of outside repairs and half the cost of all improvements and enlargements. The special committee therefore recommended that the governors should apply for voluntary status, and this recommendation was accepted.[32] There followed consultations with the Ministry, some by letter, some by deputation. The matters to be settled were chiefly those related to the constitu-

---

* See note at the end of the chapter.

tion of the governing body and the control of the school endowment income. A draft instrument and articles of government were sent to the governors for their observations in October 1946. In the letter sent by the Ministry to the Director the Ministry observed, 'These are the first Instrument and Articles which have been prepared for a voluntary controlled secondary school in the County, and it is hoped when [they] . . . have been agreed, the same provisions could be adopted for the similar documents to be prepared for other such schools in the County.' Some local disquiet was created by the suggestion that, in the event of shortage of places in the school, preference should be given to pupils from the Northwich urban area. This proposal was an attempt to maintain the special relationship of the school with the 'Chapelry of Witton'. In the event the proposal was dropped. The final instrument and articles of government were sent by the Ministry on 7 June 1947, having been signed and sealed on 27 May of that year.

In retrospect it is difficult to see what other solution to the question of the school's status could have been reached. It is abundantly clear that the income from endowment funds would have proved insufficient and that, in the political climate of 1945, the matter of increased fees was dynamite. The failure to achieve direct-grant status was a bitter blow and sad disappointment to many people, and the governors fought a hard fight to prevent this failure. But voluntary controlled status brought certain advantages, not least being the independent control by the governors—subject only to the Ministry and not to the L.E.A.—of the income from school endowment. This income has been applied to further many projects in the school—projects in such activities as games and the arts which would have received insufficient financial support from the L.E.A.

The last major matter before 1950 to be recorded concerns the school property. The old school buildings and headmaster's house in Church Road were sold to Northwich Urban Council. The present Council offices occupy the site: the actual school building—the third —was, until 1969, the Church Institute of Witton parish church. Apart from the school buildings and fields on the school site, the property consisted principally of houses and shops in Chester. The farm of sixty acres at Larton in the Wirral was sold in 1920. The Chester property was in three places—two of them Foregate Street. On the north side of the street, on the site of the ancient hostelry 'The Saracen's Head' were houses and shops, as well as premises let to the Grosvenor Motor Company. On the south side of the street there were the Swan Inn, the Swan Court, which contained eleven small tenements, and sundry shops and houses. The third site was in Queen Street, off Foregate Street. The governors bought two houses there in 1911, their object being to obtain a right of way through to the Foregate Street property and into Frodsham Street.

The care of this property created one of the major problems with which the governors had to deal. The minute books and correspondence show that the task was tackled seriously, and that the governors set themselves high standards of responsibility as landlords. They had, of course, to rely heavily on agents in Chester. Even so, sub-committees from the governing body made reasonably frequent visits, and tenants and prospective tenants were invited to meetings in Northwich to discuss specific problems and proposals. The great question the governors had to decide was whether the ownership of this property was the best way of investing the endowment. It would be reasonable to say that, throughout the 1930s, the average gross annual income was in the region of £1,000; against this, however, has to be placed average annual expenses of about £250. Thus the net income was unlikely to exceed £800 per annum. Some of this income, however, came from other sources, and it would be more realistic to assess the actual net proceeds from the Chester property at only £650 per annum. The capital value of this property was estimated to be £14,313 on 31 March 1937.[33] Thus the yield did not reach 5 per cent. Clearly the governors would have been failing in their duty to the endowment had they not given careful thought to alternative methods of investment.

As already indicated, the year 1937 saw the governors in some financial difficulty. It was at that time that Mr W. Watson, the managing director of the Grosvenor Motor Company (to whom most of the Foregate Street and Queen Street property was let) approached the governors to discuss a sale. The figure he had in mind was £15,000. The governors had placed themselves at some disadvantage by having in 1935 extended the leases to the Grosvenor Motor Company on Nos. 41, 43 and 45 to 1 June 1965 for a total rent of £610. Watson was therefore in the favourable position of a sitting tenant with a long lease to run. Perhaps he also knew that the governors were in financial difficulty. However, by the terms of the agreement they had made with the County the matter had to be referred to County Hall, and county consent was withheld. This was probably a wise decision because of the low price Watson had offered. A firm of Chester valuers put the price at not less than £16,500, and added that 'they [the governors] should give the matter very careful consideration before disposing of what must eventually be a very valuable property'.[34]

The matter was reopened in 1943; but Watson, with his strong position, was content 'to sit back on his lease'. An old boy of the school, E. Mainwaring Parkes, had been appointed County Architect, and he wrote to the governors on 20 December 1943, saying that unless Watson offered a favourable price—which he should be asked to state— he could not recommend a sale. 'You will,' he wrote, 'of course appreciate that this property is a valuable asset, and one which will proportionately increase in value as the life of the present lease is reduced.'

In 1946 A. W. Chambers—the former clerk—made an offer on behalf of a client of £15,000 for the property occupied by the Grosvenor Motor Company. The governors asked Messrs Swetenham Whitehouse & Co. to make a valuation. This document makes interesting reading.[35] They suggested that the governors should consider selling at £45,000—a figure they subsequently revised to £42,000. The governors' position was, however, weakened by the fact that in January 1947 they lost their lease on the right of way into Frodsham Street, the owner having sold to Littlewood's Mail Order Stores, who were intending to develop the site. The governors would therefore be put to some expense to find an alternative access for their tenants— probably at the expense of the Queen Street houses! But it was most unlikely that Chester City Council would have allowed them to pull down a dwelling house, because of the current housing shortage. They resolved, however, to open negotiation with the Grosvenor Motor Company on the basis of a price of £42,000.[36] Swetenham Whitehouse & Co. wrote in May to say that they could find a purchaser 'without much difficulty' at £40,000; and the governors appointed a sub-committee of the Rev. A. W. Maitland Wood and the Mr W. D. Yarwood (the present Chairman of Governors) to consult with Moss & Haselhurst* with power to proceed with negotiations for a sale. In the meantime Chambers & Co. increased their offer on behalf of their client, but would not go beyond £19,000. Chambers was also acting for the Grosvenor Motor Company in trying to get a reduction in rent because of the loss of the right of way.

The summer of 1947 saw protracted negotiations, chiefly conducted through Swetenham Whitehouse & Co., who in September came up with a 'firm offer' of £35,000, which was subsequently increased to £36,000. On 23 September the governors resolved to accept this, subject to the approval of the Ministry.[37] A. W. Chambers was, however, in touch with H. M. Moss. Acting on behalf of the Grosvenor Motor Company, he asked the governors to give an option until 15 December to purchase at £42,000. This figure was reduced to £40,500, Chambers using as arguments that there was still difficulty over the right of way—an essential amenity

* Moss & Haselhurt had succeeded Chambers & Co. as the school's solicitors. The senior partner, H. M. Moss, was also a school governor.

to the conduct of their business—and that over the years the tenants had spent over £15,000 on repairs. The Grosvenor Motor Company, finding that the governors were preparing to abide by their conditional agreement with the Swetenham Whitehouse client (Mr Dudley Beck), served a writ in February 1948 on them in the Chancery Division for breach of contract over the right of way. Mr Beck stated that he was prepared to stand by his offer, even in the face of the impending lawsuit—for which he was prepared to indemnify the governors. The clerk was accordingly instructed to apply to the Ministry for permission to sell.

There followed lengthy correspondence. The legal branch of the Ministry were severely critical of the governors over some aspects of the leases granted to the Grosvenor Motor Company, and suggested a conference at the Ministry between representatives of the governors, the Grosvenor Motor Company and the Ministry.[38] The Northwich Member of Parliament, Brigadier J. G. Foster (now Sir John Foster) was invited by the governors to attend but could not be present. However, he supported the proposal to sell and promised to use what influence he had with the Ministry. The governors were represented by the Rev. A. W. Maitland Wood, W. D. Yarwood, H. M. Moss and the clerk (E. P. Thomas), together with a representative from Swetenham Whitehouse. The governors had good reason to be grateful to the Ministry for this conference. The Grosvenor Motor Company agreed to buy at £44,000, to satisfy all claims of other tenants and to discontinue the action against the governors.[39]

It would be easy to exercise hindsight and to say that either the property ought not to have been sold at that time, or that a much higher price should have been obtained. Indeed, when one looks at the site of the property today after much of it has been developed by British Home Stores, it is tempting to dream of the tremendous increase in wealth the endowment would have received had the governors waited, say, until the Grosvenor Motor Company lease had expired in 1965. Such repinings are, of course, useless. In the light of the circumstances at that time—some of them admittedly created by previous errors—the governors had no option. The Swetenham Whitehouse valuation of 1946 looked to 1965 and thought by then the value could be of the order of £65,000, but remarked any estimate as far ahead as that was purely hypothetical —and in the intervening years the governors would have spent several thousands of pounds on repairs which were already urgently necessary in 1946. On the whole, therefore, it is fair to say that the governors came out of a very difficult and protracted affair with credit.

A word must be said about Riversdale and the school grounds.

When the old school property in Church Road was sold in 1911, it was resolved that part of the proceeds should be used to acquire a house for the headmaster. The house Riversdale had been built in the nineteenth century by the Thompson family, salt manufacturers, of Marston. Thompson was a Unitarian, and constructed a separate two-storeyed building with coach house, stables and storehouses on the ground floor and a chapel (not consecrated) and vestry on the first floor. The approach was from the south, off the lane leading to Leftwich Farm, and a lodge was built a hundred yards or so from the house. All this property, including the meadow to the north of the house, was first leased by the governors and then bought by them in 1919. Weedon and Keeble never fully occupied the house, some rooms being used for teaching and, in Keeble's day, for a few boarders. In 1950 the governors decided to spend a considerable sum on modernising the house for the new headmaster; but they failed to obtain building licences of sufficient size to put their complete plans into effect.

They were more fortunate with their plans for Riversdale meadow. In the middle of this field was a large horseshoe-shaped pond which had been part of the original course of the river Weaver. This waterway was one of the main arteries of the salt trade, and various improvement schemes had been considered in the seventeenth century. In 1721 the Weaver Navigation Act was passed, giving the Weaver Navigation trustees the power to canalise the river. Thus when the course of the Weaver was straightened Riversdale Pond was created. The meadow was virtually useless for school games, apart from occasional skating in the winter. Problems of drainage caused the governors to enter into an agreement with British Waterways (the successors of the Weaver Navigation trustees after nationalisation) in 1949 by which the level of the meadow was to be raised. The work would also strengthen the banks and help to maintain navigation on the Weaver by clearing its bed. In the next few years thousands of tons of silt were pumped by dredgers on to the meadow. In due course it became clear that the development of the site for playing fields was a practicable proposition. The help of the county authority was sought, and in 1961 a scheme was agreed. The cost was borne in a proportion of two-thirds from school endowment and one-third by the county authority—who were, however, to maintain the site when the scheme was finished. Completion was achieved in 1963, and the formal opening by the late Sir Wesley Emberton, Chairman of the County Council, took place on 11 October. The site is a natural athletics bowl. The track is 440 yards, in six lanes, with an eight-lane straight of 140 yards. Inside the track is a full-size rugby pitch. Jumping areas have been developed, and a hockey pitch established at the south end. Since the Estates Governors (as they then were) had already provided in 1961 a new boathouse and dinghy shed—the latter constructed by staff and boys from materials supplied by the governors—at the north end of the meadow, the whole area assumed a major importance in the school's physical education. When Sir John Brunner moved the school to its present site in 1908–10 he gave land behind the main buildings for playing fields to the extent of nearly seven acres. In 1921 his son, Roscoe Brunner, gave a further seven acres. Part of this is the present 'diggings', levelled by boys before the second world war. Riversdale meadow has an area of twelve acres; the total playing field space is therefore now over twenty-six acres.

Epilogue

The account of Riversdale meadow takes the record beyond 1950, the year at which this history was supposed to finish. But the record would not be complete without some final comments.

First, the next twenty years saw some important developments. The county authority, in its general policy to plan for a considerable entry into grammar schools—something of the order of 30 per cent —decided to build a new girls' grammar school in Northwich. This was completed in 1957, and the first three years of girls' entry into Sir John Deane's were transferred to the new school. The remaining girls continued their education at Sir John Deane's, the last group leaving in the summer of 1962. The school now returned to the founder's original intention of a boys' school. A wider range of courses was developed, including practical and engineering subjects. A new library was also established as part of the quatercentenary celebrations in 1957.

Many people feared that the removal of the girls would weaken the arts subjects in the school. In fact the opposite happened. English, history, languages and art became very popular subjects in the sixth, whilst music developed not only as an examination subject but also as an important activity, with choirs, orchestra and brass band. Facilities have been provided for many boys to learn a wide range of musical instruments—many of the instruments being paid for out of school endowment. The Foundation Governors (the successors to the Estate Governors) also financed the development of film-making in the school—an activity which also provided the only visual record of the rebuilding of central Northwich.

A very active Parents' Association was formed in 1951. This body has made many gifts to the school, the latest and largest being the fine swimming bath opened in 1972. The total cost was some

£28,000, the greater part of which was donated by parents. The Foundation Governors provided collateral for the bank loan. The county authority made no payment towards the capital cost, but provided architect's and other professional services free of charge, and assumed the full cost of maintenance on completion.

When the school changed its status after the 1944 Act, and the new instrument and articles of government were drawn up in 1947, no arrangements were made concerning the care of the school endowment. Indeed, it was widely—and erroneously—assumed that the intention of the Ministry was to make no provision until after the decease of all the Estates Governors. Unofficial enquiries at the Ministry's legal branch revealed that no scheme had been drawn up in 1947 simply because of the heavy load of work created by the 1944 Act. The legal branch very quickly entered into discussions with the Estates Governors, and showed every wish to draw up a scheme acceptable to them. A scheme was agreed and sealed on 29 August 1967. Its provisions strike a fair balance between all interests concerned. Of its twelve members, four are co-optative, the first four being the surviving Estates Governors, viz. W. D. Yarwood, Canon A. W. Maitland Wood, Mrs A. Whalley and E. A. W. Buckley. These four hold office for life. The remaining co-optative governors will appoint a successor when a vacancy occurs. The county authority appoint four, and Northwich Urban and Rural Councils appoint two each. The governors may apply not more than half of the endowment income in providing 'special benefits' for the school; this half may be exceeded with the permission of the Secretary of State. The rest of the income may be applied, according to very wide terms, to give help to pupils or former pupils to pursue their education. In the short time during which the present scheme has existed the Foundation Governors have given generous help both to the school and to many individuals.

In coming to the end of this history one is tempted to try to read the future. The articles of government of the 1947 scheme, at the eighth paragraph, state quite clearly that 'the Local Education Authority shall determine the general educational character of the school and its place in the local educational system'. For some five years before 1972 the reorganisation of secondary education in mid-Cheshire was hotly debated, and various proposals concerning Sir John Deane's were put forward—a mixed eleven-to-eighteen comprehensive school, a mixed eleven-to-sixteen comprehensive school, a sixth-form college. It is idle to speculate on the outcome of these proposals. Some kind of change is probable—not by any means for the first time in the long history of the school. The latest official step taken by the local authority was to ask the governors on 9 February 1972 what would be their reactions to a sixth-form college at Sir John Deane's. The governors resolved that, in the absence of any preferable and viable alternative scheme, they would be in favour of such a proposal. And there the matter must rest. If the scheme comes to fruition it will enable Sir John Deane's to continue its long tradition of sound academic work with the children of mid-Cheshire.

A note on Elizabeth Dobson's charity

In 1695 Elizabeth Dobson of Birches, near Northwich, established a fund to support a schoolmaster and two pupils, all to be Anglicans and the boys sons, respectively, of a counsellor at law and a clergyman. Originally the master and boys lived in the house provided by Mrs Dobson, but during the eighteenth century the estate was let and the money handed over to the boys' parents to educate their sons in schools of their choice. In 1837 the Charity Commissioners recommended to the trustee, Lord Delamere, a stricter control of the fund for purely educational purposes.* Subsequently, in 1891, a modification of the original trust linked the fund with 'the four ancient grammar schools of Cheshire'—Stockport, Macclesfield, Chester and Witton. Three university scholarships of £50 a year were to be competed for by pupils who had spent at least three years in one of these schools. In recent years, because of the provision of grants from public funds, the trust deed has been modified and the income used in other ways for the benefit of the four schools.†

* *C.C.R.*, 31, pp. 901–3.
† *School Recs.*, file on Elizabeth Dobson's bequest.

Notes and references

Chapter I, pp. 1–8

1 King's *Vale Royal* (1656) quoted Ormerod, III, 7–10 (the itinerary is by William Webb and can be dated 1621; see Ormerod, I, xxx and III, 290); *Calendar of the Committee for Compounding, 1643–60*, Pt, 1, 685. Wills, of Bromfield, Harl. MS. 2067, f. 80; of Farmer, Ches. Co. Rec. Off.; of Crymes, *C.S.*, third series, XI, 83.

2 See W. G. Hoskins, 'English provincial towns in the early sixteenth century', *Transactions of the Royal Historical Society*, fifth series, 6; King's *Vale Royal*, section by William Smith *c.* 1585, quoted Ormerod, I, 137; *The Historical Atlas of Cheshire*, ed. D. Sylvester and G. Nulty, p. 26.

3 A. F. Calvert, *Salt in Cheshire*, pp. 730–1 and 1073; Nantwich Chantry Certificate, quoted J. Hall, *History of Nantwich*, pp. 282–3; *The Journeys of Celia Fiennes*, ed. C. Morris, pp. 177 and 224.

4 The plan (Harl. MS. 2073) is reproduced in Calvert, *op. cit.*, p. 1087, and the organisation of the town and the salt industry is described on pp. 70–1, 78–9 and 1039–67.

5 Ormerod, III, 154–5, 159 and 187–97; J. Varley, *A Middlewich Chartulary (Chet. Soc.*, new series, 105), p. 39; *Lancashire and Cheshire Cases in the Court of Star Chamber*, Pt. 1 (*L. and C. Rec. Soc.*, 71), 108; Bretchgirdle's petition, P.R.O. C 3/15 No. 13; *Camden Miscellany*, IX, 76; Thomas Venables will (1604), *Northern Genealogist*, I, 103–4.

6 Ormerod, II, 196–7 and 199–205, and III, 165–6 and 270–3.

7 Ormerod, III, 154. In 1811 the curate of Witton reported to the Bishop of Chester that it was not certain how long Witton had enjoyed parochial rights although it appeared to have been denominated a parish in 1558. However, its curates—or, rather, occasional ministers—were furnished from Great Budworth until the time when the inhabitants of the chapelry entered into a subscription towards the maintenance of a resident, and what was then termed a preaching, minister. He thought it probable that there had never been a parsonage house (*C.D. Recs.*, EDV 7/4, 244); William Webb, quoted Ormerod III, 10; *The Life of Adam Martindale, Chet. Soc.*, IV, 220.

8 Raymond Richards, *Old Cheshire Churches*, pp. 361–2; Ormerod, III, 155.

9 Barlowe's will, *London Consistory Court Wills, 1492–1547*, ed. I. Darlington, p. 33; Blagge's will, P.C.C. 15 Maynwaring; Northwich chantry certificate, P.R.O., E 301, Cert. 8, No. 13; Deane *v.* Bromfield and Newall, P.R.O. C 1/1215, No. 31; Knottesford pedigree, Ormerod, III, 137; for the Lancashire average see F. R. Raines, *History of Lancashire*

Chantries, Chet. Soc., LIX, vol. I, xiii; John Deane refers to Thomas
Bromfield as 'nuper canteriste in Capella de Wytton' in the school feoffment; *C.P.R. Elizabeth I*, III (1563–66), p. 66, and IV (1566–69), p. 49.

10 For Hardware's dispensation see D. S. Chambers, *Faculty Office Registers
1534–49*, p. 148; *L. and P.*, XIII, Pt. I, 586. The Dean and Chapter of
Christ Church renewed, or carried on, Cotton's lease and granted a forty-
year lease to follow it to Peter Shakerley and Bryan Travers. (Harl. MSS,
index, II, 484.)

Chapter II, pp. 9–26

1 Much of the information about St Bartholomew's is taken from E. A.
Webb, *The Records of St Bartholomew's Smithfield* (1921).

2 William Webb, quoted Ormerod, III, 10; W. F. Irvine, 'The Bishop of
Chester's Visitation Book, 1592', *C.A.J.*, new series, V, pp. 418–19. The
property owned by Deane's descendants—Roger (d. 1608) and John (d.
1625)—is described in their *inquisitions post mortem* (*L. and C. Rec. Soc.*,
84, pp. 172–4).

3 The Parker Certificates, Corpus Christi College, Cambridge, MS. 122,
ff. 28 and 80–1; these are discussed in E. L. C. Mullins, *The Effects of
the Marian and Elizabethan Religious Settlements upon the Clergy of
London 1553–64*, London University M.A. thesis (1948), pp. 263 and 270.

4 *L. and P.*, XVIII, Pt. I, 533.

5 H. B. Walters, *London Churches at the Reformation*, p. 20; J. G. Ridley,
Nicholas Ridley, pp. 215–17.

6 *C.P.R. Edward VI*, IV, 223; *Chapter Acts of Lincoln Cathedral, 1547–
1549*, *Lincoln Record Society*, 15, p. 69, and further information from
Mrs D. Owen. (E. A. Webb, *op. cit.*, II, 300, wrongly states that the
prebend was that of Buckingham.) Details of Carlton cum Dalby are
given in *Lincoln Diocese Documents, 1450–1544*, ed. A. Clark, *Early
English Text Society*, original series, 149, pp. 15 and 207.

7 *Chronicle of Queen Jane and of Two Years of Queen Mary*, ed. J. G.
Nichols, *Camden Society*, 48, p. 16; J. Foxe, *Acts and Monuments*, ed.
J. Pratt (fourth edition), VI, 767, giving a reference to the 1563 edition,
p. 1000.

8 The report of 1560 in the Parker Certificates said of St Bartholomew's
'non habent rectoriam'. (C.C.C. MS. 122, f. 28.) On Coulsdon see *V.C.H.
Surrey*, IV, 204–5, and O. Manning and W. Bray, *History and Antiquities
of Surrey*, II, 458. For the Crown's presentation see *C.P.R. Philip and
Mary*, IV, 124. (I owe this reference to Mr R. A. Christopher.) There is a
further mystery connected with Coulsdon, as in A. Goodman and G.
Baskerville, 'Surrey incumbents in 1562', *Surrey Archaeological Collec-
tions*, XLV, p. 111, a different name (Robert Taylour) is given for the
incumbent. Deane's will, P.C.C. 36 Chayre.

9 H. Gee, *The Elizabethan Clergy, 1558–64*, p. 104; Mullins, *op. cit.*, p.
250.

10 Mullins, *op. cit.*, p. 288.

11 The returns on Deane concerning hospitality ran 'non fovet alimentum'
and 'non alit familiam'. (C.C.C. MS. 122, ff. 28 and 81); Mullins, *op.
cit.*, p. 242; H. B. Walters, *op. cit.*, p. 6.

12 Deane's family tree has been deduced from his will, from the inquisition
on his London property (*Inquisitiones Post Mortem of the Tudor*

Period for the City of London, II, *British Record Society*, 26, pp. 33–4) and from the inquisition on his Cheshire property (P.R.O. Wards 7/9, f. 36). For the survey of Church goods see Ormerod, III, 886. (E. A. Webb, *op. cit.*, II, 300, reads the item wrongly as implying that all three chalices were in Deane's hands.)

13 *L. and P.*, XVIII, Pt. II, p. 54, No. 107 (14) and p. 120, No. 231; *Particulars for Grants, 35 Henry 8*, John Deane, P.R.O. E 318/359; E. Owen, 'The monastery of Basingwerk at the period of its dissolution', *Flintshire Historical Society*, VII.

14 Proceedings of the Court of Augmentations, P.R.O. E 321/23/90.

15 Alicia was not, as Ormerod stated (III, 157), the daughter of Deane's brother, Richard, but of Richard's son, Laurence: the Latin runs 'filia Laurentii deane filii Ricardi deane fratris predicti Johannis dean cl'. (P.R.O. Wards, 7/9 f. 36.) The inquisition on Deane's London property (held not in chief but in free burgage) found John, son of Richard Deane, his next heir. The pardon of alienation (4 May 1564) is given in *C.P.R. Elizabeth I*, III (1563–66), p. 19, No. 106, and the grant of wardship in *ibid.*, IV (1566–69), p. 40, No. 352 (undated but apparently 1567). A 'Robert Shaw' appears in the 1565 walling book; see Calvert, *op. cit.*, p. 1070.

16 J. Brownbill, *West Kirby and Hilbre: a Parochial History*, pp. 215 and 216; Venables of Kinderton held half the manor of Newton cum Larton until 1557 (P. Sulley, *The Hundred of Wirral*, p. 262); *C.P.R. Edward VI*, V, 206; *Chapter Acts of Lincoln Cathedral 1547–59*, Lincoln Record Society, 15, p. 152.

17 *C.P.R. Philip and Mary*, I, 153.

18 *C.P.R. Edward VI*, II, 16; on Richard Crymes see *C.S.*, third series, XI, 83, and J. Youings, *Devon Monastic Lands: Calendar of Particulars for Grants, 1536–58*, pp. xxii–xxiii and 79–81; on John Crymes see *Inquisitiones Post Mortem of the Tudor Period for the City of London*, I, 147. Alice, wife of Edward Sudlow, was buried in December 1566. (Witton Par. Reg.)

19 Deane's petition, P.R.O. C 1/1215, No. 31; Bromfield's will, Harl. MS. 2067, f. 80.

20 D. Jones, *The Church in Chester 1300–1540*, Chet. Soc., third series, VII, 64–5 and 117; *C.P.R. Edward VI*, V, 56 and 57.

21 Deane *v*. Grene, P.R.O. C 1/1421, Nos. 21–4; Chancery Town Depositions Philip and Mary, P.R.O. C 24/6, bundle 36, No. 11; Combermere pension list, Ormerod, III, 419. Grene was still on the pension roll of 1568; see G. Chesters, 'Beyond the cloister', Pt. 4, *Cheshire Round*, I, 8, p. 279.

22 Deane's will and the inquisitions on his property in London and Cheshire. For bequests *to* Deane, see E. A. Webb, *op. cit.*, I, 543–4.

23 The lists are given in Calvert, *op. cit.*, pp. 1068–9, 1073–4 and 1080; Alicia and George Symcock's writs are listed in P.R.O., *Thirty-ninth Report of the Deputy Keeper*, appendix, p. 254.

Chapter III, pp. 27–52

1 W. K. Jordan, *The Social Institutions of Lancashire*, Chet. Soc., third series, XI, 51; W. K. Jordan, *Philanthropy in England, 1480–1660*, pp. 347–8. On Stockport School see B. Varley, *The History of Stockport*

Grammar School, and on Macclesfield see G. E. Wilson, *History of Macclesfield School* (unpublished Leeds University M.Ed. thesis, 1952).

2 Wilson, p. 35; John Stow, *Survey of London*, ed. C. L. Kingsford, I, 74.

3 There seems to be no foundation for the statements made by W. K. Jordan, (*The Charities of London*, p. 226), that Deane founded his school in 1561, and that he had been granted letters patent for the purpose in 1558.

4 Calvert, *op. cit.*, pp. 1068 and 1071; H. A. C. Sturgess, *Register of Admissions to the Middle Temple*, I, 29; Subsidy Roll of 1 Elizabeth, P.R.O. E 179 85/57; *Visitation of Cheshire 1580, Harleian Society*, XVIII, 252–3; for Maisterson of Nantwich see Ormerod, III, 439.

5 N. Carlisle, *Endowed Grammar Schools in England and Wales*, I, 134; *School Recs.*, box E, bundle 1; Weston, *Notebook* 3; *Minute Book* (1835–1884), 2 October 1874; *School Recs.*, box J, bundle 5.

6 Wilson, p. 44.

7 A. M. Stowe, *English Grammar Schools in the Reign of Queen Elizabeth*, pp. 57–8.

8 *Ibid.*, pp. 96–7.

9 A. F. Leach, *English Schools at the Reformation*, Pt. I, p. 114.

10 A description of 'barring out' is quoted in Stowe, *op. cit.*, p. 143.

11 Quoted in Stowe, *op. cit.*, pp. 108–9, where the comparison with Witton is made.

12 E. Fripp, *Shakespeare, Man and Artist*, p. 83, thought that Deane intended the Latin catechism. After 1570 Dean Nowell's Latin catechism became the standard prescribed version and was mentioned in Bishop Chadderton's visitation articles for Chester diocese printed in 1581 (*C.A.J.*, new series, XIII, 19), but see below, Chapter VII, pp. 141, 143.

13 A. F. Leach, *op. cit.*, Pt. I, p. 105; J. H. Brown, *Elizabethan Schooldays*, pp. 70–2.

14 Erasmus's role is described at length in T. W. Baldwin, *Shakspere's Small Latine and Lesse Greeke*, I, 77–117.

15 See T. W. Baldwin, *William Shakspere's Petty School*, chapters I and II, Foster Watson, *The English Grammar Schools to 1660*, p. 32, and F. Procter and W. H. Frere, *A New History of the Book of Common Prayer* (1949), pp. 18–20 and 126–7.

16 Ormerod, III, 10; W. K. Jordan, *The Charities of London*, p. 226.

17 For Macclesfield, see Wilson, pp. 35–6; for Rivington, Middleton and Clitheroe see M. Kay, *History of Rivington School*, pp. 34–7; Stowe, *op. cit.*, pp. 86–9.

18 M. Kay, *op. cit.*, p. 39.

19 *Report* of Sir George Rose (printed 1851), p. 10.

20 The results of these investigations appeared first in 'The Minister who baptized Shakespeare', *Hibbert Journal*, 18 (1919–20), and 'John Brownsword: poet and schoolmaster at Stratford-upon Avon', *ibid.*, 19 (1920–1), and later in *Shakespeare Studies* (1930) and *Shakespeare, Man and Artist* (1938).

21 D. S. Chambers, *Faculty Office Registers, 1534–49*, p. 290; *Clergy List, 1541–2*, ed. W. F. Irvine, *L. and C. Rec. Soc.*, 33; *C. D. Recs.* Call Book (1548), EDV 2/3 f. 8v and Correction Book (1554), EDV 1/1 f. 28v; Bretchgirdle *v.* Venables, P.R.O. C 3/15, No. 13.

22 T. W. Baldwin, *Shakspere's Small Latine* . . ., I, 491; Bretchgirdle's will is reproduced in Fripp, *Shakespeare Studies*, pp. 23–9.

23 Fripp, 'John Brownsword . . .', *Hibbert Journal*, 19. A copy of Brownswerd's poems is in the British Museum: Joannis Brunsuerdi Maccles-

feldensis Gymnasiarchae *Progymnasata quaedam Poetica*. (On the back of the dedication are four Latin poems to his memory, one by Hugh Winnington. J. P. Earwaker, *East Cheshire*, II, 518.)

24 Weston, *W.G.S.*, includes Stephen Lambert in the list of masters for the years 1561–75, but his notebooks contain no evidence for the inclusion. Presumably Fripp followed Weston: he gave no reference for the statement that Lambert followed Bretchgirdle. (*Hibbert Journal*, 19, 560.)

25 For Taylor see *Early English Text Society*, original series, lxxvii; for Mather see *C.D. Recs.*, Correction Book (1563), EDV 1/3, f. 26v. and Venn.

26 Ormerod, III, 437; Rev. H. Green, 'On the emblems of Geffrey Whitney of Nantwich in the sixteenth century', *C.A.J.*, first series, 2 (1858–64), p. 353 (Venn corrects the dates to 1570–89); *Cheshire Notes and Queries*, 1900, p. 97.

27 Gastrell, *op. cit.*, I, 319; *C.D. Recs.*, Correction Book (1563), EDV 1/3 f. 26v; *C.S.*, third series, IV, 11; *York Diocesan Recs.*, R VI A 7, f. 27, and R VI A 23 (unfoliated).

28 *C.D. Recs.*, Call Book (1701), EDV 2/12; Bishop's Act Book (1760–76), EDA 1/7 f. 12v; Visitation Queries and Replies (1778), EDV 7/1, f. 115.

Chapter IV, pp. 53–86

1 W. K. Jordan, *The Social Institutions of Lancashire, 1480–1660*, Chet. Soc., third series, 11, pp. 47 and 53.

2 Calvert, *op. cit.*, pp. 1073, 1081, 1106, 1111, 1117 and 1121.

3 *Ibid.*, pp. 1049 and 1045.

4 Par. Reg.; the jurors are given in Calvert, *op. cit.*, p. 1103; Subsidy Roll of 2 Car. I, P.R.O., E 179 85/128.

5 A list of feoffees, with dates of feoffment, was produced during the Finlow case (1719–26) in the Chester Exchequer court, P.R.O. Chester 16/122, pp. 47–50; will of Richard Dayne of Shurlach, 1617, Ches. Co. Rec. Off.; *Cheshire Inquisitions Post Mortem*, I, L. and C. Rec. Soc., 84, pp. 172–4.

6 On Hugh Winnington see J. P. Earwaker, *History of Sandbach* (1890), p. 207; F. A. Inderwick, *A Calender of the Inner Temple Records*, I, (1896), 270. There was a contemporary 'Hugh Winnington of Northwich', but since by his will (1607) he left looms and work tools he seems unlikely to have been the 'gentleman' of the Accounts.

7 Will of Henry Pickmere, Ches. Co. Rec. Off.

8 Calvert, *op. cit.*, p. 1086.

9 J. Brownbill, *West Kirby and Hilbre: a Parochial History*, pp. 216–17.

10 *C.S.*, third series, XXXIV, 104. Only an imperfect copy of the 1606 survey survives; there is also a copy of one of 1646. *School Recs.*, Schedule No. 31.

11 R. V. H. Burne, *Chester Cathedral*, pp. 93 and 122.

12 *Calendar of Chester City Council Minutes, 1603–42*, ed. M. J. Groombridge, *L. and C. Rec. Soc.*, 106, pp. 79–80; J. T. Murray, *English Dramatic Companies, 1558–1642*, II, 235.

13 W. E. Tate, 'Sources for the history of English grammar schools, II', *British Journal of Educational Studies*, 2. For the Commission of 1615 concerning the Swan, the Saracen's Head and Ball's Croft see P.R.O. C 93/6/23 and for that of 1630, P.R.O. C 93/13/16. The latter is also in Harl. MS. 2176, f. 97, part of which is printed in *C.S.*, third series, V, 24.

14 These disputes and the covenant are referred to in the schedule of documents, submitted during the Finlow case. P.R.O. Chester, 16/122, p. 51.

15 F. G. James, 'Charity endowments as sources of local credit in seventeenth and eighteenth century England', *Economic History Journal*, VIII.

16 Chester Exchequer Court, *Orders and Confessions 6–14 Charles I 1634–1638*, P.R.O. Chester 14/43, ff. 222v and 251.

17 G. L. Apperson, *English Proverbs and Proverbial Phrases*; Adam Martindale, *Life, Chet. Soc.* IV, 103.

18 Burne, *op. cit.*, p. 51. For John Bowdon see Ormerod, I, 607.

19 For the master's seat at the upper end of the room see the accounts for July 1660 and *cf.* B. Redwood, 'Audlem Free School', *C.A.J.*, new series, 51, p. 47. The upper rooms are referred to in the accounts of 1626.

20 The slate on the roof is mentioned in the accounts of 1629 and 1630, and the thatching of the master's chamber in 1611 and 1613. For Saintpoole see Ormerod, III, 156.

21 T. W. Baldwin, *Shakspere's Small Latine . . .*, I, 429–31; 'Bishop Chadderton's Visitation Articles', *C.A.J.*, new series, XIII, 19.

22 Foster Watson, *The English Grammar School to 1660* (1908), pp. 389–91; Burne, *op. cit.*, p. 64; on Boston see Stowe, *op. cit.*, p. 140.

23 Wilson, pp. 98 and 313; Thomas Pierson's will, P.C.C. 103 Russell; *Divin Pierson's Life and Sermons*, Harl. MS. 7517. After the Restoration Kington School was said to have a *small* library of about a hundred books, W. A. L. Vincent, *The Grammar Schools: their Continuing Tradition, 1660–1714*, p. 83.

24 Venn; Par. Reg. The Keeper of the Records of St John's College kindly informed me that Webster's admission as sizar gives Cheshire as his county of origin. For his admission as master at Witton see *York Diocesan Records*, R VI A 7, f. 27.

25 Quoted by W. F. Irvine, 'Bishop of Chester's Visitation Book, 1592', *C.A.J.*, new series, V, 403.

26 Hugh T. Dutton, 'The adventures of an Elizabethan headmaster', King's School, Chester, *Year Book*, 1913–14; Venn; Ormerod, I, 237.

27 Only one Tilman at Oxford or Cambridge fits the date: he is Isaac, B.A. 1572, Magdalen Hall, Oxford, M.A. Sup. 1574 (Foster): Isaac Tilman was admitted master at Congleton in 1578, *York Diocesan Records*, R VI A 7, f. 27v. Starkey may well have been the master at King's School, Chester, in 1589; see Burne, *op. cit.*, p. 64. Humfrey Venables, though in orders, is not among the curates of Witton Chapel. He figured in a charge at the Visitation of 1592–3, *C.D. Recs.*, Correction Book, EDV 1/10 f. 71v.

28 *C.C.R.*, V, 578; Venn. There was a contemporary Thomas Farmer at Oxford who supplicated B.A. in 1572 and again in 1575, but was not awarded the degree; A. Clark, *Register of the University of Oxford*, II, Pt. III (*Oxford Historical Society*, XII), p. 18. For Farmer's admission at Great Budworth in 1578 see *York Diocesan Records*, R VI A 7, f. 27. Farmer's will, now missing, was transcribed for me by the former Cheshire County Archivist, Major F. J. C. Rowe.

29 *Miscellanies Lancashire and Cheshire*, I, *L. and C. Rec. Soc.*, 12, pp. 62–3; *C.D. Recs.*, Correction Book (1619–28), EDV 1/22, f. 45.

30 Harl. MS. 1994, f. 290; P.R.O. c 93/18/4.

31 Weston, *N.P.C.*, p. 25; *Northwich Guardian*, 30 July 1887.

32 Venn, III, 363, and IV, 535; J. Peile, *Biographical Register of Christ's College, Cambridge*, I, 297–8; (for Pigott's teaching at Halton see Venn,

under 'Benjamin Winnington'); J. P. Earwaker, *East Cheshire*, II, 519 n.; J. B. Oldham, *History of Shrewsbury School, 1552–1952*, pp. 52–4.

33 J. S. Purvis, *Tudor Parish Documents*, p. 132; Oldham, *op. cit.*, p. 53; W. A. Shaw, *A History of the English Church, 1640–60*, II, 407; A. G. Matthews, *Calamy Revised*, p. 389.

34 Urwick, *Nonconformity in Cheshire*, p. xi; P. Collinson, *The Elizabethan Puritan Movement*, p. 211; the wills of Margery Pigott and Richard Mather, Ches. Co. Rec. Off.; the Remonstrance, Harl. MS. 2107, ff. 217–220. *York Diocesan Records*, R VI A 22 (visitation of 1630), A 23 (visitation of 1633).

35 Accounts of William Leftwich, Harl. MS. 1999, f. 313v; transcript of the Constable's account, Weston, *Notebook* No. 8.

36 *Local Gleanings*, II (1877–8), 256; Pigott's will, National Library of Wales, Aberystwyth.

37 Venn. Simon Savage may well have been the man of that name who appears as 'presbyter' at Davenham in 1612, 1618 and 1623. (Ormerod, III, 241 and 243.)

38 Par. Reg., December 1633 and March 1636. Further information on the Berchenheads from P. W. Thomas, 'John Berkenhead in literature and politics' (D.Phil. thesis, Oxford, 1962) and *Sir John Berkenhead: a Royalist Career in Politics and Polemics* (1969), and from Mr D. A. Iredale; see also D. A. Iredale, 'A multitude of interesting anecdotes', *The Wittonian*, summer 1960.

39 *Brasenose College Register, 1509–1909, Oxford Historical Society*, LV, 174; Foster; the Jeffrey Harrison who, presumably as a feoffee, gave evidence against Swinton in 1663 seems to have been the Oxford matriculant, for their ages tally. Thomas Harrison appeared in the Subsidy Roll of 1626, P.R.O. E 179 85/128.

40 Foster; Ormerod, III, 162. In 1630 Bentley was presented by the Witton churchwardens at the Visitation of the Archbishop of York for practising 'physick' without a licence, but the Court Book reveals that the case was dismissed because he exhibited his licence at Manchester during the visitation. (*York Diocesan Records*, R VI A 22.) J. H. Raach, *A Directory of English Country Physicians, 1603–43*, omits Bentley but shows the small number of provincial doctors. The list of books purchased by Bentley is given in William Leftwich's accounts, Harl. MS. 1999, f. 280v.

41 Venn; J. Peile, *Biographical Register of Christ's College; St John's Coll. Admissions; Life* of Thomas Pierson, Harl. MS. 7517; Ormerod, I, 660. Richard Wrench is the only student of that surname at Oxford or Cambridge whose dates coincide with the grant of Farmer's money; Gastrell, I, 245; *C.C.R.* 31, p. 463. A William Norcott of Northwich appears in the Subsidy Roll of 1626, P.R.O. E 179 85/128.

42 The master was Joseph Allen, referring to Macclesfield School, of which he later became master. (Allen to John Ward, Esq., Bromley Davenport MSS., John Rylands University Library of Manchester.) Thomas Sudlow's will, Ches. Co. Rec. Off.; on the Leftwich's see E. Calvert, *Shrewsbury School Registrum Scholarium, 1562–1635*, pp. 71 and 75, and the 1580 *Visitation of Cheshire, Harleian Society*, XVIII, 142. Thomas Berchenhead's burial is recorded in the Par. Reg.; see also Guildhall MS. 6538 and information from Mr A. H. Hall. For the Chester apprenticeships see *C.S.*, third series, VIII, 7, and XXVI, 31. William Hewitt of Witton appears in the Subsidy Roll of 1626, P.R.O. E 179 85/128, and his will (1641), which mentions another son apprenticed in Chester, is in the Ches. Co. Rec. Off.

43 W. K. Jordan, *The Social Institutions of Lancashire*, pp. 32, 36 and 45. The Speaker is quoted in A. L. Rowse, *The England of Elizabeth*, p. 496.
44 P. W. Thomas, *op. cit.* (1969), *passim*; *Mercurius Aulicus*, ed., with an introduction by F. J. Varley; C. V. Wedgwood, *Seventeenth Century English Literature*, pp. 96–7.
45 *Life* of Pierson, Harl. MS. 7517; Pierson's will, P.C.C. 103 Russell.
46 Venn; *St John's Coll. Admissions*; W. F. Irvine's transcript of the 1665 Visitation, Ches. Co. Rec. Off., DFI 183, p. 22; A. G. Matthews, *Calamy Revised*, pp. 461–2; R. Schlatter, *Social Ideas of Religious Leaders, 1660–88* (1940).
47 W. Haller, *The Rise of Puritanism* (Harper Torchbook edition, 1957), p. 52.

Chapter V, pp. 87–101

1 Par. Reg., f. 105v; the account of the Civil War in relation to Northwich is based on Ormerod, III, 162, *Civil War Memorials, L. and C. Rec. Soc.*, 19, and *Cheshire Civil War Tracts, Chet. Soc.*, new series, 65.
2 *Cheshire Quarter Sessions Records, 1559–1760, L. and C. Rec. Soc.* 94, p. 141.
3 *Cal. Committee for Compounding*, 1643–60, Pt. 1, 685; Ormerod, III, 196; *Cal. Committee for Advance of Money*, 1642–56, Pt. 1, 103; P. W. Thomas, *Sir John Berkenhead*, pp. 10–12, and information from Mr D. A. Iredale.
4 *Cheshire Quarter Sessions Records*, p. 159.
5 Copy of the survey, *School Recs.*, Schedule No. 31; signed copy of the petition in the school; J. Hemingway, *History of the City of Chester* (1831), I, 178 and 197.
6 P.R.O. C 93/24/7.
7 Will of Richard Mather, Ches. Co. Rec. Off.; for Leftwich see Harl. MS. 1999, ff. 107 *et seq.*, 240 *et seq.*, 260 *et seq.* and 313 *et seq.*, and *Cal. Committee for Compounding*, Pt. 1, 685 and 687.
8 On Lowe see Ormerod, III, 181, and Par. Reg.; on Bentley, see Foster, Ormerod, III, 162, *Cheshire Visitation Pedigrees, Harleian Soc.*, XCIII, p. 8, *Chester Marriage Licences*, VI, *L. and C. Rec. Soc.*, 69, p. 191, and Martindale, *Life*, p. 100; Bentley's will, Ches. Co. Rec. Off.; for Sworton see *St John's Coll. Admissions*, Pt. 1, 142.
9 On Guest see A. G. Matthews, *Calamy Revised*, p. 238, and his will, 'of Aston by Budworth', Ches. Co. Rec. Off.; his burial is entered in Great Budworth Par. Reg., 19 February 1681. On Liptrott see Chester City Rec. Off., M/L/6/183, C. Nickson, *History of Runcorn*, p. 229, and A. G. Matthews, *op. cit.*, p. 325.
10 Foster; *Mun. Glas.*, III, 27. An entry of 1657 in *Registers of Church Minshull* (typescript at Ches. Co. Rec. Off.), describes Higginson as minister of Sutton and schoolmaster of Tarvin in 1654. *C.D. Recs.*, Call Book (1671), EDV 2/6, f. 1 v; Par. Reg., 2 July 1664; P.R.O. Chester 16/122, p. 39. A 'Samuel Higgenson, clerk' was admitted a freeman of Chester in 1668. (*Chester Freemen Rolls*, Pt. 1, *L. and C. Rec. Soc.*, 51, p. 155.) Some of these identifications are incompatible. The Church Minshull minister, who seems definitely to have been the Witton master, was twenty-nine in 1657 (*C.S.*, third series, XVIII, 52) and could not have been the Oxford matriculant, aged seventeen in 1642.

11 Foster; *Plundered Ministers' Accounts*, I, *L. and C. Rec. Soc.*, 28, p. 213, and II, *Rec. Soc.*, 34, p. 47; Venn; *St John's Coll. Admissions*, Pt. I, 116.

12 Venn; Coulton's will, Ches. Co. Rec. Off.; Audlem Free School papers, Ches. Co. Rec. Off., s 1/8–11 (I am grateful to Mr B. Redwood for drawing my attention to these); Ormerod, III, 471.

13 Foster; Venn; *St John's Coll. Admissions*, Pt. I, 142.

14 On Peter Berkenhead see Foster, I, 128, and addenda, p. iv, and P. W. Thomas, *op. cit.*, p. 8. In 1660 Sir John Berkenhead was appointed by the Archbishop of Canterbury to be Master of Faculties, a position with responsibility for dispensing Lambeth Degrees (*Ibid.*, p. 209). Thomas Knight may well have returned to the Northwich area: John Greenhalgh, a later master at Witton, left 20s in his will, of 1674, to 'Thomas Knight of Castle Northwich, clerk'.

Chapter VI, pp. 102–36

1 The decay of the common brine pit is dated in Thomas Finlow's petition of *c.* 1719 as about forty-four years earlier, P.R.O. Chester 15/119; Fishwick's report to the bishop, 10 May 1717, *C.D. Recs.*, EDA 6/4; Nash is quoted in E. Hughes, *Studies in Administration and Finance*, p. 379; Brancker's report on Macclesfield School's salt rights is quoted in J. Hall, *Nantwich*, pp. 259–62; *C.D. Recs.*, Terriers, Witton (1663); Gastrell, I, 326; 'The inhabitants of Witton etc. case', *C.D. Recs.*, EDP 305/5; J. Varley, *A Middlewich Chartulary, Chet. Soc.*, new series, 105, p. 34.

2 Hughes, *op. cit.*, pp. 389–93; *C.D. Recs.*, Terriers, Witton (1718).

3 For Bloore see Par. Reg., 11 August 1688 and 6 November 1693; for Penny see *C.D. Recs.*, Call Book (1716), EDV 2/16, f. 22v; on the Charity School, *Local Gleanings*, I, 224; for Harper see *St John's Coll. Admissions*, Pt. II, p. 140, Par. Reg. and *C.D. Recs.*, Call Book (1671), EDV 2/6, f. 1v; for his licence (1672) as 'a literate person' to be parish clerk of Davenham see *Chester Marriage Licences*, VI, *L. and C. Rec. Soc.*, 69, p. 114.

4 E. Lloyd, *Nantwich and Acton Grammar School* (1960); on Lymm see Kay, pp. 47–9; on Darnhall see *C.S.*, third series, IV, 105–7.

5 *D.N.B.*; Henrietta Brady Brown, *Some Venables of England and America* (1961); P.R.O. Chester 16/122, p. 49; *Calendar of State Papers Domestic, James II* (February–December 1685), p. 235.

6 P.R.O. Chester 16/122, p. 48; P. W. Thomas, *John Berkenhead in Literature and Politics, 1640–63*, p. 3.

7 Par. Reg.: there is some mystery here, for no Thomas Torbocke is given in the feoffments produced in the Finlow case, P.R.O. Chester 16/122. On Thomas Pigott see 'The inhabitants of Witton etc. case', *C.D. Recs.*, EDP 305/5; on Mouldsworth, P.R.O. Chester 16/122, p. 14, and on the Lowes, Ormerod, III, 181.

8 Starkey's will is in the Bishop's Register (1660–1704), *C.D. Recs.*, EDA 2/3, f. 70; the list of feoffees in 1707 is given in Terriers, Witton (1718).

9 Finlow's petition, P.R.O. Chester 15/119.

10 Lease of 1713, *School Recs.*, Schedule No. 5; *C.D. Recs.*, Terriers, Witton (1718).

11 Draft of proposed subscription, *School Recs.*, box A; lease to Thomas Urmston, 18 February 1715, *School Recs.*, Schedule No. 6; for the suggested exchange of land see *Account Book*, November 1714.

12 Gastrell, I, 327–8.

13 Wilson, pp. 68–9 and 103.

14 *C.D. Recs.*, Terriers, Witton (1718). For evidence that Cotton was a Witton pupil see P.R.O. Chester 16/122, p. 43, and for his epitaph J. P. Earwaker, *History of the Church and Parish of St Mary on the Hill* (1898), p. 54.

15 J. Hoole, *A New Discovery of the Old Art of Teaching School*, ed. E. T. Campagnac (1913), p. 266.

16 D. Ogg, *England in the Reign of Charles II* (1934), II, 430; P.R.O. E 179/86/150, f. 17. In 1665 the feoffees proved to the King's Auditor that the school lands were not subject to chief rent. (*Account Book.*)

17 *B.N.C.* Reg., p. 195. It is difficult to identify Thomas Swinton with complete certainty, as there were contemporaries of the same name in Cheshire and at Cambridge, but this identification seems the most probable. The age of the Brasenose entrant tallies with the baptism in December 1634 of the son of Thomas Swinton of Knutsford, who had two younger sons, James and Peter, baptised in 1640 and 1641. (Knutsford Par. Reg.) These names tally with those in the wills of Thomas Swinton, clerk, of Wallasey (1702) and of Peter Swinton, bookseller, of Knutsford (1698). For Swinton's marriage see *Chester Marriage Licences*, V, *L. and C. Rec. Soc.*, 65, p. 21.

18 *C.D. Recs.*, Consistory Court Book (1663–4) EDC 1/67, unfoliated; Consistory Court Miscellaneous Papers (1663) EDC/5, unnumbered.

19 *York Diocesan Recs.*, R VI C 13a, f. 17; *C.D. Recs.*, Call Books 1674) EDV 2/7, f. 1 v, and 2/8, f. 4v, and (1677) EDV 2/9, f. 4v; Chester Apprenticeship Indenture Reg., 1690–1794, Chester City Rec. Off. A/Ap/ B/2/3; E. C. Woods and P. C. Brown, *The Rise and Progress of Wallasey*, p. 78.

20 Rycroft may have been the Ellis Rycroft who was at Ormskirk School in 1673, *Hist. Soc. L. and C.*, LXXVI, 107. For Greenhalgh see Venn and *St John's Coll. Admissions*, Pt. I, 11. Varley (pp. 96–8) thought that the other Greenhalgh (of Brandlesome Hall), who had been ejected from his Cambridge fellowship, was the man recommended for Stockport School; incidentally Bradley Hayhurst, master at Stockport, 1634–44, had become vicar of Leigh in 1645. On Greenhalgh's early career see A. Gordon, *Ancient Days at Atherton*, pp. 5 *et seq.*, J. Lunn, *History of Leigh Grammar School*, pp. 9 and 18, and *Christ's College Register*, I, under James Livesey (1645).

21 *Plundered Ministers' Accounts* Pt. I, *L. and C. Rec. Soc.*, 28, pp. 194–5 and 217; *Christ's College Reg.*, I, under Thomas Venables (1650). For Greenhalgh's dismissal see Chester City Rec. Off., A/B/2/106v; the reference to his fidelity to the king is in *King's School Year Book*, 1913–14; J. Hall, *Nantwich*, p. 411; Greenhalgh's burial entry, Great Budworth Par Reg. 1 December 1674; his will (1674), Ches. Co. Rec. Off.

22 *C.D. Recs.*, Subscriptions, 1669–71, EDA 4/1, f. 7; Simon Steward's will, Ches. Co. Rec. Off.; Venn; *C.D. Recs.*, Call Books (1671) EDV 2/6, f. 1 v, and (1674) EDV 2/7, f. 5v.

23 Foster; *C.D. Recs.*, Call Books (1674) EDV 2/7, f. 5v, and (1677) EDV 2/9, f. 8; C. Wase, *Considerations concerning Free Schools in England* (1678), p. 68; Ormskirk School, *Hist. Soc. L. and C.*, LXXVI, 109; Frodsham School, *C.S.*, third series, I, 89; Adam Martindale, *Life*, p. 216; Visitation of Archbishop of York, 1684, transcript by the kindness of the late Dr J. S. Purvis.

24 P. J. Wallis, 'The Wase School collection', *Bodleian Library Record*, IV; Witton return, Bodleian Library MS. C.C.C. 390/1, f. 67r.

25 Adam Martindale, *Life*; Kay, p. 24; *Mun. Glas.*, III, 37 and 118 for Martindale and 119 for Fishwick.

26 Venn; Par. Reg. (In January 1695, at the baptism of a daughter, Deane was styled 'clericus', whereas previously he had been 'generosus'.) E. Axon informed Venn (Venn, IV, 518) that Gerard Deane was perhaps vicar of Weaverham, 1693–1702, but this seems to be a mistake.

27 *Warrington Parish Church Registers, 1591–1653, Lancs. Parish Reg. Soc.*, 70, p. 299; *Mun. Glas.*, III, 120; *C.D. Recs.*, Call Books (1674) EDV 2/7, f. 21v, (1677) EDV 2/9, f. 17, (1705) 2/13, f. 21v, and 1709 2/14, f. 22v; *Register of Farnworth Chapel*, Pt. II, *Lancs. Parish Reg. Soc.*, 97, p. 179; *C.D. Recs.*, EDP 305/11. On the identification of the pupils see my note in *C.S.*, third series, LVIII, 8–9; William Pullen's admission to Hale Chapel, May 1695. *C.D. Recs.*, Subscriptions, 1689–96, EDA 4/3, p. 30.

28 Venn; *St John's Coll. Admissions*, Pt. II, 139–40.

29 Copy of articles of agreement with Nichols, *School Recs.*, Schedule No. 32; the funeral expenses are detailed in the *Account Book*.

30 For the subscription see P.R.O. Chester 16/122 and 15/119. These doubtless refer to the draft of May 1710 in the *School Recs.*, box A. This was not unique: compare the 'very generous subscription' entered into 'for my encouragement by the nobility, Dean, Chapter and gentry' mentioned by the master of the King's School, Chester, in 1768. (*C.S.*, third series, XIII, 24.) On Allen see Venn, *Trinity Coll. Admissions*, III, 16, and D. Robson, *Some Aspects of Education in Cheshire in the Eighteenth Century*, *Chet. Soc.*, third series, 13, p. 192.

31 N. Hans (*New Trends in Education in the Eighteenth Century*, p. 221) states that Allen had a private school at Peover, but Finlow (P.R.O. Chester 15/119) said that Allen was preferred 'both to the Parochial Chapel of Lower Peover and also to the school there', which suggests an existing foundation: see also Gastrell, I, 323 and *C.C.R.* 31, pp. 436–7. Witton Churchwardens' Accounts; Wilson, appendix IVC, p. 307; *Chester Marriage Bonds*, Pt. IV, *L. and C. Rec Soc.*, 101, p. 59; Venn; *Trinity Coll Admissions*, III, especially under John Morgan, Robert Banks, John Gleave and John Tovey; Wilson, pp. 90–1.

32 Kay, p. 57.

33 *C.D. Recs.*, EDP 305/11; Par. Reg.

34 Venn.

35 *Mun. Glas.*, III, 52, 56, 220 and 255; A. Gordon, *Cheshire Classis Minutes, 1691–1745*, pp. 190–1 and 197–8; C. J. Street, 'The old nonconformity at Norton, Derbyshire', *Trans. Unitarian Hist. Soc.*, I, 49–54; Ormerod, III, 181 and 210; W. Urwick, *Nonconformity in Cheshire*, pp. 392–3.

36 *Alumni Dublinenses* (1924), ed. G. D. Burtchaell and T. U. Sadleir, p. 40; Venn; *Clergy List, 1691*, in *Chetham Miscellanies*, III, *Chet. Soc.*, new series, 73; *St John's Coll. Admissions*, Pt. II, 139–40; Ormerod, III, 181; will of John Low of Northwich (1702), Ches. Co. Rec. Off.

37 Sandwich School statutes, quoted in J. Brown, *Elizabethan Schooldays*, p. 112; the record of acting at Nantwich is in Roger Wilbraham's diary, quoted in J. Hall, *Nantwich*, p. 375. For abuses relating to barring out at Ormskirk see *Hist. Soc. L. and C.*, LXXVI, 113–14; M. Claire Cross, *The Free Grammar School of Leicester*, p. 33. On Darnhall School see *C.S.*, third series, IV, 106.

Chapter VII, pp. 137–51

1 *The Answer of Thomas Mouldsworth, Ralph Broome, John Hewitt, James Cheney, Ralph Livesey and William Barker. Chester Exchequer Pleadings* (paper), 1724–5, P.R.O. Chester 16/122, pp. 16–19 and 25–8.

2 *Ibid.*, pp. 40–1.

3 On Frodsham School see *C.S.*, third series, I, 89; John Brinsley, *Ludus Literarius* (ed. E. T. Campagnac, 1917), pp. 12–13.

4 P.R.O. Chester 16/122, pp. 41 and 59–63. There are nineteenth-century copies of most of the documents in the case in the *School Records*, box A: they are accurate, except, occasionally, for the exact date of the month.

5 P.R.O. Chester 16/122, p. 21; *C.D. Recs.*, EDP 305/11.

6 Finlow's petition, attached to the *Joint and Several Answers of Nathaniel Leftwich, Ralph Nickson and Thomas Done. Chester Exchequer Pleadings*, 1720, P.R.O. Chester 15/119; *Trinity Coll. Admissions*, III, 45.

7 Witton Churchwardens' Accounts, 1716 and 1717.

8 Finlow's petition, P.R.O. Chester 15/119; P.R.O. Chester 16/122, pp. 35–6.

9 *C.D. Recs.*, EDP 305/5; Witton curate's return (1811) EDV 7/4, No. 244; Terriers Witton (1663); Gastrell, I, 326; P.R.O. Chester 16/122, p. 37.

10 *St John's Coll. Admissions*, Pt. III, 10; P.R.O. Chester 16/122, pp. 33–4, and Chester 15/119; the Relators' Bill was recited in *Chester (Exchequer) Order Book*, 1716–23, 16 October 1721, P.R.O. Chester 14/30, pp. 130–3.

11 Thomas Finlow to Bishop Gastrell, 24 August 1719, *C.D. Recs.*, EDP 305/11; Call Book (1725) EDV 2/21, f. 25v.

12 P.R.O. Chester 14/30 and 16/122. Thomas Wright, son of Thomas, of Thornhall, Staffs., matriculated in 1712, aged nineteen; B.A. 1715. (Foster.)

13 See P.R.O. Chester 13/70 (*Decrees and Orders Original*), 9 November 1720: the case of Finlow *v.* Ralph Higginson *et al.* was mentioned, and Higginson *et al.* were ordered to stay their proceedings against Finlow until they had answered his Bill.

14 The charges and defences are taken from P.R.O. Chester 13/70 (16 October 1721), Chester 15/119 and 16/122.

15 The date of Finlow's death is given in P.R.O. Chester 13/70 (*Decrees and Orders Original*) 11 July 1723.

16 Partington to Bishop Gastrell, 12 December 1720, *C.D. Recs.*, EDP 305/11; on Spencer see Kay, p. 56, and *St John's Coll. Admissions*, Pt. III, 10–11.

17 The nomination of Bradshaw was quickly made, but in fact he was rapidly succeeded by Thomas Hughes, who himself almost at once resigned all claim to Witton in March 1722, and was succeeded by James Copland. (*C.D. Recs.*, EDP 305/1, Pt. 1.) On Cottrell see P.R.O. Chester 16/122, p. 34, and 13/20, 26 February 1724.

18 The course of the case can be traced among the decrees and orders of the Chester Exchequer Court, P.R.O. Chester 13/70, under the dates mentioned. See also Partington to Gastrell, 8 September 1722, on the nomination of Cholmondeley, a compromise candidate: Partington had wished the bishop to nominate a temporary master, while his opponents wanted Captain Warburton to arbitrate. (*C.D. Recs.*, EDP 305/11.)

Chapter VIII, pp. 152–69

1 T. S. Willan, *The Navigation of the River Weaver in the Eighteenth Century, Chet. Soc.*, third series, III; W. H. Chaloner, 'Salt in Cheshire', *Trans. Lancs, and Ches. Antiquarian Soc.*, 71, p. 69; Calvert, *op. cit.*, p. 284; D. and S. Lysons, *Magna Britannia*, II (1810), 410–11.

2 Lysons, *op. cit.*, II, 537; W. Tunnicliffe, *Topographical Survey of Cheshire* (1787), p. 65.

3 Ormerod, III, 5; Lysons, *op. cit.*, II, 332; *C.D. Recs.*, EDV 7/1 No. 117 and 7/6 No. 209; D. A. Iredale, 'The rise and fall of the Marshalls of Northwich', *Hist. Soc. of Lancs. and Ches.*, 117

4 Willan, *op. cit.*, p. 60; Church Minshull case, P.R.O. Chester 14/32, pp. 110–18; on Farmer's legacy see P.R.O. Chester 16/122, p. 43 and Gastrell, I, 329, fn. by 'Mr Speed', deputy registrar, who added that the schoolmaster was 'presented' to the bishop in 1785 in connection with the loss: no record of this has been found.

5 *C.C.R.* 31, p. 458; on John Barrow see Weston, *Notebook* No. 11, *N.P.C.*, p. 65, and J. H. Cooke, *Bibliotheca Cestriensis*, p. 39; on the Mort-Wakefields see Iredale, *op. cit.*, p. 68.

6 Ormerod, II, 203, and III, 196; Lysons, *op. cit.*, II, 537–9.

7 Gastrell, I, 327; *C.D. Recs.*, EDV 7/1 No. 117; memoranda of William Cragg, Tabley MSS; *C.D. Recs.*, Bishop's Act Book (1777–90), EDA 1/8, ff. 134–6 and 157–8; reply to Visitation queries (1811) EDV 7/4 No. 244.

8 Urwick, *Nonconformity in Cheshire*, pp. 392–8; draft return to Visitation Queries, 1778, Tabley MSS; *C.D. Recs.*, EDV 7/4 No. 244.

9 *C.D. Recs.*, EDP 305/11.

10 The names of the feoffees survive in the school records on masters' bonds, leases, and on new feoffments of 1746, 1767, 1772 and 1784; Hadfield's memorandum, Tabley MSS.

11 Rough notes of the feoffees' meeting, 12 August 1765, *School Recs.*, Schedule No. 42; Weston, *N.P.C.*, pp. 47–51; Sir Peter Leicester's lease (1766), *School Recs.*, Schedule No. 19; Sir John Fleming Leicester's lease (1790), Schedule No. 58; the feoffees received £51 19*s* 6*d* (misprinted in Weston, *N.P.C.*, p. 51), Account Book, 1805.

12 The order of 1747 was listed for the first time in a schedule of papers, for use as evidence in the Hand case, sent to the feoffees' solicitor, Hostage, in March 1834 (*School Recs.*, box A), and a copy of it is attached to T.I.B. Hostage's affidavit of 10 January 1846; Shuttleworth's bond, 5 April 1748, *School Recs.*, Schedule No. 37.

13 On the relation to the churchyard see Weston to the Charity Commissioners, 23 July 1867, P.R.O. Ed. 27/298.

14 Foster; Kay, pp. 64–5; *C.D. Recs.*, *Call Books* (1728) EDV 2/24, f. 29v, and (1733) 2/27 f. 39v; Harrison's bond, 1 September 1741, *School Recs.*, Schedule No. 33; feoffees to Bishop of Chester, 30 October 1741, *C.D. Recs.*, EDP 305/11.

15 Foster; Williamson's bond 30 October 1741, *School Recs.*, Schedule No. 34; Wilson, p. 107; Kay, p. 55: the bond at Lymm was raised to £400 in 1813, *ibid.*, p. 79 (for the bishop's dislike of such bonds as an infringement of his authority see *ibid.*, p. 53); Head, *History of Congleton*, p. 243; *C.D. Recs.*, EDA 1/6, f. 12v.

16 *Adam's Weekly Courant*, No. 775, 1 March 1748; *School Recs.*, Schedule Nos. 35, 36 and 37; Venn; *St John's Coll. Admissions*, Pt. III, 101 and 515; *C.D. Recs.*, Bishop's Act Book, EDA 1/7, f. 123B.

17 Par. Reg.; affidavit of George Leigh, 18 September 1826, *School Recs.*,

box E, bundle 2. Two schoolmasters figure in the Par. Reg. in 1773—
Thomas Richardson and James Newton (also organist): it is impossible
to say if either was an usher.

18 Eccles's bond, 20 November 1750, *School Recs.*, Schedule No. 38;
nomination of same date, etc., *C.D. Recs.*, EDP 305/11; Foster; *B.N.C.
Reg.*, p. 334; Ormerod, III, 143, gives him as curate at Lower Peover,
1748–54.

19 Venn; *Trinity Coll. Admissions*, III, 133; *School Recs.*, Schedule Nos. 39
and 40; *C.D. Recs*, EDP 305/11 and EDA 1/6, f. 12v; Witton Churchwardens' Accounts, 1745.

20 J. P. Earwaker, *History of Sandbach*, p. 78; Varley, pp. 177–8; M. Kay,
History of Rivington School, p. 91; Wilson, p. 125; W. Beamont, *An
Account of Winwick* (second edition), pp. 98–100.

21 *C.D. Recs.*, Bishop's Act Book (1760–76) EDA 1/7, f. 17; Davenham
Parish bundle, EDP 102/1 and 102/7.

22 Nomination, 12 April 1755, testimonial and certificate, *C.D. Recs.*, EDP
305/11; licensing, EDA 1/6, f. 21v; Foster; letter to Lord Fauconberg,
quoted in Wilson, pp. 282–3; *B.N.C. Reg.*, p. 344; *C.D. Recs.*, Call Books
(1760) EDV 2/36, f. 44, and (1766) 2/37, f. 30.

23 Foster; J. P. Earwaker, *East Cheshire*, II, 522–3; Macclesfield governors'
recommendation to Witton, EDP 305/11; Jones's agreement to the feoffees'
proposals, his bond and licence, *School Recs.*, Schedule Nos. 43, 44 and
45; W. E. Tate, 'The episcopal licensing of schoolmasters in England',
Church Quarterly Review, CLVII; *C.D. Recs.*, Bishop's Act Book (1760–76)
EDA 1/7, ff. 92 and 104; Robson, *op. cit.*, p. 89; for Jones at Little Leigh
see EDV 7/1, No. 116.

24 *Adam's Weekly Courant*, Nos. 1765 and 1766, 11 and 18 September 1770;
Hadfield's agreement and bond, *School Recs.*, Schedule Nos. 46 and 47;
Venn; *St John's Coll. Admissions*, Pt. IV, 1 and 286; *Manchester School
Reg.* 1 (1730–75), *Chet. Soc.*, LXIX, 100; Tabley MSS.; Hadfield's wife's
name is given on a plaque in Northwich parish church.

25 Replies to Visitation Queries, Tabley MSS. and *C.D. Recs.*, EDV 7/1, No.
117; lists of pupils, *School Recs.*, box A; copies of affidavits of Samuel
Edge of Over and John Norbury of Witton, *ibid.*, box B; *Trinity Coll.
Admissions*, III, 277, 286 and 295.

26 Copies of affidavits of R. P. Hadfield and John Barnes in the Hand case,
School Recs., Brief Depositions, box B; *Manchester School Reg.*, I, 70, 93
and 95, and II, Chet. Soc., LXXIII, 52 and 176.

27 *C.D. Recs.*, EDV 7/1, No. 117, and EDV 2/40, f. 49; plaque in Northwich
parish church; proposals to candidates, 13 April 1786, *School Recs.*,
Schedule No. 52; Minute Book (1784–1835), 13 April 1786 and 27
December 1800.

Chapter IX, pp. 170–89

1 S. J. Curtis, *History of Education in Great Britain*; N. Hans, *New Trends
in Education in the Eighteenth Century*; J. W. Adamson, *English Education, 1789–1902*; for Hull and Beverley see J. Lawson. *A Town Grammar
School through Six Centuries*; Wilson, pp. 111–12 and 138–47; Varley,
p. 186.

2 E. Hughes, *Studies in Administration and Finance*, p. 403; D. A. Iredale,
'The rise and fall of the Marshalls of Northwich', *Hist. Soc. of Lancs. and*

Ches., 117; letter from John Dawson to John Barker, 14 November 1815, *School Recs.*, box A; 1811 feoffment, *School Recs.*, Schedule No. 82.

3 J. Aikin, *A Description of the Country from Thirty to Forty Miles round Manchester* (1795), p. 427; Account Book (1785–1811); for Wettenhall, see *C.S.*, third series, XXXIV, 104; 'Minutes taken from Mr Hadfield respecting Witton School and Church', 10 March 1786, Tabley MSS.; 1785 rental, *School Recs.*, Schedule No. 49.

4 Printed 'Proposals' to candidates for the mastership, 1816, copy signed by Whitworth, *School Recs.*, box A; Ormerod, III, 157; letter to the trustees from Messrs Statham and Foster, 15 April 1818, *School Recs.*, box D; Minute Book, 17 August 1818 and 22 January 1819.

5 The feoffees' Minute Book was not kept between January 1811 and August 1816, but copies of the resolutions of 11 May and 6 August 1811 are in the *School Recs.*, box A; for the sale of stock see *C.C.R.*, 31, p. 447.

6 Johnson's reports, *School Recs.*, Schedule Nos. 57, 61 and 63; Weston, *N.P.C.*, pp. 57 and 58; Weston, *Notebook* No. 14; copies of the Vestry resolutions (11 April 1814 and 1 December 1817), *School Recs.*, box A, and of Hand's letter to the bishop, 10 October 1825, box D.

7 Foster; *Manchester School Reg.*, III, Pt. I, *Chet. Soc.*, XCIII, 104, and Pt. II, *Chet. Soc.*, XCIV, 229; documents relating to Litler's appointment, including his bond dated 10 May 1786, *School Recs.*, Schedule Nos. 52, 53 and 54; nomination to bishop, 21 July 1788, *C.D. Recs.*, EDP 305/11; 1786 rules, *School Recs.*, box E, bundle 1, and box J, bundle 10.

8 Numbers of pupils, Minute Book (1784–1835); R. Rawson, 'Memoir of Eaton Hodgkinson', *Memoirs of the Manchester Literary and Philosophical Society*, third series, II, 145; *D.N.B.*

9 Account Book (1785–1811), 8 November 1799.

10 Venn; lists of Whitworth's pupils, 17 June and 16 December 1817, *School Recs.*, box A, and 21 December 1818, box E, bundle 1; Carlisle I, 136.

11 Foster; Winstanley to Hunt and Barker, undated, but of 1812; Winstanley to Barker, 7 August 1812 and 5 October 1819, *School Recs.*, box A; minutes of feoffees' meetings of 7 August 1813 and 26 December 1815, box A; on the temporary character of masters after Litler see letter (copy) from the feoffees to James Kelsall, 21 February 1816, box A; Venn.

12 For Allen see Cash Book (1812–32), *School Recs.*, box J, bundle 9 and Peter Barker's affidavit. On the bishop's attempted intervention and the feoffees' reaction see Kelsall to John Barker, 23 February 1816, and copy of the feoffees' letter to the bishop, 25 June 1816, *School Recs.*, box A; resumed Minute Book, 31 August, 1816.

13 Deposition of Peter Barker, nephew of Thomas Barker, Brief Depositions, *School Recs.*, box B; Minute Book (1784–1835).

14 Advertisement in the *Chester Chronicle*, 1 July 1796, quoted in Robson, *op. cit.*, p. 56.

15 Lists of pupils: 1785–1817, *School Recs.*, box A; 1821–2 box E, bundle 1; *C.C.R.* 31, p. 453; affidavit of R. P. Hadfield, 1846, *School Recs.*, box B. On Rivington, see M. Kay, *op. cit.*, pp. 72 3, 84 and 109; Varley, p. 117.

16 Affidavits in the Hand case, Brief Depositions, *School Recs.*, box B; Dawson was described as a printer on his appointment (Minute Book, 19 September 1785); Carlisle, I, 136; M. Kay, *op. cit.*, p. 110; Dawson's affidavit in 1826 *School Recs.*, box E, bundle 2.

17 Affidavits of Peter Barker and John Coates, Brief Depositions, *School Recs.*, box B.

18 Winstanley to John Barker, 25 September, 5 and 29 October 1819, *School Recs.,* box A. It is interesting to note that the two Marshalls, John and Thomas (both school feoffees), took a large part in establishing an Anglican church at Hartford to combat Methodism (D. A. Iredale, *op. cit.,* p. 71.

19 Letters of application: Allen to Barker, 23 November 1822; Allen to John Marshall 23 November 1822; Hand to Barker, 21 November 1822, *School Recs.,* box A. Hand to Barker, 3, 9 and 12 December 1822, 5 and 17 February 1823, box D; Minute Book, 13 December 1822; Hand's nomination and testimonial, *C.D. Recs.,* EDP 305/11; Foster; for Hand's father see George Slater, *Chronicles of Lives and Religion in Cheshire* (1891), p. 153.

Chapter X, pp. 190–216

1 *S.I.C.* XVII (1869), p. 104.

2 Copies of affidavits of Hostage (January 1846) and James Dean (November 1836), *School Recs.,* box B; *C.D. Recs.,* EDV 7/7 No. 489 (1821) and EDA 6/58 (1815).

3 This account is based on the feoffees' Minute Book (1784–1835) and on the statements made by Hand and the feoffees, summarised in *C.C.R.* 31, pp. 448–54. Hand's bond, *School Recs.,* box E, bundle 1.

4 Minute Book (1784–1835); copy of Hand's letter to the bishop, 10 October 1825, and Hand to John Barker, 10 November 1827, *School Recs.,* box D.

5 List of Hand's pupils, *School Recs.,* box E, bundle 1; affidavit of Jane Pennington in Brief Depositions, *School Recs.,* box B; on Stockport, see Varley, p. 187; *C.C.R.* 31, pp. 448–9; on Malpas see *C.S.,* third series, XXIX, 87; affidavits of Edward Carnes, John Siddeley Saxon, George Saxon and Samuel Plant (the ushers between 1824 and 1832 were as Griesback, Nicholson, Francis and Atkinson), Brief Depositions.

6 Copy of the Vestry Meeting resolutions, 23 November 1826, *School Recs.,* box B.

7 *C.C.R.* 31, pp. 449–55; Minute Book, 1 January and 19 October 1830.

8 Copy, 'Case of Witton School with the opinion of Mr Wilbraham', 8 July 1831, *School Recs.,* box C; on Ashby de la Zouch see Levi Fox, *A Country Grammar School: a History of Ashby de la Zouch Grammar School through Four Centuries, 1567–1967;* Minute Book, 24 September, 5 November 1831 and 25 November 1833; foundation documents and statutes, printed 1831 at Northwich by F. Carnes; Thomas Jones's testimonials, etc., box E, bundle 1, and card giving previous posts, box A. The bitterness is revealed in letters of Hand to Barker, 9 June 1831, and Barker to Hand (copy), 11 June 1831 (box A) and later in the respective returns of Hand and the feoffees to the Secretary of State, November 1833.

9 *C.C.R.* 31, p. 449; printed notice of Jones's appointment, *School Recs.,* box E, bundle 1; documents in the action of trespass Jones *v.* Hand in the King's Bench (writ served August 1833), box A; Minute Book, 19 February 1835, 2 February and 25 October 1836.

10 *C.C.R.* 31, pp. 455–6. (There is some evidence that in 1832 Hand hoped to use the Charity Commission's investigations as a weapon against the feoffees: Hand to Barker, 14 March, and to trustees, 4 July 1832, *School*

Recs., box D.) For a description of Chancery procedure see W. S. Holdsworth, *A History of English Law*, IX, 340–60.

11 Brief Depositions, *School Recs.*, box B. Several of the parents had themselves been pupils and gave evidence of past usage.

12 Samuel Plant, who was at Witton from 1829 to 1833, went to Manchester School in February 1834: he was a remote descendant of John Hulse, founder of the Hulsean lectures and a former incumbent of Witton (*Manchester School Register*, III, Pt. II, 257); for his and other affidavits see *School Recs.*, box B. Of the private schools mentioned, only one, Edward Rothwell's, figured in Pigot's *Cheshire Directory* of 1828: it proved to be well established and figured in a series of directories.

13 Minute Book, 8 March and 12 November 1839; copy, letter of Barker to Vawdrey, 8 March 1839, *School Recs.*, box A; *Chester Courant*, 8, 15 and 22 October 1839.

14 *C.C.R.* 31, pp. 449–54; copy, Mutual Admissions of Evidence, *School Recs.*, box B.

15 Sir George Rose's *Report* (printed 1851), p. 14; Minute Book, 21 April 1832, 21 July 1835, 30 April and 16 October 1847; *C.C.R.* 31.

16 Minute Book, 13 June 1833, 2 February 1836, 20 May 1836, 5 March 1841, 30 August 1841 and 14 June 1843.

17 Minute Book, 8 March 1839; letters of Charles F. Barker to John Barker, 8 December 1838, copy, letter of Froggatt (London agent) to Hostage, 25 January 1839, and of Barker to Vawdrey, 11 March 1839, *School Recs.*, box A.

18 Minute Book, 30 August and 6 October 1841; *The Times* law reports, 7 December 1843 and 22 June 1844; recital of the decree in 'Brief on behalf of the defendants on further directions', 18 February 1852, *School Recs.*, box C; *Report* of Sir George Rose.

19 Minute Book, 18 March 1845, 4 December 1846, 6 March 1846; copies of the three schemes, some with marginal comments, *School Recs.*, box C.

20 Rose's *Report* was printed by F. Carnes, Northwich, 1851.

21 Minute Book, 30 September 1851: no meeting of the trustees was recorded between this one and 15 February 1853. The Attorney General's scheme is summarised in *The Times* law report, 11 February 1853. 'Suggestions of the Defendants for amending the proposed scheme of the Attorney General', *School Recs.*, box C.

22 Froggatt to Hostage, 10 February 1853, *School Recs.*, box C; *Order* of Vice-chancellor Stuart, printed 1855 by Shaw & Sons, London.

23 Minute Book, 15 February and 19 July 1853; 10 July 1855; 18 October 1856 and 3 January 1857; Froggatt to Hostage, 14 July 1854 and 4 July 1856, *School Recs.*, box C; 24 September 1857, box D.

24 Weston, *W.G.S.* (1885), p. 16.

25 Affidavits of George Saxon, James Dean, George Beckett and Frances Carnes, Brief Depositions, *School Recs.*, box B; on Leeds School see A. C. Price, *History of Leeds Grammar School*, p. 139.

26 *S.I.C.*, XVII, 417. See letter of Lee Porcher Townshend to ? Hostage, 29 February [probably 1852]: 'I have been told that Mr Hand wishes to recommence the suit in Chancery; if he succeeds in this, the school can be of no use to any of the present generation.' (*School Recs.*, box C.) Report of the Vice-chancellor's speech, *The Times* law report, 11 February 1853.

Chapter XI, pp. 217–41

1 J. M. Cohen, *The Life of Ludwig Mond*; John I. Watts, *The First Fifty Years of Brunner, Mond & Co., 1873–1923*; Ormerod (ed. T. Helsby), II, 197, 199, 204, and III, 163.
2 E. Hampden-Cook, *The Register of Mill Hill School, 1807–1926*, p. 113; J. M. Lee, *Social Leaders and Public Persons: a Study of County Government in Cheshire since 1888*, p. 60.
3 Hilda M. Rooke, 'The effect of the growth of an industrial concern (Brunner, Mond & Co.) on local politics and affairs in the Weaver valley 1873–1898', Manchester University M.A. Econ. thesis, 1965); *Northwich and Winsford Chronicle*, 22 July 1885; S. Koss, *Sir John Brunner: Radical Plutocrat*, pp. 64, 168, 172 and 202.
4 Morris, *Cheshire Directory* (1874), p. 147 of the advertisements; *S.I.C.* XVII, 105.
5 Minute Book (1835–1884), 24 April 1862, 27 March 1874 and 4 December 1882; P.R.O. Ed. 27/299 and 27/300 No. 34.
6 P.R.O. Ed. 27/303; *S.I.C.* XVII, 104; Weston *W.G.S.* (1885 and 1899 editions).
7 Obituary of Hand, *Northwich Guardian*, 13 September 1873; *S.I.C.* XVII, 4 and 122; P.R.O. Ed. 27/303.
8 Venn; Linthwaite's testimonials, *School Recs.*, box D; Weston, *W.G.S.* (1885), p. 16; F. S. Moller, *Alumni Felstedienses, 1564–1931*, p. 79; *S.I.C.* XVII, 106.
9 S.I.C. XVII, 104–5.
10 *S.I.C.* VIII, 622, note 3.
11 Weston, *Notebook*; P.R.O. Ed. 27/296; Minute Book, 29 September 1857, 29 March 1867 and 31 March 1871.
12 P.R.O. Ed. 27/298; Minute Book, 1866–71.
13 Minute Book, 6 October 1871; *School Recs.*, box I, Bundle 1; Weston, *W.G.S.* (1885), p. 12.
14 *School Recs.*, rough copy of return to Charity Commissioners, 31 October 1877.
15 Fearon's report, 1873. P.R.O. Ed. 27/300 No. 34; Minute Book, 1876–7; the trustees sold Consols to the value of over £1,000 and later borrowed £1,500 for the house, P.R.O. Ed. 27/301; Leach's report, 1892, P.R.O. Ed. 27/303.
16 Reply of the Commissioners to Witton Local Board, P.R.O. Ed. 27/300 No. 2; Minute Book 30 September 1870.
17 The whole process leading up to the new scheme occupies P.R.O. Ed. 27/300, on which the following paragraphs are based.
18 P.R.O. Ed. 27/297.
19 Minute Book, 15 June 1872; the memorial is given in P.R.O. Ed. 27/300 No. 27.
20 Weston, *W.G.S.* (1885), gives the scheme of 1874. The trustees' Anglican leanings are evident in their correspondence with the Commissioners, e.g. P.R.O. Ed. 27/300 No. 45.
21 Venn; obituary of Rounthwaite, *Northwich and Winsford Guardian*, 26 January 1884; letters of Rounthwaite to the governors, 1872, *School Recs.*, box J, bundle 9, and 4 May 1881, No. 61 in indexed Book of Letters Received, *School Recs.*, box I; copy of return to Charity Commissioners, 1877, *School Recs.*; P.R.O. Ed. 27/300 No. 29; Minute Book, 24 October 1881.

22 Minute Book, 21 June and 5 July 1872; obituary of Whitley, *Northwich Guardian*, 22 April 1903.
23 Venn; four boys from Scarborough were admitted at Witton in August 1882, *School Register*; obituary of Whitley; account of school prize-giving, *Northwich Guardian*, 30 July 1887; Webb, *op. cit.*, II, 301; on the name of the school see P.R.O. Ed. 27/303; the opening of the Brunner Library is described in the *Northwich and Winsford Guardian*, 22 July 1885.
24 Minute Book, 26 April 1883 and 30 January 1884; P.R.O. Ed. 27/303; Weston, *W.G.S.* (1899).
25 P.R.O. Ed. 27/303; *The Manchester Grammar School, 1515–1965*, ed. J. A. Graham and B. A. Phythian, pp. 57–8; on Tweedy's retirement see *School Recs.*, box I, bundle 4 (Report of Committee of Governors, 1896–7) and box G, Letter Book (1896–9), ff. 106, 135 and 276.
26 P.R.O. Ed. 27/303. Leach noted the special preparation for the public school entrance examination to which (with university entrance) Whitley, himself a public school man, devoted great attention.
27 Morris, *Directory* (1874), p. 147 of advertisements; J. Brunner, *Public Education in Cheshire* (1890), pp. 68–9; *School Recs.*, box G, Letter Book (1896–9), f. 535, letter to the Department of Science and Art, 8 September 1898; Cheshire County Council Minute Book No. 5, p. 240.
28 P.R.O. Ed. 27/303; *School Recs.*, box G, Letter Book, f. 236a, letter to the Department of Science and Art, 15 October 1897, and f. 689, to R. P. Ward, 10 March 1899.
29 Trustees to Leach, 9 December 1892, P.R.O. Ed. 27/303; Verdin Technical Schools commemorative booklet, 1897; *School Recs.*, box G, Letter Book, f. 61, letter to Northwich Urban District Council, 7 October 1896; Weston, *W.G.S.* (1899); Letter Book, ff. 535 and 649, letters to Department of Science and Art; 1904 report, P.R.O. Ed. 109/479.
30 Obituary of Whitley; P.R.O. Ed. 27/303; *School Recs.*, box G, Letter Book, ff. 241, 555, 218 and 355.
31 *School Recs.*, box I, bundle 4, report of 1897 (new furniture was bought, Letter Book, f. 268); box G, Letter Book, ff. 628 and 634; Cheshire County Council Minute Book No. 10 (1899–1900), p. 235.
32 Venn.
33 P.R.O. Ed. 109/479.
34 J. M. Lee, *op. cit.*, p. 50; S. Koss, *op. cit.*, p. 168.
35 Minute Book, 30 July 1881 and 8 April 1884; P.R.O. Ed. 27/303; School Register.
36 Minute Book, 25 October 1883; Weston, *W.G.S.* (1885 and 1899); P.R.O. Ed. 27/305 and 303.
37 P.R.O. Ed. 53/16 (Dufton's notes, *c.* 1903); Cheshire County Council Minute Book No. 5 (1893–5), p. 241, and *ibid.*, No. 7 (1896–7), pp. 81–3; Cheshire Education Committee Minute Book No. 2 (1904–5), pp. 580–1 and 788; P.R.O. Ed. 53/19.
38 Cheshire Education Committee Minute Book No. 2, pp. 581, 485 and 652.
39 P.R.O. Ed. 53/16 (Dufton's notes are undated, but from minutes on them appear to be of December 1903); John I. Watts, *op. cit.*, p. 92; *School Recs.*, box J, bundle 5.
40 P.R.O. Ed. 53/20, Lloyd (H.M.I., Cheshire) to Schuster, 7 November 1907.
41 Cheshire County Council Minute Book No. 10, p. 235; P.R.O. Ed. 109/479 and 426.
42 School Register; P.R.O. Ed. 27/303; Weston *W.G.S.* (1899); *School Recs.*,

box G, Letter Book (1896–9), ff. 535, 650, 683, 689 and 727; Cheshire County Council Minute Book No. 10, p. 235; *School Recs.*, box J, bundle 5 (Brunner's supporters were Brandrith, Deacon, Williams, Cliff and Fletcher). The meeting was held; see Cheshire Education Committee Minute Book no. 2, p. 715.

43 Minute Book of Administrative Sub-committee for Education for Northwich and District, CED 4/1/2, p. 48; P.R.O. Ed. 53/17; *School Recs.*, Report of Headmaster, November 1908.
44 P.R.O. Ed. 109/479 (1904 inspection); P.R.O. Ed. 109/426 (1914 inspection); Cheshire Education Committee Minute Book No. 2, p. 485; *ibid.*, No. 4, p. 453; obituary of Russell Wright, *Northwich Guardian*, 3 August 1907; School Register; Kelly's *Directory of Cheshire* (1906), p. 482.
45 P.R.O. Ed. 53/16 (R. P. Ward, Director of Education, Cheshire, expressed to Dufton the county's distrust of the governing bodies of most of the grammar schools, 16 December 1903); Cheshire Education Committee Minute Book No. 1, p. 368 (meeting of 15 February 1904).
46 P.R.O. Ed. 53/17; Cheshire Education Committee Minute Book No. 2, p. 715; P.R.O. Ed. 53/19 and 20.
47 Cheshire Education Committee Minute Book No. 4, pp. 301 and 453; Board of Education *Regulations for Secondary Schools* (Cd. 3592); Cheshire Education Committee Minute Book No. 5, p. 743.
48 Cheshire Education Committee Minute Book No. 6, pp. 4–5 and 401; CED 4/1/3, p. 142.
49 Obituary of Russell Wright; P.R.O. Ed. 109/426; the number of boys is given in the headmaster's report of 1910.

Chapter XII, pp. 242–68

1 *School Recs.*, box I, bundle 5.
2 Weedon's reports to governors.
3 Minute Book, 23 June 1910.
4 Letter from Alleyn's School, 12 December 1967.
5 Letter from Dean of Christ Church, 7 December 1967.
6 Minute Book, 21 November 1911.
7 Letter from Board of Education, 16 November 1928.
8 Minute Book, 8 July 1929.
9 *School Recs.*, box I, bundle 5.
10 1910 scheme, clauses 41 and 42.
11 Minute Book, 21 September 1910.
12 Minute Book, 30 November 1910, and Weedon's report.
13 1910 scheme, clause 44.
14 1910 scheme, clause 34.
15 Minute Book, 20 December 1911.
16 Minute Book, 22 November 1914.
17 Weedon's report to governors, April 1908.
18 Weedon's report to governors, 13 July 1910.
19 Minute Book, 16 July 1914.
20 Details given to writer by Dr Frank Towers, who joined the school in 1905.
21 Weedon's report to governors, 10 June 1912.
22 Weedon's report to governors, and Minute Book, September 1910.

23 *School Recs.*, box E, bundle F.
24 *School Recs.*, box E, bundle F.
25 Minute Book, p. 165.
26 Minute Book, pp. 170–2.
27 Minute Book, p. 403.
28 EPT file marked '1944'.
29 Minute Book, p. 426.
30 EPT file marked '1944'.
31 Minute Book, p. 447.
32 Minute Book, p. 409.
33 File, Financial crisis, 1937.
34 Property file, letter from Messrs Wickham and Beckett.
35 Property file.
36 Minute Book, p. 490.
37 Minute Book, p. 519.
38 Ministry letter dated 23 June 1948 (property file).
39 Minute Book, p. 540.

Appendix I

The school records to 1908

The school records are extensive, though they do not form a continuous record. Until recently they were scattered, but they have now been united, and, with the exception of the framed statutes which are still in the school, have all been deposited in the Cheshire County Record Office. There they are in process of being classified and catalogued, but the references in this book follow the previous arrangement, that is, by numbers for the scheduled documents and by boxes for the rest of the material.

Before the discovery of a mass of documents in 1968 the school records consisted primarily of an ordered, though not continuous, series of central documents going back to the sixteenth century. Many of them had been cited in lawsuits involving the school, so that various schedules listing them existed: the Finlow case schedule, *c.* 1722, is now in the Public Record Office, while that of the Chantler case, *c.* 1811, was printed in *The Cheshire Sheaf*, third series, III. Almost all the documents mentioned in these schedules survive. A valuable collection of these scheduled records was in the hands of the school's solicitors, Messrs Moss and Haselhurst: they included feoffments, leases and numerous papers relating to the appointment of masters, chiefly in the eighteenth century. These records are referred to by their schedule numbers. Other scheduled documents were in the school, and they included the statutes, Deane's letter and the petition of *c.* 1650. The first account book was not in existence at the time of the Finlow case schedule: the first surviving one, marked No. 2, runs from 1578 to 1630, and the second, marked No. 3, from 1631 to 1718. The central series then stopped until the Minute Book of 1784–1835, which is followed by that of 1835–84; after which, curiously, there is a gap until 1910. The later Account Books in the original school collection ran from 1785 to 1811 and from 1836 to 1841.

Apart from these staple official records, there was at the school a great mass of miscellaneous papers, many of which had been produced as evidence in the Hand case. They included the accounts of John Partington from 1718 to 1726, lists of pupils of the late eighteenth and early nineteenth centuries, papers connected with the Chantler case, a Register of 1876 to 1909, letters covering the whole of the nineteenth century, and above all a great quantity of material relating to the Hand case and covering the period *c.* 1822–57. (These are in boxes A–D and in box K.)

In spite of searches it was not until 1968 that a very large number of documents came to light in the office of Messrs Chambers, solicitors,

Northwich. These form a valuable, though again a discontinuous, collection, mainly of the nineteenth century. The records are of many types, including estate papers, papers relating to the appointment of masters, lists of pupils, copies of rules, Letter Books and indexed letters received of the late nineteenth century, governors' reports and resolutions, miscellaneous drafts, and more documents relating to Hand and the Chancery case. There were also Account Books of varying dates—1801–11, 1812–32, 1832–35, and 1858–79. (These are in boxes E–J.)

Appendix II
The foundation documents

The original feoffment, with its schedule, by which Deane founded the school was still in the possession of the feoffees in 1722, when it was included in a schedule of documents drawn up during the Finlow case. In 1836, however, the Charity Commissioners found that they were unknown 'within the period of living memory'. During the Hand case the Court of Chancery accepted as evidence a copy in the Harleian MSS, in the British Museum. It is strange that an official and almost contemporary copy entered in the Bishop of Chester's Register (1525–75)* was not used: it is this which is reproduced below. Although there is also a copy of the statutes in the Register, the copy which still hangs in the school has been used, since it is one of the original copies and has John Deane's signature. John Deane's letter of 1561, which was found in 1708 by John Partington at the bottom of the school chest and included in the 1722 schedule, is damaged in places, but its meaning is clear. When it was printed in 1812 (and reprinted in 1826) it was preceded by an account of its discovery by 'T.' (an error for 'J.') Partington, signed by him in June 1713, relating how 'by reason of its craziness I have pasted [it] to this parchment'.

The feoffment

Omnibus Christi fidelibus ad quos hoc presens scriptum indentatum tripartatum pervenerit Johannes Deane clericus Rector ecclesie parochialis divi Bartholomei magni iuxta Westsmithefelde London salutem in domino sempiternam. Sciatis me prefatum Johannem Deane ad honorem Dei omnipotentis et in nomine Jhesu Christi necnon pro bona et cristiana institucione puerorum infra villam de Wytton iuxta Northwyche in comitatu palatino Cestrie in virtute et bonis litteris perpetuis temporibus in futuris habenda et villam predictam inviolabiliter manntenenda dedisse concessisse et hoc presenti scripto meo confirmasse dilectis mihi in cristo Ricardo Deane de Shurlach in comitatu Cestrie yoman, Johanni Deane, Ricardo Deane et Rogero Deane, filiis predicti Ricardi Deane, Thome Masterson de Wyvyngton in comitatu predicto generoso, Willelmo Walley de Herford in comitatu predicto yoman, Roberto Wyvyngton de Northwyche in comitatu predicto generoso, Philippo Downes de eadem mercero, Georgio Sudlowe de Crosse in comitatu predicto yoman, Hugoni Cowe de eadem yoman, Edwardo

---

* *C.D. Recs.*, EDA 2/1, ff. 388–402. Continuous in the original: here paragraphed for convenience.

Sudlowe de Lostocke in comitatu predicto yoman, et Johanni Wyvyngton consanguineo et heredi Roberti Wyvyngton de Byrches totum illud messuagium et tenementum meum cum pertinentiis vocatum The Sygne off the Swanne ac unum gardinum meum scituatum et existentem in vico vocato Foregate strete in civitate Cestrie ac unum clausum terre inde in eodem vico ac omnia et singula shopas, cellar, solar, edificia, terras, tenementa et hereditamenta mea cum omnibus et singulis proficuis commoditatibus eseamentis eorundem cum suis pertinentiis in predicta civitate Cestrie modo vel nuper in tenura sive occupacione Petri Nicholas et Alicie uxoris eius vel assignatorum suorum ac etiam omnia illa tria messuagia sive tenementa mea cum pertinentiis vocata De Sarsons head in predicta civitate Cestrie ac omnia shopas, sellar, solar, edificia, gardina, terras, tenementa et hereditamenta mea cum omnibus et singulis suis juribus, membris et pertinentiis modo vel nuper in tenura sive occupacione Johannis Hankye vel assignatorum suorum scituata iacentia et existentia in predicta civitate Cestrie Que omnia et singula premissa superius expressa et specificata cum suis pertinentiis dudum spectabant et pertinebant nuper fraternitati Sancte Anne in dicta civitate Cestrie ac parcellae possessionum inde nuper fuerunt.

Sciatis insuper me prefatum Johannem Deane, clericum, pro consideracionibus et causis supra dictis dedisse concessisse et per hoc presens scriptum meum indentatum confirmasse prefatis Ricardo Deane . . . Johanni Wynyngton totum illud croftum meum terre cum pertinentiis iacens et existens super le Dye Bankes in campis dicte civitatis Cestrie nuper in tenura sive occupacione Thome Ball vel assignatorum suorum ac nuper Collegio Sancti Johannis Baptiste in dicta civitate dudum spectans et pertinens ac parcellam possessionum inde nuper existentem. Ac omnes illas duas partes unius saline vulgariter vocate a Salthowse in tres partes dividende cum omnibus et singulis suis juribus membris et pertinentiis in Northwyche predicto modo vel nuper in tenura sive occupacione Thome Bromefeld nuper canteriste in Capella de Wytton in parochia de Budworthe in comitatu predicto dudum spectantes et pertinentes ac parcellam possessionum inde nuper existentium. Ac omnia illa terras tenementa et hereditamenta mea cum pertinentiis in Acton in predicto comitatu palatino Cestrie modo vel nuper in tenura sive occupacione Johannis Venables. Ac etiam omnia illa terras tenementa et hereditamenta mea cum pertinentiis in Pever in predicto comitatu palatino Cestrie modo vel nuper in tenura sive occupacione Edwardi Richardson vel assignatorum suorum. Ac Ac etiam omnia illa terras tenementa et hereditamenta mea cum pertinentiis in Laghton Werall in dicto comitatu palatino Cestrie modo vel nuper in tenura sive occupacione Roberti Weryngton nuper monasterio de Bassyngwarke in comitatu Flynt quomodam spectans et pertinens ac parcellam possessionum inde nuper existentium. Ac omnia et omnimoda domos edificia structuras hortos pomaria gardina terras tenementa prata pascua pasturas boscos subuscos redditus reverciones servicia ac cetera commoditates emolumenta proficia et hereditamenta mea quecumque cum omnibus et singulis pertinentiis universis dictis messuagiis sive tenementis et premissis cum pertinentiis seu alicui parcellis quoquomodo spectantibus nel pertinentibus. Habendum tenendum et gaudendum omnia et singula predicto messuagia terras tenementa prata pascua pasturas ac cetera omnia et singula premissa superius expressa et specificata cum suis pertinentiis universis prefatis Ricardo Deane ... Johanni Wynyngton heredibus et assignatoris suis imperpetuum ad opus usum et intencionem in quadam sedula tripartita indentata huic presenti scripto annexata contentata specificata et declarata De capitalibus dominis feodi illius per redditus et servicia inde prius debita et de iure consueta.

Et ego vero prefatus Johannes Deane clericus et heredes mei predicta messuagia terras tenementa prata pascua pasturas ac cetera omnia et singula premissa cum pertinentiis prefatis Ricardo, Johanni, Ricardo, Rogero ... et Johanni Wynyngton, heredibus et assignatis suis, ad opus et intencionem supradictum contra me prefatum Johannem Deane et heredes meos warrantizabimus et imperpetuum defendimus per presentes.

Insuper Sciatis me prefatum Johannem Deane fecisse, ordinasse, constituisse, locoque meo posuisse, dilectos mihi in Christo Petrum Paver de Northwyche predicto et Ricardum Wylbram de Crosse yoman meos veros et legittimos Attornatos coniunctim et devisim ad intrandum pro me vice et nomine meo in predicta messuagia terras tenementa ac cetera omnia premissa cum pertinentiis et in qualibet inde parcellas. Ac plenam et pacificam possessionem statum et seisinam inde vice et nomine meo capiendum et postea ad deliberandum vice et nomine meo prefato Ricardo Deane; ... Johanni Wynyngton aut suo certo in hac parte attornato plenam et pacificam possessionem statum et seisinam de et in premissis et de et in qualibet inde parcellis secundam formam et effectum huius presentis cartis mee indentate Ratum et gratum habent et habiturum totum et quicquid dicti Attornati mei fecerint seu eorum alter fecerit in premissis seu in eorum aliquo. In cuius rei testimonium unicuique partu huius presentis scripti tripartiti indentati ego prefatus Johannes Deane sigillum meum apposui. Dat vicesimo sexto die Octobris annis regnorum Philippi et Marie dei gracia regis et regine Anglie Hispanie Francie Utriusque Cicilie Jerusalem et Hibernie Fidei Defensores Archiducum Austrie ducum Burgundie Mediolani et Brabanc Comitum Haspurgi Flaundrie et Tirolis Quarto et Quinto.

per me Johannem Deane clericum

Sigillat et Deliberat in presentia Ranulphi
Cholmondeley Recordatoris civitatis London
Rolandi Bulkeley, Hugonis Haughton et
Ricardi Shrowbrydge.

The schedule to the feoffment

The declaration off this present dede off feoffement hereunto annexed and the very full mynde and meaninge off me the sayd Sir John Deane is that the same feoffement and all estates and assurance from hensfourthe to be had or made of all the messuages, lands, tenements and hereditaments with ther appurtenances in the same dede of feoffement specyfyed and every parcell theroff shalbe to the oneley uses, purposes and intents hereafter in thys present Sedule indented, specyfyed and declared, and to none other use, purpose or intent, and that Rychard Deane and all other his cofeffees named in the same dede and ther heyres and assigneys for ever shall from the tyme off the state off the premisses delyvered accordinge to purport off the sayd dede stand and be feoffees and seased off and in all the sayd messuages, lands, tenements and hereditaments and off every part thearoff to the onlye uses, purpooses and intents hereafter in this present Sedule declared and lymytted and not otherwyse nor in any other maner. That is to witt whereas I, the sayd Sir John Deane, perceyvinge and well consyderinge howe very godly, vertuous and necessary itt is to provyde that youthe shall and maye be brought uppe in vertue, learninge and good order and obedyence, wherbye they maye the better knowe and serve God and proffitt ther countrey, have fullye determyned with mye self, by goddes furtherance, to ordeyne, take order and establyshe that a free grammer scoole shalbe by me founded and erected within the towneshipe of Wytton nere to the sayd vylledge off Northwyche within the sayd countie palatyne off Chester beinge in mye owne natyve countrey, to have contynuaunce and endure for evermore. And for that onelye intent and purpose I have made and caused to be executed the sayd dede off feoffement herunto annexed. And to thentent that my true intent and meaninge towchinge the premisses may be from tyme to tyme knowen, understanden and publyshed universcallye aswell in those parties as elles where I have annexed to everye parte off my sayd dede off feoffement indented trypartyte one sedule conteynynge and declarynge my sayd mynde, intent and purposes in manner and forme folowynge, that is to wytt:

Fyrst my mynd and intent is that mye sayd twelve feoffees and ther heyres shall stand and be seased off and in all the premisses to ther onelye use for ever upon this condicion, confydence, trust and consyderacyon, nevertheles, that they, the same feoffees, ther heyres and assygnes, shall with part off mye rents, issues and proffytts off my sayd messuages, lands and tenements with ther appurtenances kepe and meyneteyne all the necessary reparacions off the premisses in suche good and convenyent wyse as to theym or they most parte off theym shalbe thowght mete and convenient, and to do, execute and performe all suche other thinges as shalbe by me the sayd Sir John Deane in thes presents or by mye last will in wrytinge or otherwyse hereafter declared and wylled.

And my mynde and intent is that my sayd twelve feoffees, ther heyres and assignes shall yearely for evermore from and after the Feast off St Mychaell tharchangell next ensuenge the date hereoff in the dayes off the Feasts off St Mychaell tharchaungell and the Annuncyacyon off our Blessed Ladye, or within the space off twelve dayes next ensuenge any off the sayd Feasts, well and trewlye paye or cause to be payd off they revenues, issues and proffytts off the premisses to the handes off they churchwardens off the churche off Northwyche for the tyme beynge, the somme off twelve powndes off lawfull money off England by equall porcions, which somme I wyll shalbe holly bestowed by the sayd churchwardens for the tyme

beynge to and for the stypend, wages and lyvinge off one good, able and
sufficient scoolemaster teachinge grammer scoole wythin the sayd towne-
shippe off Wytton.

And my mynde and intent is that the same scoolemaster shalbe named,
examined, appointed, placed, removed and removeable from tyme to
tyme durynge the lyffe off me, the sayd Sir John Deane, by me the sayd
Sir John, or by suche other person or persons as I shall therunto assygne
and appoint by my wrytinge, sealed with my seale and subscribed with my
hande.

And my full mynde and intent is that after the decease off me the said
Sir John Deane, the said scoolemaster shalbe named, examyned, appointed,
placed, removed and removeable from tyme to tyme* by the reverend
father in God, the Bisshopp of Westchester and his successours and the
scoolemaster off the same cittie off Chester for the tyme beinge.

And mye mynd and full intent is that iff anye greater somme or proffytt
then the sayd twelve powndes may be convenyentlye obteyned or levyed
yerely off the premisses with ther appurtenances in the sayd dede indented
annexed specyfyed, that then the same shalbe employed by the discrecion
off the churchewardeins off the churche aforsaid for the tyme beynge eyther
towards the fyndinge off one ussher within the sayd scoole for ever, or ells
to some other suche good purpose as they, the same churchwardeins for the
tyme beynge, shall thinke good and necessary for the preservacion, maynetenance and contynuance off the sayd free scoole forevermore.

And to avoyd suche daungers, perylls and inconvenyences as myght
happen and chaunce if itt shall fortune all my sayd twelve feoffees to dye and
no feoffement or further assuraunce to be made over in the meane tyme
off all the premisses with the appurtenances in the sayd dede off feoffement
herunto annexed specyfyed, my full mynde and intent is, and I specyallye
requyre mye sayd feoffees in good behalff, that so sone as itt shall fortune
eyght off mye sayd twelve feoffees to dye, that then those foure feoffees, or
so many off them as shall so fortune to survyve, shall wythin the space off
fouretene dayes next ensueinge the deathe of the last off my sayd eyght
feoffees, shall make a newe feoffement in fee to certen other persons, to the
nomber off twelve, off all the premysses with ther appurtenances in the
sayd dede off feoffement herunto annexed specyfyed and shall therunto
cause to be annexed one scedull conteyninge the effect off this sedule word
for worde. And so I will that when eyght off the same twelve feoffees shall
fortune to dye, that then they foure survyvinge or soe manye off them as
shall fortune to survyve shall make a feoffement over annexinge one
scedule herunto conteynynge the effect off this scedule word for worde.

And I do ordeyne and will this order to be from tyme to tyme truely
and invyolably kept for evermore withowte fraude, deceyte, colour or
covyn. And I wyll and straytely charge in goddes behalff as well all those
which nowe be by me putt in trust for this purpose as also all those which
hereafter shall have any doinge or entermedlynge in or anywyse, concernynge
the premysses, that they do truely, upryghtly and honestly in all thinges

* Here the scribe, in beginning a new page, accidentally repeated the
preceding paragraph before continuing as given.

performe, fullfyll and accomplishe thys my good and godly purpose and intent as they wyll and shall answer before almyghtie God when he come to judge bothe the quycke and the deade. In wyttness wherof I the sayd Sir John Deane, to everye parte off thys my present scedule indented trypartyte have sett mye seale,* the syx and twentie daye off October, in the yeare off our Lord God a thowsand, fyve hundrethe, fyftye and seven, and in the fourthe and fyfte yeres of the raygnes off our soveraygne Lord and Lady Phylyp and Mary, by the grace off God Kynge and Qwene off England, Spayne, Fraunce, both Cycylls, Jerusalem and Ireland, Defendor off the Faythe, Archeduke off Austria, Duke off Burgundy, Myllayne and Braband, Comites of Haspurge, Flaunders and Tyroll.

        per me Johannem Deane, clericum.

A 'memorandum'† in Latin records that on 6 November 1557 Peter Paver and Richard Wilbram, after the reading and declaration in English of the deed and annexed schedule, took possession of the properties named. They then, in the name of John Deane, delivered possession to Robert Wevyngton of Northwich and George Sudlowe, representing all the feoffees, in the presence of Edward Golborne, Thomas Werberton, William Golborne, Thomas Wevyngton Jr (all described as 'generosi'), Homfrey Yate, John Madocke, Roger Paver, William Cleaton, Homfrey Taylor, Robert Hiccoke, William Res, John Nicholl, and Christopher Birchehall and others.

The statutes

I Sir Iohn Deane Prest one of the sonnes of Laurence Deane late of Shurlache in the parisshe of Davenham in the Countie of Chester Prebendary in Lincolne and person of great Saint Batholomewes neere Smythfeilde in London Founder of the Free Grammer Scole att Northwyche in the Countie of Chester aforesaid erected in the name of Jhesus at the feaste of Sainte Michell tharchaungell in the yere of our Lorde god a thousande fyve hundrethe fyftye and aightte Forasmoche as goddes glorye his honor and the welth publyke is advaunced and mainteyned by no meanes more then by virtuose educacion and bringinge upp of youth under suche as be lerned and vertuose scolemaisters whoose good examples maie aswell enstructe them to lyve well, as their doctrine and lerninge maie furnysshe their myndes with knowledge and connynge Have thought it good not onlye to erecte the said Free Grammer Scoole and to provide a reasonable and a competente stypende for the scoolemaister of the same (And that in the respecte of the zeale that I have to goddes glorye and for the love that I beare to my native countrey) but also for that nothinge can endure and contynewe longe in good ordre without lawes and statutes do ordeyne

---

* At the end of the copy in the Harleian MSS. there is a rough drawing of a seal, presumably Deane's: it shows a seated figure with a trident.

† *C.D. Recs.*, EDA 2/1, f. 389v.

and appoynte certeyne orders rules statutes and lawes to be observed and
kepte for ever aswell of the Feoffees as also of the scolemaister and scollers
of the said Free scole And the rather bycause that in processe of tyme suche
might happen to be rulers or teachers as eyther thrughe a singularytie or
els necligence wolde not observe such good customes ordres statutes and
lawes as their predecessors have used And as are used in the great scoles to
the great hinderance of the scollers.

The Qualities of the Scolemaister

Inprimis I do ordeyne and will that the scolemaister be lerned, sobre,
discrete, and unmaryed, suche a one hath taken degree or degrees in the
universitie of Oxforde or Cambridge ondefamed and of thage of thirtie
yeres at least, to thende that experience maie appeare in his conversacion
and lyffe, and that moore obedyence maie be used towardes hym for the
same.

The Electours or Chosers of the Scolemaister

Also because frendshipp and ignoraunce might be an occasion that often-
tymes the scollers might be frustrate of suche a scolemaister as is aforesaid,
I will that the Feoffees and certeyn honeste men of the Parisshe of Wytton
aforesaid shall presente suche one as theye procure and electe before his
admission into the scoole to the Bisshopp of Chester and to the scoolemaister their, for the tyme beinge to be examyned of them and to be
founde and thought mete for that vocacion as well for discression as for
lerynynge And so beynge by them founde, then to be admytted and placed
in the scoole.

The Ordre of thadmission of the Scholemaister

Also I will that the scolemaister of Chester with the Feoffees and thother
honest men of the Parisshe of Wytton as aforesaid shall admytte hym,
shall bringe hym to the scole, And then and their shall reade theis Ordres
rules and statutes to hym, lettinge hym understaunde his chardge and what
is required at his handes And shall shewe hym the commodyties of the
scoole and his lodginges their And the lands and houses apperteynynge to
the scoole, wheare they lye, And in whoose handes and occupacion they
are And what interest and yeres the tenantes and occupyers have in them
And for their paynes in this doinge, they shall receyve fortie shillinges
emongest theym at the placinge of everye scoolemaister in such lawfull
sorte as is aforesaide at the handes of the churchewardens.

The Removing of the Scholemaister and the causes whie

Also even as the continuaunce of a scholemaister that dooth his duetie
tendereth the profyte of his scholers and maketh them prouspere aswell
in maners as in lernynge is profytable and commendable and nothinge
more is, Soo lykewyse is it the greatest hinderaunce and discommoditie to
the scholers to have a scholemaister that is necligent in his office or dooth
not profyte the scholers dissolute in maners a drunkerde a horemaister or
intangeled with other occupacions repugnaunt to his vocacion A dyser or

a common gamster I will therfor that if enny such chaunce their to be placed, That thoose which have or shalhave auctoritie to place and admitte hym shall lykewyse after examynacion and due prooffe theirof made have auctoritie to remove hym.

The warnyng that shalbe geven to the Scholemaister
and that he shall geve also

Also I will that the Feoffees and thothers as aforesaid beinge disposed to remove the scholemaister uppon iuste occasion as aforesaid shall gyve to hym warnynge half a yere to provide for hym selfe And likewise if hee be disposed to departe hee shall gyve to theym openlye in the church on the sondaie or summe festyval daie warnynge theirof half a yere before his departure, If a shorter tyme willnot serve booth the partyes more conveny-ently, And if hee neclect to gyve the said warnyng I will that their shalbe stayed in the handes of the Feoffees that have at that tyme the collecyon of the rentes of his wageis fourtye shillings which I will shalbe gyven to fortye poore people of the said Parisshe of Wytton.

The absence of the Scholemaister

Also because nothinge that is perpetuall is plesaunt I will that the schoole-maister shalhave liberty once in everye yere thirtie daies togethere to be absent to recreate hym selfe requiringe licence therfore at thandes off the Feoffees Soo it be for reasonable occasions and urgent busynes Hee alwaies providinge that his schollers loose no tyme in his absence but that they be occupyed and exercysed at their bookes till his returne at his chardges, Uppon which consideracions the said Feoffees shall graunt hym licence as is aforesaid.

What Aucthours are to be redde in the Schoole

As touching In this scoole what shalbe taught of the maister and lerned of scollers, It passeith my wytte to devyse and determyne in perticuler, But in generall to speeke, and sumwhat to saie my mynde I will they were taught allwaies the good lytterature both laten and greeke, And good Auc-thours such as have the veraie Roman eloquence Joyned with wysdome specyally christyane Aucthours that wrote their wysdome with cleane and chaste laten eyther in verse or in prose, For myne entente is by Foundinge of this schoole specyallye to encrease knowledge and worshipp of god and our Lorde Jhesu christe And good christian lyffe and maners in the children And for that entent I will the children lerne the Chatechisme And then the accidence and grammer set out by kinge Henrye theight or some other if enny can be better to the purpose to Induce children more spedelye to laten speche And then Institutum christiani hominis that lerned Erasmus made And then Copia of the same Erasmus Colloquia Erasmi Ovidius methamorphoseis Terence Mantuan Tullye Horace Saluste Virgill and such other as shalbe thought moost convenyent to the purpose unto true laten speche All barbary all corrupcion and fylthynes and such abusion which the blinde worlde brought in I utterlye abanysshe and exclude out of this schoole and chardge the maister that hee teache alwaie that is beste and reade to them suche authours as have with wysdom joyned the pure chaste eloquence.

The admission of the Schollers

Also I will that the schoolemaister admytte no scholler into the schoole under the age of syxe yeres And that the schoolemaister reade the statutes orders rules and lawes belonginge to the schollers at thadmission of everye scholler, which their freindes presentinge theym and hearinge, shall undertake and promise to see perfourmed by the children by them presented, which doon, the scholemaister shall admytte hym and wryte his name in a rolle of parchement. And for thadmission and entringe of eny scholler in the rolle to receyve and take iiij d. onste for ever, of everye of theym, And if their parentes or freindes will not paye the same willingly I will then their children to be refused and unreceyved till such tyme that it be payeed.

The schoolemaisters stypend or wageis and vayles*

Also I will that the shoolemaister [*sic*] shalhave yerely twelve poundes standing, besides his vayles And that hee shall receyve and have it quarter-lye by iii li. a quarter at thandes of the Feoffees and churchwardeyns of Wytton for the tyme beinge, which vayles is iiij d. each at thadmission of every scholler And on the firste Thursdaie after the begynnyng of schoole after Christmas of every scholler a penny commonlye caulled a cock pennye.

The correccion and causes of expulcion of the schollers

Also I will that all the scollers of what estate condicion or degree so ever they be shall submytte them selves to due correccion of the scholemaister, which at their entraunce shalbe promysed as well by their freindes as by themselves, which correccion shalbe alwaies referred to the discression of the schoolemaister And not to the opynyon and mynd of the schollers And for disobedyence and resestence theirof, they shalbe expelled the schoole for ever onlesse their freinds be ernest sutours to the schoolemaister and can prevail with hym And yet in such sorte that their humble obedyence at their returne shall recompence their fourmer stubbornes But ... inge the great inconvenyence and enormytie that dooth aryse by wylfull persons and ignoraunt, whoo can suffer their children, through dissolutenesse and over moche libertie, shuld commytte offenses worthye greatt punisshement to their shame and undoinge, then to have theym corrected by the dis-cression of the scholemaister according to the qualytie quantitie and gravitie of their offences And uppon complaynt of the children, their parentes doo seeme to moleste and disquyet the scholemaister against reason and ordre, I will that all such mens children after due proffe of such follye and fondnesse of the parentes herein shalbe utterlye expelled from the scole for ever, unless they shalbe hable to prove that the correccion doon was unreasonable And that to be provedd before and to the Feoffees of the schole and overseers for the tyme beinge.

* An occasional emolument or fee in addition to a salary.

The preferment of the founders kynred and schollers

Also I will that my kynsfolke whearsoever they dwell comyng to this schoole shalbe freely taught And that if their be enny of theym hable and meete to teach or comparable to those which may be gottin when the place is voide, that theye shalbe preferred And for lack of theym I will that such as have been born in the parisshe or brought upp in this schoole, and after hable and meete for this funcion shalhave the preferment thereof before others.

Olde orders and customes to be observed

Also to thende that the schollers have not an evell opynyon of the schoole-maister nor the schoolemaister shulde not myslyke the schollers doinge for requiringe of customes and ordres I will that uppon thursedaies and satur-daies in thafternoones and uppon hollydaies they refresshe themselves And that a weeke before Christynmas and Easter accordinge to the olde custome they barre and keepe forth of the schoole, the schoolemaister in suche sorte as others scollers doo in great schooles And that as well in the vacacions as the daies aforesayed, they use their bowes and arrowes onlye, And eschewe all bowling cardinge dysinge quytinge and all other unlaufull gammes, uppon payne of extreame punysshement to be doon by the schoolemaister And that every scholler have and use in the churche his prymer wherin is conteynyd the vii psalmes the psalmes of the passion and suche like.

For prayer and observinge of tyme

Also I will that the schollers come to the schole by vii of the clock in the mornynge, And goo to dyner at xi And after dyner returne at one of the clock And departe home at v of the clock And that theye thrise a daie serve god within the schoole, Rendring hym thanks for his goodnes doon to theym, Craving his specyall grace that they maie profyte in vertuose lernynge to his honor and glorye, Prayinge for the soull of their founder by name, And for the soules of his father and mother, and all Christian soules, And onste every week, that is to saie on the Frydaye to saie the seven penytencyall psalmes, with the latenye suffrags and collects. And every second Frydaie the psalmes of the passion, with the psalmes of [mercy]* and de profundis, with a collet [*sic*] at thende theirof, And onste a yere (that is to saie) uppon Jhesus daie in thafternone (In whoose name this schoole is erected) in the parisshe church aforesaied to saie the dirige and commendacions.

Whan theis Estatutes shalbe redde

Also I will that theis estatutes be redde in the churche at every feaste before the breaking upp of the schoole to all the schollers to thintent the schollers maie the better theirby remembre their duetie, in the tyme of their absence And that the schoolemaister do gyve them an exortacon in the schoole before they break upp schoole howe they shall ordre them selves, till their returne, At which tyme I will that foure of the Feoffees

* A blank in the school copy but 'mercy' in the Bishop's Register.

and the churchewardeyns be present To thintent they maie gyve warninge
to suche schollers as they shall see to offend against the said exortacion
or against enny of theis estatutes.

The electyon of the Feoffees

Also because all men be mortall And that throughe the lack of the numbre
of them, Feoffees beinge deade, there might happen sume disordre not
onlye in the schoole but also the landes and tenementes hereunto gyven by
the founder aforesaid might fall to sume ruyne and decaie or the schoolehouse wante suche furnyture as appertayneth Therfore I will that as often
as iiij of the Feoffees bee deade, the reste of the Feoffees survivinge within
one quarter of a year shall assemble them selves at the schoolehouse aforesaid And shall not onlye then and their elect and choose iiij others of the
Founders next kynsfolke to be Feoffees in the steade and place of the other
iiij Feoffees before deade if there be then so manye of his kynnesfolkes
alyve, And if not then to choose foure of the mooste honeste sage and
discretest persons beynge inhabytants of the parisshe of Wytton aforesaid
And specyallye such as wilhave a vigilant Iye and beare a good zeale to the
mayntenance and contynuaunce of this Free Grammer schoole, but shall
then and their allso enfeffe the foure so by them chosen in all the landes
and tenementes gyven to the schoole aforesaid, to thuse lymyted
by the founder In such sorte as they them selves be enfeoffed by the feoffement of the founder And this ordre and eleccion to be contynuied for ever.

Who shall receyve the rents yerely and paie the wages and chardge

Also I will that ij of the Feoffees onely shall receyve and paye all maner
of rentes wages and chardges concernyng the premysses And theirof shall
yelde accoumpt every yere uppon Jhesus even to the rest of the Feoffees
and to the churchewardeyns of Wytton aforesaid for the tyme beinge and
those ij to receave and paie the said rents and charges for ij yeares and
then to be removed from the busynes therof and other two of the feoffees
to be chosen in their stedes by the eleccion of the rest of the feoffees and
of the said churchewardens for the tyme being.

A specyall remembraunce

And be it remembryd and knowen to all the inhabitaunts of the parisshe
of Wytton that I the said Sir John Deane by my last wyll and testament
remeanyng in writing have geven to the poore householders in the same
parisshe fyve marks to be paid within one quarter of a yeare next after my
deceasse.

Also I have geven and provyded in my said last wyll that of thissues and
profitts of my wychehouses in Northwiche and of other my landes in
Shorlache and Budworth there shalbe yearely for ever geven disterbute and
bestowed amongest the poore scolers and poore folks of this my Frescole
and parisshe of Wytton tenne shillings in the viggil or even of the birthe
of our lord God, the one half therof amongest the said poore scolers and the
other half therof amongest the said poor folks. And thus I byd you all fare
well and desire you all to pray for me   By me Sir John Deane parson
of great [St Bartholomew's] in London.

John Deane's letter

After my hertie commendacions whereas I am crediblie enformed by th[e] [re]porte of Mr John Maisterson and Phillipp Downes your neyboures and parisshioners that their is contencion emongest you about the nominatinge and chosinge of a scolemaister in your towne, I have thought good as one to whome me thinke, the thinge beinge by [me] founded apperteyneth to require and will you that in your con[tencion] you have summe regard to my meanynge in the Foundacion. And therwithall to dispose the same uppon summe v[ertu]ose lerned and hable man for that purpose, leavinge your affecions [assi]de. And bynde your eleccion simplie uppon the statutes of the same scole which were not devised without the godlye and discrete advise of the learned. And the same statutes hanginge in the scole were openlye redde in your churche at my last beinge their, theffecte whereof in this parte is that he shalbe chosen and admytted by the Bysshop of Chester for the tyme beinge, or els by the scole maister of the Free scole in the citie of Chester foresaid, which ordre methinks you shuld not breake. The premisses well wayed and consideredd I praie you send me upp the statuts hither to London, to thintent I maye set my hande to them in confyrmacion. And in the meanetyme those that you have to hange theym upp in the scol[e]. Further you shall understand my meanyng and will is that [two] Feoffees [shall be] chosen to receyve the rentes of the l[ands] and shall [give account] yerelye for the same to the other fe[offee]s and to the [church-warden]s of Wytton for the tyme beinge. And that those twoo [bailiff Fe]offees, together with the church[wardens] foresaied [shall from ty]me to tyme yerely surveye the [repa]racion[s] [n]ecessary [to be done] And make declaracion theirof to the reste of the Feoffees. [And be]sides theis myn entent and meanyng is that this my l[etter shall be red]de in the churche to thende your hoole parisshe maie kn[owe my intent] in the same. And thus I bydd you hertilye Farewell [   ] the xxxth daie of August 1561 from

Your loving Freind Sir John Deane parson of Great Seynt Bartylmewes

Appendix III

The masters

?John Bretchgirdle	M.A. Oxford	–?1560
?Richard Mather	B.A. Cambridge	In 1563
—	—	—
Henry Webster	B.A. Cambridge	1578–1584 (died)
John Albright	B.A. Cambridge	1584
——Dicson (?Robert)	?M.A. Oxford	1584–1585
——Tilman (?Isaac)	?M.A. Oxford	hired but not paid
Thomas Farmer	B.A. Cambridge	1586–1625 (died)
Richard Pigott	M.A. Cambridge	1625–1643
Randle Guest	No degree known	*c.* 1646 for about two years
William Liptrott	No degree known	probably *c.* 1648
Samuel Higginson	?M.A. Glasgow	*c.* 1648–*c.* 1651
John Holme or Hulme	Probably matric. Oxford	*c.* 1652–1656
Thomas Coulton or Colton	B.A. Cambridge	1656–1659
Thomas Swinton	?admitted Brasenose College, Oxford	1659–1663 (ejected)
John Greenhalgh	B.A. Cambridge	1663–1669
James Steward	B.A. Cambridge M.A., 1672	1669–1673
Peter Woodnoth	B.A. Oxford	1673–1679
Thomas Martindale	M.A. Glasgow	1679–1680 (died)
John Fishwick	Glasgow ?M.A.	1680 (for one quarter)
Gerard Deane	B.A. Cambridge	1681–1693
Aaron Nichols	Glasgow ?M.A.	1693–1710 (died)
Joseph Allen	B.A. Cambridge	1710–1715
Thomas Finlow	Admitted Trinity College, Cambridge	1715–1720 (died)
Samuel Harrison	B.A. Oxford	1727–1741
Samuel Williamson	M.A. Oxford	1741– before March 1748 (or possibly March 1747)
Barton Shuttleworth	B.A. Cambridge	1748–?
John Eccles	M.A. Oxford	1750– by 1754

John Tench	B.A. Cambridge	1754– before April 1755
Henry Mayer	B.A. Oxford	1755–1767
Thomas Jones	B.A. Oxford	1767– before November 1770
William Hadfield	Matric. St John's College, Cambridge	1770–1786 (died)
Robert Litler	Matric. Brasenose College, Oxford	1786–1812
John (?) Robinson Winstanley	Matric. St Alban Hall, Oxford	1812–1813
Frederic Gwynne	B.A. Cambridge M.A. 1815	1814–1815
Edward Allen	No degree	part of 1816
William Whitworth	No degree	1816–1819
Charles Hand	B.A. Oxford	1823–1853
Henry Linthwaite	M.A. Cambridge	1857–1872
John Rounthwaite	M.A. Cambridge	1872–1882
Arthur Whitley	M.A. Cambridge	1882–1903 (died)
Herbert Russell Wright	M.A. Cambridge	1903–1907 (died)
Frank Charles Weedon	B.Sc. Oxford	1908–1929
Cyril Francis Allan Keeble	M.A. Cambridge	1929–1950
Louis Albert Hopkins	M.A. Cambridge	1950–1973

Appendix IV

The site of the original school

The identification of this site has proved very difficult, and even now it cannot be established beyond all doubt. The uncertainty about it is shown in the statements of the usually accurate and well informed Weston. He changed his mind on the subject between 1885,* when he placed it on 'the easterly side of the churchyard', that is, presumably, on the same site as the second school, and 1908 when, in his book on the church, he referred to the 'sites' of the school and placed the first building outside the churchyard on the south side and at the western end of a plot later incorporated into the churchyard. The school feoffees, in the course of their conflict with Hand in Chancery, had maintained that the second school was not built on the site of the old school, which adjoined the churchyard, but in the churchyard.

There are various reasons for the uncertainty about the site of the original school. First, there is no reference to the site or the original building in Deane's foundation documents. Second, there are no title deeds nor any record of payment of rent for the first school building between the sixteenth and the eighteenth centuries, but this applies equally to the second school. Third, the relative positions of the school and the master's 'chamber' (later his house), for which rent was paid to Venables of Kinderton, are not clear, and this is further confused by ambiguity of terminology. In the accounts the school is sometimes called the 'school house', but normally it seems to have been distinguished from the 'school house' which was the master's house:† hearth money payments, for instance, were made for the school, which had one chimney, and for the school house, where the master lived, which had two.

Two points seem to emerge clearly from contemporary records. First, the master's chamber was succeeded by a new house (the rent payments going on continuously to the same landlord), and this was sometimes called in the early eighteenth-century accounts the Church House: the Church House stood on a plot lying south of the churchyard and outside it, which was called in 1766 the 'school house croft'. In 1718, after listing the school lands,‡ John Partington noted the 'dwelling house', rented from the Baron of Kinderton's heirs, 'which has been the usuall habitacion of such masters

---

* *W.G.S.* (1885).
† The *O.E.D.* gives both meanings for 'school house'.
‡ *C.D. Recs.*, Terriers, Witton (1718).

as have been housekeepers, with a garden and a little croft of ground adjoyning'. (When the master did not occupy it himself he let it for 10*s* a year: if he let it to the curate, who had no parsonage house, this could explain the term 'Church house'.) The master's house, according to Partington, was 'near the school'—the first building. Secondly, by 1766, when Sir Peter Leicester had reasserted his rights over the 'school house croft', there was apparently no house on the plot, which was subsequently, in two stages, incorporated into the churchyard. The part of this plot which was leased to the feoffees in 1766 was described as being 'near to the said school'—in this case the second school.

Where, then, was the first school? There are two main pieces of evidence. The first is a map of the manor of Witton made in 1721 but surviving only in an attested copy of 1829, now in the Brunner Library, Northwich. The second is a set of depositions taken in 1826, probably in connection with the vestry resolution about the school, which are among the school records.

The map of 1721 (in its 1829 copy) shows a long plot running along the south side of the churchyard: part of it is named 'yord', and at the west end is a building.* This appears to correspond with the holding given as 'Church House' in the contents list, and to be what was later called the 'school house croft'.† On the east side of the churchyard, on what appears to be the site of the second school, a building is marked which corresponds with a building marked on an 1828 survey map and on the tithe map of 1846. If this is not the first school, what is it? If it was not the school, and was demolished to make way for the second school, there would surely be some reference to this. The order of 1747 states that the first school was 'taken down in order to be rebuilt', which may suggest the same site. A small piece of evidence may also support the theory of an identical site. In his will of 1624 Thomas Farmer asked to be buried on the bank before the school door. Weston (*N.P.C.*, p. 25) records that during Hand's mastership thieves tried to remove the brass plate on Farmer's tombstone, 'which lay under the school window'. Absence of evidence may also support this theory: there appears to be no change in the school records (though they are not continuous) which might suggest a change of site or title, and there is no reference to the matter in the churchwardens' accounts or the vestry minutes, although the digging out of the new school's foundations was said later to have involved disturbing graves.

Apparently decisive evidence in favour of a different site for the second school is contained in depositions taken in 1826 by the Rev. G. Okell from four old men.‡ The Rev. George Leigh, the son of a writing master at the school, and then in his eighty-second year, claimed to remember the dwelling house and school room 'erected by Dean' at the west end of a small croft adjoining the chapel yard. John Dawson, writing master from

---

* See plate IV. The 'yord', later the 'school house croft', is to be distinguished from the 'school croft' shown on the map: the origin of the latter name is not clear.

† In 1668 the feoffees had bought seventy sycamore plants to set round the schoolmaster's croft or *yard*. (Account Book.)

‡ *School Recs.*, box E, bundle 2.

1785 to 1795, particularly remembered the site of the former school at the west end of a close running along the whole length of the south side of the chapel yard, from the remains of the foundation stones visible at the time of his appointment. John Walton of Leftwich, wool comber, born in Witton in 1744, had similar memories and, like Dawson, hearsay evidence of the removal of corpses during the laying of the foundations of the new school. (This would, perhaps, not be incompatible with digging out new foundations on the same site.) The most specific was Thomas Baguley of Shurlach, who deposed that 'he well remembers' 'the ancient school house' 'a timber built edifice' on the west side of the plot, with the principal entrance from the lane on the east side. The plot where the old school house lay was, he said, made into a garden and eventually incorporated into the churchyard. Only two of these witnesses claimed to remember the actual school building and only one mentioned the house as well: the others had seen foundation stones and relied on hearsay evidence. All were dealing with a period eighty years earlier. Were they remembering the original school pulled down in 1744 or the master's 'school house'? Was the master's house pulled down later than the school, or were these two buildings adjoining and were they pulled down together?

The evidence of these old men was produced in 1826 when the parish wished to assert its claims over the school. It was later cited by the feoffees when, in opposing Hand's claims, they tried to prove that the freehold of the second school lay in the incumbent of Witton.* It may represent a valid local tradition, but it has to be weighed against the evidence of the map of 1721 and against the absence of contemporary or near-contemporary evidence suggesting a change of site or title. Even if the first school was on the same site as the second, changes in the size of the churchyard between the sixteenth and eighteenth century make it difficult to say whether it was within the churchyard.

---

* See the letter from John Barker to Hostage, 21 December 1833. But later, in 1866, when it came to selling the site of the second school, the trustees asserted that the freehold of the school lay with the Charity. P.R.O. Ed. 27/298.

Index

Masters, headmasters and ushers of Sir John Deane's Grammar School are described as 'master', etc.; masters of other local schools are described as 'schoolmaster'.
Curates and vicars of Witton are described as 'curate' or 'vicar'.
Pupils named on lists are not indexed unless they appear in the text.